MATHEMATICS EDUCATION

in Secondary Schools and Two-Year Colleges

Sourcebooks on Education
Vol. 15

Garland Reference Library
of the Social Sciences
Vol. 377

MATHEMATICS EDUCATION

in Secondary Schools and Two-Year Colleges

A Sourcebook

Paul J. Campbell

Louise S. Grinstein

Garland Publishing, Inc. • New York & London
1988

Library of Congress Cataloging-in-Publication Data

Mathematics education in secondary schools and two-year colleges ; a
source book / [edited by] Paul J. Campbell, Louise S. Grinstein.
      p.   cm. — (Garland reference library of social science ; vol.
377. Source books on education ; vol. 15)
    Includes bibliographies and indexes.
    ISBN 0-8240-8522-1 (alk. paper)
    1. Mathematics—Study and teaching (Secondary). 2. Mathematics—
Study and teaching (Higher) 3. Mathematics—Study and teaching
(Secondary)—Bibliography, 4. Mathematics—Study and teaching
(Higher)—Bibliography. I. Campbell, Paul J. II. Grinstein,
Louise S. II. Series: Garland reference library of social science
; v. 377. IV. Series: Garland reference library of social science.
Source books on education ; vol. 15.
QA12.W377 1988
510'.7'11—dc19   88-2322
                                                  CIP

Printed on acid-free, 250-year-life paper
Manufactured in the United States of America

To Melanie
and
To Jack

Table of Contents

Preface

The quality of education in general, and of mathematics education in particular, has been severely criticized in recent years. Published reports from government commissions and task forces have repeatedly stressed the need for educational reform in our schools and colleges. The erosion of our nation's technological supremacy must be stemmed and reversed.

To address these issues, this volume has been designed as a reference work for all those desiring to improve instruction in mathematics at the secondary and two-year-college levels. The aim throughout has been to present a spectrum of available material that can be of value in making mathematics education more meaningful and effective.

The overall scope of the volume is comprehensive in nature and encompasses major areas in mathematics education. The volume is topically organized into 20 chapters. These chapters consist of cogent essays followed by annotated, evaluative bibliographies.

The individual essays provide orientation to the various chapters. They focus attention on related problems and background information.

The bibliographic materials presented (all in English) were selected on the basis of significance, timeliness, and relevance to both parents and educators. The entries include books, periodical literature, and non-print material (i.e. booklets, videotapes, software). The vast majority of bibliography items are from the 1970s and 1980s.

Each chapter reflects the insights and viewpoints of its contributors. For purposes of stylistic uniformity and consistency in the volume as a whole, however, contributors were requested to follow a set structural format. Since each contributor attempted to provide a complete presentation of pertinent and available material, there was perforce considerable overlap in various discussions. As a result, part of the editing process entailed consolidation and merging. When entries and annotations had to be moved, the identity of the specific contributor has been indicated by use of initials in parentheses. In addition, complete bibliographic citations to frequently referenced materials, such as NCTM yearbooks, general bibliographies, periodicals, distributors, and publishers, can be found in the Resources chapter; and a dictionary of abbreviations follows that chapter.

References noted as published by ERIC are available from the ERIC Clearinghouse on Science, Mathematics, and Environmental Education (address in Resources chapter) and are most easily obtained with the help of a librarian.

This volume could not have been brought to fruition without the efforts of our contributors. We wish to express our thanks and appreciation for their suggestions, advice, understanding, and participation.

Not to be forgotten is the commitment of the editorial committee — Drs. Peter Lindstrom, Joseph Malkevitch, Warren Page, and Bruce Vogeli. Their comments were always insightful and their criticisms constructive. They served to give direction to the work as a whole.

Special recognition must be given to Marie Ellen Larcada who initiated the idea and provided invaluable guidance throughout the various stages of the book's development.

We wish to acknowledge the assistance of Brenda Michaels and the librarians at Kingsborough Community College in the task of cross-checking and indexing citations. Finally, we wish to thank David Heesen of Beloit College for skilled typing and formatting, which accommodated the intentions of the contributors, the deadlines of the publisher, and the high hopes of the editors.

Paul J. Campbell   **Louise S. Grinstein**

Beloit College   **Kingsborough Community College**

Beloit, WI 53511   **Brooklyn, NY 11235**

Contributors

Douglas B. Aichele
Oklahoma State University
Stillwater, Oklahoma

Bonnie Averbach
Temple University
Philadelphia, Pennsylvania

Bettye Anne Case
Florida State University
Tallahassee, Florida

Orin Chein
Temple University
Philadelphia, Pennsylvania

James Choike
Oklahoma State University
Stillwater, Oklahoma

R. S. Cunningham
Software Reviews Editor
College Mathematics Journal
California State College
  at Stanislaus
Turlock, California

Robert B. Davis
University of Illinois at Urbana/
  Champaign
Urbana, Illinois

Frank Demana
Ohio State University
Columbus, Ohio

John A. Dossey
President, National Council of
  Teachers of Mathematics
Illinois State University
Normal, Illinois

Wade Ellis, Jr.
West Valley College
Saratoga, California

Elizabeth Fennema
University of Wisconsin–Madison
Madison, Wisconsin

Ross L. Finney
Massachusetts Institute of
  Technology
Cambridge, Massachusetts

Anna O. Graeber
University of Maryland
College Park, Maryland

Peter J. Hilton
State University of New York
Binghamton, New York

John W. Kenelly
Clemson University
Clemson, South Carolina

Sally I. Lipsey
Brooklyn College
City University of New York
Brooklyn, New York

Calvin T. Long
Washington State University
Pullman, Washington

Margaret R. Meyer
University of Wisconsin–Madison
Madison, Wisconsin

Thomas A. Romberg
University of Wisconsin–Madison
Madison, Wisconsin

Mark E. Saul
Bronxville Schools
Bronxville, New York

Doris W. Schattschneider
Moravian College
Bethlehem, Pennsylvania

Alan H. Schoenfeld
University of California
Berkeley, California

Martha J. Siegel
Towson State University
Towson, Maryland

Lynn A. Steen
Past President, Mathematical
  Association of America
St. Olaf College
Northfield, Minnesota

Lindsay A. Tartre
California State University
  at Long Beach
Long Beach, California

Pamela Trim
State Technical Institute
  at Memphis
Memphis, Tennessee

Ann E. Watkins
Pierce College
Woodland Hills, California

Stephen F. West
State University College
  of Arts and Sciences
Geneseo, New York

EDITORIAL COMMITTEE

Peter A. Lindstrom
North Lake College
Irving, Texas

Joseph Malkevitch
York College
City University of New York
Jamaica, New York

Warren Page
New York City Technical College
City University of New York
Brooklyn, New York

Bruce Vogeli
Teachers College
Columbia University
New York, New York

Foreword

Mathematics education is once again on the public agenda, as it was in the post-Sputnik period. Newspaper headlines echo an avalanche of foundation and government reports: performance of United States students in mathematics is not what it should be, whether measured by international norms or by societal needs.

Several themes emerge repeatedly in the many recent commentaries on U.S. mathematics education:

- that the changing role of mathematics in society requires a different mathematics curriculum in the schools;
- that the ubiquitous role of computers and calculators alters priorities within school mathematics;
- that advances in research on the process of learning reveal modes of teaching that are more effective than traditional methods;
- that U.S. students learn less mathematics than students in other countries;
- that far too few women and minority students make it through the mathematics pipeline well prepared for advanced work;
- that the emergence of a worldwide market for trade compels the United States to ensure that its work force is well educated in mathematics.

In response to these frequent exhortations, at least three major national groups are working on new standards for school mathematics. The National Council of Teachers of Mathematics, the American Association for the Advancement of Science, and the Mathematical Sciences Education Board of the National Academy of Sciences are currently preparing new objectives for school mathematics. These recommendations express the leading edge of an emerging national consensus that only a dramatically different mathematics curriculum will ensure that *all* students learn school mathematics sufficient for their lives and appropriate to their times.

Curriculum builders are already at work in many school districts and on several university campuses constructing pieces of the new school mathematics program. Some work on elementary school mathematics, others on high school; some focus on curriculum, others on teacher training, still others on testing. Many diverse components for this new curriculum are being fabricated, tested, and revised. During the next decade policy leaders will begin to implement parts that are ready for classroom use, thereby gradually erecting a new structure for mathematics education in United States classrooms.

To last, this new curriculum must be properly situated on a firm foundation of experience and research. This *Sourcebook* provides access to that foundation, to the scores of articles that describe research and innovative experience in mathematics education primarily during the last 15-20 years. References to virtually all major issues of school and two-year-college mathematics that have been explored in recent years can be found in this volume.

One will not find in this sourcebook an elixir to remedy our curricular ills. No one has a magic answer for what is an enormously complex problem. Undoubtedly no single answer exists, since different communities, different students, and different schools are situated very differently within the vast terrain of current mathematics curriculum and practice.

What one *will* find are clues and examples, bits of evidence that can be assembled by creative teachers into whole new approaches to teaching mathematics. Each of the 20 chapters contains a wealth of information that can provide firm foundation for any new curricular endeavor. A timely volume, this *Sourcebook* gives curriculum reformers a platform on which to build. It is a healthy and valuable contribution to an important national enterprise — the revitalization of school mathematics.

Lynn Arthur Steen

Introduction

The present role of mathematics as a "critical filter" for entry into our technologically-based society presents those involved with the teaching of mathematics with a variety of opportunities and problems. The opportunities are based on the myriad of choices concerning materials, approaches, and assistance available. The problems arise from coping with the conditions of the teaching environment, the lack of articulation between levels of schooling, and the rapid growth of mathematical knowledge.

The present volume provides a source for starting to both understand and gain control over some of the factors operating in and on the mathematics curriculum of secondary schools and two-year colleges. Its major sections deal effectively with the questions of general curricular goals, instruction in the core areas of the mathematics curriculum, and concern for special populations in the mathematics classroom. In addition to providing an overview in each of these areas, the authors have worked to provide also a solid bibliography of sources related to the major chapter themes.

The balance of tensions covered by the topics selected illustrate a modern dynamic view of mathematics and of its teaching and learning. Classroom teaching of mathematics must come to reflect this vibrancy and the rapid growth of the mathematical sciences. The opening chapters also provide cogent treatments of the historical roots of the mathematics curriculum and the forces that have moved to shape it. These forces act in the work of the National Council of Teachers of Mathematics (NCTM), the Mathematical Association of America (MAA), and other professional organizations. However, attempts at curriculum reform and change in teacher education are also presently being informed by research results coming from cognitive psychology and instructional theory. These findings suggest exciting alternatives concerning the placement and appropriate approaches to topics across the secondary school and two-year-college mathematics curriculum.

These new alternatives place mathematics educators in a precarious position. Effecting curricular change is a difficult task. The past ten years have seen the gradual introduction of problem solving as a major curricular objective in secondary schools and two-year college programs. This change resulted from the heavy emphasis given the topic by the NCTM's *Agenda for Action* in 1980. Recommendations calling for the reorganization of objectives, grade placement of topics, and approaches to instruction require careful planning, implementation, and evaluation. The successful implementation of new and revised programs of study will call for a wide-scale agreement on objectives, instructional approaches, and modes of evaluation. Such plans will have to be carefully orchestrated both in time and order of implementation, articulation within and between levels of the curriculum, and societal acceptance of the changes. All of these activities call for a solid commitment from the mathematics community and its allied professional groups.

Mathematics educators must begin to think of themselves as facilitators of student learning rather than as transmitters of a static body of knowledge. This will require substantial change in classroom methods. Teachers will need opportunities to grow in terms of their ability to observe, question, challenge, evaluate, and motivate their students as they pass through the various stages of mathematical development required by the core areas of the curriculum. Likewise, students will have to grow in their ability to observe, record, create, validate, and generalize in their study of quantitative and spatial situations.

These changes have significant ramifications for the teaching of algebra, geometry, precalculus, calculus, and other core/elective areas of the secondary and two-year-college mathematics curriculum. These ramifications and related choices are carefully detailed in the chapters dealing with the major areas of the curriculum. However, the work does not stop here. One must also make choices about dealing with varying levels of student ability, selection of instructional materials, and other special needs of students. These topics are covered in the concluding chapters of the text.

The contemporary reaction to the NCTM's *Curriculum and Evaluation Standards for School Mathematics* reflects the beginning of the discussion that will lead to change in the K-12 portion of the curriculum. The debate revolving about the MAA's discussion of the calculus and the infusion of discrete mathematics into the undergraduate curriculum portrays the possibility for great change in the curriculum at the undergraduate level. These opportunities for change make the discussion of current knowledge in mathematics education involving the curriculum, methods of instruction, and allied topics even more important. The present text serves to illuminate several of these needs. Not only does it provide the focus on central points of discussion, it also provides guidance toward the major works describing current levels of knowledge in these areas. Informed change is dependent on leadership that is both informed and creative. The contents of this sourcebook help in both areas. First, it provides the resources through which one can become informed on the issues confronting the profession today. Second, the overviews provide a setting to begin the discussion that will assist one in forming a personal philosophy and alternatives to deal with the hurdles facing quality mathematics instruction.

The years to the turn of the century will be exciting years for mathematics education. This period of time will see the gradual infusion of calculators and computers into the mathematics classroom, the development of probability and statistics as a major strand across the curriculum from the early grades through the collegiate level, and a nationwide consensus on what the goals of mathematics education are. The emerging view of these goals reflects the contents and concerns covered in this volume. Read it and the recommended readings with care, discuss their contents, and resolve to use this sourcebook as a first step in becoming a contributing member to positive change in mathematics teaching and learning in the coming years.

John A. Dossey

REFERENCES

National Council of Teachers of Mathematics. 1980. *An Agenda for Action*. Reston, Va.: National Council of Teachers of Mathematics.

National Council of Teachers of Mathematics. 1987. *Curriculum and Evaluation Standards for School Mathematics*. Reston, Va.: National Council of Teachers of Mathematics.

Mathematics Education

in Secondary Schools and Two-Year Colleges

1. Historical Overview

DOUGLAS B. AICHELE

This historical overview of secondary and junior college mathematics education is presented chronologically and highlights significant factors and trends from the very early days of formal American education to the present. We begin by partitioning the history of mathematics education in the United States into five periods (Jones 1970) according to some of the significant events that occurred.

Prior to Mid-1820s

Publication of Warren Colburn's first books on arithmetic (1822) and algebra (1825) and with them a new concern for pedagogical issues.

Mid-1820s — Mid-1890s

Establishment and development of several professional organizations, e.g., American Mathematical Society (AMS), and the role of the National Education Association (NEA) in appointing the Committee of Ten on Secondary School Studies. The report of the latter (NEA 1894) focused attention on mathematics-specific curricular questions particularly related to college entrance requirements.

Mid-1890s — 1920

Founding of the National Council of Teachers of Mathematics (NCTM), the Mathematical Association of America (MAA), and the release of *The Reorganization of the First Courses in Secondary School Mathematics* (National Committee ... 1920), which reflected the continuing concern of college-level mathematicians for the secondary-school curriculum as preparatory for meeting college requirements.

1920 — 1945

Period characterized by economic depression and war, forces affecting the mathematics curriculum beyond the control of professional educators.

1945 — Present

Release of the NCTM's reports of the Commission on Post-War Plans (Commission ... 1945a, 1945b). These motivated serious attempts to remedy the shortcomings in mathematics education that had surfaced during World War II and linked pre-war issues with the reforms that began in the early 1950s. Though there was activity in the early 1950s, the period from 1957 to the mid-1970s is generally regarded as the era of "new math" or "modern math," a time characterized by experimentation and reform in mathematics education. The junior-college movement in mathematics education emerged in the mid-1970s with the establishment of the American Mathematical Association of Two-Year Colleges (AMATYC).

Though many of the same issues in mathematics education continued to surface during each of these periods, significant changes have occurred during the last three decades. Further, there are considerable similarities in the mathematics education setting today and 30 years ago. "Mathematics education is largely the effect of the past, especially the recent past since about 1960; the future will undoubtedly be influenced by the issues and concerns of the present" (Aichele 1978).

To better understand the factors and trends of the recent past, we focus our attention more closely on the situation in the mid-1950s. The public sector was generally dissatisfied with the mathematical preparation of entering college students and was fearful that the Soviet Union would gain supremacy in space. Also, there was a critical shortage of qualified mathematics teachers, and many of those who were teaching school mathematics were in need of upgrading in both content and pedagogy. The changes that were appearing in the content of school mathematics at this time were so far-reaching and profound that they appropriately characterized a revolution, which was caused principally by advances in mathematical research, automation, and computers (NCTM 1961).

The response to the launching of Sputnik in 1957 was the commitment of unprecedented amounts of federal monies to upgrade the scientific education curricula of our schools. The first large-scale project aimed specifically at the secondary school mathematics curriculum was the University of Illinois Committee on School Mathematics (UICSM) in 1951 (Beberman 1958; NCTM 1963; Seyfert 1968). Other projects representative of the host of those funded and aimed at various school-age groups included the University of Maryland Mathematics Project (UMMaP) in 1957, the School Mathematics Study Group (SMSG) in 1958, the Stanford Program in Computer Assisted Instruction in 1963, and the Comprehensive School Mathematics Program (CSMP) in 1963 (NCTM 1963; Seyfert 1968).

The professional learned societies were actively involved in the change process through conferences, institutes, and the widespread dissemination of committee reports. For example, the National Science Foundation (NSF) supported thousands of mathematics teachers to upgrade their mathematics and teaching skills from the "modern mathematics" perspective. In 1955 the Commission on Mathematics of the College Entrance Examination Board (CEEB) studied the secondary mathematics curriculum and recommended "relatively minor changes in content, but tremendously important changes in the points of view of instruction, and major changes in teaching emphases" (CEEB 1959). The Cambridge Conference on School Mathematics in 1963 resulted in the much-discussed and debated "Cambridge Report" (Educational Services 1963), which delineated the broad goals for school mathematics and proposed school mathematics curricula.

The emphasis and thrust of the programs was clear during these times: to produce quality mathematics curricula for the college-bound student. This would soon change, however, as attention would be given to developing programs for less-able students and generally to expanding the educational opportunities for all youth.

A classic critique of "new math" is Morris Kline's book *Why Johnny Can't Add* (1973). Kline is a strong advocate of applications in mathematics. Strong resistance to "new math" emerged earlier, however, in the "basic skills" or "back-to-the-basics" movement of the late 1960s. The "basic skills" movement (applied to mathematics) actually included only computational skills and thus prescribed a very limited mathematics curriculum. With this movement came such issues as tests of minimal competence for entering employment, school and teaching accountability with achievement testing, and the related pedagogical theories based on behavioral objectives. The underlying theories of learning associated with this movement were clearly inconsistent with those of the "new math" movement that preceded it and warranted an organized response from the mathematics education profession.

Of significant importance in this response was the appointment of the National Advisory Committee on Mathematical Education (NACOME) in 1974 by the Conference Board of the Mathematical Sciences, and its subsequent report (National Advisory Committee ... 1975), which included an overview and analysis of U.S. school-level mathematical education – its objectives, current practices, and attainments. The NACOME Report was a conscious attempt by the mathematics education profession to address the growing resistance to "new math" that was a consequence of the "back-to-the-basics" movement. The Report concluded: "From a 1975 perspective the principal thrust of change in school mathematics remains fundamentally sound, though actual impact has been modest relative to expectations." It was asserted by the NACOME Committee that this modest impact may have been due to the curriculum's less-than-widespread acceptance by classroom teachers.

The mathematics profession also responded to the "back-to-the-basics" movement by defining the basic skills required of an enlightened citizenry. A rather widely accepted position paper was prepared by the National Council of Supervisors of Mathematics (NCSM 1978) that acknowledged problem solving as the fundamental skill and recognized its integral interrelationship with each of nine other identified skills.

The junior-college movement also flourished during the late 1960s and the 1970s and became recognized as an important educational option for students. Since the developments and changes in the two-year college mathematics curriculum appear to have been linked directly to their companion programs in the secondary school, we are able to understand much of its history and evolution through our scrutiny of secondary mathematics education.

Heightening the tension were reports in the media reporting the terrible state of student achievement: steadily declining college aptitude (SAT) test scores, high failure rates on tests of minimal competence, and lower student performance at many grade levels when compared to previous national norms (NAEP 1975, 1979, 1983). It was clear that the perceptions of the mathematics education profession and the general public were not aligned at this time; this is an important observation if we believe that history is valuable in charting the future.

The pressure for reform of the mathematics curriculum precipitated NCTM's 1980 *Agenda for Action* (NCTM 1980). It included recommendations (many calling for curricular revision) that were realistic and responsible and were written to advise society of the directions of mathematics education during this decade.

Since 1980 there has been a clamor, largely from outside of the mathematics community, calling for improved student performance in mathematics and for curricular revision in mathematics. Reform in education was briefly a political issue in the 1984 presidential election.

We can recognize many similarities between today and the mid-1950s: public dissatisfaction with student performance; new advances in mathematical research not yet included in the curriculum; a critical shortage of mathematics teachers; and competition with the Soviet Union for military and space supremacy. The pervasiveness of computers and technological advances, together with the pressures of worldwide economic competition, are new and important factors that are shaping society's demands on the mathematics education curriculum.

The stage is set for another revolution in mathematics education! Usiskin has identified several noteworthy principles for implementing the coming revolution: specifying the new curriculum by intended grade level in as much detail as the current content, making materials available to implement the recommendations, and holding students accountable for the new content (Usiskin 1985). A successful revolution will require leadership from the teaching profession; financial encouragement from local, state, and national governments; and greater support for teachers from the general public.

REFERENCES

Aichele, Douglas B. 1978. Mathematics teacher education: An overview in perspective. In *Mathematics Teacher Education: Critical Issues and Trends*, edited by Douglas B. Aichele, 9-24. Washington, D.C.: National Education Association.

Beberman, Max. 1958. *An Emerging Program of Secondary School Mathematics*. Cambridge, Mass.: Harvard University Press.

Colburn, Warren. 1822. *First Lessons in Arithmetic on the Plan of Pestalozzi, with Some Improvements.* 2nd ed. Boston: Cummings and Hilliard.

––––––. 1825. *An Introduction to Algebra upon the Inductive Method of Instruction.* Boston: Cummings, Hilliard & Co.

College Entrance Examination Board, Commission on Mathematics. 1959. *Program for College Preparatory Mathematics.* New York: College Entrance Examination Board.

Commission on Post-War Plans of the NCTM. 1945a. *The Role of Mathematics in Consumer Education.* Washington, D.C.: Consumer Education Study.

Commission on Post-War Plans [of the NCTM]. 1945b. The Second Report of the Commission on Post-War Plans. *Mathematics Teacher* 38 (5) (May 1945): 195-221.

Educational Services Incorporated. 1963. *Goals for School Mathematics – The Report of the Cambridge Conference on School Mathematics.* Boston, Mass.: Houghton Mifflin. Review: *Mathematics Teacher* 58 (4) (April 1965): 353-360.

Jones, Phillip S., ed. 1970. *NCTM Yearbook 32.*

Kline, Morris. 1973. *Why Johnny Can't Add: The Failure of the New Math.* New York: St. Martin's.

National Advisory Committee on Mathematical Education. 1975. *Overview and Analysis of School Mathematics, Grades K-12.* Reston, Va.: National Council of Teachers of Mathematics.

National Assessment of Educational Progress. 1975. *The First National Assessment of Mathematics – An Overview.* Denver, Colo.: National Assessment of Educational Progress (distributed by U.S. Government Printing Office).

––––––. 1979. *Changes in Mathematics Achievement, 1973-1978.* Denver, Colo.: National Assessment of Educational Progress (distributed by U.S. Government Printing Office).

————. 1983. *The Third National Mathematics Assessment: Results, Trends, and Issues.* Report No. 13-MA-01. Denver: Education Commission of the States. Columbus, O.: ERIC/SMEAC. ERIC: ED 228049.

National Committee on Mathematical Requirements of the MAA. 1920. *The Reorganization of the First Courses in Secondary School Mathematics.* USBE Secondary School Circular no. 5. Washington, D.C.: U.S. Government Printing Office.

National Council of Supervisors of Mathematics. 1978. *Position Paper on Basic Mathematical Skills.* Reprinted in *Mathematics Teacher* 71 (February 1978): 147-152.

National Council of Teachers of Mathematics. 1961. *The Revolution in School Mathematics, A Report.* Washington, D.C.: National Council of Teachers of Mathematics.

————. 1963. *An Analysis of New Mathematics Programs.* Washington, D.C.: National Council of Teachers of Mathematics.

————. 1980. *An Agenda for Action: Recommendations for School Mathematics of the 1980s.* Reston, Va.: National Council of Teachers of Mathematics.

National Education Association. 1894. *Report of the Committee of Ten on Secondary School Studies with the Reports of the Conferences Arranged by Committees.* New York: American Book Co.

Seyfert, Warren C., ed. 1968. *The Continuing Revolution in Mathematics.* Washington, D.C.: National Council of Teachers of Mathematics.

Usiskin, Zalman. 1985. We need another revolution in secondary school mathematics. In *NCTM Yearbook 1985*, 1-21.

BIBLIOGRAPHY

The selected references included below are presented according to the five historical periods cited in the accompanying essay. The period 1945-present has been subdivided, however, into 1945-1975 and 1975-present. The sections, then, are:

- Prior to Mid-1820s
- Mid-1820s – Mid-1890s
- Mid-1890s – 1920
- 1920 – 1945
- 1945 – 1975
- 1975 – Present.

Prior to Mid-1820s

Jones, Phillip S. and Arthur F. Coxford, Jr. 1970. From discovery to an awakened concern for pedagogy: 1492-1821. In *NCTM Yearbook 32*, 11-23.

> Discusses the issues that arose and the forces that were at work during this period.

Rash, Agnes M. 1975. Some topics in the mathematics curriculum since colonial days. *School Science and Mathematics* 75 (5) (May-June 1975): 423-444.

> Discusses the mathematics curriculum of the 18th and 19th centuries, emphasizing arithmetic and algebra, with comparisons to current practices.

Mid-1820s – Mid-1890s

Greenwood, J. M. 1894. Conference report on mathematics. *Education* 15 (2) (October 1894): 65-74.

Jones, Phillip S., and Arthur F. Coxford, Jr. 1970. From Colburn to the rise of the universities: 1821-94. In *NCTM Yearbook 32*, 24-35.

National Education Association. 1894. *Report of the Committee of Ten on Secondary School Studies with the Reports of the Conferences Arranged by Committees*. New York: American Book Co.

Seerly, H. H. 1894. The report of the Committee of Ten. *Education* 15 (4) (December 1894): 239-241.

Mid-1890s — 1920

Agris, Myrna Skobel, and Joe Dan Austin. 1984. Women in *School Science and Mathematics*—the early years. *School Science and Mathematics* 84 (5) (May-June 1984): 386-394.

Early issues of *School Science and Mathematics* were examined to investigate the writings of women educators and their role in education from 1902 to 1906.

Austin, Charles M., et al., eds. 1926. *NCTM Yearbook 1.*

Highlights the work of the International Commission on the Teaching of Mathematics, the National Committee on Mathematical Requirements, and the College Entrance Examination Board. Modifications in the arithmetic and algebra curricula are discussed at some length, and changes in the geometry curriculum are indicated. Includes developments in the testing movement as related to mathematics education, with particular attention paid to standardized achievement tests, their misuses, and their correct place in mathematics education. The history of the junior-high-school movement and the development of its mathematics curricula are traced.

Deatsman, Gary A. 1976. "New Math" in the Gay Nineties. *Arithmetic Teacher* 23 (7) (March 1976): 165-166.

A grammar-school arithmetic textbook published in the 1890s is described, and elements of "modern" mathematics programs that were present in this book are identified.

Fishman, Joseph. 1965. Trends in secondary school mathematics in relation to educational theories and social changes: 1893-1964. Doctoral diss., New York University.

Jones, Phillip S., and Arthur F. Coxford, Jr. 1970. First steps toward revision: 1894-1920. In *NCTM Yearbook 32*, 36-45.

National Committee on Mathematical Requirements of the MAA. 1920. *The Reorganization of the First Courses in Secondary School Mathematics.* USBE Secondary School Circular no. 5. Washington, D.C.: U.S. Government Printing Office.

Osborne, Alan R., and F. Joe Crosswhite. 1970. Emerging issues: 1890-1920. In *NCTM Yearbook 32*, 155-196.

1920 — 1945

Ahlfors, Lars, et al. 1962. On the mathematics curriculum of the high school. *Mathematics Teacher* 55 (3) (March 1962): 191-195. Also in *American Mathematical Monthly* 69 (3) (March 1962): 189-193.

Betz, William. 1923. The confusion of objectives in secondary mathematics. *Mathematics Teacher* 16 (8) (December 1923): 449-469.

————. 1936. The reorganization of secondary education. In *NCTM Yearbook 11*, 22-135.

————. 1940. The present situation in secondary mathematics with particular reference to the new national reports on the place of mathematics in education. *Mathematics Teacher* 33 (8) (December 1940): 339-360.

————. 1950. Five decades of mathematical reform — evaluation and challenge. *Mathematics Teacher* 43 (8) (December 1950): 377-387.

Commission on Post-War Plans [of the NCTM]. 1945b. The Second Report of the Commission on Post-War Plans. *Mathematics Teacher* 38 (5) (May 1945): 195-221.

Hancock, John D. 1961. The evaluation of the secondary mathematics curriculum: A critique. Doctoral diss., Stanford University.

Jones, Phillip S., and Arthur F. Coxford, Jr. 1970. Abortive reform — depression and war: 1920-45. In *NCTM Yearbook 32*, 46-66.

Kilpatrick, Jeremy, and J. Fred Weaver. 1977. The place of William A. Brownell in mathematics education. *Journal for Research in Mathematics Education* 8 (November 1977): 382-384.
    Gives a tribute to William A. Brownell, along with a brief sketch of his academic career and professional activities, and selected references illustrating his philosophy of education and research.

Oakes, Herbert I. 1965. Objectives of mathematics education in the United States from 1920 to 1960. Doctoral diss., Columbia University.

Oakley, Cletus O. 1942. The coming revolution – in mathematics. *Mathematics Teacher* 35 (7) (November 1942): 307-309.

Osborne, Alan R., and F. Joe Crosswhite. 1970. Mathematics education on defensive: 1920-45. In *NCTM Yearbook 32*, 197-234.

Reeve, William David, ed. 1929. *NCTM Yearbook 4*.

————. 1933. *NCTM Yearbook 8*.

————. 1940. *NCTM Yearbook 15*.

Schorling, Raleigh. 1945. The need for cooperative action in mathematics education. *American Mathematical Monthly* 52 (4) (April 1945): 194-201.

1945 – 1975

Adler, Irving. 1966. The Cambridge Conference Report: Blueprint or fantasy? *Arithmetic Teacher* 13 (3) (March 1966): 179-186.

Allendoerfer, Carl B. 1965. The second revolution in mathematics. *Mathematics Teacher* 58 (9) (December 1965): 690-695.

Beberman, Max. 1958. *An Emerging Program of Secondary School Mathematics*. Cambridge, Mass.: Harvard University Press.

————. 1962. The old mathematics in the new curriculum. *Educational Leadership* 19 (6) (March 1962): 373-375.

Begle, Edward G. 1962. Some remarks on "On the mathematics curriculum of the high school." *Mathematics Teacher* 55 (3) (March 1962): 195-196.

————. 1963. The reform of mathematics education in the United States of America. In *Mathematical Education in the Americas*, edited by Howard Fehr. New York: Bureau of Publications, Teachers College, Columbia University.

————. 1968. SMSG: The first decade. *Mathematics Teacher* 61 (3) (March 1968): 239-245.

————. 1973. Some lessons learned by SMSG. *Mathematics Teacher* 66 (3) (March 1973): 207-214.

————, ed. 1970. *Mathematics Education.* 69th Yearbook of the National Society for the Study of Education (Part I). Chicago: University of Chicago Press.
> Explains the educational and psychological problems in the selection, organization, and presentation of mathematics materials, at all levels from kindergarten through high school.

————, and J. W. Wilson. 1970. Evaluation of mathematics programs. In Begle (1970).

Bidwell, James K. 1968. A new look at old committee reports. *Mathematics Teacher* 61 (4) (April 1968): 383-387.

————, and Robert G. Clason, eds. 1970. *Readings in the History of Mathematics Education.* Washington, D.C.: National Council of Teachers of Mathematics.
> Presents a cohesive view of the evolution of mathematics in the United States from approximately 1828 to 1959, emphasizing historical continuity.

College Entrance Examination Board, Commission on Mathematics. 1959. *Program for College Preparatory Mathematics.* New York: College Entrance Examination Board.

Committee on the Undergraduate Program in Mathematics. 1969. *Qualifications for Teaching University Parallel Mathematics Courses in Two-Year Colleges.* Washington, D.C.: Mathematical Association of America.

————. 1969. *A Transfer Curriculum in Mathematics for Two Year Colleges.* Washington, D.C.: Mathematical Association of America.

Conference Board of the Mathematical Sciences, Committee on Computer Education. 1972. *Recommendations Regarding Computers in High School Education.* Washington, D.C.: Conference Board of the Mathematical Sciences.

Davis, Robert B. 1967. *The Changing Curriculum: Mathematics.* Washington, D.C.: Association for Supervision and Curriculum Development, National Education Association.

Educational Services Incorporated. 1963. *Goals for School Mathematics — The Report of the Cambridge Conference on School Mathematics.* Boston, Mass.: Houghton Mifflin. Review: *Mathematics Teacher* 58 (4) (April 1965): 353-360.

Edwards, P. D., Phillip S. Jones, and Bruce E. Meserve. 1952. Mathematical preparation for college. *Mathematics Teacher* 45 (5) (May 1952): 321-330.

Elkins, John. 1977. The quiet revolution in mathematics. *Australian Mathematics Teacher* 33 (October-December 1977): 211-218.

Investigates the meaning of the ambiguous term "new math" in the light of past developments in teaching theories, media, and content.

Fehr, Howard F. 1972. Why mathematics should be taught in a contemporary setting. *Australian Mathematics Teacher* 28 (September 1972): 79-91.

Overviews of classical mathematics and of modern mathematics, with implications for secondary school curriculum and instruction.

Fremont, Herbert. 1967. New mathematics and old dilemmas. *Mathematics Teacher* 60 (7) (November 1967): 715-719.

Hale, William T. 1961. UICSM's decade of experimentation. *Mathematics Teacher* 54 (9) (December 1961): 613-619.

Hartung, Maurice L. 1955. Modern methods and current criticisms of mathematical education. *School Science and Mathematics* 55 (2) (February 1955): 85-90.

Kline, Morris. 1958. The ancients versus the moderns, a new battle of the books. *Mathematics Teacher* 51 (6) (October 1958): 418-427.

———. 1966. A proposal for the high school mathematics curriculum. *Mathematics Teacher* 59 (4) (April 1966): 322-330.

————. 1973. *Why Johnny Can't Add: The Failure of the New Math.* New York: St. Martin's.

Jones, Phillip S. 1970. Epilogue: Summary and forecast. In *NCTM Yearbook 32*, 451-465.

————, and Arthur F. Coxford, Jr. 1970. Reform, "revolution," reaction: 1945-present. In *NCTM Yearbook 32,* 67-89.

McQualter, J. W. 1974. Some influences on mathematics curriculum making: An historical review. *Australian Mathematics Teacher* 30 (February 1974): 15-26.
    Presents a brief overview of the history of mathematics and mathematics education and describes the impact of learning theories. Identifies first-round curriculum projects in the United States, England, and Australia.

Meder, Albert E., Jr. 1958. The ancients versus the moderns — a reply. *Mathematics Teacher* 51 (6) (October 1958): 428-433.

Monroe, Charles R. 1972. *Profile of the Community College.* San Francisco, Calif.: Jossey-Bass.
    Introductory textbook that reviews the history and characteristics of the community college.

National Council of Teachers of Mathematics. 1954. *Emerging Practices in Mathematics Education.* Washington, D.C.: National Council of Teachers of Mathematics.

————. 1959. Secondary School Curriculum Committee. The secondary mathematics curriculum. *Mathematics Teacher* 52 (5) (May 1959): 389-417.

————. 1961. *The Revolution in School Mathematics: A Challenge for Administrators and Teachers, A Report.* Washington, D.C.: National Council of Teachers of Mathematics.

————. 1963. *An Analysis of New Mathematics Programs.* Washington, D.C.: National Council of Teachers of Mathematics.

National Institute of Education. 1975. *The NIE Conference on Basic Mathematical Skills and Learning,* 2 vols. Euclid, Ohio; Washington, D.C.: National Institute of Education.

Osborne, Alan R., and F. Joe Crosswhite. 1970. Reform, revolution and reaction. In *NCTM Yearbook 32*, 235-297.

Rosskopf, Myron F. 1970. Mathematics education: Historical perspectives. In *NCTM Yearbook 33*, 3-29.
Examines important factors that have contributed to the present mathematics curriculum.

Seyfert, Warren C., ed. 1968. *The Continuing Revolution in Mathematics*. Washington, D.C.: National Council of Teachers of Mathematics.

Shuster, Carl N. 1948. A call for reform in high school mathematics. *American Mathematical Monthly* 55 (8) (October 1948): 472-475.

Suydam, Marilyn N., and Alan Osborne. 1977. The status of pre-college science, mathematics, and social science education: 1955-1975. Columbus, O.: ERIC/SMEAC. ERIC: ED 153878.
Historical study on the status of precollege mathematics education from 1955 through 1975, based on a review, analysis, and synthesis of the literature.

White, Edwin P. 1978. Problem solving: Its history as a focus in curriculum development. *School Science and Mathematics* 78 (3) (March 1978): 183-188.
Traces the historical attention problem solving has received as a major curriculum goal, from the Dewey School of 1896 to the 1970s.

Wooton, William. 1965. *SMSG: The Making of a Curriculum*. New Haven, Conn.: Yale University Press.

Wren, F. Lynwood. 1969. The "new mathematics" in historical perspective. *Mathematics Teacher* 62 (8) (November 1969): 579-585.

1975 — Present

Aichele, Douglas B. 1978. Mathematics teacher education: An overview in perspective. In *Mathematics Teacher Education: Critical Issues and Trends*, edited by Douglas B. Aichele, 9-24. Washington, D.C.: National Education Association.

Albers, Donald J. 1985. New directions in two-year college mathematics. *Mathematics Teacher* 78 (5) (May 1985): 373-375.

Summarizes the conference of July 1984 to discuss the state of mathematics in two-year colleges. Main topics included: case for curricular change; technical mathematics; influence of new technologies on learning mathematics; faculty renewal; collaboration with secondary schools, colleges and universities.

Alexanderson, G. L. 1979. George Pólya interviewed on his ninetieth birthday. *Two-Year College Mathematics Journal* 10 (1) (January 1979): 13-19.

Discusses Pólya's contributions, influences on his work, and past and future directions of mathematics and mathematics education.

American Mathematical Association of Two-Year Colleges. 1984. *A History of AMATYC, 1974-1984.* Santa Rosa, Calif.: American Mathematical Association of Two-Year Colleges.

Includes a brief history of AMATYC, its relationship with NSF and CBMS, and the founding of the *AMATYC Review.*

Cohen, Arthur M., and Florence B. Brawer. 1982. *The American Community College.* San Francisco, Calif.: Jossey-Bass.

Traces the history of community colleges in the U.S. and examines several facets of their endeavors.

Conference Board of the Mathematical Sciences. 1983. *New Goals for Mathematical Sciences Education.* Washington, D.C.: Conference Board of the Mathematical Sciences

Summarizes the conference of November 1983 to improve the quality of mathematics education in elementary and secondary schools and colleges. Gives recommendations on: curriculum, teacher support networks, communication of standards and expectations, mathematical competence and achievement, remediation, faculty renewal.

Dessart, Donald J. 1981. Curriculum. In *Mathematics Education Research: Implications for the 80's,* edited by Elizabeth Fennema, 1-21. Alexandria, Va.: Association for Supervision and Curriculum Development with National Council of Teachers of Mathematics.

Review of the events in research related to the revolution in mathematics education. Includes discussion of mathematical content, instructional procedures, the evolving mathematics curriculum, evaluation of programs, curricular variable identification and study, meaningful instruction and drill, and the textbook.

Fey, James T. 1979. Mathematics teaching today: Perspectives from three national surveys. *Mathematics Teacher* 72 (7) (October 1979): 490-504.

————. 1982. Status and prospects. In *Education in the '80s: Mathematics*, edited by Shirley A. Hill, 15-23. Washington, D.C.: National Education Association.

Cites significant differences among the priorities of the public, classroom teachers, administrators, and innovators in mathematics education, and encourages a spirit of cooperation among those with interest in mathematics education.

Hart, Eric W. 1985. Is discrete mathematics the new math of the eighties? *Mathematics Teacher* 78 (5) (May 1985): 334-338.

Attempts to define discrete mathematics and discusses the parallels between "new math" and discrete mathematics.

Hirsch, Christian R., and Marilyn J. Zweng, eds. 1985. *NCTM 1985 Yearbook.*

Howson, A. G. 1984. Seventy five years of the International Commission on Mathematical Instruction. *Educational Studies in Mathematics* 15 (February 1984): 75-93.

Describes the origins, history, work, and aims of the ICMI.

Jones, Chancey O., and John A. Valentine. 1984. The College Entrance Examination Board and mathematics education. *Mathematics Teacher* 77 (5) (May 1984): 369-371.

Gives history of the College Board to help explain the relationship between Board activities and mathematics education today. Notes the development of the Advanced Placement computer science course description and examination.

Kansky, Bob. 1985. One point of view: Looking back, I think I see the future. *Arithmetic Teacher* 32 (5) (January 1985): 2-3.

Lists lessons the author learned from the "new math" curriculum reform era. Focuses on curricular change rather than revision, the need to start at the elementary-school level, and how to select topics, interweaving throughout the role of technology.

National Advisory Committee on Mathematical Education. 1975. *Overview and Analysis of School Mathematics, Grades K-12.* Reston, Va.: National Council of Teachers of Mathematics.

National Assessment of Educational Progress. 1975. *The First National Assessment of Mathematics – An Overview.* Denver, Colo.: National Assessment of Educational Progress (distributed by U.S. Government Printing Office).

————. 1979. *Changes in Mathematics Achievement, 1973-1978.* Denver, Colo.: National Assessment of Educational Progress.

————. 1983. *The Third National Mathematics Assessment: Results, Trends, and Issues.* Report No. 13-MA-01. Denver: Education Commission of the States. Columbus, O.: ERIC/SMEAC. ERIC: ED 228049.

National Council of Teachers of Mathematics. 1980. *An Agenda for Action: Recommendations for School Mathematics of the 1980s.* Reston, Va.: National Council of Teachers of Mathematics.

————. 1981. *Priorities in School Mathematics: Executive Summary of the PRISM Project.* Reston, Va.: National Council of Teachers of Mathematics.

————, and the Mathematical Association of America. 1977. *Recommendations for the Preparation of High School Students for College Mathematics Courses.* Reston, Va., and Washington, D.C.: National Council of Teachers of Mathematics and Mathematical Association of America.

National Council of Supervisors of Mathematics. 1978. *Position Paper on Basic Mathematical Skills.* Reprinted in *Mathematics Teacher* 71 (2) (February 1978): 147-152.

National Science Board Commission on Precollege Education in Mathematics, Science and Technology. 1983. *Educating Americans for the 21st Century, A Report to the American People and the National Science Board.* Washington, D.C.: National Science Foundation.
    Presents "a plan of action for improving mathematics, science, and technology education for all American elementary and secondary students so that their achievement is the best in the world by 1995." The changes proposed by the NSB Commission are sweeping and drastic, emphasizing the teaching and learning of mathematics, science, and technology in schools.

————. 1983. *Educating Americans for the 21st Century, Source Materials.* Washington, D.C.: National Science Foundation.

Source documents that report activities sponsored by the NSB Commission, deliberations of a subgroup of the NSF Engineering Advisory Committee, and a paper prepared for the Pfizer Corporation.

National Science Foundation. 1980. *Science Education Databook.* Washington, D.C.: National Science Foundation.

————, and the Department of Education. 1980. *Science and Engineering Education for the 1980s and Beyond.* Washington, D.C.: National Science Foundation (distributed by U.S. Government Printing Office).

Peng, Samuel S., William B. Fetters, and Andrew J. Kolstad. 1981. *High School and Beyond: A Capsule Description of High School Students.* Washington, D.C.: U.S. Department of Education, Office of Educational Research and Improvement, National Center for Educational Statistics.

Reeve, William David. 1955. The need for a new national policy and program in secondary mathematics. *Mathematics Teacher* 48 (1) (January 1955): 2-9.

Science Education in Two-Year Colleges: Mathematics. 1980. Los Angeles: Center for the Study of Community Colleges and ERIC Clearinghouse for Junior Colleges. Columbus, O.: ERIC/SMEAC. ERIC: ED 187386.

Shufelt, Gwen, and James R. Smart, eds. 1983. *NCTM 1983 Yearbook.* Includes articles under each of the eight recommendations in the *Agenda for Action* (NCTM 1980) to improve mathematical instruction. Serves as a reference and source of new mathematical ideas and activities.

Usiskin, Zalman. 1980. What should not be in the algebra and geometry curricula of average college-bound students? *Mathematics Teacher* 73 (6) (September 1980): 413-424.

Weiss, Iris R. 1978. *Report of the 1977 National Survey of Science, Mathematics, and Social Studies Education.* Research Triangle Park, N.C.: Center for Educational Research and Evaluation (distributed by U.S. Government Printing Office).

Wirtz, William Willard, et al. 1977. *On Further Examination. Report of the Advisory Panel on the Scholastic Aptitude Test Score Decline.* New York: College Entrance Examination Board.

Zelinka, Martha. 1978. Edward Griffith Begle. *American Mathematical Monthly* 85 (8) (October 1978): 629-631.

2. The Theories of Mathematical Learning

THOMAS A. ROMBERG

This chapter is about the learning of mathematics. When they are faced with the task of teaching a mathematics topic, all teachers make implicit assumptions about how their students learn. Based on those assumptions, teachers make decisions about how instruction should proceed, the nature of the mathematical topic, and other practical considerations such as available time and number of students. The intent of this chapter is to provide an overview of the theories of learning that have been posed by psychologists, to relate those theories to the learning of mathematics, and to provide an annotated listing of relevant books and articles.[1]

Theories of Learning

Notice the plural—theories of learning. There are many different theories, because how humans learn is extremely complex. First, there is no general agreement on a definition of learning. Some say it is "change in behavior," others "acquisition of new knowledge" or "gaining a new understanding." In addition, there is no agreement on either the details of how learning takes place or what constitutes reasonable evidence that learning has taken place. The latter is necessary if theories are to be tested—validated or falsified.

Second, part of the reason for lack of agreement on a learning theory is that there are lots of different kinds of learning. For example, learning

1 The research reported in this chapter was funded by the Wisconsin Center for Education Research, which is supported in part by a grant from the National Institute of Education (Grant No. NIE-G-84-0008). The opinions expressed in this chapter do not necessarily reflect the position, policy, or endorsement of the National Institute of Education.

how an ellipse is defined and the form of an equation that can be used to represent it is different from learning how to solve simultaneous equations using matrices, and both are different from learning how to use trigonometric ideas to solve a surveying problem. Thus, depending upon what kind of learning a psychologist studies — concepts, skills, problem solving — a different theory may be developed.

Third, psychologists have made different philosophic assumptions about the nature of the learning process. These contrasting assumptions include the following: whether learning occurs by passive reflection or by active construction, whether limits of learning are biologically determined or environmentally determined, whether learning is a rational process or an irrational process.

Thus, given that there are different things to be learned and that psychologists have made such differing assumptions about learning, it should not be surprising that they have proposed many different explanations of how learning occurs.

I have chosen to concentrate on seven general theories that were developed during this century and currently influence the way the learning of mathematics is studied. Each of the first six theories has explained some aspect of mathematical learning well, yet each is inadequate on other aspects. Following these six perspectives, I present the seventh theory, which has become dominant in psychological work in the last decade but has as yet had little impact on mathematics instruction. Thus, no theory is "true" or "best." Nevertheless, if one understands the basic ideas of each theory, its strengths and limitations, then one could plausibly follow instructional procedures appropriate to the kind of learning.

Behaviorism

This theory, which evolved during the early part of this century, focuses on the outcomes of learning (behaviors) rather than on how learning occurs. It assumes learning occurs by passively, but rationally, reflecting on stimuli from the environment. And it has been used by scholars to study how desired responses to stimuli (outcomes) become fixed by practice and praise (reinforcement). Learning is viewed as change in behavior (or performance), and change scores (pre- vs. post-test differences) on some measure of performance are often used as evidence for learning.

This theory, in its many forms, has strongly influenced all education in the United States and mathematics education in particular. From the publication of Edward L. Thorndike's *The Psychology of Arithmetic* (1922) through Robert Gagné's *The Conditions of Learning* (1965), mathematics educators have utilized principles drawn from behaviorism. For example, drill-and-practice routines (e.g., to memorize multiplication facts, or factor trinomials, or solve linear equations) follow the tenets of this theory.

Differential (or Mediational) Behaviorism

In the 1930s a variant of behaviorism was developed in response to a major flaw in classical behaviorism. It had been assumed that different individuals would exhibit the same behaviors if they were given the same stimuli and reinforcements. However, data failed to support this assertion. Different individuals learned faster, retained more, and showed other variations in learning. To explain these variations, many hypotheses were posed and examined. Explanations gradually focused on genetically determined biological or neurological differences in how information was absorbed. They argued that individuals differ in learning because of predetermined aptitudes, abilities, capacities, or styles which mediate how information is processed. One major line of research based on this theory has been "aptitude-by-treatment interaction (ATI) studies" (Cronbach and Snow 1977). In such studies, students with different aptitudes receive different treatments. Schools today form ability groups and tracks, for instance, based on these ideas. Again, learning involves a change in performance, and change scores constitute the usual evidence of learning for this theory.

Gestalt Constructivism

While behaviorism in its many forms was an adequate model for many forms of learning (particularly low-level concepts and skills), it was totally inadequate in explaining how one discovered a relationship, proved a theorem, and solved complex problems. Repeated practice and reinforcement cannot make someone a creative mathematician; they do not foster invention of new ideas. Learning is not simply change in performance. Therefore, change scores, the increases in number of correct answers, fail to capture changes in strategies or ways of thinking about a problem. Thus, in the 1930s, Gestalt theory developed. The word "Gestalt" means organization or configuration. This theory posits that learning involves active construction rather than passive absorption from the environment; and it implies that students experience the world in meaningful patterns and then construct meanings from those patterns. For this theory, evidence of learning has been in terms of changes in how persons said they thought about problems (coded from think-aloud interviews). The best examples of this approach can be found in the work of Wertheimer (1959) who was interested in the problem of "productive think-ing" in mathematics. Most early work on mathematical problem solving (e.g., Pólya 1945, Hadamard 1945) is rooted in this theory. Also, in con-trast to the behaviorists, the place of meaning was of particular interest to these psychologists. The work of William Brownell (1972a, 1972b) and his influence on mathematics instruction are of particular importance on this topic.

Developmental Constructivism

As differential behaviorism grew out of a need to explain why per-sons differ in responses, developmental constructivism grew out of a need to explain why the same persons at different ages constructed different meanings from the same environment. The explanation for this phenomenon, due in large part to Jean Piaget, also was based on biologi-cal traits. He argued that human learning differs and changes in various evolutionary stages which he called preoperational, concrete operation-al, and formal operational. Piaget's work first became widely known in the United States in the 1960s (Flavell 1963) and since that time has profoundly influenced mathematics education research. The influence has been particularly strong on the study of young children's learning; it is now well-documented that they see and operate on the world different-ly than do adults. Learning, for Piaget, involves the restructuring of knowledge. Furthermore, in this theory, change or restructuring is de-pendent upon the notion of maintaining balance or equilibrium and the processes of assimilation and accommodation needed to maintain that balance. Evidence of learning for Piaget was based on his *méthode clini-que*: this involved interviews of children as they worked on clever sets of problems.

Dialectic Constructivism

In contrast to Piaget's explanation of differential construction over time, Soviet psychologists (notably, Luria 1979, Vygotsky 1962, and Leont'ev 1981) posed an alternate theory where imbalance not equi-librium is considered normal. Change—a student's language develop-ment, in particular—is dependent on dialectic synthesis, one's environment, and the actions or activities in which the subject is involved. Again, evidence is typically based on data from interviews of individual subjects. Interest in this theory for mathematics teaching is in part due to the publication of the volumes of *Soviet Studies in the Psychology of Learn-ing and Teaching of Mathematics* (Kilpatrick and Wirszup 1969-1975) and the publication in English of Krutetskii's *The Psychology of Mathematical Abilities in School Children* (1976).

Psychoanalytic Behaviorism

This theory, which assumes that learning is based on the irrational desires, fears, and other emotions of humans, is rooted in the work of Sigmund Freud at the turn of the last century. It assumes that biological drives (hunger, sexuality, self-concept) are at the basis of learning. Humans construct attitudes and perspectives based on these drives. Erikson (1968) has proposed stages of development from this perspective. Evidence supporting this theory comes from clinical psychoanalysis (a special form of clinical interview). This theory has become prominent in mathematics education in the study of mathematics phobias and similar phenomena.

Cognitive Science

Although each of the above six general theories has contributed significantly to our understanding of the learning of mathematics, most current psychological research is based on very recent notions about how humans process information. Behaviorists ignored processing; differentialists argued for global aptitudes; and others gave other general biological or environmental explanations for how learning takes place. Cognitive scientists, on the other hand, have built (and are building) elaborate models to explain the details of processing using the analogy that the brain operates in a manner similar to a computer (Gardner 1985). Technically, cognitive science is not a theory of learning, since its emphasis is not on changed behavior, but on how information is processed. Only very recently has there been much work on change in processing (Nason and Cooper 1985).

Cognitive science is multifaceted in that it has incorporated important ideas from many of the prior theories. Figure 2.1 indicates some of the key notions of cognitive science. Processing begins with stimulus information, but in this theory information is not considered to be isolated pieces but a coherent network of ideas from a content domain. The best example comes from the research on young children's learning of addition and subtraction. That domain has a semantic and a syntactic structure (Carpenter et al. 1982). Information is filtered by a perceptual mechanism that involves the beliefs and attitudes held by an individual with respect to that information. This activity is referred to as the metacognitive component of learning. In this mechanism, mediating vari-

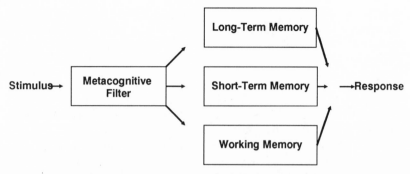

Figure 2.1. Basic notions about how information is processed in cognitive science.

ables from both differential and psychoanalytic behaviorism have been considered.

Next, mediated information is organized and stored in memory. A critical aspect of cognitive theory is that it distinguishes three types of memory: working memory, short-term memory, and long-term memory. Working memory involves the amount of information that one can actually process at one point in time. The units of information may be individual pieces or "chunks" of related pieces (chunked information). Information is stored in short-term memory if it is to be used in a relatively short period of time. Then it is either dumped (forgotten) or stored in long-term memory. Long-term memory consists of schemas (like computer programs) of several different types. One type involves the existing semantic networks and data structures the individual has developed (his or her organized knowledge of the world). Such schemas may be organized in several different ways, such as in scenes, scripts, stories, or classifications. A second type of schema consists of the Piagetian rules of thinking. A third type includes control processes, the rules and strategies (heuristics) available for memorizing, solving problems, and so on.

Some of this system is assumed to be biological in origin (hardwired), and some evolves as a result of acting upon the environment (software). Also, according to the theory, the content of what is to be learned (stimulus) and its relationship to what is stored in long-term memory are critical.

The implications of this theory are only now being drawn for mathematics instruction. However, it is certainly clear that teachers should take into account misconceptions (inappropriate schemas) some students have about new information being presented. For example, many algebra students, when they see the expression $a + b = \_$, assume that the equal sign means *find* an answer. This misconception, undoubtedly reinforced by the handheld calculator, must be dealt with when trying to teach students to write equivalent expressions such as $a + b = b + a$.

Summary

This brief overview of the theories of learning posed by psychologists illustrates the complexity of the topic. We do not know how learning occurs for each student. However, some knowledge of the complexity of learning, and how theorists have conceived and studied it, should be helpful to teachers in planning adequate mathematics instruction.

The Learning of Mathematics

The general theories discussed in the previous section have been developed to encompass all areas of learning. The question being raised in this section is: What is unique about mathematics? The concepts of mathematics are similar to those of science, social studies, and so on; its processes, while algorithmic, are probably little different from learning to conjugate regular verbs or solve chemical equations; problem solving is not unique to mathematics. The question of uniqueness may be associated first with what is involved in *doing* mathematics and second with the *structure* of mathematics.

Activities of Mathematics

When non-mathematicians, such as sociologists, psychologists, and many teachers, look at mathematics, what they often see is a static and bounded discipline. This vision is perhaps a reflection of the mathematics they studied in school rather than an insight into the discipline itself. Mathematics should be viewed as activities people do, but those activities are not carried out solely by following predetermined rules. Even with superficial knowledge about mathematics, it is easy to recognize four related activities common to all of mathematics: *abstracting, inventing, proving,* and *applying*.

The *abstractness* of mathematics is easy to see. We operate with abstract numbers without worrying about how to relate them in each case to concrete objects. The farther one proceeds in mathematics, the more remote from experience are the concepts introduced. This process of abstracting, characteristic of each branch in mathematics, is distinguished by three features. In the first place, it deals with quantities and spatial forms, abstracting them from other properties of objects. Second, increasing degrees of abstraction go very much further than abstractions in other sciences. Finally, mathematics moves almost wholly in the field of abstract concepts and their interrelationships. While the natural scientist turns to experiments for proof of his assertions, the mathematician applies only argument. For mathematicians, abstracting involves construction. However, we all expect naive learners to acquire the common abstractions used in mathematics; teachers may find ideas from both constructive and behavioral psychological theories helpful.

Inventing is a second aspect of what mathematicians do. There are two aspects to all mathematical inventions: The conjecture, or guess, about the relationship, followed by the demonstration of the logic of the assertion. All mathematical ideas — even new abstractions, like irrational numbers — are inventions. To assist in the invention of their abstractions, mathematicians make constant use of theorems, mathematical models, methods, and physical analogies, and they have recourse to various completely concrete examples. Clearly, inventing is a constructive process.

The third activity that mathematicians engage in is *proving*. No proposition is considered a mathematical product until it has been rigorously proved by a logical argument. The results of mathematics are distinguished by a high degree of logical rigor, and the mathematical argument is conducted with sufficient scrupulousness to make it incontestable and completely convincing to anyone who understands it. But the rigor of mathematics is not absolute; it is continually developing. Unfortunately, the writings of mathematicians often give a misleading view of their work. The processes of abstraction and invention are ignored in most published articles, and only the proof of an invention is usually presented. The process of building logical proofs has not been the object of much psychological research; however, notions of heuristics from constructivism undoubtedly bear on how students discover the connections between ideas that are so essential for proofs.

The final activity that mathematicians are involved in is *applying*. The importance of mathematics arises from the fact that its abstractions and theorems originate in the actual world. In one way or another, abstract mathematics is applied in almost every science, from mechanics to political economics. The work on problem solving from a constructivist (or a cognitive science) perspective applies here.

Structure of Mathematics

It is now commonly believed that learners construct understanding. They do not simply mirror what they are told or what they read. They look for meaning and will try to find regularity and order in the events of their world. This means that naive theories will always be constructed by each individual as a part of the learning process. Thus, to understand something like mathematics is to know the relationships between ideas in mathematics. This knowledge is stored in clusters and organized into schemas that individuals use to interpret familiar situations and reason about new ones. If the bits of information which are typically taught to students are related to each other via structures that become accessible in memory, they are likely to be retained. Thus, new ideas should be related to established schemas so that naive theories can be changed and adapted. This network of interrelated ideas needs to be developed by students and must be a central part of the learning process. Since the structure of the discipline of mathematics deals with the interrelatedness of abstract ideas, this structure must be part of what students gradually acquire over time. Obviously, ideas from cognitive science are most appropriate here.

In summary, the notions from the various general theories of learning often do not apply to the learning of mathematics in direct and obvious ways. Nevertheless, each theory has influenced and will continue to influence the way scholars and teachers view the learning of mathematics.

REFERENCES

Brownell, William A. 1972a. The place of meaning in mathematics instruction: Selected research papers. In *Studies in Mathematics*, vol. 22, edited by J. Fred Weaver and Jeremy Kilpatrick. Stanford, Calif.: School Mathematics Study Group.

―――. 1972b. The place of meaning in mathematics instruction: Selected theoretical papers. In *Studies in Mathematics*, vol. 21, edited by J. Fred Weaver and Jeremy Kilpatrick. Stanford, Calif.: School Mathematics Study Group.

Carpenter, Thomas P., James M. Moser, and Thomas A. Romberg, eds. 1982. *Addition and Subtraction: A Cognitive Perspective*. Hillsdale,

N.J.: Erlbaum.

Cronbach, Lee J., and Richard E. Snow. 1977. *Aptitudes and Instructional Methods: A Handbook for Research on Interactions*. New York: Irvington.

Erikson, Erik H. 1968. *Identity, Youth, and Crisis*. New York: Norton.

Flavell, John H. 1963. *The Developmental Psychology of Jean Piaget*. New York: Van Nostrand.

Gagné, Robert M. 1965. *The Conditions of Learning*. New York: Holt, Rinehart & Winston.

Gardner, Howard. 1985. *The Mind's New Science: A History of the Cognitive Revolution*. New York: Basic Books.

Hadamard, Jacques. 1945. *An Essay on the Psychology of Invention in the Mathematical Field*. New York: Dover.

Kilpatrick, Jeremy, and Izaak Wirszup, eds. 1969-1975. *Soviet Studies in the Psychology of Learning and Teaching Mathematics*. 14 vols. University of Chicago Survey of East European Mathematics Literature. Chicago: University of Chicago Press.

Krutetskii, Vadim A. 1976. *The Psychology of Mathematical Abilities in School Children*. Translated by Joan Teller. Edited by Jeremy Kilpatrick and Izaak Wirszup. Chicago: University of Chicago Press.

Leont'ev, A. N. 1981. The problem of activity in psychology. In *The Concept of Activity in Soviet Psychology*, edited and translated by James V. Wertsch. Armonk, N.Y.: Sharpe.

Luria, Aleksandr R. 1979. *The Making of Mind: A Personal Account of Soviet Psychology*. Edited by Michael Cole and Sheila Cole. Cambridge, Mass.: Harvard University Press.

Nason, R., and T. Cooper. 1985. A theory of mathematics education: An information processing view. Paper given at the International Conference on the Foundation and Methodology of the Discipline Mathematics Education. University of Bielefeld (FRG), July 1985.

Pólya, George. 1945. *How to Solve It: A New Aspect of Mathematical Method.* 1957. 2nd ed. Garden City, N.Y.: Doubleday. 1971. Reprint. Princeton, N.J.: Princeton University Press.

Thorndike, Edward L. 1922. *The Psychology of Arithmetic.* New York: Macmillan.

Vygotsky, Lev S. 1962. *Thought and Language.* Edited and translated by Eugenia Hanfmann and Gertrude Vakar. Cambridge, Mass.: MIT Press.

Wertheimer, Max 1959. *Productive Thinking.* Edited by Michael Wertheimer. New York: Harper & Row.

BIBLIOGRAPHY

The references have been organized into three categories. A small number of references cover all the theories outlined in the essay. They are followed by references specific to each theory. Finally, a few other references specifically on mathematical problem solving are presented. (These annotations were prepared with the help of Nancy Mack and Sufian Kamal). The sections, then, are:

- Theories of Learning – General References
- Behaviorism
- Differential Behaviorism
- Gestalt Constructivism
- Developmental Constructivism
- Dialectic Constructivism
- Psychoanalytic Behaviorism
- Cognitive Science
- Mathematical Problem Solving.

Theories of Learning — General References

Fehr, Howard F. 1953. Theories of learning related to the field of mathematics. In *NCTM Yearbook 21*, 1-41.

> Out-of-date but classic example of how psychological theories can be related to mathematics. Examines three theories of learning: association, conditioning, and what field psychologies say about learning.

Gardner, Howard. 1985. *The Mind's New Science: A History of the Cognitive Revolution*. New York: Basic Books.

> Presents a well-argued account of the philosophical and psychological issues which underlie the recent cognitive revolution (pp. 49-137), tracing the problems psychologists have faced in studying how the mind works, reasons, and learns.

Hilgard, Ernest R., and Gordon H. Bower. 1975. *Theories of Learning*. 4th ed. Englewood Cliffs, N.J.: Prentice-Hall.

> The classic text on learning theories, written for graduate students in psychology, so it is both historically detailed and technical. The first chapter is an excellent introduction; it describes two opposing views of epistemology, empiricism and rationalism, as a background for comparing and classifying modern learning theories.

Langer, Jonas. 1969. *Theories of Development* New York: Holt, Rinehart & Winston.

> Text for psychology students on the psychological theories of development. Langer presents three developmental perspectives (behaviorism, constructivism, and psychoanalytic), with excellent contrasts of their intent and limitations.

Philips, Denis C., and Jonas F. Soltis. 1985. *Perspectives on Learning*. New York: Teachers College Press.

> Presents an overview of theorizing about learning, and is an excellent introduction to the problems of building theories. Directed toward classroom teachers, it can be used as a textbook for studying learning theories. The aim is to induce teachers to think about learning, how it happens, and what it is. The last chapter presents several vignettes concerning arguments and issues of learning theories, which can be used for classroom discussion.

Resnick, Lauren B., and Wendy W. Ford. 1981. *The Psychology of Mathematics for Instruction*. Hillsdale, N.J.: Erlbaum.

> The best single book on the learning of mathematics. Traces psychologists' efforts to discover and explain the nature of learning and thought processes in mathematics. Also gives some insight about how expert thought in mathematics proceeds, how expertise develops, and how instruction can enhance the process of mathematics learning.

Skemp, Richard R. 1971. *The Psychology of Learning Mathematics*. Baltimore, Md.: Penguin Books.

The first section handles questions such as "What is understanding?" and "How can we help bring it about?" Psychological ideas are discussed in this section with references made to mathematics. The second part relates specific areas of knowledge in mathematics to psychological ideas.

Behaviorism

Gagné, Robert M. 1965. *The Conditions of Learning*. New York: Holt, Rinehart & Winston.

Presents a classification of eight types of learning based on "S-R" (stimulus-response) theories, characterizing each in terms of the conditions of learning; then draws educational implications, in terms of planning, managing, instructing, and selecting media. Probably the reference most influential on current schooling practices.

Langer, Jonas. 1969. The mechanical mirror. Chapter 3 in *Theories of Development*, 51-86. New York: Holt, Rinehart & Winston.

Pp. 51-73 elucidate the behaviorist theory of learning, which conceives of all psychological phenomena as behavior stimulated by the environment, not as mental processes. Discusses the basic assumption of this theory that the child is like a machine that must respond to the stimuli of an outside force and increasingly conform its responses to the demands of that force. Goes on to treat the mechanisms of transmitting the environmental content to the child (respondent and operant conditioning) and the formation of associations, which constitute the growth and memory of the child.

Shulman, L. S. 1970. Psychology and mathematics education. In *Mathematics Education*, edited by Edward G. Begle, 23-71. 69th Yearbook of the National Society for the Study of Education (Part I). Chicago: University of Chicago Press.

Discusses the learning theories of Bruner, Gagné, and Ausubel, particularly with regard to the areas of instructional objectives, entering characteristics of students, and teacher-learning activities and procedures.

Sowder, Larry. 1980. Concept and principle learning. In *Research in Mathematics Education*, edited by Richard J. Shumway, 244-285. Reston, Va.: National Council of Teachers of Mathematics.

Discusses various definitions of the terms *concept* and *principle*. Presents an overview of typical research variables as related to concept and principle, with research trends and issues in the learning of concepts and principles.

Suydam, Marilyn N., and Donald J. Dessart. 1980. Skill learning. In

Research in Mathematics Education, edited by Richard J. Shumway, 207-243. Reston, Va.: National Council of Teachers of Mathematics.

> Reviews research on skill learning involving whole numbers, fractions, and decimals, and presents a clinical research model for developing a skill theory in mathematical learning.

Thorndike, Edward L. 1922. *The Psychology of Arithmetic.* New York: Macmillan.

> The classic text on the application of behaviorist principles to school subjects. Presents ten tasks for relating psychology and mathematics, then illustrates these tasks with aspects of mathematics, including meanings of numbers, arithmetical language, problem solving, and arithmetical reasoning.

Differential Behaviorism

Anastasi, Anne. 1958. *Differential Psychology: Individual and Group Differences in Behavior.* 3rd ed. New York: Macmillan.

> Basic graduate psychology text on differential mediation and its mechanisms. Chapter 1, "Origins of differential psychology," introduces the theory and traces individual differences in psychological theory from Plato to the early 1900s. Efficient statistical techniques for analyzing data are presented as a method that has greatly contributed to differential psychology.

Cronbach, L. J., and R. E. Snow. 1977. *Aptitudes and Instructional Methods.* New York: Irvington.

> Presents the basic perspectives about ATI research and its methods, a review of studies, and a summary of what has been learned.

Fennema, Elizabeth, and Merlyn J. Behr. 1980. Individual differences and the learning of mathematics. In *Research in Mathematics Education*, edited by Richard J. Shumway, 324-355. Reston, Va.: National Council of Teachers of Mathematics.

> Reports the status of knowledge about individual differences in variables related to mathematics learning and instruction, and discusses and examines new trends in examining individual differences. Some areas are identified in which research might significantly improve learning mathematics.

Kulm, Gerald. 1980. Research on mathematics attitude. In *Research in Mathematics Education*, edited by Richard J. Shumway, 356-387. Reston, Va.: National Council of Teachers of Mathematics.

> Defines *attitude* and procedures for assessing attitude, with hypotheses for future research on mechanisms by which attitudes impact learning behavior.

Langer, Jonas. 1969. The mechanical mirror. Chapter 3 in *Theories of*

Development, 51-86. New York: Holt, Rinehart & Winston.

Pp. 74-86 introduce the problem of non-observable mediational processes which influence overt responses, with ties to differential psychology and the Soviet dialectical notions.

Gestalt Constructivism

Brownell, William A. 1972. The place of meaning in mathematics instruction: Selected research papers. In *Studies in Mathematics*, vol. 22, edited by J. Fred Weaver and Jeremy Kilpatrick. Stanford, Calif.: School Mathematics Study Group.

Commentaries on measurement evaluation and research methods, critiquing behavioral methods of inquiry. Ten empirical studies follow, including the classic "Borrowing in subtraction," which made "fair trading" rather than "equal additions" the subtraction algorithm used in American schools.

_____. 1972. The place of meaning in mathematics instruction: Selected theoretical papers. In *Studies in Mathematics*, vol. 21, edited by J. Fred Weaver and Jeremy Kilpatrick. Stanford, Calif.: School Mathematics Study Group.

Includes 17 of Brownell's theoretical papers, grouped under meaning theory, broader contexts, and readiness. For the student interested in the application of psychological ideas to mathematics by one of the most influential thinkers of this century, this collection of papers should be mandatory reading.

Hadamard, Jacques S. 1945. *An Essay on the Psychology of Invention in the Mathematical Field*. New York: Dover.

Raises various questions concerning origination of ideas, the role of the unconscious, etc., by presenting the author's own views and those of other prominent mathematicians. Mathematics teachers usually find it easy to relate to the ideas in this book since it deals with mathematical problem solving – a nice example of how the Gestalt perspective of learning relates to mathematics.

Hilgard, Ernest R., and Gordon H. Bower. 1975. Gestalt theory. Chapter 8 in *Theories of Learning*. 4th ed. Englewood Cliffs, N.J.: Prentice-Hall.

Introduces theory of Gestalt constructivism. The way in which a subject structures or "sees" problem situations and how salient the correct action is within the structure, are of primary importance to Gestalt psychologists. Laws of "perceptual" organization are discussed and then examined in relation to six different and typical problems of learning.

Developmental Constructivism

Carpenter, Thomas P. 1980. Research in cognitive development. In *Research in Mathematics Education*, edited by Richard J. Shumway, 146-206. Reston, Va.: National Council of Teachers of Mathematics.

Describes organismic and mechanistic models of cognitive development and research in the development of mathematical concepts, with educational applications of research findings.

Flavell, John H. 1963. *The Developmental Psychology of Jean Piaget.* New York: Van Nostrand.

Summarizes Piaget's basic theories and research and evaluates the theories both methodologically and in the light of related work done by others.

Langer, Jonas. 1969. The organic lamp. Chapter 4 in *Theories of Development.* New York: Holt, Rinehart & Winston.

Discusses the constructivist theory of development, which assumes that development is a process of interaction between organismic and environmental factors. Numerous examples of children's responses are presented to clarify the components of the theory, and the work of Piaget and of Werner is discussed in relation to this theory.

Dialectic Constructivism

Krutetskii, Vadim A. 1976. *The Psychology of Mathematical Abilities in School Children.* Translated by Joan Teller. Edited by Jeremy Kilpatrick and Izaak Wirszup. Chicago: University of Chicago Press.

Reports the details and the outcomes of a 12-year theoretical and experimental research program begun in 1955 with the aim of investigating the structure and formation of mathematical abilities in schoolchildren. According to Krutetskii, mental activities involved in mathematical problems may be divided into three stages: gathering information, processing information, and retaining information about the solution. To each one of these stages corresponds one or more abilities that influence the nature of the pupil's performance at that stage. The importance of Krutetskii's work stems not only from his thoughtful analysis and discussion of a critical aspect of mathematics learning, but also from the diversity of methods he utilized in his research, the variety and ingenuity of the employed tasks, and the comprehensiveness of the review of related literature he presented.

Menchinskaya, N. A. 1969. Fifty years of Soviet instructional psychology. In *Soviet Studies in the Psychology of Learning and Teaching Mathematics*, edited by Jeremy Kilpatrick and Izaak Wirszup, vol. 1, 5-27. University of Chicago Survey of East European Mathematics Literature. Chicago: University of Chicago Press.

Provides an overview of Soviet research studies concerning changes that occur in mental activity under the influence of instruction. The studies are presented chronologically to illustrate the stages in Soviet instructional psychology.

Riegel, Klaus F. 1979. *Foundations of Dialectical Psychology*. New York: Academic.

Basic text on dialectic psychology for graduate students. However, Chapter 1, "The dialectic of human development," is a good introduction to the theory. In that chapter the importance of dialogue in dialectical psychology is discussed and an interpretation of development is given which focuses upon simultaneous movements along four dimensions. Piaget and traditional psychology are critiqued with respect to these features of dialectical psychology. Finally, a manifesto for dialectical psychology is discussed.

Psychoanalytic Behaviorism

Langer, Jonas. 1969. The psychoanalytic perspective. Chapter 2 in *Theories of Development*. New York: Holt, Rinehart & Winston.

Discusses an approach to development related to behavioral theory by learning but influenced by psychoanalytic hypotheses. According to this approach, conditioned reflexes do not adequately explain many of children's behaviors, like imitation, wanting specific things, and concept learning. It maintains that covert responses attributable to the child mediate production of other overt responses. It claims that what is needed for adequate explanation of children's behavior is a conception of a machine with complex programs for observation, storage, desire, conceptualization, and performance.

Cognitive Science

Anderson, John R. 1980. *Cognitive Psychology and Its Implications*. San Francisco, Calif.: W. H. Freeman.

Textbook for graduate students in psychology. Discusses elements of information processing theory with references to research studies, and presents numerous examples. Also examines problem solving, reasoning, and three aspects of language from an information-processing view.

Behr, Merlyn J., Richard Lesh, Thomas R. Post, and Edward A. Silver. 1983. Rational number concepts. In *Acquisition of Mathematics Concepts and Processes*, edited by Richard Lesh and Marsha Landau, 91-126. New York: Academic.

Describes the NSF-supported Rational Number Project, which was conducted by the authors to investigate "the development of cognitive structures of rational number thinking within a well-defined, theoretically-based instructional program" (p. 98). In particular, this project investigated the mechanisms children in grades 2-8 use to achieve functional use of rational numbers, and the role played by representational systems to serve that end.

Biggs, John B., and Kevin F. Collis. 1982. *Evaluating the Quality of Learning: The SOLO Taxonomy.* New York: Academic.

Presents a criterion-referenced taxonomy for measuring the quality of learning, which grew out of an attempt to develop implications for teachers based on Piaget's notions. The taxonomy is called a Structure of the Observed Learning Outcomes (SOLO).

Bishop, Alan J. 1983. Space and geometry. In *Acquisition of Mathematics Concepts and Processes*, edited by Richard Lesh and Marsha Landau, 175-204. New York: Academic.

Reviews the available research on space and geometry after identifying two different thrusts within it. The first is concerned with children's understanding of spatial and geometric concepts, and the other with spatial abilities and visual processing. Using this framework of understandings and abilities, the chapter analyzes data gathered from a research study done in Papua, New Guinea, and discusses its results. Concludes by pointing out some important issues in the domain of space and geometry that need to be researched. Places particular emphasis in this respect on the interpretations of children's meanings and on the development of the abilities of interpreting figural information and visual processing.

Carpenter, Thomas P., and James M. Moser. 1983. The acquisition of addition and subtraction concepts. In *Acquisition of Mathematics Concepts and Processes*, edited by Richard Lesh and Marsha Landau, 7-44. New York: Academic.

Reviews and analyzes recent developments in research on the acquisition by young children of basic whole-number addition and subtraction concepts and skills. Particularly focuses on the analysis of solution processes and their development. Describes the authors' research program on addition and subtraction in grades 1-3 and relates it to other programs with similar objectives. As a background to discussion of the recent developments referred to above, the chapter also reviews earlier investigations on how children solve different basic addition and subtraction problems and discusses why some problems are more difficult than others.

Chi, M. T. H., R. Glaser, and E. Rees. 1982. Expertise in problem solving. In *Advances in the Psychology of Human Intelligence*, edited by Robert J. Sternberg, 7-76. Hillsdale, N.J.: Erlbaum.

Excellent presentation of an important method of identifying problem-solving processes in cognitive science. Presents theoretical and artificial intelligence models of physics problem solving. Examines in the light of theoretical models approaches taken by "experts" and "novices" in solving various physics problems.

Davis, Robert B. 1983. Complex mathematical cognition. In *The Development of Mathematical Thinking*, edited by Herbert P. Ginsburg, 253-290. New York: Academic.

Discusses an "alternative" paradigm about how humans think about mathematical problems, which regards mathematical thought processes as fundamental. The paradigm is based upon data of several researchers, and its analysis is based upon information-processing conceptualizations.

Gardner, Howard. 1985. *The Mind's New Science: A History of the Cognitive Revolution*. New York: Basic Books.

A very readable history of cognitive science, required reading for all who want to understand cognitive science. Includes a well-drawn picture of the revolt against behaviorism and then traces the influences of philosophy, psychology, artificial intelligence, linguistics, anthropology, and neuroscience on the converging ideas dominant in cognitive science. Illustrates work in visual processing, mental imagery, classification, and rationality. Concludes with an analysis of strengths and limitations of cognitive science.

Groen, Gary, and Carolyn Kieran. 1983. In search of Piagetian mathematics. In *The Development of Mathematical Thinking*, edited by Herbert P. Ginsburg, 351-375. New York: Academic.

To examine the shift from the Piagetian framework of research on children's mathematics to information-processing theory, a set of questions regarding Piaget and school mathematics is presented. The questions are not directly answered, but they present ideas to lead to more questions which will allow reasonable inferences to be made regarding the nature of Piagetian mathematics.

Karplus, Robert, Steven Pulos, and Elizabeth K. Stage. 1983. Proportional reasoning of early adolescents. In *Acquisition of Mathematics Concepts and Processes*, edited by Richard Lesh and Marsha Landau, 45-90. New York: Academic.

Presents research on the development of proportional reasoning in early adolescent students. Focuses on investigating the factors causing difficulty in proportional reasoning and the diversity of reasoning approaches used by students, and attempts to explain them in terms of cognitive and attitudinal variables. Reviews previous research on proportions and describes teaching approaches for enhancing proportional reasoning capabilities of early adolescents.

Resnick, Lauren B. 1983. A developmental theory of number understanding. In *The Development of Mathematical Thinking*, edited by Herbert P. Ginsburg, 109-151. New York: Academic.

Outlines a theory of number representation for three periods of development. Proposes levels of understanding to be achieved through an active interplay between schematic and procedural knowledge.

Riley, Mary S., James G. Greeno, and Joan I. Heller. 1983. Development of children's problem-solving ability in arithmetic. In *The Development of Mathematical Thinking*, edited by Herbert P. Ginsburg, 153-196. New York: Academic.

Research studies reviewed in this chapter show interactions between conceptual and procedural knowledge in problem solving. Also discusses models concerning the nature of conceptual development.

Romberg, Thomas A., and Thomas P. Carpenter. 1985. Research on teaching and learning mathematics. In *Handbook of Research on Teaching*, 3rd ed., edited by Merlin C. Wittrock, 850-873. New York: Macmillan.

Reviews research drawn from two disciplines of scientific inquiry (learning and teaching), then draws implications from current work in both disciplines with respect to current practice, research, and curricular reform.

Skemp, Richard R. 1979. *Intelligence, Learning, and Action.* Chichester, England: Wiley.

Discusses a theory on the conception of intelligence from the point of view of the function of intelligence. The first part presents an overview of the nature of intelligence while the second presents a model based upon director systems. The last section compares this model with others and suggests applications to education.

Sternberg, Robert J. 1982. A componential approach to intellectual development. In *Advances in the Psychology of Human Intelligence*, edited by Robert J. Sternberg, 413-464. Hillsdale, N.J.: Erlbaum.

Provides a description of components of information processing and how these components develop and change over time. Compares components of this information processing system with alternative views of information processing.

Thorndike, Robert L. 1984. *Intelligence as Information Processing: The Mind and the Computer.* Bloomington, Ind.: Phi Delta Kappa's Center on Evaluation, Development, and Research.

A brief introduction to cognitive science. Thorndike examines the emphasis that cognitive psychology puts on human problem-solving processes in relation to traditional psychometric approaches to studying human abilities. The author recognizes the computer as a model for understanding cognition and focuses on the use of flowcharting for the purposes of developing intelligent human behavior — in particular, problem solving. The assumption is that a chart can help in focusing the attention of psychologists on aspects of information processing capability which must be mastered by the competent problem solver. Much space is devoted to research relating to the steps of flowcharting, with possible educational implications.

VanLehn, Kurt. 1983. On the representation of procedures in repair theory. In *The Development of Mathematical Thinking*, edited by Herbert P. Ginsburg, 197-252. New York: Academic.

Discusses repair theory and "core procedures" in reference to students attempting to correct their errors. Discusses "perfect prefix learning" as a representative model for repair theory.

Vergnaud, Gerard. 1983. Multiplicative structures. In *Acquisition of Mathematics Concepts and Processes*, edited by Richard Lesh and Marsha Landau, 127-174. New York: Academic.

Introduces the framework of a conceptual field and defines it as "a set of problems and situations for the treatment of which concepts, procedures, and representations of different but narrowly interconnected types are necessary" (p. 127). Utilization of this framework is believed to facilitate the study of inter-related concepts over a period of time. Multiplicative structures constitute a main conceptual field whose operations and notions are of the multiplicative type, like multiplication, division, fractions, ratios, and similarity. Relations among these concepts must be pointed out during the course of study.

Mathematical Problem Solving

Hill, Claire Conley. 1979. *Problem solving: Learning and Teaching, An Annotated Bibliography*. New York: Nichols.

Presents an annotated bibliography of a large collection of references on problem solving, classified into 13 sections, each of which reflects a different conception of problem solving or an issue relating to the learning/teaching of it. Each section is preceded by a concise discussion relevant to the focus of the annotations in that section. This book is particularly valuable to mathematics educators and researchers in mathematics education, and equally valuable for all interested in problem solving, such as psychologists, scientists, and engineers.

Lesh, Richard, Marsha Landau, and Eric Hamilton. 1983. Conceptual models and applied mathematical problem-solving research. In *Acquisition of Mathematics Concepts and Processes*, edited by Richard Lesh and Marsha Landau, 263-344. New York: Academic.

Discusses the authors' theoretical construct called "conceptual model" that underlies their research program on applied mathematical problem solving. A conceptual model is defined as an adaptive structure consisting of four components: (1) within-concept networks of relations and operations, (2) systems of representations, (3) between-concept systems, and (4) systems of modeling processes. The discussion focuses only on the first two components and is illustrated by rational number concepts. Also discusses results from interviews in which fourth- to eighth-graders solved tasks based on the same arithmetical structure but varying in format and results from the written testing program of the

Rational Number Project. The discussion shows how these results contribute to the understanding of the development of children's conceptual models.

Lester, Frank K., Jr. 1980. Research on mathematical problem solving. In *Research in Mathematics Education*, edited by Richard J. Shumway, 286-323. Reston, Va.: National Council of Teachers of Mathematics.

Presents an overview of representative research on mathematical problem solving with respect to four categories of interacting variables: subject variables, task variables, process variables, and instruction variables. Issues for future research are also presented.

————. 1983. Trends and issues in mathematical problem-solving research. In *Acquisition of Mathematics Concepts and Processes*, edited by Richard Lesh and Marsha Landau, 229-262. New York: Academic.

Presents the nature of mathematical problem solving and then analyzes the relevant research according to five categories of factors that affect problem-solving performance: task factors, process factors, environment factors, instrumentation, and research methodology. Two main conclusions are drawn: the current mathematical problem solving research "is being thoughtfully and systematically conducted" (p. 257), and there is a need for more focus on determining the cognitive demands upon the problem solver.

Schoenfeld, Alan H. 1983. Episodes and executive decisions in mathematical problem solving. In *Acquisition of Mathematics Concepts and Processes*, edited by Richard Lesh and Marsha Landau, 345-396. New York: Academic.

Distinguishes between strategic (executive or managerial) decisions and tactical ones in problem solving. Focuses on the importance of managerial decision making, which must be made at points separating the episodes of a solution, for the success or failure of the solving process. Describes the nature of the major episodes of problem-solving performance, discusses a full protocol, and presents an informal analysis of two other protocols. The aim behind these extended protocol analyses is twofold: to emphasize the critical role of metacognitive or managerial behaviors during problem solving, and to characterize the metacognitive aspects of expert and novice problem-solving behaviors at college level.

3. Curriculum Development

MARTHA J. SIEGEL

Secondary Schools

Curriculum development in the secondary schools of the United States has progressed at varying rates and has been influenced by various factors. The impetus for change in the mathematics curriculum usually is rooted in pressures brought on by the society, the political situation, educational theorists, college and university requirements, the mathematical community, and/or new technological advances. Professional organizations of mathematicians and educators have reflected those pressures and played a central role.

In the colonial period the mathematics curriculum of the schools was primarily arithmetic. Private schools, established in the eighteenth century to produce clergy, navigators, merchants and surveyors, emphasized the mental discipline and practical nature of arithmetic. Church schools were patterned after Latin grammar schools, the university preparatory schools of England. Early colleges included in their curricula the natural sciences and logic. By the latter part of the eighteenth century, the academies were established as egalitarian schools that emphasized the practical subjects. Mathematics was an important component of the curriculum. By the 1850s there were more than 6,000 of these private schools in the United States, enrolling about 300,000 students.

College requirements have always had a great influence on the offerings of the secondary schools. In the early 1700s Harvard required that students know arithmetic, and the high-school curriculum adapted. In 1820 Harvard required algebra and in 1844 geometry. By 1875 geometry was being taught in most high schools, but college entrance requirements differed from school to school. State associations of mathematics teachers in the secondary schools and in the colleges began to form and to issue guidelines for a more uniform secondary school curriculum. These early groups heavily affected the curriculum of the nation's schools. The Committee of Ten of the National Education Association (NEA) reported in 1892 that arithmetic studies should be completed by age 13, algebra should begin at grade 9 and continue for three years, and formal study of geometry, beginning at grade 10, should be studied concurrently with algebra for the next two years. All students would be required to take the first-year algebra course, while those who were not college-bound could go on to bookkeeping and technical mathematics instead of studying the college-preparatory second-year algebra (U.S. Bureau of Education 1893).

The Report of the Committee [of the NEA] on College Entrance Requirements attempted to standardize the college-preparatory curriculum. It expanded the 1892 recommendations of the Committee of Ten by recommending that geometry and algebra be taught in grades 7 through 10, with solid geometry and trigonometry offered to 11th graders and advanced algebra to 12th graders. The advanced algebra course would include elementary treatment of series, the binomial theorem (for fractional and negative exponents), logarithms, determinants, and theory of equations (National Education Association 1899). This program became standard only in the country's best college-preparatory high schools of the day.

In the same year the Chicago section of the American Mathematical Society recommended that all students be required to study mathematics at least two hours per week in grades 9 through 12 (American Mathematical Society 1899). It recommended that geometry should come before algebra and that when algebra studies began they should continue side by side with geometry through 12th grade. Surprisingly, the report emphasized that trigonometry and advanced algebra were college subjects. It is interesting to note that in 1911 fewer than 20% of the high schools in the country offered more than 1 1/2 years of algebra (International Commission on the Teaching of Mathematics 1911).

The College Entrance Examination Board was established in 1900. Today as then, shaping the high-school curriculum to correspond to college entrance tests and requirements is a major part of its work, and a major consideration for secondary schools.

The International Commission on the Teaching of Mathematics presented a survey of mathematics in the public and private secondary schools of the United States in the American Report of 1911 (International Commission ... 1911). The survey of textbooks from the late 1800s to the year 1911 reveals some positive changes in the mathematics curriculum. Geometry continued to follow a year's work in algebra, although there were a few books offering combined work. In geometry there was still a reliance on the five books of Euclid as prepared by Legendre. The trigonometry textbooks varied greatly on the emphasis given to various topics. There had been steady pressure to include the use of Cartesian coordinates in elementary algebra; some textbooks in 1898 did. By 1911 most texts used them, although there was not widespread use of the idea of a locus of points or of functions. There were more equations and more word problems that give rise to equations. But, as earlier, there were very-involved manipulative exercises for transforming unduly-complicated algebraic expressions, which had no application to any of the fairly simple forms growing out of the practical word problems. There continued to be a lack of emphasis on the computational questions concerning degrees of accuracy. Calculations of long division and square roots were treated at length and without discussion about the accuracy of approximate answers.

Many individuals and groups of the time (1800-1930) recommended that the mathematics curriculum stress the use of graphs, computation skills such as approximation, clear and simple notation and vocabulary, and problem solving in algebra as opposed to excessive manipulation drill. There is frequent mention of requiring less formal proof and fewer memorized geometry propositions. The proposal of the MAA National Committee on Mathematical Requirements also includes the need for adding statistics to the curriculum, both in the middle grades and as a senior-level high-school course (National Committee ... 1923).

The early part of the twentieth century saw rapid expansion in secondary enrollments. In 1900, a mere 11% of the appropriate age group in the United States was attending secondary school. By 1934, however, 64% of the eligible youth were in attendance (Progressive Education Association 1940). Learning theorists were beginning to dominate the curriculum reform movement. The behaviorists thought that the activities of the school should reflect the needs of the society and these should be the prevailing guidelines in curriculum construction. The application of the behaviorist approach to the mathematics curriculum can be traced to the classical text, *The Psychology of Arithmetic* (Thorndike 1922) and the handbook *How to Make a Curriculum* (Bobbit 1924). There was a reliance on completely defined teaching tasks designed to stimulate certain responses.

But in the late 1920s the economy was not healthy; unemployment was widespread. The schools were pressured to teach for the vocations instead of concentrating on courses for the college-bound (Progressive Education Association 1940). The place of mathematics in the curriculum was related to democracy, socialization, and the teaching of freedom of thought. By 1940 minimal education for the masses was coming into vogue. John Dewey's "learn by doing" philosophy shaped the progressive era of education (1930-1940). The goal was integration of the curriculum into the entire scope of the students' awareness. There should be no division into different subjects, since this was not realistic. The Final Report of the Joint Commission of the MAA and NCTM (Reeve 1940) urged that the curriculum demonstrate the usefulness of mathematics through applications. Here was acknowledgment that students at every level of cognitive skill development should be taught the subject, with adequate time for review and overviews.

An important role, played by mathematicians — acting individually at that time — led to changes in the geometry syllabus, with a marked effect lasting even into today. George Birkhoff and Ralph Beatley advocated revised (and more defensible) postulates for Euclidean geometry and stressed the use of coordinate geometry and Riemannian geometry. Their textbook *Basic Geometry* (1941), and the earlier books *Elementary Mathematics from an Advanced Viewpoint* (1932, 1939) by Felix Klein, helped to mold the kind of geometry course we see today: an eclectic course with coordinate, descriptive, some Euclidean, and projective geometry, with vector and analytic methods.

The AMS and the MAA, along with the pivotal National Council of Teachers of Mathematics (NCTM), continue to sponsor many individual and joint committees to improve school mathematics. Recommendations by the Joint Commission in 1942 established the typical high-school curriculum which remained in place until the 1960s (Table 3.1) (Kinney and Purdy 1960). The right-hand sequence of Table 3.1 was the more rigorous, while the left-hand side was designed for the terminal or non-science student.

In the years immediately after the start of World War II, the national posture was for a "back to basics" curriculum. The young recruits of the country had shocked the military with their inability to handle many basic mathematical concepts. Although the furor passed, the Second Report of the Commission on Post-War Plans of the NCTM further established the need for all students to study mathematics (1945). There was clearly a need for a two-track system, better evaluation of progress, and an emphasis on building the curriculum around key concepts. The sequential courses meant for the better students, the report suggested, should not be "emasculated" to provide for weaker students; the weaker students should be enrolled in general mathematics courses instead. Studies in

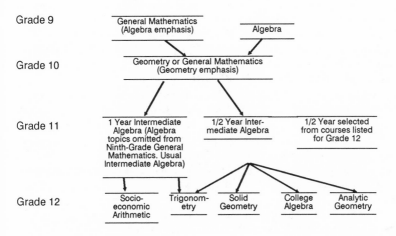

Table 3.1. From Kenney and Blair (1960), with permission.

1948-1949 revealed that about 25% of all high-school pupils were taking either algebra or general mathematics, and only 5% of that population was taking mathematics past plane geometry.

Major changes in mathematics curricula took place in the early 1960s. The launching of Sputnik in 1957 and subsequent federal support of curriculum reform in mathematics and science made new programs possible. The structural approach, due largely to Jerome S. Bruner, was based primarily on the notion of building cognitive structures by using a spiral approach in adding new concepts (Bruner 1960). This spiral structure is found in many of the "new math" materials we associate with the 1960s. Research such as J. Piaget's, although concerned with young children, led to the formative approach, which encouraged the manipulation of real objects and applications to allow the student to make his or her own discoveries. This type of program was quite open-ended and activity-oriented.

Modern mathematics for the research mathematician was undergoing tremendous changes, and university mathematicians objected to the old-fashioned nature of the preparation of the high-school students. Besides proper vocabulary and an appreciation for the general structures in mathematics, the reformers wanted a more-integrated curriculum, an attempt to unify the discipline. The Bourbaki group in France led early reform in an indirect way by presenting a clear and cohesive structured approach to higher-level mathematics. Dieudonné's 1959 speech to the Organisation for European Economic Cooperation seminar at Royaumont was a landmark in the launching of the "new math." He pleaded for the secondary schools to recognize the modern language of mathematics. He stressed that the most concise summary of the plan he could give would be "Euclid must go!" (Howson et al. 1981, 101-107).

The "new math" on the secondary level omitted Euclidean geometry and advanced trigonometry and introduced probability, statistics, and some computer science. There was an attempt by the mathematicians to teach more than rote number and geometric facts. The objective was to show the student the *structure* of mathematics and to give the student an appreciation for the unity of many mathematical ideas through their basic structural similarities. Abstract ideas, correct mathematical terminology, and the introduction of both discovery and generalization characterized the reforms. Dieudonné advocated the replacement of "pure geometry" with matrices and determinants, elementary calculus, graphing of functions, curves given in parametric form, complex numbers, and polar coordinates.

The largest of the U.S. programs, the School Mathematics Study Group (SMSG), directed by Edward G. Begle, may be credited with many elements of today's curriculum. Grades 9 and 10 were to contain SMSG's Elementary Mathematics I and II. There was an increase in emphasis on the properties of a number field, although intuitive and concrete examples were to be presented initially for the student to "discover" many of the abstract rules. While manipulative skills were considered necessary, the goal was to attain *both* manipulative skill and knowledge of concepts. The goals in algebra were generalizations about numbers, use of absolute values, familiarity with inequalities, and appreciation of equations and their loci. Geometry was to be revised to be more defensible and to make the logical flow easier. There was to be a reduction in the number of memorized theorems, with emphasis concentrated in three areas: deductive reasoning, creating original proofs, and knowledge about the geometric figures in the plane and in space. Coordinate geometry was to be included, with a shift to analytic as well as synthetic methods. In trigonometry, logarithm computations were omitted. A shift to the use of vectors, coordinates, and computations involving functions was recommended. Suggestions for the senior year deemphasized calculus and included courses in linear algebra and matrices, probability and statistics, or an introduction to modern algebra, as well as the popular elementary functions (precalculus) (Begle 1968).

Since the late 1960s, National Educational Assessment Test results and declines in the College Entrance Board SAT scores have led many communities to cry for a "back to basics" program with heavy emphasis on drill in arithmetic skills. Additional reform in the secondary-school offerings in mathematics has been stimulated by moves to upgrade the education of the non-college bound and to provide opportunities and encouragement for girls and racial minorities to study more mathematics. Recent efforts of the American Statistical Association (ASA) in its Quantitative Literacy Project have the potential to make significant changes in the emphasis placed on exploratory data analysis, statistics, probability and simulation in grades K-12 (American Statistical Association ... 1986). Perhaps the most significant of the NCTM's Agenda for Action proposals for the 1980s is the proposed increased role of problem solving in the K-12 curriculum (National Council of Teachers of Mathematics 1980). Other groups had proposed this change even at the beginning of the century, yet the role of problem solving in the day-to-day curriculum is still not well-defined.

The pressure of new technology is frequently a major motivating force in the reform of curriculum. First, it may be that the new technology (such as the hand calculator) may change what we accept as important activities in the mathematics classroom. Second, new technologies may present new professional and vocational choices to students. Third, the technology may have the potential to "take over" some of the teaching, such as drill or perhaps acceleration for gifted students.

The availability of hand calculators has raised questions, not yet answered, of what to teach about arithmetic. Estimation has gained new importance; understanding of concepts remains essential. In recent NAEP examinations, questions such as: "How many buses are needed to transport 1,000 students if every bus holds 45 students?" showed that students could do the division, but that the correct answer was rarely chosen: students either did not realize that the answer had to be an integer or they rounded their calculation (in this case, incorrectly) down (Carpenter et al. 1983). The curricula in algebra and trigonometry no longer include computation from logarithmic and trigonometric tables. The notion of interpolation is not needed as early, and the necessity of checking for the reasonableness of an answer has grown in importance.

The most dramatic effect of technology, of course, has been the availability in almost every school in the country of the microcomputer. Although the teaching of computer science takes place under the auspices of the mathematics faculty in many schools, we shall not discuss computer science as a discipline here. The impact of the computer on the teaching of mathematics is due primarily to its speed, its graphics capabilities, and its ability to use randomness for illustration and experimentation in geometry (of two and three dimensions), probability, statistics, and graphing of relations and functions. Software such as Logo has changed the way in which geometry is taught in many schools. As better software becomes available, the classroom will become more experiential, leading students to generalize and come to conclusions about relationships in mathematics which might very well be a revival of the best parts of the "new math." Computers are an essential part of the modern mathematical experience (Hansen and Zweng 1984).

The recent availability of calculators that can display graphs (such as the Casio fx-7000G, the Sharp EL-5200, and the Hewlett-Packard 28C) and do symbolic calculation (the Hewlett-Packard 28C) may soon end the need for drill-and-practice in some of the standard algebra curriculum. Similar software has been available on microcomputers for some time, e.g., muMath (Wilf 1982); but it is portability and widespread student ownership that will force the curriculum to confront and adapt to the technology. Since the software can find the roots of equations, factor polynomials, calculate derivatives and integrals, and find critical points and points of inflection of a function, educators need to question many facets of the high-school curriculum. Testing to assess students' skills might also undergo radical changes. The emphasis must be changed from routine manipulative exercises to thought-provoking conceptual problems.

Educating for study and careers in the new technologies is another problem facing the schools. Traditionally, the high-school curriculum for college-bound youngsters has led to the calculus. However, the age of computers requires the study of discrete mathematics. The pervasiveness of mathematical modeling and the use of the computer in all fields of study makes the study of discrete mathematical structures important to the social scientist, the chemist, and the physicist, as well as to the computer scientist and engineer.

Discrete mathematics deals primarily with finite and countably infinite structures such as networks, graphs, and trees as well as combinatorics (counting) problems of all types. The notion of recursion and the correctness of algorithms (programs) are central to the study of computing. Calculus is still important in the education of all science students. But because of the computer, many mathematicians and scientists are finding that they are using the discrete (as opposed to continuous) methods in applying notions of calculus. Recent conferences on the state of college mathematics (Ralston and Young 1983) and reports of an MAA committee investigating the role of discrete mathematics (Report of the

Committee ... 1986) indicate that there is a definite place in the high school for an increased role of discrete methods and ideas. That coupled with interest in adding to the curriculum more material in probability and statistics may lessen the role of calculus in the high school. Discrete mathematics also allows for the increase in the number of non-standard problems that a student sees, perhaps supplying new problem-solving experience as a by-product.

Recurrent objectives in proposals for curricular reform are more conceptualization, better computational common sense, and mathematical maturity to read, write, and create mathematics.

Two-Year Colleges

Great unemployment in the 1930s and the post-War period after 1945 brought many people to the nation's two-year colleges. During the last twenty years no sector of education has experienced more rapid growth. Today more than one-third of all college students are enrolled at two-year colleges. The population of the two-year colleges has changed also. The Conference Board of the Mathematical Sciences (CBMS) studies indicate that in 1966 students intending to transfer to four-year schools accounted for 74% of the two-year college population, while by 1980 that figure was reduced to 48% (Fey et al. 1981). Thus the majority of the population considers the two-year college as a vocational training ground. Once consisting mostly of single, white, male, 18- to 19-year-old, full-time students, the population is now mostly part-time, over 21 years old, and married, with more than 25% minorities and more than 50% women.

The two-year college mathematics curriculum has traditionally been both an extension of the high-school curriculum, perhaps leading to transfer to four-year programs, and a vocational program, flexible enough to offer the vocational and technical training as needed in the local community (Kidd 1948).

The transfer curriculum is largely determined by the four-year colleges and universities. There is cooperation on a local level, with most two-year colleges coming to some agreement with the large public institutions about what courses will be transferable. Articulation on a national level is encouraged by the close cooperation between the MAA Committee on the Undergraduate Program in Mathematics (CUPM) and the MAA Committee on the Two-Year Colleges. In addition, the American Mathematical Association of Two-Year Colleges (AMATYC) plays an active role as an affiliate of CBMS.

In the early history of the two-year colleges, all students took algebra, trigonometry, analytic geometry, and calculus. That picture has been changing since 1940. In 1980 analytic geometry courses were almost non-existent and only 10% of all mathematics enrollments were in the calculus (Fey et al. 1981).

Mathematics offerings in the 1940s began to include applied courses such as mathematics of finance, business mathematics and statistics. Many of these courses can be transferred to four-year schools. Later, courses in technical mathematics were added for the large numbers of students pursuing a terminal degree for a vocation. In the 1960s, courses in liberal-arts mathematics and finite mathematics were added, paralleling a movement in the four-year schools; and recently courses in mathematics for data processing have become popular. The question of the role of discrete mathematics in the two-year college, especially for the potential mathematics, computer science, or electrical engineering bachelor's candidate, is one of immediate concern.

The most dramatic change, however, has been the growth of the remedial programs at two-year colleges. In 1980 42% of all mathematics enrollments were in remedial mathematics (arithmetic, high-school geometry, elementary and intermediate algebra, and general mathematics). Courses in arithmetic were taught in one-third of all two-year colleges (Fey et al. 1981). Advanced courses in calculus, linear algebra, differential equations, and liberal-arts mathematics are becoming less available.

New developments in two-year college curricula can be expected to follow (or even lead) four-year college trends in using calculators and computers more in the classroom. The growth of computer-science and data-processing programs in the two-year colleges has been exceptionally large, and the concomitant emphasis on related mathematics should increase. One noticeable trend, however, is that departments of business and computing have been teaching their own mathematics. Large numbers of part-time faculty and weakened control by mathematicians may significantly reduce the quality of these offerings.

The most recent material on the state of the mathematics curriculum at two-year colleges can be found in the proceedings of a conference held in 1984 on the subject (Albers et al. 1985).

BIBLIOGRAPHY

ACM Task Force on Curriculum for Secondary School Computer Science and ACM Task Force on Teacher Certification. 1985. Computer science in secondary schools: Curriculum and teacher certification. *Communications of the Association for Computing Machinery* 28 (3) (March 1985): 269-279.

Describes two year-long courses and also outlines two 1/2-year courses (Introduction to High-Level Computer Languages and Applications, and Implications of Computers). Includes implications for teacher training and certification. The mathematics required of students in the year-long course and one of the 1/2 year courses is likely to affect curriculum design.

Ahlfors, Lars V., et al. 1962. On the mathematics curriculum of the high school. *Mathematics Teacher* 55 (3) (March 1962): 191-195. Also in *American Mathematical Monthly* 69 (3) (March 1962): 189-193.

Warns that stressing content at the expense of pedagogy is dangerous. The fundamental principles of curriculum development should be: the mathematics curriculum should provide for all students and aim to provide cultural background to some and professional preparation for others; and knowing is doing — students need to see that mathematics solves problems, the structural approach is not sufficient.

Albers, Donald J., Stephen B. Rodi, and Ann E. Watkins, eds. 1985. *New Directions in Two-Year College Mathematics*. New York: Springer-Verlag.

Contains a series of papers presented at the Sloan Foundation Conference on New Directions in Two-Year College Mathematics. Each paper deals with some phase of curriculum: statistics, discrete mathematics, technical mathematics, and remedial work are included.

American Mathematical Society. 1899. Report of the Committee of the Chicago Section of the American Mathematical Society. Reprinted in Bidwell and Clason (1970), 195-209.

American Statistical Association — National Council of Teachers of Mathematics Joint Committee on the Curriculum in Statistics and Probability. 1986. Quantitative Literacy Project. Four booklets: *Exploring Data* by James M. Landwehr and Ann E. Watkins. *Exploring Probability* by Claire M. Newman, Thomas E. Obremski, and Richard L. Scheaffer. *The Art and Techniques of Simulation* by Mrdulla Gnanadesikan, Richard L. Scheaffer and Jim Swift. *Exploring Surveys and Information from Samples* by James M. Landwehr, Jim Swift, and Ann E. Watkins. Palo Alto, Calif.:

Dale Seymour.
> A series of handbooks and lessons for improving students' ability to gather and interpret data.

Begle, Edward G. 1968. SMSG: the first decade. _Mathematics Teacher_ 61 (3) (March 1968): 239-245.

Bidwell, James K., and Robert G. Clason, eds. 1970. _Readings in the History of Mathematics Education._ Washington, D.C.: National Council of Teachers of Mathematics.
> Contains readings and committee reports dating from 1828 to 1959 that shed perspective on the development of the curriculum.

Birkhoff, George, and Ralph Beatley. 1941. _Basic Geometry._ New York: Chelsea.

Bobbitt, John Franklin. 1924. _How to Make a Curriculum._ Boston, Mass.: Houghton Mifflin.

Bruner, Jerome S. 1960. On learning mathematics. _Mathematics Teacher_ 53 (8) (December 1960): 610-619.
> Explains the author's theory of the structural approach to mathematics, emphasizing the continuity of the subject matter in the ideal curriculum. Discusses the place of discovery and intuition.

Carpenter, Thomas P., Mary M. Lindquist, Westina Matthews, and Edward A. Silver. 1983. Results of the third NAEP mathematics assessment: Secondary school. _Mathematics Teacher_ 76 (9) (December 1983): 652-659.
> Compares the third NAEP results to previous assessments.

College Entrance Examination Board. 1959. _Program for College Preparatory Mathematics, Report of the Commission on Mathematics._ New York: College Entrance Examination Board.
> Presents a nine-point program designed for the "college-capable" which takes into account modern mathematics. The nine points are: (1) strong preparation, in concepts and skills, for calculus; (2) understanding deductive reasoning in algebra and geometry; (3) appreciation of structure including properties of natural, rational, real and complex numbers; (4) judicious use of unifying ideas — sets, variables, functions and relations; (5) treatment of inequalities along with equations; (6) incorporate coordinate geometry, solid geometry and space perception; (7) 11th grade trigonometry centered on vectors, coordinates, complex numbers; (8) 12th grade: functions; (9) alternatives for 12th grade: introduction to probability and statistics or introduction to modern algebra.

Commission on Post-War Plans [of the NCTM]. 1945. The Second Report of the Commission on Post-War Plans. *Mathematics Teacher* 38 (5) (May 1945): 195-221.

Committee on the Undergraduate Program in Mathematics. 1965. *A General Curriculum in Mathematics for the Colleges: A Report.* 1972. *Commentary on a General Curriculum in Mathematics for Colleges.* 1981. *Recommendations for a General Mathematical Sciences Program.* Washington, D.C.: Mathematical Association of America.

> Here are three reports that influenced American collegiate education in a significant way. The 1965 report was prepared in close cooperation with many SMSG representatives to create a well-articulated program with the secondary schools. This program was attacked as being too demanding, leaving no time for applications and no room for the average student. The 1972 report answers these criticisms and gives revisions for the introductory courses. The 1981 report shows the influence of computing, the demand for mathematicians trained in applicable mathematics, and the need to attract students who may prefer applied to pure mathematics. New directions in the teaching of calculus, and emphasis on discrete methods, probability, statistics, operations research, applied algebra, and actuarial science are reflected in the 1981 report.

Committee on the Undergraduate Program in Mathematics, Panel on Mathematics Appreciation. 1983. Mathematics appreciation courses. *American Mathematical Monthly* 90 (1) (January 1983): 44-53.

> Discusses the work of the MAA panel on the development of guidelines and suggestions for the liberal arts mathematics course offered at many colleges for the liberal learning requirements. Extensive bibliography on pp. C11-C20 of the same issue (January 1983).

Committee to Implement the Recommendations of *An Agenda for Action.* 1985. *Alternative Courses for Secondary School Mathematics.* Reston, Va.: National Council of Teachers of Mathematics.

> Details 74 new courses representing the "flexible curriculum" recommended by the National Council of Teachers of Mathematics *An Agenda for Action* (1980). (PJC & LSG)

Davis, Robert B. 1984. *Learning Mathematics: The Cognitive Science Approach to Mathematics Education.* Norwood, N.J.: Ablex.

> An account of at least two decades of the author's research into the mysteries of learning mathematics. Several chapters (especially chs. 23 and 24) deal with the implications for curriculum development. Discusses all grade levels and ability levels, with subject matter including arithmetic, geometry, algebra, and calculus.

Dessart, Donald J. 1981. Curriculum. In *Mathematics Education Research: Implications for the 80's,* edited by Elizabeth Fennema, 1-21. Alexandria, Va.: Association for Supervision and Curriculum Development and National Council of Teachers of Mathematics.

> Discusses mathematical content of the curriculum relative to psychological, sociological, and structural factors. Also contains information on evaluation of both programs and of textbooks with the hope of limiting the significant variables.

Douglas, Ronald G., ed. 1987. *Toward a Lean and Lively Calculus: Report of the Conference/Workshop to Develop Curriculum and Teaching Methods for Calculus at the College Level.* MAA Notes no. 6. Washington, D.C.: Mathematical Association of America.

> An important collection of reports of three workshops held in January 1986 in New Orleans. Three major areas of concern are addressed: the curriculum, the teaching and the implementation in plans to improve the teaching of calculus.

Edwards, E. L., Jr., Eugene D. Nichols, and Glyn H. Sharpe. 1972. Mathematical competencies and skills essential for enlightened citizens. *Mathematics Teacher* 65 (7) (November 1972): 671-677.

> Helpful to those who are trying to construct meaningful curricula for the average student.

Fey, James T., Donald J. Albers, and Wendell H. Fleming. 1981. *Undergraduate Mathematical Sciences in Universities, Four-Year Colleges and Two-Year Colleges, 1980-1981.* Report of the Survey Committee, vol. 6. Washington, D.C.: Conference Board of the Mathematical Sciences.

> Contains a great deal of information gathered by the Survey Committee about the nature of undergraduate education. Contains information on the curriculum, the student population, the faculty, and students' interests and contrasts this with the results of the 1967, 1972 and 1975-1976 surveys.

Goddard, Roy W. 1944. Basic issues for junior colleges in the postwar period. *North Central Association Quarterly* 19 (2) (October 1944): 184-189.

> Describes characteristics and goals of two-year colleges in the period following World War II, explaining the qualities which make public support for these schools important.

Hansen, Viggo P., and Marilyn J. Zweng, eds. 1984. *NCTM 1984* Yearbook.

> Shows how the computer has entered the mathematics classroom at all levels, including several articles on the use of programming as a technique to teach mathematical concepts.

Heid, M. Kathleen. 1983. Calculus with muMath: Implications for curriculum reform. *Computing Teacher* 11 (4) (November 1983): 46-49.
> Presents the results of teaching an applied calculus course with the software muMath, an excellent introduction to the practical use of symbolic manipulators in the college classroom. Shows particularly well how one might teach for understanding of concepts with the aid of muMath.

———. 1983. Characteristics and special needs of the gifted student in mathematics. *Mathematics Teacher* 76 (4) (April 1983): 221-226.
> Discusses the challenges to the curriculum in trying to give the gifted a sense of achievement. Stresses the role of discovery, open-ended questions, flexibility, depth, and independence in planning for the talented.

Henderson, Kenneth B., ed. 1973. *NCTM Yearbook* 36.
> Aids in the placing of geometry in the grades K-12.

Hill, Shirley A. 1976. Issues from the NACOME report. *Mathematics Teacher* 69 (6) (October 1976): 440-446.
> Recommended the addition of applied areas to the curriculum.

Hilton, Peter J. 1982. The emphasis on applied mathematics today and its implications for the mathematics curriculum. In *New Directions in Applied Mathematics*, edited by Peter J. Hilton and Gail S. Young, 155-163. New York: Springer-Verlag.
> Warns that problem solving does not substitute for mathematics, and advises that broad knowledge of mathematical concepts helps one to find suitable strategies.

Hlavaty, Julius H., et al., eds. 1963. *NCTM Yearbook* 28.
> Can be used by teachers, curriculum planners, parents and students themselves as the range of the articles covers all the high-school years and the transition to college, with some novel and fascinating suggestions for activities and techniques to deal with the mathematically gifted. Contains an excellent bibliography.

House, Peggy A. 1983. Alternative educational programs for gifted students in mathematics. *Mathematics Teacher* 76 (4) (April 1983): 229-233.
> Discusses alternatives to the curriculum for the gifted, including the options for delivery.

Howson, Geoffrey, Christine Keitel, and Jeremy Kilpatrick. 1981. *Curriculum Development in Mathematics*. Cambridge, England:

Cambridge University Press. Review: *American Mathematical Monthly* 91 (2) (February 1984): 150-151.

> Extremely good resource for survey of curriculum development from the historical, theoretical and practical viewpoints. Contains careful review of the development, dispersion, and evaluation of several important programs since the 1950s, concentrating on strengths and weaknesses of each. Includes programs outside of the U.S., such as CSMP. Has excellent bibliography and guide to the alphabet soup of mathematics programs.

International Commission on the Teaching of Mathematics. 1911. *Mathematics in the Public and Private Secondary Schools of the United States.* Washington, D.C.: U.S. Government Printing Office. Also in Bidwell and Clason (1970), 328-360.

Joint Committee of the Mathematical Association of America and the National Council of Teachers of Mathematics. 1980. *A Sourcebook for Applications of School Mathematics.* Reston, Va.: National Council of Teachers of Mathematics.

> Helpful volume of applications that can be used in the mathematics curriculum at a range of grade levels. Could be used to glean ideas to supplement the standard curriculum.

Kantowski, Mary Grace. 1981. Problem solving. In *Mathematics Education Research: Implications for the '80s*, edited by Elizabeth Fennema, 111-126. Alexandria, Va.: Association for Supervision and Curriculum Development and National Council of Teachers of Mathematics.

> Discusses research in problem solving of both the routine and the non-routine types. Explains the difficulties of finding good problems and then the barriers to change, such as the existence of standardized tests that do not test for such skills directly, the need for individual attention to students in teaching problem solving, flexibility in dealing with approaches to problems, etc.

Kidd, Kenneth Paul. 1948. *Objectives of Mathematical Training in the Public Junior College.* Nashville, Tenn.: George Peabody College for Teachers.

> A comprehensive text on the two-year colleges at the time that their enrollments were growing quite rapidly.

Kilpatrick, Jeremy. 1970. Evaluating a unified mathematics curriculum. In the Symposium: Problems of Evaluation in Developing Mathematics Curriculum Programs. Meeting of the American Educational Research Association, Minneapolis, Minn. Columbus, O.: ERIC/SMEAC. ERIC: ED 042811.

> Stresses the problems in evaluating any innovative mathematics curriculum.

————. 1985. *Academic Preparation in Mathematics: Teaching for Transition from High School to College.* New York: College Entrance Examination Board.

A follow-up on the 1983 College Entrance Examination Board publication *Academic Preparation for College: What Students Need to Know and Be Able to Do.* The book offers suggestions on a three year course for a curriculum that will help attain desired outcomes of the original proposal. There is reference to curriculum in computing, statistics, algebra, geometry, and functions for secondary schools.

Kinney, Lucien Blair, and C. Richard Purdy. 1960. *Teaching Mathematics in the Secondary School.* New York: Holt, Rinehart & Winston.

Presents a historical review of curriculum development and a perspective on the authors' view of the problems of that era.

Klein, Felix. 1932, 1939. *Elementary Mathematics from an Advanced Viewpoint* 2 vols. New York: Macmillan.

Kline, Morris. 1973. *Why Johnny Can't Add: The Failure of the New Math.* New York: St. Martin's.

An indictment of the new mathematics curricula of the 1960s, expressing a popular view of the failures of those programs to teach "basic" skills.

Knuth, Donald E. 1985. Algorithmic thinking and mathematical thinking. *American Mathematical Monthly* 92 (3) (March 1985): 170-181.

The buzzword of 1984-1985 was to teach "algorithmic" thinking, especially because of its applications to discrete mathematics and computer science. Knuth researches the differences and similarities in the thinking styles of standard mathematics texts.

Koffman, Elliott B., Philip L. Miller, and Caroline E. Wardle. 1984. Recommended Curriculum for CS1, 1984. *Communications* of *the Association for Computing Machinery* 27 (10) (October 1984): 998-1001.

Recommendations of the Task Force of the ACM on the content of the first college course in computer science for serious students of computer science. The mathematics prerequisites and corequisites demanded make this required reading for anyone designing mathematics curricula at the senior-high-school or college level.

Koffman, Elliott B., David Stemple, and Caroline E. Wardle. 1985. Recommended Curriculum for CS2, 1984. *Communications* of *the Association for Computing Machinery* 28 (8) (August 1985): 815-818.

Recommendations of the ACM Task Force for the curriculum of the second course in the college computer science sequence. Mathematics prerequisites should be noted: discrete mathematics is a necessity.

Krulik, Stephen, and Robert E. Reys, eds. 1980. *NCTM 1980 Yearbook*.
The primary goal in the NCTM Agenda for Action (NCTM 1980) was to introduce problem solving into the curriculum. This yearbook is an excellent introduction to what can be done.

Maurer, Stephen. 1985. The algorithmic way of life is best. *College Mathematics Journal* 16 (1) (January 1985): 2-18 (includes responses by other authors).
Presents algorithmic thinking as one of the primary goals of mathematics education.

McGarvey, Craig. 1981. Mathematics and miseducation: toward the next school curricula. *Mathematics Teacher* 74 (2) (February 1981): 90-95.
Attacks some of the choices we made in the curricula of the 1950s and suggests new models are needed that integrate the teaching of mathematics and science, avoid the compartmentalization of algebra and geometry, and teach a mode of thought rather than axiomatics.

McIntosh, Jerry A., ed. 1971. *Perspectives on Secondary Mathematics Education*. Englewood Cliffs, N.J.: Prentice-Hall.
Contains reprints of articles from various sources, with many on curriculum development. They focus on structure, geometry, linear algebra, and 12th-grade course recommendations from college professors (who suggested including limits but not doing calculus).

National Advisory Committee on Mathematical Education (NACOME). 1975. *Overview and Analysis of School Mathematics Grades K-12*. Washington, D.C.: National Council of Teachers of Mathematics.

National Committee on Mathematical Requirements. 1923. *The Reorganization of Mathematics in Secondary Education*. Lancaster, Pa., and Ann Arbor, Mich.: Mathematical Association of America.

National Council of Teachers of Mathematics. 1959. *The Growth of Mathematical Ideas K-12*. Washington, D.C.: National Council of Teachers of Mathematics.
Articles arranged by subject matter trace mathematical concepts through the curriculum: a good way of studying the structural approach to the curriculum.

————. 1963. *An Analysis of New Mathematics Programs*. Washington, D.C.: National Council of Teachers of Mathematics.

Serves as a short guidebook to several important mathematics programs of the "new math" era. Includes Boston College Mathematics Institute, Greater Cleveland Mathematics Program, Syracuse University—Webster College Madison Project, University of Maryland Mathematics Project, Ontario Mathematics Commission, School Mathematics Study Group, Developmental Project in Secondary Mathematics at Southern Illinois University, and University of Illinois Committee on School Mathematics.

————. 1980. *An Agenda for Action: Recommendations for School Mathematics of the 1980's*. Reston, Va.: National Council of Teachers of Mathematics.

Recommendations of the NCTM for improvement of mathematics education include several related to the curriculum: that "problem solving be the focus of school mathematics in the 1980's," "basic skills be defined to encompass more than computational facility," "mathematics programs take full advantage of the power of calculators and computers at all grade levels," "more mathematics study be required for all students and a flexible curriculum with a greater range of options be designed to accommodate the diverse needs of the student population," and "public support for mathematics instruction be raised to a level commensurate with the importance of mathematical understanding to individuals and society."

————. 1981. *Priorities in School Mathematics: An Executive Summary*. Reston, Va.: National Council of Teachers of Mathematics.

Results of national NCTM survey called the PRISM project, of parents, administrators, and elementary, high-school and college teachers, as to their priorities relative to the NCTM's Agenda for Action (NCTM 1980). Answers to questionnaires provide insight into what diverse segments of the population think should be highlighted in the mathematical education of the young.

————. 1987. *Curriculum and Evaluation Standards for School Mathematics*. Reston, Va.: National Council of Teachers of Mathematics.

National Education Association. 1899. *Journal of Proceedings and Addresses of the Thirty-eighth Annual Meeting, Report of the Committee on College Entrance Requirements*. Reprinted in Bidwell and Clason (1970), 189-194.

National Institute of Education. 1984. *Involvement in Learning: Realizing the Potential of American Higher Education*. Final Report of the Study Group on the Conditions of Excellence in American Higher Education, October 1984. Washington, D.C.: National Institute of Education. Columbus, O.: ERIC/SMEAC. ERIC: ED 246833.

Investigates undergraduate education in light of the contribution of the first two years to the liberal education of American students. Challenges higher education to enhance education for the masses of students attending the nation's colleges and universities. Among the goals of liberal learning should be to give each student ample experience in analysis and problem solving.

National Research Council, Panel on Undergraduate Education in Mathematics. 1968. *The Mathematical Sciences: Undergraduate Education.* Washington, D.C.: National Academy of Sciences.

Recommendations for undergraduate mathematics education. Addresses special problems of the era (staffing, women in mathematics, high-school preparation, etc.). Eight case studies of collegiate programs show the spectrum of possibilities. Heavy emphasis on the practical nature of mathematical sciences.

National Science Board Commission on Precollege Education in Mathematics, Science and Technology. 1983. *Educating Americans for the Twenty-First Century: Source Materials.* Washington, D.C.: National Science Foundation.

Source materials of proceedings of various commissions and boards seeking to improve secondary (and elementary) education. Includes:

- "The mathematical sciences curriculum K-12: What is still fundamental and what is not" (Conference Board of the Mathematical Sciences),
- "A revised and intensified science and technology curriculum, grades K-12, urgently needed for our future" (Conference on Goals for Science and Technology Education Grades K-12),
- "Integrating concepts of engineering and science into instruction in grade levels K-12" (Ad hoc Subcommittee of the NSF Engineering Advisory Committee),
- "Fundamentals in precollege technology education" (Junior Engineering Technical Society),
- "Report on educational technology" (Conference on the Uses of Technology in Education),
- "Research on cognition and behavior relevant to education in mathematics, science and technology" (Federation of Behavioral, Psychological and Cognitive Sciences),
- "Results of a 50-state survey of initiatives in science, mathematics and computer education" (Education Commission of the States).

National Science Foundation and the Department of Education. 1980. *Science and Engineering Education for the 1980's and Beyond.* Washington, D.C.: National Science Foundation (distributed by U.S. Government Printing Office).

Investigates the basic scientific and technical education of all citizens, and also considers necessary professional training for those going into mathematics, science, and engineering. Useful as guide to what the college program should be and consequently sheds light on the preparatory role of the high schools in these areas.

Nicely, Robert F. Jr. 1985. Higher-order thinking skills in mathematics textbooks. *Educational Leadership* 42 (7) (April 1985): 26-30.
> Report of a study of the higher-order thinking skills emphasized by textbooks in general use in the 1960s to 1980s. A rating scale indicates that there is a decline in the opportunities presented to students for involvement and a concomitant decrease in the higher-order skills and behaviors demanded of them in the texts from 1960 to 1970. From the 1970s to the 1980s there has been an increase, but the level in 1980 is still below that of 1960. The curriculum generated and derived from these books might be expected to show similar scoring on this special scale.

Organisation for European Economic Co-operation. 1961. *New Thinking in School Mathematics*. Paris, France: Organisation for European Economic Cooperation.
> A report on the Royaumont seminar considered important in the development of "new math" curricula. One of the French delegates was Dieudonné, whose influential address to the seminar is included.

Page, Warren, ed. 1984. *American Perspectives on the Fifth International Congress on Mathematical Education (*ICME 5). MAA Notes no. 5. Washington, D.C.: Mathematical Association of America.
> Reviews papers presented at ICME 5 in August, 1984 in Adelaide, Australia.

Progressive Education Association, Committee on the Function of Mathematics in General Education for the Commission on Secondary School Curriculum. 1940. *Mathematics in General Education*. New York: D. Appleton-Century.

Råde, Lennart, ed. 1970. *Proceedings of the First CSMP International Conference on the Teaching of Probability and Statistics*. New York: Wiley.
> Useful for good ideas on the enrichment of the curriculum with probability and statistics. The ideas range from simple activities to complex units on probability.

Ralston, Anthony. 1984, 1985. Will discrete mathematics surpass calculus in importance? *College Mathematics Journal* 15 (5) (November 1984): 371-382; 16 (1) (January 1985): 19-21 (includes responses by other authors).
> Provocative article on the subject of changes in the first two years of the college curriculum.

Ralston, Anthony, and Gail Young, eds. 1983. *The Future of College Mathematics*. New York: Springer-Verlag. Review: Peter J. Hilton, *Amer-*

ican Mathematical Monthly 91 (7) (August-September 1984): 452-455.

> Reproduces papers presented at a conference at Williams College in the summer of 1983. Includes transcripts of discussion sessions and course outlines for proposed discrete mathematics courses. The papers are very provocative on the role of mathematics for the culture, for technology, and for intellectual growth in the computer age.

Reeve, William D., ed. 1940. *NCTM Yearbook 15.*

Report of the Committee on Discrete Mathematics in the First Two Years. 1986. Washington, D.C.: Mathematical Association of America.

> Contains suggestions for the first course in discrete mathematics, to be offered at the same level as calculus during the first two years of college. Contains bibliography of possible textbooks, and suggestions for changes in the high-school curriculum which might help students entering discrete mathematics courses as freshmen.

Roberts, Fred S. 1984. The introductory mathematics curriculum: misleading, outdated and unfair. *College Mathematics Journal* 15 (5) (November 1984): 383-399 (includes responses by other authors).

> Helps to illuminate the current difficulties with designing a modern and solid mathematics program for colleges.

Rosskopf, Myron F. 1970. Mathematics education: Historical perspectives. In *NCTM Yearbook 33,* 3-29.

> Historical approach to curriculum contained in article with the long-range point of view.

Schoenfeld, Alan H. 1983. *Problem Solving in the Mathematics Curriculum: A Report, Recommendations and an Annotated Bibliography.* MAA Notes, no. 1. Washington, D.C.: Mathematical Association of America.

> Under the auspices of the Committee on Teaching Undergraduate Mathematics (CTUM) of the MAA, Schoenfeld and a subcommittee have compiled a useful guide to the known research on teaching and learning how to solve problems. Includes recommendations of CTUM to encourage an open and questioning attitude toward mathematics, to offer courses at the college level (even at the first-year level) in problem solving, to offer courses in problem solving to teachers at all grade levels, and to encourage development of textbooks for courses of this type. Bibliography should be especially helpful to those interested in all aspects of the subject, since it contains problem books as well as books and articles about problem solving.

School Mathematics Study Group. 1959. *Report of an Orientation Conference for SMSG Experimental Centers.* New Haven, Conn.: Yale

University.

> Gives the flavor of the SMSG, its method of training, and its structure. The conference participants included SMSG personnel, teachers, and teachers teaching teachers how to use the materials in the classroom.

Sharron, Sidney, and Robert E. Reys, eds. 1979. *NCTM 1979 Yearbook*.

> Good resource for applications and their use in the curriculum.

Shufelt, Gwen, and James R. Smart, eds. 1983. *NCTM 1983 Yearbook*.

> Introduction plus 27 essays focusing on the NCTM Agenda for Action (NCTM 1980). Recommendations are reviewed with an eye toward assessing progress toward goals of the 1980s. For each of the Agenda recommendations there is at least one article. Articles on problem solving, evaluation, and teaching for understanding are most numerous.

Stanley, Julian C., Daniel P. Keating, and Lynn H. Fox, eds. 1974. *Mathematical Talent: Discovery, Description and Development*. Baltimore, Md.: Johns Hopkins Press.

> Serves as an introduction to the Search for Mathematically Precocious Youth, a program that seeks mathematically-gifted seventh-graders through the quantitative part of the SAT. Might serve as helpful resource in developing curriculum for the gifted.

Suydam, Marilyn N. 1979. *Calculators: A Categorized Compilation* of *References*. Columbus, O.: ERIC Clearinghouse.

> Useful as a guide to all research up to 1979 done on the use of calculators in the schools.

Thorndike, Edward L. 1922. *The Psychology of Arithmetic*. New York: Macmillan.

United States Bureau of Education. 1893. *Report of the Committee on Secondary School Studies of the National Education Association*. Washington, D.C.: U.S. Government Printing Office. Reprinted in Bidwell and Clason (1970), 129-141.

Usiskin, Zalman. 1980. What should not be in the algebra and geometry curriculum of average college-bound students? *Mathematics Teacher* 73 (6) (September 1980): 413-424.

> The curriculum has become packed with suggestions from the 1959 CEEB "9-point program for college-capable students," the NACOME report, and other curricular revisions. Addresses the issue of what can be deleted, and argues the case against the critics who cite the CEEB tests.

Weaver, J. Fred. 1981. Calculators. In *Mathematics Education Research: Implications for the 80's,* edited by Elizabeth Fennema, 154-168. Alexandria, Va.: Association for Supervision and Curriculum Development and National Council of Teachers of Mathematics.

> Can be seen as an assessment of the state of the art of bringing calculators into the classroom. Expresses a need for research and development so that curriculum can be written with calculators as a meaningful part of mathematics courses.

Whitesitt, John. 1982. Mathematics for the average college-bound student. *Mathematics Teacher* 75 (2) (February 1982): 105-107.

> Students in 9th and 10th grade who are college-capable, but not necessarily college-bound, do not get what they need from the high-school curriculum. Citing the many students at universities like Berkeley and Montana State who need remedial work leads the author to ask: what do their secondary schools lack?

Wilf, Herbert S. 1982. The disk with the college education. *American Mathematical Monthly* 89 (1) (January 1982): 4-8.

> Investigates the versatility of muMath, a symbolic manipulator that does algebra and calculus symbolically. Should lead one to question why we teach many of the topics now occupying a large portion of the high-school curriculum.

4. Testing and Evaluation

ANNA O. GRAEBER
and
JOHN W. KENELLY

We approach the topic of testing and evaluation from the viewpoint of mathematics classroom teachers. Although we drew on our background and experiences in the construction and administration of national tests, we tried to restrict this discussion and the accompanying resources to suggestions that could be used in any mathematics classroom. The comments and bibliography are constrained by that assumption, and no attempt was made to write a comprehensive reference document. It is, by design, a resource chapter for classroom teachers, with information and suggestions that will be of special benefit for them in their day-to-day teaching and testing activities.

The opening comments are organized around three topics. We first look at individual test questions and their role as singular assessment devices. Then we examine the interaction of test items in collections, i.e., tests as groups of individual questions. Finally, we look at the above as a means to improve the teaching of mathematics.

Individual Test Questions

The first rule of evaluation is to know what the individual question is testing. There are times when you want to test a single idea and times when you want to test the interaction of concepts—but there is never a time when you want to know how well the students perform on an unknown.

Good test items are simple! Long discussion questions often test reading skills more than they test the desired mathematics. Intricate arithmetic may suggest that the question is hard and thought-provoking, when in fact the intricate arithmetic dominates the measurement and obscures the testing of the intended concept. "Trick questions" are especially weak — they focus on the pathological exceptions and typically miss important rules. Basic guidelines for constructing a variety of types of mathematical items appear in Merwin (1961), Suydam (1974), and Swadener and Wright (1975). Gay (1980), while not devoted exclusively to mathematics, also uses a commonsense approach to item construction.

Good test items are carefully designed to measure at predetermined skill levels. Definitions of various skill levels and examples of mathematical items constructed for specific levels are contained in Cooney et al. (1975) and presented in more detail with more examples in Wilson (1971). An important point to remember is that if you want to measure routine technique, then make the item require *only* routine techniques for its solution. If you want to measure spatial properties, then try to write the question with a maximum use of figures and a minimum use of words. In the latter case, try to avoid formula-dependent situations and make the widest possible use of estimations and comparisons.

Questions that require the integration of two ideas often provide a good way to measure comprehension of concepts. When a test question relies on a single concept, it is very difficult for the question to measure more than factual recall; and it is hard to write on a single concept and separate comprehension from recall. A gear analogy illustrates this point very well. It is hard to tell whether there are rusty spots on two gears when you individually roll them along a surface. However, when you ask the gears to mesh and roll together, then all their imperfections are immediately apparent. In a similar manner, two concepts tested side-by-side in separate questions may not finely differentiate between the knowledgeable students and the students with casual familiarity. If the same two concepts are needed to answer a single question, students must truly comprehend both concepts. Such questions make it unlikely that students will be successful if they only memorize rhetoric and established routines. Exemplary items that test more than one concept are frequently found on the SATs (College Entrance Examination Board 1983a). Pedersen and Ross (1985) also provide some excellent examples from more-advanced high-school mathematics.

"Upper-level" and "lower-level" questions are the hardest to write. It is difficult for most teachers to write routine simple questions, and it is even more difficult for them to write straightforward nonroutine questions that test insight, ingenuity, and higher-order mental processes. The low-end questions require a singular focus and must lack distracting elements.

Albrecht and Carnes (1982) as well as Hopkins and Antes (1985) offer guidelines for writing high-level (essay and problem solving) questions. Schoenfeld (1982) includes suggestions to ameliorate the difficulty caused when time needed to solve problems and the time available for testing do not match.

Good high-level questions should be hard for the student, but they should not be long, intricate, or logically complex. The key point is that they should be _thought-provoking._ They can require a sequence of logical steps and the application of conclusions to yield additional conclusions, but they should not be so involved that it takes a logician to follow the pattern. They should be clever, but at the same time they should avoid tricks and gimmicks.

The Test As a Collection of Questions

Most teachers think that there is a fundamental equity in equally-weighted test questions. As a result, they write their questions at a "balanced" level and they assign the same number of points to each problem. Since they typically call time at the end of the testing period, the end result is a speed test and not a power test. Without realizing it, they are measuring how _fast_ the students perform and not how _well_ they can perform. This approach assigns grades on a "problems per hour" basis; it does not measure the students' level and depth of comprehension.

A well-designed test includes questions that cover the full spectrum of levels of difficulty. There should be routine problems that require nothing more than factual recall and familiar manipulations. There should be intricate questions that require the demonstration of comprehension of the ideas and concepts. There should also be several upper-level problems that require insight and higher mental processes. The test should be loaded with the middle-level items — about 50% — and also include coverage of the extremes. The test should be short and leave time for the students to check their work and ponder for a second time the difficult problems that they could not readily solve. In one of the authors' classes, the students label the routine questions the "thank you for coming" questions and the upper-level sorting questions the "I wished that I hadn't come" questions. Examples of "I wished that I hadn't" questions can be found in Artino et al. (1983), Jones et al. (1975), and the College Entrance Examination Board publications (1983a and 1983b).

A hurdles race is a good analogy for a well-designed test. If all the hurdles are the same height, then you have a timed test of ability to jump hurdles. Racers win or lose on the basis of the speed with which they jump rather than on the basis of the heights to which they jump. Anyone who could start the race and clear the first hurdle would finish the race if given a sufficient amount of time. A race with increasingly-high hurdles would differentiate on the basis of one's power to handle hurdles, and the results would measure just how well the individuals had mastered hurdle-jumping.

How To Improve Classroom Tests

If items and item statistics are reviewed and saved for future use, learning from our testing history can make the process a little easier, a little better, and may even help us look at our teaching. What do the steps above suggest for such procedures?

First of all, avoid the pitfall of the bank of equal questions with equal difficulty. Cover the wide range of problem types and difficulty levels. After you have changed your test banks to a varied collection of questions, then try to improve and refine each question. Note each question's precise measurement objectives — see that the question stands the careful scrutiny of the singular nature of their purpose. On essay examinations try to include questions that get progressively deeper into the subject. Make part A simple and routine, part B a non-trivial application of the concepts, part C a real test of the student's in-depth knowledge of the topic, and part D a separator to see who could have taught the class that week.

Look at the statistics, review the face validity of each question, and listen to students' comments. Even the professional test-writers write some items that don't fly. The item statistics may identify such questions for you, but it may be the comments of a student that give you insights into the question's pitfalls.

While it is true that the students are ultimately responsible for their learning, at least consider the role your teaching might have played in the results. Accept praise where due, and also ask yourself if you provided the foundation for any items that everyone (or nearly everyone) missed. Was too much class time devoted to the routine? Are there points essential to upcoming topics that few in the class have grasped?

Keep statistics on your students and on the test items as well. See if you cover the extremes in both the reported student scores and the challenge questions that you ask on the examinations. Admittedly, the political elements of today's school might require that you call these "bonus" problems and "super A's," but a good teacher will always try to challenge their brightest students on tests.

BIBLIOGRAPHY

Albrecht, James E., and DuWayne Carnes. 1982. Guidelines for developing, administering the essay test. *NASSP Bulletin* 66 (November 1982): 47-53.

>Argues that the ease of scoring short answer tests and the apparent exactness in reporting scores from such tests has resulted in a decline in the use of essay tests. The pros and cons of essay tests are reviewed, and the authors include a helpful set of guidelines for writing and scoring essay questions. Although the article is not specific to the mathematics area, the current emphasis on teaching for understanding and problem solving may encourage teachers to investigate and use some essay type questions in the mathematics class.

Artino, Ralph A., Anthony M. Gaglione, and Niel Shell, comps. 1983. *The Contest Problem Book IV.* New Mathematical Library no. 29. Washington, D.C.: Mathematical Association of America.

>Includes problems and solutions from the Annual High School Mathematics Examinations 1973-1982. This is a collection of higher-level multiple-choice items that can be solved with high-school mathematics. An index to the problems allows the reader quick access to problems with a particular content. Three earlier volumes in the New Mathematical Library Series (nos. 5, 17, 25) include items from previous examinations.

College Entrance Examination Board. 1983a. *10 SATs.* New York: College Entrance Examination Board.

>Contains complete recent Scholastic Aptitude Tests. Carefully-developed multiple-choice items cover relatively standard arithmetic, first-year algebra, and geometry in problem-solving settings. Here the reader will find questions that each require understanding of two concepts. For example, some items necessitate combining concepts from algebra and geometry. Teachers discussing test-taking strategies with their own students may find helpful the discussion of the consequences of guessing at or omitting answers.

———. 1983b. *The College Board Achievement Tests: 14 Tests in 13 Subjects.* New York: College Entrance Examination Board.

>Includes actual Level I and Level II Mathematics Achievement Tests. Provides excellent examples of well-constructed multiple-choice items covering college-preparatory high-school and precalculus college-level mathematics.

Cooney, Thomas J., Edward J. Davis, and Kenneth B. Henderson. 1975. Evaluating student and teacher performance. In *Dynamics of Teaching Secondary School Mathematics*, 410-441. Boston, Mass.: Houghton Mifflin.

>Provides a discussion of test construction which concentrates on aligning

test items with instructional objectives and examining the cognitive level of the items. These steps are illustrated with examples from secondary-school mathematics.

Diederich, Paul B. 1973. Short-cut statistics for teacher-made tests. Princeton, N.J.: Educational Testing Service.

> Explains the meaning, use, and interpretation of item analysis, standard error (of scores, of an average, between averages), reliability, and correlation. Explains short-cut methods of computing these statistics and their assumptions. Provides examples for both the short-cut and standard computation of each statistic. Although the title might suggest a "cookbook" approach, much of the paper is devoted to developing understanding.

Educational Testing Service. 1973. Information for test construction. Princeton, N.J.: Educational Testing Service.

> Explains the standard terminology related to multiple-choice items, gives suggestions for preparing and reviewing them, and lists types of information that can be tested by them. Includes simple guidelines for essay questions, completion items, true-false items, and matching items, plus "dos and don'ts" in regard to sex and ethnic fairness. Concludes with a list of considerations in constructing a test from individual items.

————. 1980. Guidelines for writing multiple-choice questions in mathematics. Princeton, N.J.: Educational Testing Service.

> Illustrates the value of 15 guidelines for writing multiple-choice items by providing an original and revised item to illustrate each guideline.

Farrell, Margaret A., and Walter A. Farmer. 1980. The proof of the pudding: Evaluation of instruction. In *Systematic Instruction in Mathematics for the Middle and High School Years*, 194-241. Reading, Mass.: Addison-Wesley.

> Presents guidelines for writing various types of test items, after illustrating the pitfalls of poorly-constructed items. Steps in planning test content and format are included, as are directions for obtaining and interpreting item difficulty and discrimination index. This is one of the few simple treatments of item analysis which includes directions for the case in which partial credit is given. The directions are simple, straightforward, and accompanied by clear examples. Also of value are practical methodological hints on preparing the class, scoring tests, reviewing results with the class, and storing items for retrieval.

Gay, L. R. 1980. *Educational Evaluation & Measurement: Competencies for Analysis and Application.* Columbus, O.: Charles E. Merrill.

> Includes comprehensive and straightforward discussions on test item construction (Chapter 9), and on test revision (Chapter 11). Although the examples included in the two chapters are not confined to secondary-school mathematics, mathematical essay and objective items are represented. The author's common-

sense approach to characteristics of good items lends cohesiveness to the guidelines for various types of items. The chapter on test revision may at first look sophisticated, but the reader will find the writing clear and will appreciate the practical classroom approach to item difficulty and discrimination the author eventually offers.

Hassett, Matt, and Harvey Smith. 1983-1984. A note on the limitations of predictive tests in reducing failure rates. *Placement Test Newsletter* 7 (Winter 1983-1984): 1-5.

Reports on the use of placement tests for counseling college students with little chance of success in a course and for informing students at moderate risk. The authors combine theory and data from their situation to explain why placement tests currently rated as "good" do not result in dramatic changes in course completion rates.

Hopkins, Charles D., and Richard L. Antes. 1985. Constructing problem items. In *Classroom Measurement and Evaluation*, 2nd ed., 187-206. Itasca, Ill.: Peacock.

Reviews the advantages and disadvantages of test items that require mathematical problem solving. Includes "guides to writing mathematical problem items" that can be used as a basic but useful checklist for reviewing test items. A few exemplary items for secondary school are included.

Although not specific to mathematics, other chapters include comprehensive discussions of planning a test, guidelines for the construction of various types of items, and test appraisal methods.

Jones, Chancey O., John W. Kenelly, and Donald L. Kreider. 1975. The Advanced Placement Program in Mathematics — update 1975. *Mathematics Teacher* 68 (8) (December 1975): 654-670.

Provides a readily-accessible sample of both routine and higher-level multiple-choice and free-response questions related to elementary functions and beginning calculus. For those unfamiliar with the Advanced Placement mathematics courses, the authors include brief descriptions of the AB and BC calculus courses. Changes from earlier versions of the two courses are highlighted.

Kenelly, John W. 1978. Grading the Advanced Placement Examination in Mathematics: 1977 and 1978. Princeton, N.J.: Educational Testing Service.

Contains several complete Calculus AB and BC exams, the scoring scales used to grade answers, and sample graded answers. This provides both high-school and college calculus teachers examples of multiple-choice and free-response questions that range from routine to high-level. The scoring scales provide a good model of an "objective" approach to grading free-response items. The College Board's grading process is explained. While the classroom teacher will not be able to replicate these procedures exactly as described, the accompanying guidelines and rationale will help the teacher adapt the procedures to meet needs and resources. Similar guides are available for later years, with varying authors. The 1985 version is available in two parts. One part is entitled "The Entire 1985 AP Calculus AB Examination and Key," and the second is a similarly-titled booklet for the BC exam.

Kubiszyn, Tom, and Gary Borich. 1984. *Educational Testing and Measurement: Classroom Application and Practice.* Glenview, Ill.: Scott, Foresman.

Not specific to mathematics, but the chapters on test design, item writing, and test analysis provide clear, general guidelines. In Chapter 5 the authors describe a test "blueprint" to chart content domains and level of cognitive behavior. Chapters 6 and 7 present guidelines for writing and scoring objective and essay items. Chapter 9 includes clear steps for calculating the difficulty level and discrimination index of items. The sample discussions about the advisability of eliminating or modifying items on the basis of these statistics serve to highlight the meaning and interpretation of the statistics.

McLaughlin, Kenneth F. 1971. Interpretation of test results. In *Studying Teaching,* 2nd ed., edited by James Raths, John R. Pancella, and James S. Van Ness, 148-156. Englewood Cliffs, N.J.: Prentice-Hall.

Discusses and explains the use of item difficulty and item discrimination. Includes some quick methods for having pupils participate in the needed data-collection process. The article includes a clear and careful explanation of the calculations and their interpretations. The procedures described are most appropriate for short-answer and multiple-choice tests.

Merwin, Jack C. 1961. Constructing achievement tests and interpreting scores. In *NCTM Yearbook 26*, 43-70.

Reviews general procedures for planning a test, guidelines for writing items, and the use of test data to obtain information about the test. Item difficulty, item discrimination, and the effectiveness of discriminators are explained simply, with examples and clear interpretations.

Nimmer, Donald N. 1983. Multiple true-false classroom tests. *Clearing House* 56 (6) (February 1983): 257-258.

Provides examples (including some from mathematics) of items that combine the true-false and multiple-choice format: students are asked to read each of several statements about a single topic and respond T or F to each. Describes the benefits of this type of item and guidelines for writing them.

————. 1984. Measures of validity, reliability, and item analysis for classroom tests. *Clearing House* 58 (3) (November 1984): 138-140.

Claims that for the classroom teacher, measures of reliability and computation of a standard deviation may frequently be of little value. Argues that two elements, content validity and item difficulty, are widely applicable in classroom teaching. Simple procedures for constructing a table of specifications for a test (to encourage content validity) and for tallying responses (to determine item difficulty) are described and explained.

Nitko, Anthony J. 1983. Item analysis: Using information from pupils to improve the quality of items. In *Educational Tests and Measurement: An Introduction*, 283-303. New York: Harcourt Brace Jovanovich.

> Presents a more-detailed and thorough explanation of the calculation and use of item-difficulty and the item-discrimination indices than do many of the other references included here. Nitko carefully distinguishes interpretations of statistics between criterion-referenced and norm-referenced test situations. He also describes the use of data from multiple-choice questions for the purpose of identifying poor distractors, ambiguous alternatives, and/or miskeyed answers. Although this chapter is comprehensive, it is easy to read and suggests shortcuts and rules of thumb for the classroom teacher.

Pancella, John R. 1971. Grading alternatives. In *Studying Teaching*, 2nd ed., edited by James Raths, John R. Pancella, and James S. Van Ness, 158-162. Englewood Cliffs, N.J.: Prentice-Hall.

> Describes and clarifies some of the assumptions underlying grading systems based on fixed percentages, normal-curve distribution, a combination of fixed percentages and the normal curve, and mastery-learning constructs (pass/fail).

Pedersen, Jean, and Peter Ross. 1985. Testing understanding and understanding testing. *College Mathematics Journal* 16 (3) (June 1985): 178-185.

> Makes the case that test questions that probe for understanding and meaning are not always easy to compose. Includes a sample of problems for beginning calculus, analytic geometry, and elementary functions courses which illustrate testing for meaning. All of the examples given involve graphing in the presentation or in the solution, but this set of model problems may help the reader write testing-for-meaning items in different areas of mathematics.

Schoenfeld, Alan H. 1982. Measures of problem-solving performance and of problem-solving instruction. *Journal for Research in Mathematics Education* 13 (1) (January 1982): 31-49.

> Addresses two of the frequently-discussed "difficulties" of testing mathematical problem solving ability: the difficulty of establishing scoring rules, and the relatively small number of problems that can be given in one testing session. Includes some scoring techniques and a testing strategy (plan and describe solutions, don't carry them out) that he feels can be used as they are, or adapted by classroom teachers evaluating students' achievement in problem solving. The problems and techniques illustrated were used at the college (freshman, sophomore) level.

Suydam, Marilyn N. 1974. *Evaluation in the Mathematics Classroom:*

From What and Why to How and Where. Columbus, O.: ERIC Information Analysis Center for Science, Mathematics and Environmental Education.

Brief and to-the-point compendium of guidelines and techniques. Three simple steps in test construction are followed by general suggestions for writing items and specific guidelines for short-answer, multiple-choice, true-false, matching, and essay items. Unsophisticated means of item analysis (difficulty and discrimination) are discussed briefly. Examples of good and faulty items and in-depth treatment of test analysis are left for the reader to pursue in the extensive (if now somewhat dated) list of references.

Swadener, Marc, and D. Franklin Wright. 1975. Testing in the mathematics classroom. *Mathematics Teacher* 68 (1) (January 1975): 11-17. Reprinted under the title "More on testing—some specific suggestions" in *Readings in Secondary School Mathematics*, 2nd ed., edited by Douglas B. Aichele and Robert E. Reys, 452-461. Boston: Prindle, Weber & Schmidt, 1977.

Offers a simple listing of guidelines for writing essay, completion, true-false, multiple-choice and matching items. The authors describe the calculation and use of standard scores to reflect a student's relative standing in a group. Simple directions for calculating item difficulty and item discrimination are included.

Travers, Kenneth J., Len Pikaart, Marilyn N. Suydam, and Garth E. Runion. 1977. Evaluating: How did they do/how did I do? In *Mathematics Teaching*, 155-181. New York: Harper & Row.

Contains much of the same material as Suydam (1974).

Williams, S. Irene, and Chancey O. Jones. 1974. Multiple-choice mathematics questions —how students attempt to solve them. *Mathematics Teacher* 67 (1) (January 1974): 34-40. Reprinted in *Readings in Secondary School Mathematics*, 2nd ed., edited by Douglas B. Aichele and Robert E. Reys, 462-471. Boston: Prindle, Weber & Schmidt, 1977.

Reports on a field test of items for ETS's Level I and II Mathematics Achievement Tests. The authors' experience with oral interviews led them to some specific observations about students' use (or non-use) of information in the problem and about students' use of the test author's intended method of solution. Gives some useful insights into the problems of test construction and illustrates the type of information that statistical item analysis does not give but that a discussion with test-takers can provide.

Wilson, James W. 1971. Evaluation of learning in secondary school mathematics. In *Handbook on Formative and Summative Evaluation of Student Learning*, edited by Benjamin S. Bloom, J. Thomas Hastings, and George F. Madaus, 643-696. New York: McGraw-Hill.

Argues that mathematics learning ought to be, but frequently is not, measured over a broad range of levels of behavior. Included are many sample items, drawn from different areas of secondary mathematics and different grade levels, which illustrate defined subcategories of the cognitive levels — computation, comprehension, application, and analysis.

5. Problem Solving

ALAN H. SCHOENFELD

The question of how to define "problem solving" – obviously the appropriate first question for the author of a literature review on the topic to ask – brings to my mind a scene from a Hollywood movie version of *Alice in Wonderland* made in the late 1930s. The movie starred, among others, W.C. Fields as Humpty Dumpty and Cary Grant as the White Knight. In the relevant scene Alice asks Humpty Dumpty what he means by a particular word. "My dear little girl," says Fields as only Fields can, "Words mean exactly what I want them to mean – not a little bit more and not a little bit less."

It's much the same with problem solving. Though the phrase has been bandied about quite a lot, it has many different meanings to its many different users. Unfortunately those meanings are often contradictory, and a fair amount of confusion is caused by the miscommunications that result from the different ways that people use the term. For that reason this review begins with a review of some different perspectives regarding the nature of problem solving. It concludes with some of my own biased views on the subject.

In early 1981 the Mathematical Association of America's Committee on the Teaching of Undergraduate Mathematics (CTUM) distributed a questionnaire on problem-solving courses to every college-level mathematics department in the United States and Canada, and to others who were known by the Committee to be involved with problem-solving courses. The responses to the questionnaire indicated the diversity of the enterprise that goes under the name of "problem solving." The largest percentage of respondents, comprising groups 1 and 2 below, indicated that they taught "general problem solving courses." The goals of their courses were to provide students with experience in problem solving, to develop their problem solving ability, to train them to think creatively, and to learn to generate their own problems. This was a large part, but hardly all, of the story. All told, the following six groups of courses were distinguished from the responses.

Group 1. About 22% of all problem-solving courses were offered for general audiences (liberal arts majors, science majors, etc.) at the advanced high-school or freshman-sophomore level, usually focusing on "non-standard" problems solvable by Pólya-type heuristics. The idea behind most of these courses was that "learning problem solving" meant learning the strategies, which one did by working suitable problems.

Group 2. Another 18% of the courses surveyed consisted of upper-division offerings for mathematics majors, where for the most part the students worked on collections of problems that had been compiled by their individual instructors. In such courses the emphasis was on learning by doing, without an attempt to teach specific heuristics: the students worked lots of problems because (according to the implicit instructional model behind such courses) that's how one gets good at mathematics.

Group 3. Another 17% of the courses were devoted to training students for problem-solving competitions. Many of these were not formal offerings as in groups 1 and 2, but once-a-week problem sessions or otherwise informal training that often ceased as soon as the exam—be it the Putnam Competition (cited most frequently for college courses), one of various Olympiads, or one of various MAA contests—was given. Training for contests is serious business, and there are those who will argue that the only measure of problem solving that counts is performance on exams like the Putnam. I have some difficulties with this kind of approach. It's like arguing that "physical fitness" must be seen as "having an ideally proportioned body," and that you're not physically fit if you don't look like Arnold Schwarzenegger. Nonetheless that point of view has its adherents, and books that such people favor should be listed in a collection such as this.

Groups 4, 5, 6. Another 18% of the courses were designed to train in-service and preservice school teachers to teach problem solving. Most of these were at the secondary level, with goals similar to those of courses in Group 1. The spirit of Pólya, and a solid sampling of his books, were universal in such offerings. Yet another 15% were specialized courses in applied mathematics or mathematical modeling, algebra, probability, etc. The point is that their instructors thought of them as problem-solving (rather than subject-matter) courses; it was the approach that defined the nature of the course. Finally, 10% of the courses could be considered "basic" or "remedial" in some sense. Half of these used problems as a way of reintroducing and teaching remedial mathematics, and the other half focused on developing "critical thinking skills" or "analytical reasoning."

There are, indeed, more perspectives than those listed above. The CTUM survey was mostly at the college level, and it covered just one part of the spectrum. Since the mid-1970s problem solving has been a major theme of the National Council of Teachers of Mathematics and a significant focus of both elementary and secondary mathematics. At the elementary level the phrase is often taken to mean working word problems of the following type: "John has eight apples. He gives four apples to Mary. How many apples does John have left?" At the secondary level "problem solving" may mean working more word problems in algebra (e.g., digit problems or rate problems); it may mean learning to use certain heuristics like "when you see an integer parameter, n, plug in values of $n = 1,2,3,4,5$, and look for a pattern."

It has generally come to mean a distillation of Pólya-type heuristics, all too frequently watered down for younger students' consumption. There is more, but these examples suffice to make the point. Given the kind of diversity reflected above, it is difficult to make sense of what problem solving is all about. Any bibliography, this one included, must necessarily reflect the incoherence of the field. But it has to reflect more as well. As diverse as the categories above may seem to be, they do not cover enough.

To bring some focus to the discussion, let us return to a truly basic question: Why do we teach the mathematics that is taught in the schools? For its utility, perhaps? Some of the mathematics is, of course, directly useful. We'd all be in pretty bad shape if we didn't know arithmetic, and a fair amount of other mathematics can be similarly justified on the basis of its utility. But that argument hardly covers most of algebra, trigonometry, or calculus (to name just a few). One could argue that the few people who really need that particular specialized knowledge could get it in vocational courses, just as architects gain certain kinds of technical knowledge in their mechanical drawing courses. That argument just doesn't feel right, however. It's not solely for its utility that we teach mathematics—at least, not for the utility of the specific subject matter.

Another line of argument with the same conclusion is as follows. If you're not in a technical field, when did you last use the quadratic formula? Most likely, when you last studied it or taught it—and never outside the classroom! Why, in that case, should you have learned it? The answer to that question, discussed below, is part of the reason. What holds for utility holds for esthetics as well. We do not teach mathematics primarily for the esthetics of the discipline, though that's important too. Similar arguments can be used about the need for "quantitative literacy," or any of a number of other such plausible answers.

By analogy, why do we teach history? It isn't because historical dates and events are important in and of themselves, but because having an understanding of historical events helps an individual to better understand the world. As historians are fond of reminding us, people who fail to understand history's lessons are doomed to repeat history's mistakes. I think that in a similar way the primary reason for teaching mathematics is that *thinking mathematically* is a valuable (if not essential) skill.

Broadly speaking, thinking mathematically consists of having the ability to apply mathematical ideas in situations for which the mathematics is appropriate, and—equally importantly—of having the propensity to do so. It means being able to take an analytic perspective in problematic situations, trying to figure out what makes things tick. It means being able to see things that can be appropriately quantified in quantitative terms, and then using the mathematics one knows to help make sense of them. Using mathematics in this way is a very active, adaptive process; few of the situations one encounters in the real world are carbon copies of situations that one was taught to handle in the classroom. (Thank goodness, we do not try to teach "applied mathematics" by providing prepackaged solutions to problems. Whatever skills that students learned in that fashion would be obsolete in short order.) Indeed, the virtue of mathematics is that it is a flexible and adaptable tool. The mathematics that we know applies to a broad range of situations—once, that is, we have been able to characterize those situations in the appropriate mathematical ways.

If one accepts the perspective expressed in the previous paragraph, it follows that learning mathematics should consist in large part of learning to see things mathematically—so that one can then apply the mathematical tools that one has taken so much trouble to master! It also follows that learning mathematics should include lessons at learning to use one's mathematical knowledge with efficiency, since hitting a thumbtack with a sledgehammer (or failing to hit it because one has chosen to use a pickaxe) is no more appropriate in mathematics than in any other area. Finally, it also means that learning to do mathematics should include learning to reflect on one's use of the mathematics—on how successfully one (or it) has been, and why, so that things will go more smoothly the next time around. Such reflection is the primary catalyst for improvement, and the primary safeguard against the inappropriate waste of time and energy.

To return to the central theme of this essay, what does the preceding discussion have to do with problem solving? As far as I am concerned, the answer is "just about everything."

If you think of real problems in mathematics—both pure and applied – as situations in which the student has to stretch what he or she knows in order to make progress, then real problem solving is the ideal vehicle for developing the kinds of skills mentioned above. By "real problems," of course, I mean mathematical tasks that pose an honest challenge to the student and that the student needs to work at in order to obtain a solution.

I do not wish to demean rote exercises, for they play an important role in skill development – but working such exercises has been confused with "problem solving," and that confusion has had negative consequences. Of course students must master the relevant subject matter, and exercises are appropriate for that. But if rote exercises are the only kinds of problems that students see in their classes, we are doing the students a grave disservice. In classroom situations where students face honest-to-goodness problems, we can help them to develop the skills they can transfer to the honest-to-goodness problems they encounter outside the classroom. The problems we use may be "applied" and have real world content, but that is not necessary (although when the problems are not artificial, their relevance to the real world is a nice plus). Problems from pure mathematics such as the following are quite rich on their own terms.

1. Using straightedge and compass, can we construct a triangle given: the length of a side, of the triangle, the measure of the angle opposite the side, and the length of the median to the side?

2. How can we find the greatest common divisor of two numbers?

The problems we use need not be advanced. A favorite of mine, and one that turns out to have some real mathematical substance, consists of figuring out how to fill in a 3 x 3 magic square. Of course, what makes the problem worthwhile is what we do with it in the classroom. If we approach a problem with a spirit of inquiry – "Now, how does one make sense of this?" – rather than with a sense of conveying information "This is how one solves this kind of problem" – then we can begin to convey to our students one of the most important aspects of thinking mathematically.

It should be stressed that this kind of inquiry approach can be taken to a large percentage of the mathematical subject matter that appears in virtually all of the courses we teach. One need not wait until separate problem-solving courses to talk about problem-solving methods. Although separate problem-solving courses are nice, they are a luxury few can afford. If we taught enough mathematical thinking in our regular course offerings, separate problem-solving courses might even be redundant!

Finally, a few comments are in order regarding the choice of books listed in the bibliography. As the preceding discussion indicates, there is a lot of ground to cover in any review of problem solving. One must do justice to the constituencies represented by the six groups of problem-solving courses discussed above, and also to the burgeoning literature on problem-solving at the secondary level. The literatures for these groups are mostly mathematical, somewhat pedagogical. In addition there is a comparably important psychological literature, one which has to do with understanding the thought processes that comprise "problem-solving skills."

As an example, consider the field of artificial intelligence (AI), in which attempts are made to have computer programs behave in intelligent ways. A program called General Problem Solver, given the definitions of sets and a strategy called means-ends analysis, managed to prove a large number of the theorems at the beginning of Russell and Whitehead's *Principia Mathematica*. Perhaps most impressively, it proved one of the theorems in fewer steps than Russell and Whitehead — with a proof that Russell has reputedly called elegant.

Then there is a program called AM (for "Automated Mathematician"), which was armed with a set of heuristics for finding "interesting" mathematical ideas. Given sets, it discovered arithmetic, primes, unique factorization, and a number of other things. Playing with the primes it had discovered, AM made Goldbach's conjecture, and — its biggest coup — it also conjectured a theorem that appeared to be brand new, until it was discovered that Ramanujan had made the same conjecture.

Other AI programs are capable of predicting the incorrect answers that students will make on subtraction problems, before the students work the problems! All of these computer programs were written on the basis of insights about human problem solving, and have implications for our understanding of human problem solving behavior. Yet these represent merely the tip of the cognitive iceberg. The field of cognitive science, of which AI is a part, is making deeper and deeper inroads into the way the mind works and how our understanding of that can help us to understand how students learn.

Unfortunately, given the plethora of relevant work, it is impossible for any reasonably short bibliography to provide more than a tasting of the literature. I have chosen some of my favorites for the collection that follows, but the collection hardly does justice to either the mathematical or the psychological literature on problem solving. My view of what problem solving is all about, and a fair amount of psychological evidence regarding the issue, are given in my *Mathematical Problem Solving* (1985). A nuts-and-bolts discussion of teaching problem solving, and a substantial bibliography of problem solving journals, articles, and books, are given in my *Problem Solving in the Mathematics Curriculum* (1983). I hope the reader finds the references listed here of sufficient interest to continue to delve more and more deeply into the fascinating world of problem solving.

BIBLIOGRAPHY

Alexanderson, Gerald L., Leonard F. Klosinski, and Loren C. Larson, comps. 1986. *The William Lowell Putnam Mathematics Competition (1965-1984)*. Washington, D.C.: Mathematical Association of America.
See also Gleason et al. (1980).

Artino, Ralph A., Anthony M. Gaglioni, and Neil Shell, comps. 1983. *Contest Problem Book IV*. New Mathematical Library no. 29. Washington, D.C.: Mathematical Association of America.
For earlier contests, see Salkind (1961, 1966) and Salkind et al. (1973).

Averbach, Bonnie, and Orin Chein. 1980. *Mathematics: Problem Solving Through Recreational Mathematics*. San Francisco, Calif.: W. H. Freeman.
Entertaining and well-written text with a fair number of interesting problems. Logic puzzles, cryptarithmetic, number theory, graph theory, games, and other aspects of recreational mathematics. Designed to serve as the text for an introductory college mathematics course.

Ball, W.W. Rouse, and H.S.M. Coxeter. 1987. *Mathematical Recreations and Essays*. 13th ed. New York: Dover.
A marvelous collection of problems and entertainment, compiled by eminent scholars and mathematicians.

Barbeau, E., M. Klamkin, and W. Moser. 1976. *1001 Problems in high school mathematics*. 4 vols. Ottawa: Canadian Mathematical Society.
Problems from a variety of mathematical domains, some of which are quite challenging. Compiled by three of Canada's most active and dedicated problemists.

Begle, Edward G. 1979. *Critical Variables in Mathematics Education: Findings from a Survey of the Empirical Literature.* Edited by James W. Wilson and Jeremy Kilpatrick. Washington, D.C.: Mathematical Association of America and National Council of Teachers of Mathematics.

> A brief overview of major results in mathematics education. It's hardly an encouraging survey, but it gives one a major figure's sense of where the discipline was in the mid-to-late 1970s.

Bold, Benjamin. 1969. *Famous Problems of Geometry and How to Solve Them.* New York: Dover.

> A classic collection of problems.

Brooke, Maxey. 1969. *150 Puzzles in Crypt-arithmetic.* 2nd rev. ed. New York: Dover.

> The following is a typical (and famous) cryptarithmetic problem. Each of the letters S, E, N, D, M, O, R, N, and Y stands for a different digit between 0 and 9. Identify the choice of digits with the property that, when you substitute the value of the digits for the letters, the following sum is numerically correct:

$$
\begin{array}{r}
\text{S E N D} \\
\text{+ M O R E} \\
\hline
\text{= M O N E Y}
\end{array}
$$

> If you like this kind of problem, there is much in this book to entertain you.

Brousseau, Brother Alfred. 1972. *Saint Mary's College Contest Problems.* Mountain View, Calif.: Creative.

> Some good contest problems, many clever and unusual.

Brown, Stephen I. and Marion I. Walter. 1983. *The Art of Problem Posing.* Philadelphia, Pa.: Franklin Institute.

> If you want to learn to think mathematically, you have to learn to ask questions as well as answer them. This volume offers some nice strategies for generating interesting problems.

Bryant, Stephen J., George E. Graham, and Kenneth G. Wiley. 1965. *Non-Routine Problems in Algebra, Geometry, and Trigonometry.* New York: McGraw-Hill.

> Though the problems in this book were ostensibly composed for 10th and 11th graders, they'll keep more advanced students busy as well.

Burkhardt, Hugh. 1981. *The Real World and Mathematics.* Glasgow, Scotland: Blackie.

> This is an introduction to applied mathematics for secondary school stu-

dents. Topics include descriptions of problems from everyday life, tackling real problems in the classroom, and a variety of applications techniques.

Butts, Thomas. 1973. *Problem Solving in Mathematics: Elementary Number Theory and Arithmetic.* Glenview, Ill.: Scott, Foresman.
A nice exposition on problem solving, written before the term got fashionable. The book is currently out of print, but worth searching out.

Charles, Randall, Frank Lester, and Phares O'Daffer. 1987. *How to Evaluate Progress in Problem Solving.* Reston, Va.: National Council of Teachers of Mathematics. (PJC & LSG)

Charosh, Mannis, comp. 1965. *Mathematical Challenges.* Washington, D.C.: National Council of Teachers of Mathematics.
A selection of problems from the *Mathematics Student Journal,* including "miscellaneous brevities," geometric, algebraic, and inferential problems. Intended for students in grades 7 through 12.

Committee on the Undergraduate Program in Mathematics. 1981. *Recommendations for a General Mathematical Sciences Program.* Washington, D.C.: Mathematical Association of America.
For a fair number of mathematicians, "problem solving" includes mathematical modeling. The section on modeling in this report is extensive.

Curcio, Frances R., ed. 1987. *Teaching and Learning: A Problem-Solving Focus.* Reston, Va.: National Council of Teachers of Mathematics.
A tribute to George Pólya. Includes essays on problem solving.

Descartes, René. 1980. *Philosophical Essays.* Indianapolis, Ind.: Bobbs-Merrill.
Much recent work in problem solving is based on Pólya's writings, which were at least partly inspired by Descartes — this volume contains Descartes' rules for the direction of the mind, his most serious attempt to outline productive strategies for thinking mathematically.

Dörrie, Heinrich. 1965. *100 Great Problems of Elementary Mathematics; Their History and Solution.* Translated by David Antin. New York: Dover.
The title summarizes the contents. Good choice of problems, very nice exposition.

Dynkin, E.B., S.A. Molchanov, A.L. Rosental, and A.K. Tolpygo. 1969. *Mathematical Problems: An Anthology.* Edited and translated by Richard A. Silverman. New York: Gordon & Breach.

A lovely collection of problems from all sorts of domains. You'll be certain to find some that please you.

Gardner, Martin. 1978. *Aha! Aha! Insight.* San Francisco, Calif.: W. H. Freeman.

Like most of Gardner's books, this is quite entertaining. It's a collection of "insight" problems that have cute solutions. Check out the various collections of Gardner's columns from *Scientific American* also. There's a series of them, published as *The (nth) Scientific American Book of Mathematical Puzzles and Diversions.*

Gleason, Andrew M., R.E. Greenwood, and L.M. Kelly. 1980. *The William Lowell Putnam Mathematical Competition: Problems and Solutions: 1938-1964.* Washington, D.C.: Mathematical Association of America.

The Putnam exam is the most prestigious national undergraduate mathematics competition. For the exams from 1965 to 1984, see Alexanderson et al. (1986). Discussions of subsequent exams, including problems and solutions, can be found in the *American Mathematical Monthly.*

Goldin, Gerald A., and C.E. McClintock. 1984. *Task Variables in Mathematical Problem Solving.* Philadelphia, Pa.: Franklin Institute.

A mainstream effort in mathematics education problem solving research in the late 1970s was to characterize the variables that affect problem solving performance, and to trace their effects. This book is the most comprehensive summary of that effort.

Greitzer, Samuel L., comp. 1978. *International Mathematical Olympiads, 1959-1977.* New Mathematical Library no. 27. Washington, D.C.: Mathematical Association of America.

The problems discussed here are tough. The International Mathematical Olympiads are designed to discriminate among the brightest kids in the world, so many an older and more-experienced problem solver can expect to be frustrated by them. Klamkin (1986) covers years 1978-1985.

Harvey, J. G., and T. A. Romberg, eds. 1980. *Problem Solving Studies in Mathematics.* Madison, Wis.: Wisconsin Research and Development Center for Individualized Schooling.

Nine doctoral studies in problem solving undertaken at Wisconsin, covering most of the 1970s, are given here. Reading this book gives one a good sense of the mathematics education perspective on problem solving during that decade.

Hayes, John R. 1981. *The Complete Problem Solver.* Philadelphia, Pa.: Franklin Institute.

An interesting and useful book, this isn't limited to mathematics. Chapters on problem solving theory and practice, memory and knowledge acquisition, decision making, and creativity and invention.

Hill, Claire Conley. 1979. *Problem Solving: Learning and Teaching, an Annotated Bibliography*. New York: Nichols.

Extensive annotations for more than 250 items on problem solving. Broad and general coverage.

Hill, Thomas, comp. 1974. *Mathematical Challenges II, Plus Six*. Reston, Va.: National Council of Teachers of Mathematics.

A sequel to Charosh (1965), this book offers a selection of problems from the *Mathematics Student Journal*, including some from geometry, algebra, number theory, probability, and trigonometry. Six little essays are included as a bonus.

Hughes, Barnabas. 1976. *Thinking Through Problems — A Manual of Heuristics*. Palo Alto, Calif.: Creative.

A text for teaching heuristics. Useful and straightforward.

Joint Committee of the Mathematical Association of America and the National Council of Teachers of Mathematics. 1980. *A Sourcebook for Applications of School Mathematics*. Reston, Va.: National Council of Teachers of Mathematics.

This volume offers a collection of "real" applications of mathematics, so that the teacher challenged to make problem solving relevant can do so with integrity. Broad range of applications at the secondary level.

Joint Matriculation Board, Shell Centre for Mathematics Education. 1984. *Problems with Patterns and Numbers: An O-Level Module*. Nottingham, England: University of Nottingham.

A useful collection of problems for middle- and secondary-school children, with enough annotations so that teachers can feel comfortable.

Kahneman, Daniel, Paul Slovic, and Amos Tversky, eds. 1982. *Judgment under Uncertainty: Heuristics and Biases*. Cambridge, England: Cambridge University Press.

Not problem solving per se, but a fascinating collection of articles on people's misconceptions of various mathematical (mostly statistical) notions. It shakes your belief in "rational thinking" — as it should.

Kilpatrick, Jeremy, and Izaak Wirszup, eds. 1969-1975. *Soviet Studies in the Psychology of Learning and Teaching Mathematics*. 14 vols. University of Chicago Survey of East European Mathematics Literature. Chicago: University of Chicago.

Russian teaching experiments described here are hardly objective descriptions of problem solving behavior in the sense of "science" as we take it, but they provide lots of interesting ideas.

Klamkin, Murray S., comp. 1986. *International Mathematical Olympiads, 1978-1985 and Forty Supplementary Problems.* New Mathematical Library no. 31. Washington, D.C.: Mathematical Association of America.
    Greitzer (1978) covers earlier years.

Kraitchik, Maurice. 1953. *Mathematical Recreations.* 2nd revised ed. New York: Dover.
    A classic of recreational mathematics.

Krulik, Stephen, and Robert Reys, eds. 1980. *NCTM 1980 Yearbook.*
    A good book to read as an introduction to problem solving. The NCTM made problem solving its top curricular goal for the 1980s, and this 1980 yearbook was the NCTM's attempt to provide its membership with up-to-date information about the topic.

Larson, Loren C. 1983. *Problem-Solving through Problems.* New York: Springer-Verlag.
    A fairly high-powered collection of problems, organized according to solvability via various problem solving heuristics. There are problems in arithmetic, algebra, series, intermediate real analysis, inequalities, and geometry.

Lesh, Richard, Diane Mierkiewicz, and Mary Kantowski, eds. 1979. *Applied Mathematical Problem Solving.* Columbus, O.: ERIC/SMEAC. ERIC: ED 180816.
    Research monograph containing a number of studies with direct implications for the classroom.

Lester, Frank K., and Joe Garofalo. 1982. *Mathematical Problem Solving: Issues in Research.* Philadelphia, Pa.: Franklin Institute.
    Papers from a conference on problem solving.

Lidsky, Viktor B., L. Ovsyannikov, A. Tulaikov, and M. Shabunin. 1973. *Problems in Elementary Mathematics.* Translated by V. Volosov. Moscow: Mir (distributed by Imported Publications).
    Varied problems from algebra, geometry, trigonometry. Some are routine, some are boring; some are interesting problems for sharpening skills.

Lochhead, Jack, and John Clement, eds. 1979. *Cognitive Process Instruction: Research on Teaching Thinking Skills.* Philadelphia, Pa.: Franklin Institute.
    The proceedings of a 1978 conference, this volume offers an early view of

instruction that focuses on what students do (i.e., cognitive processes) rather than solely on the subject matter the students are expected to learn.

Luchins, Abraham S., and Edith H. Luchins, eds. 1970. *Wertheimer's Seminars Revisited: Problem Solving and Thinking.* 3 vols. Albany, N.Y.: Faculty-Student Association, State University of New York at Albany.

Notes based on the Gestaltist Max Wertheimer's seminars on problem solving. Possibly the deepest exposition of the Gestalt view on the topic.

Mason, John, Leone Burton, and Kaye Stacey. 1982. *Thinking Mathematically.* London: Addison-Wesley.

A very nice book with an excellent selection of problems, this is one of the few books on problem-solving that really focuses on problem-solving processes. I wish I'd written it.

Maxwell, Edwin A. 1959. *Fallacies in Mathematics.* Cambridge, England: Cambridge University Press.

Fun reading, and a lot of good, thought-provoking examples.

Mayer, Richard E. 1983. *Thinking, Problem Solving, Cognition.* New York: W. H. Freeman.

A good introductory summary of the psychological literature related to problem solving.

Papert, Seymour. 1980. *Mindstorms: Children, Computers, and Powerful Ideas.* New York: Basic Books.

Papert is the inventor of Logo, a powerful computer language accessible to young children. *Mindstorms* presents the rationale behind the work and a good case for Papert's epistemological views. You may or may not agree, but you should read what he says.

Pólya, George. 1945. *How to Solve It: A New Aspect of Mathematical Method.* 1957. 2nd ed. Garden City, N.Y.: Doubleday. 1971. Reprint. Princeton, N.J.: Princeton University Press.

This is the book that started it all, a classic that should be on everyone's bookshelf. Pólya introduced the notion of "heuristic" in this book, which offers an exploration of problem solving strategies written in his unique and fascinating style. If you own one book on problem solving, this should be it — although Pólya's *Mathematical Discovery* (1981) is richer than this first, introductory book, and gives it a good run for the money.

————. 1954. *Mathematics and Plausible Reasoning.* Volume 1: *Induction and Analogy in Mathematics* Vol. 2: *Patterns of Plausible Inference.* Princeton, N.J.: Princeton University Press.

A thorough and complex study of mathematical reasoning processes, written by the man who, more than anyone else, is responsible for the rejuvenation of "mathematical problem solving" in this century.

————. [1962-1965] 1981. *Mathematical Discovery: On Understanding, Learning and Teaching Problem Solving*. 2 vols. Combined ed. New York: Wiley.

This book, too, is a must for every bookshelf. It's often used in teacher-training courses, but it should be much more widely read. It contains good problems, interesting subject matter, and the wisdom of a master problem solver.

————, and Jeremy Kilpatrick. 1974. *The Stanford Mathematics Problem Book*. New York: Teachers College Press.

Problems and solutions from the Stanford competitive examinations for high-school seniors, given 1946 through 1965.

Rapaport, Elvira, trans. 1963. *The Hungarian Problem Books I, II*. New Mathematical Library nos. 11, 12. Washington, D.C.: Mathematical Association of America.

Problems from the Eötvös competitions, notably difficult tests that were offered annually from 1894 through 1928. A good source of challenging problems, with nice discussions.

Reeves, Charles A. 1987. *Problem-Solving Techniques Helpful in Mathematics and Science*. Reston, Va.: National Council of Teachers of Mathematics. (PJC & LSG).

Salkind, Charles T., comp. 1961, 1966. *Contest Problem Book I, II*. New Mathematical Library nos. 5, 17. Washington, D.C.: Mathematical Association of America.

————, and James M. Earl, comps. 1973. *Contest Problem Book III*. New Mathematical Library no. 25. Washington, D.C.: Mathematical Association of America.

Collected problems from the annual MAA high-school contests. See also Artino et al. (1983).

Schoenfeld, Alan H. 1983. *Problem Solving in the Mathematics Curriculum: A Report, Recommendations, and an Annotated Bibliography*. MAA Notes no. 1. Washington, D.C.: Mathematical Association of America.

Includes a 50-page "how to" section on teaching a problem solving course, and an 80-page annotated bibliography of references on problem solving. Offers useful advice and a large collection of resources.

————. 1985. *Mathematical Problem Solving.* New York: Academic.
> This book explores what it means to "think mathematically," and how one might teach students to do it. It lays out a framework for analyzing mathematical behavior, describes research in the area, and discusses the kinds of things we can do to help students become better problem solvers. The book is based on ten years of research, closely coupled with the development of a problem-solving course.

Shumway, Richard J., ed. 1980. *Research in Mathematics Education.* Reston, Va.: National Council of Teachers of Mathematics.
> The NCTM's definitive research volume summing things up as of the late 1970s; includes a large chapter on problem solving.

Silver, Edward A., ed. 1985. *Teaching and Learning Mathematical Problem Solving: Multiple Research Perspectives.* Hillsdale, N.J.: Erlbaum.
> An excellent, up-to-date compendium of a variety of research views on problem solving. This book, together with my *Mathematical Problem Solving* (1985), provides a comprehensive overview of work in the field. (They're the two books I use in a course on the nature of mathematical thinking.)

Sleeman, D., and J.S. Brown, eds. 1982. *Intelligent Tutoring Systems.* New York: Academic.
> The most detailed summary of work in artificial intelligence with implications for mathematics education—problem solving included. Some of the articles are fairly technical, but it's worth wading through.

Stacey, Kaye, and Susie Groves. 1985. *Strategies for Problem Solving: Lesson Plans for Developing Mathematical Thinking.* Victoria, Australia: VICTRACC LTD.
> A very practical, useful set of materials that help the secondary school teacher develop lessons for teaching problem solving. Not at all faddish, but very solid work by two people who've thought long and hard about problem solving. We need more materials like this, so that problem solving can become a reality in our classrooms.

Stacey, Kaye, and Beth Southwell. 1983. *Teacher Tactics for Problem Solving.* Canberra, Australia: Curriculum Development Centre.
> More very solid and useful materials.

Steinhaus, Hugo. 1964. *One Hundred Problems in Elementary Mathematics.* New York: Dover.
> Lovely problems, nice exposition; this is one of the great problem books. This too belongs on your bookshelf.

Tuma, David T., and Frederick Reif, eds. 1980. *Problem Solving and*

Education: Issues in Teaching and Research. Hillsdale, N.J.: Erlbaum.

These are the proceedings of a conference held at Carnegie-Mellon University in 1978. You get a good sense of the perspective of information-processing psychologists on what's important in problem solving.

Whimbey, Arthur, and Jack Lochhead. 1980, 1984. *Problem Solving and Comprehension: A Short Course in Analytic Reasoning. Beyond Problem Solving and Comprehension.* Philadelphia, Pa.: Franklin Institute Press.

These two volumes offer a course in "analytical thinking" that focuses on reasoning skills, and on taking problems apart carefully.

Yaglom, Isaak M., and Y. Yaglom. 1977. *Challenging Mathematical Problems with Elementary Solutions.* San Francisco: Holden-Day.

Excellent source of problems for high-school students or beginning college students. Broad range of topics: algebra, geometry, number theory, probability.

6. Instruction in Introductory Algebra

ROBERT B. DAVIS

Some General Considerations

$\mathbf{M}$ajor changes in the mathematics curriculum in the United States are slowly being implemented. The changes are of fundamental importance, and everyone concerned with the teaching of introductory algebra should be thinking in somewhat dynamic terms – the field is no longer entirely static. More importantly, some of the changes ought to be incorporated into how we teach our classes this week and this year. This chapter deals both with teaching *now*, and with the nature and implications of these changes, changes that should become more evident over the next few years.

Efforts to improve algebra teaching relate to at least eight important aspects:

The Separation of Algebra from the Rest of Mathematics

Introductory algebra is commonly taught in the United States as a separate subject, not closely integrated into the rest of mathematics. This approach is very limiting and has been abandoned by nearly all other nations (Travers 1985, 83). The teaching of algebra becomes more powerful and more effective when it is combined with arithmetic, graphing, the study of functions, portions of geometry (especially analytic geometry), computer programming, and other topics. A few U.S. textbooks approach the subject this way (Stein and Crabill 1972; Dwyer and Critchfield 1975). If a slightly stronger previous knowledge of algebra can be presupposed, even more "unified" texts can be considered, such as Carmony et al. (1984). Many journal articles offer suggestions for relating algebra to other parts of mathematics (see, e.g., Kimberling (1985)). Computer courseware relevant to a more unified approach is becoming available (Dugdale 1982).

Understanding vs. Rote

In the past a substantial proportion of algebra learning was mainly by rote. For some students this approach succeeds, but for many others the result is a detailed study of procedures that do not make sense and do not seem worthwhile. Many commentaries, and a few actual studies, deal with the distinction between "rote learning"—where one merely follows "cookbook" direction or one-step-at-a-time-even-though-I-don't-know where-it-all-leads—vs. decisions and strategies based on the student's conceptual understanding. "Understanding" takes many forms, among which *conceptual understanding*, learning from relevant *experience*, clarity of *goals*, appropriate *analyses* of ways to reach these goals, and the use of *heuristics* are especially important (Davis et al. 1982; Davis 1984; Zukav 1979, 7-8; Pólya 1957; Kantowski 1981; Papert 1980; Alderman et al. 1979; and Erlwanger 1973).

Grade-Level Placement

In the United States introductory algebra has traditionally been taught in grade 9, with a second course in grade 11, and with remedial courses offered for older students at the college level. In recent years one has begun to see algebra courses in grades 7 and 8 for able students, with more and more introductory material moving into elementary-school grades. (Davis 1985b; Freudenthal 1974.)

Content

The content of introductory algebra is being reconsidered and revised. Among topics considered for possible inclusion are review of arithmetic, introduction to matrices, determinants, logic, graphs and functions, combinatorics, topics from analytic geometry, vectors, beginning ideas of calculus, and computer-programming (in BASIC, Logo, Pascal, APL, TUTOR, or other languages). Stein and Crabill (1972), for example, combine a review of arithmetic, an initial introduction to algebra, and certain topics from calculus, which may sound an unlikely combination, but one which they meld very successfully. Calculators are also beginning to have an impact on instruction in algebra (Weaver 1981; Shumway 1981).

New Ideas About Mathematical Thought

The traditional view among teachers of algebra has been that "doing mathematics" means writing certain symbols on paper, by following explicit rules that have been presented to you by natural language statements. Careful studies of student behavior have shown this to be a somewhat dangerous view, often resulting in poor student performance (Erlwanger 1973; Davis 1984).

In recent years a second view has emerged, which sees learning mathematics as a process of building up mental representations and acquiring skill in using these representations, modifying them, and synthesizing new ones (Thompson 1982; Davis 1984; Kilpatrick 1985).

These two views suggest quite different priorities for teachers. The first, the *verbal/symbolic view*, implies teacher responsibility for showing or telling students what to do, especially what to write. The second view, often called *constructivism*, implies that showing and telling will often fail, because the teacher may not make effective contact with the actual ideas in the student's mind. Instead — according to this second view — the teacher has three important responsibilities: (i) to provide *experiences* from which students can synthesize appropriate mental representations; (ii) to make effective contact with the student's mental representations; (iii) to recognize when the student's mental representations are inappropriate and help the student to correct them (Rosnick and Clement 1980; Matz 1980; Madell 1985).

Teaching and Scholarship

Traditionally there have been three common positions on the relation between the activity of teaching introductory algebra and the various activities that are usually called "scholarly."

1. The two are unrelated: teaching algebra has nothing much to do with any form of scholarly activity. Indeed, we do not ordinarily expect high-school teachers of algebra to pursue scholarly activity.
2. The *activities* were largely unrelated, but the *people* who teach

algebra at the college level should pursue some form of scholarly work within the area of traditional mathematical research: they should prove theorems and publish the results, or at least solve problems in the _American Mathematical Monthly._

3. Algebra teachers, at both high-school and college levels, should develop effective ways of teaching various topics, and share their inventions with other teachers through journals such as the _Mathematics Teacher._

In recent years, because of the emergence of mathematics education as a worthy discipline in its own right, a fourth position has appeared: Those who teach algebra can engage in _the scholarly study of the processes of teaching and learning algebra_ — and can publish the results in journals such as the _Journal for Research in Mathematics Education, Educational Studies in Mathematics,_ or the _Journal of Mathematical Behavior._ This fourth possibility can be of great importance; scholarly productivity is a valuable form of personal professional growth. That it should be closely related to our day-to-day work, that it should lead to improvements in our daily teaching, seems eminently reasonable and clearly desirable (Rosnick and Clement 1980; Schoenfeld 1985; Lesh and Landau 1983; Young 1982).

Gender

By now one hopes that everyone who teaches mathematics at any level is aware that females tend to perform, on the average, less well than males; that black and Hispanic students tend to perform less well, on the average, than white non-Hispanic students; and that special efforts need to be directed toward the elimination of these inequalities (Pedersen et al. 1985). The root causes of such unequal performances are not entirely clear, but the situation is one more matter that those who teach algebra need to bear in mind. We who teach must be careful that we are not ourselves the cause of these problems, whether by having lower expectations for female or minority students, by advising them differently, or by other actions or attitudes that may interfere with their advancement.

Goals

There has been extensive discussion, in recent years about the _goals_ of teaching mathematics. In the case of introductory algebra, when teachers of eighth-graders were asked to identify the main goals, the highest-rated goal was "developing a systematic approach to solving problems." The second-highest-rated goal was "developing an awareness of the importance of mathematics in everyday life." Tied for third were "developing an attitude of inquiry" and "understanding the logical structure of mathematics" (Travers et al. 1985, 13). These are sophisticated and appropriate goals; unfortunately, the prevalence of relatively meaningless rote instruction in many classrooms is not consistent with these goals. Many teachers are rethinking their goals in a useful and promising way, but results of this rethinking have not as yet had much impact on day-to-day classroom instruction.

Practical Aids for Day-to-Day Teaching

The application of the above considerations requires reflective thought and considerable imagination.

We turn now to another kind of discussion whose relevance to day-to-day teaching is more immediate, beginning with the need to teach heuristic analytical skills to students at every level:

Heuristics

One of the most important improvements in mathematics teaching comes from a greater effort to teach students to use various *heuristics* (i.e., strategies for making sensible decisions in attacking a problem that we initially do *not* know how to solve) (Hughes 1974; Pólya 1957; Schoenfeld 1979).

One important heuristic is to *try some easy cases*. If we are concerned with finding a simpler way to write

$$1 + 2 + 3 + \ldots + n$$

we might try studying the patterns in "easy" special cases:

$$1 = 1$$
$$1 + 2 = 3$$
$$1 + 2 + 3 = 6$$
$$1 + 2 + 3 + 4 = 10$$

Perhaps we can find the key pattern underlying these special cases (and we *can*, if we know something about finite difference methods (Davis 1967)).

Another heuristic is: *Can you write or represent the problem in a different way?* In our preceding example, if we notice that the sum can be written either as

$$1 + 2 + 3 + \ldots + (n-2) + (n-1) + n$$

or else as

$$n + (n-1) + (n-2) + \ldots + 3 + 2 + 1,$$

and if we think to *add* the two expressions together as separate vertical-column sums, we get the same result in each column:

1	+	2	+	3	+	...	+	$(n-2)$	+	$(n-1)$	+	n
n	+	$(n-1)$	+	$(n-2)$	+	...	+	3	+	2	+	1
$n+1$		$n+1$		$n+1$				$n+1$		$n+1$		$n+1$

or:

$$
\begin{aligned}
1 + n \;\;\;\;\; &= n + 1 \\
2 + (n-1) &= n + 1 \\
3 + (n-2) &= n + 1 \\
&\cdot \\
&\cdot \\
&\cdot \\
(n-2) + 3 &= n + 1 \\
(n-1) + 2 &= n + 1 \\
n + 1 &= n + 1 \; .
\end{aligned}
$$

Then we need only notice that there are n such sums, so that the total is $n(n+1)$. Since this is twice the result we sought, we deduce that:

$$1 + 2 + 3 + \ldots + n = n(n+1)/2.$$

An even more suggestive alternative representation is possible; represent K as the area of a rectangle K cm. by 1 cm., for $K = 1, 2, 3, \ldots, n$.

Then $1 + 2 + 3$ can be represented as the area shown in Figure 6.1.

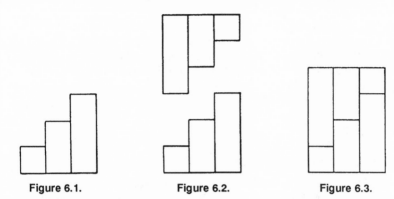

Figure 6.1.   Figure 6.2.   Figure 6.3.

Two shapes like Figure 6.1 can be fitted together (as in Figures 6.2 and 6.3), from which we see that

$$1 + 2 + 3 + 3 + 2 + 1 = 3 (3 + 1),$$

or

$$1 + 2 + 3 = 3(3 + 1)/2$$

More generally,

$$(1 + 2 + 3 + \ldots + n) + (n + (n-1) + \ldots + 3 + 2 + 1) = n(n + 1),$$

or

$$1 + 2 + 3 + \ldots + n = n(n + 1)/2.$$

This single example hardly does justice to the important topic of heuristics. One fact, however, is worth emphasizing: most children do not invent heuristics on their own. Teachers cannot expect students to acquire on their own skill in the habitual use of heuristics.

For some examples of the effective use of heuristics, see O'Daffer (1985a, 1985b), Davis (1985a), Pólya (1957), and Schoenfeld (1979). For alternative representations, see Edwards (1974).

Student Creativity

Teaching becomes far more effective when a *creative* role is assigned to students (Madell 1985; Stodolsky 1985). This creative role can involve preliminary exploration of trial examples, seeking to discover generalizations, or even just talking the task over in a small-group discussion setting.

Making Mathematics Meaningful

Most present-day instruction in algebra is perceived by most students as meaningless. Students seem to fall into three groups: (i) those who find this meaninglessness acceptable; (ii) those who are able (perhaps on their own) to *find* appropriate meanings; (iii) those who are alienated or incapacitated by this meaninglessness.

What alternatives are possible? "Meaning" can take any of several different forms. A task may be "meaningful" because it is part of a larger task that we find fascinating (Boas 1980, 1981); or because it is a symbolic translation of a situation we understand in some other form (e.g., the geometric demonstration of the distributive law); or because we ourselves have devised a strategy for attacking the problem (Holcomb 1980).

With young children, physical materials and geometric pictures are commonly used as a foundation for most mathematical ideas — recall the familiar "pie" pictures to illustrate fractional parts. Such materials are rarely used with older students, but there is evidence that such use would often be helpful.

Activities

There are many classroom activities that encourage students to take an active role (Vance 1981; Grinstein 1981; Edwards 1974; Bhattacharya and Lucchese 1980). Even more interesting activities become possible when calculators and computers are available (Dugdale 1982; Kimberling 1985; Norris 1981).

Student Errors

We now know that student errors are not so random as we used to assume. There are regular patterns of errors and increasingly powerful ways of dealing with such very common errors as

$$A \times (B + C) = (A \times B) + C$$

and

$$\sqrt{A^2 + B^2} = A + B$$

(Davis 1984; Matz 1980; VanLehn 1982; Radatz 1979). The research literature on student errors is increasingly exciting and valuable and deserves attention.

Five conceptual difficulties merit explicit mention here: first, in algebra we use the same notation to *describe a procedure* and also to *name the result* of using that procedure. Thus, $x + 2$ tells us to add 2 to whatever the value of x may be, but it is also a name for the answer. Similarly, $\sqrt{19}$ tells us to find the square root of 19, but it is also a name for the result. A discussion of this situation, and an indication of the student misconceptions that can result, is presented in Davis (1975, 17-20).

Second, there is the question of *how to write variables*. The traditional use of x and y is satisfactory to some students but misleads others. David Page has demonstrated the superiority in some situations of "$\square$" and "$\triangle$", as in

$$(\square \times 3) + 7 = \triangle$$

(Harkin and Rising 1974; Davis 1984, 48-51). Papert, in his work with Logo, uses English words to name variables, such as "height," "length," "area," etc. Thus the formula

$$A = b \times h$$

for the area of a rectangle might be written:

$$AREA = BASE \times HEIGHT$$

Something similar is quite common in computer programming.

Third, there are several different ideas about what variables "really are." Sometimes they are used to represent *generalizations*, as when

$$1 + 2 = 2 + 1$$
$$1 + 3 = 3 + 1$$
$$2 + 3 = 3 + 2$$

and so on, is written as:

$$\square + \triangle = \triangle + \square \quad,$$

or as

$$x + y = y + x \quad.$$

There are other meanings; in the earlier example, the variables referred to *measurements* made on a rectangle (and A, b, and h must be measured correctly, on the *same* rectangle, if we are to be guaranteed that $A = b \times h$).

Variables may refer to "unknowns," as in

$$3x + 7 = 22 \quad.$$

These alternatives cannot be discussed further here; perhaps the best advice to teachers is to be as honest as possible in discussing how you yourself think about the variables in the given situation.

Fourth, students are sometimes confused by the distinction between what is *legal* vs. what is *strategically useful*. Thus, if we are trying to solve the equation

$$3x + 7 = 22 \quad,$$

it is *legal* to add the same thing to both sides of the equation, and to thus obtain

$$4x + 7 = 22 + x \quad,$$

or alternatively,

$$3x + 9 = 24 \quad;$$

but neither of these steps is *strategically useful.*

Fifth, in mathematics the statement "If P, then Q" is false *only* when P is true and Q is false. Thus a statement such as "If it rains Saturday, I won't go to the picnic" — which, to the lay person, usually implies that if it does not, you will — has, for mathematicians, the clear meaning that, if it does not rain, you have made absolutely no commitment in either direction.

This convention is used consistently throughout mathematics and has important consequences. Thus, David Page's statement of the usual rule for numerical replacement of variables — "If the shape is the same, the numbers must be the same" — means that the open sentence

$$\square + \square = 8$$

has the truth set {4}. On this, lay usage and mathematical usage agree. But when we confront

$$\square + \triangle = 8 \ ,$$

we run into trouble. Many students assume that using 4 as a replacement for *both* variables is illegal. Of course it is not. If the shapes are *not* the same, no restriction applies.

A very large collection of student errors and misconceptions is presented in Davis et al. (1978).

Ways of Presenting Specific Topics

Finally, we turn to what some people would expect to be our main concern. Every now and then somebody does manage to find an unusually effective way of presenting some specific topic (Crowley and Dunn 1985). It is very helpful when these discoveries are shared with colleagues.

We have not made this our main concern in this chapter because of our firm conviction that good teaching comes not merely from some sort of "bag of tricks," but more importantly from a careful thinking out of goals, values, and assumptions about the nature of learning and even about the nature of mathematics itself.

BIBLIOGRAPHY

Adda, Josette. 1982. Difficulties with mathematical symbolism: Synonymy and homonymy. *Visible Language* 16 (3) (Summer 1982): 205-214.
  Shows how serious scholarship can be applied to problems in the teaching and learning of algebra (and other parts of mathematics). The focus is on written symbolism, a matter which surely deserves careful thought (and often does not get it, as one sees from the inappropriate notations in many textbooks).

Alderman, Donald L., Spencer Swinton, and James S. Braswell. 1979. Assessing basic arithmetic skills and understanding across curricula: Computer-assisted instruction and compensatory education. *Journal of Children's Mathematical Behavior* 2 (Spring 1979): 3-28.
  Shows how deficient the *understandings* of many students actually are. Despite the word "arithmetic" in its title, this article is relevant to the teaching and learning of algebra. It was one of the earliest studies to demonstrate that for many children mathematics is nothing more than a meaningless "dance of the symbols." (Cf. also Erlwanger (1973), and Rosnick and Clement (1980)).

Bagnato, Robert A. 1973. Teaching college mathematics by question-and-answer. *Educational Studies in Mathematics* 5 (2) (June 1973): 185-192.
  Presents one of the most powerful techniques for teaching algebra, or any other part of mathematics. Every mathematics teacher needs to consider the limitations of "telling" students or "showing" them (that is to say, of *lecturing*), vs. the strengths of engaging students in a dialogue or discussion.

Bhattacharya, Dipendra N., and Concetta R. Lucchese. 1980. An application of the complete square identity. *Mathematics Teacher* 73 (2) (February 1980): 116.
  Shows how some students accidentally "stumbled on an interesting" pattern and were able to analyze it algebraically. This discovery could be presented as a challenge to students, provided they are left to work it out for themselves.

Boas, Ralph P. 1980, 1981. Snowfalls and elephants, pop bottles and pi. *Two-Year College Mathematics Journal* 11 (2) (March 1980): 82-89. Reprint. *Mathematics Teacher* 74 (1) (January 1981): 49-55. Revised from article in *Arts and Sciences* (Northwestern University) 2 (1) (1979).
  Presents a mathematical analysis of such extremes as "the coldest day on record." How many times in your life should you expect to see more snow than you have ever seen before? Boas is a major research mathematician with an unfailing eye for finding interesting questions that can be answered in interesting ways. The methods used in this analysis are worth knowing; the excitement and challenge are hard to match anywhere else. (Although probability plays a role,

there is nothing in this article that precludes its use in an introductory algebra course.)

Carmony, Lowell A., Robert J. McGlinn, Ann Miller Millman, and Jerry P. Becker. 1984. *Problem Solving in Apple Pascal*. Rockville, Md.: Computer Science Press.

> Presents problem solving simultaneously with an introduction to the computer-programming language Pascal. This is one of the new textbooks that challenge the notion that one must do certain things *before* attempting certain others. Such consecutive sequencing is often unnecessary; it is frequently possible to pursue both goals *simultaneously*. In particular, introductory algebra can be taught simultaneously with *arithmetic* (Davis 1985b), with a *review* of arithmetic (Stein and Crabill 1972), with *computer programming* (Dwyer and Critchfield 1975), with an introduction to some key concepts of *calculus* (Stein and Crabill 1972), or – at a somewhat more sophisticated level – with learning *Pascal* (in the present book).

Corbitt, Mary Kay, ed. 1985. The impact of computing technology on school mathematics: Report of an NCTM conference. *Mathematics Teacher* 78 (4) (April 1985): 243-250.

> Suggests how substantial the changes in introductory algebra need to be if the curriculum is going to accommodate the emerging role of computers.

Crowley, Mary L., and Kenneth A. Dunn. 1985. On multiplying negative numbers. *Mathematics Teacher* 78 (4) (April 1985): 252-256, (6) (September 1985): 408, (9) (December 1985) 665, 707.

> Provides helpful background on the infamous problem of multiplying two negative numbers.

Davis, Robert B. 1967. *Explorations in Mathematics. A Text for Teachers*. Palo Alto, Calif.: Addison-Wesley.

> Shows how many topics from algebra can be combined with arithmetic, geometry, and logic to create a whole that is more powerful, and more fun to learn, than the separate parts usually are. Contents include graphs, matrices, finite difference methods, truth tables, and inference schemes.

———. 1975. Cognitive processes involved in solving simple algebraic equations. *Journal of Children's Mathematical Behavior* 1 (3) (Summer 1975): 7-35.

> Shows some of the intellectual difficulties students have in thinking about algebraic notations: in particular, the question about the notation "$x + 2$": "How can I add 2 to x when I don't know what x is?"

———. 1980. *Discovery in Mathematics: A Text for Teachers*. New Rochelle, N.Y.: Cuisenaire Company of America.

Shows how algebra can be combined with arithmetic and geometry and taught to younger students. Also shows the use of manipulatable physical materials, especially geoboards.

————. 1984. *Learning Mathematics: The Cognitive Science Approach to Mathematics Education.* Norwood, N.J.: Ablex.
Shows several aspects of the teaching and learning of algebra, including common student error patterns, alternative notations, the effects of misconceptions about algebraic symbolism, studies of how humans think about mathematical problems, and evidence that most students *could* learn substantially more mathematics if curricula and instructional procedures were altered in a suitable way.

————. 1985a. The role of representations in problem solving: Case studies. *Journal of Mathematical Behavior* 4 (1) (April 1985): 85-97.
Shows how alternative representations may simplify the task of solving problems.

————. 1985b. ICME-5 report: Algebraic thinking in the early grades. *Journal of Mathematical Behavior* 4 (2) (October 1985): 195-208.
Reports on sessions at the Fifth International Congress on Mathematical Education, held at Adelaide, Australia, August 1984, that dealt with the development of algebraic thinking in younger students and the creation of effective syntheses of arithmetic and algebra.

————, Elizabeth Jockusch, and Curtis McKnight. 1978. Cognitive processes in learning algebra. *Journal of Children's Mathematical Behavior* 2 (Spring 1978): 10-32.
Contains an extensive list of the errors and misconceptions of secondary school students who are studying algebra, together with some analysis of the thought processes that may have led to these errors. It also contains some evidence that many students have the ability to learn far more mathematics than is usually taught to students of their age. In both directions it gives a more-than-usually detailed description of how students are thinking about the algebra they are trying to learn.

Davis, Robert B., Stephen Young, and Patrick McLoughlin. 1982. *The Roles of "Understanding" in the Learning of Mathematics.* Urbana, Ill.: Curriculum Laboratory, University of Illinois.
Uses examples from arithmetic, algebra, geometry, and calculus to examine what it means to "understand" various topics in mathematics. It also shows examples of the kinds of errors that students often make when they do not understand the ideas or techniques that they are working with.

Dossey, John A. 1981. Do all graphs have points with integral coordinates? *Mathematics Teacher* 74 (6) (September 1981): 455-457.

Presents a problem—stated in the title and its solution. Probably the best use of this article would be for a teacher to read it, then present *only the problem* to students, leaving the students the task of inventing a method for solving the problem. Only when students run into trouble should one offer hints, such as suggesting that they consider the graph of $3x + 6y = 7$.

Dugdale, Sharon. 1982. Green Globs: A microcomputer application for graphing of equations. *Mathematics Teacher* 75 (3) (March 1982): 208-214.

Presents one of the most interesting algebra-related activities ever programmed for a classroom computer. Points on a graph are located by random numbers, and students try to pass a single curve through the greatest possible number of points. Curves are specified by typing their equations into the computer. This report also discusses the rationale for different uses of activities (including some presented via computer) in support of courses in introductory algebra (also Kimberling (1985)).

Dwyer, Thomas A., and Margot Critchfield. 1975. *Computer Resource Book: Algebra*. Boston, Mass.: Houghton Mifflin.

Makes possible the *simultaneous* study of introductory algebra and computer programming (in the BASIC language). *Simultaneous* study of two or more mathematical topics—instead of the traditional sequence of doing first one, then the other—is one of the exciting and valuable developments of recent years. Frequently it is *easier* to study the two topics simultaneously—the study of one assists the study of the other.

Eddy, Roland H. 1985. Behold! The arithmetic-geometric mean inequality. *College Mathematics Journal* 16 (3) (May 1985): 208.

Presents probably the neatest proof ever given that:

$$(a + b)/2 \geq \sqrt{ab}$$

with equality only if $a = b$. This important result follows immediately from examining a simple geometric figure—whence the use of "Behold!" in the title of this article. One more demonstration of the value of unifying algebra and geometry!

Edwards, Ronald R. 1974. Summing arithmetic series on the geoboard. *Mathematics Teacher* 67 (5) (May 1974): 471-473.

Shows how algebraic ideas can be related to arithmetic and to geometry; also shows how the use of manipulatable physical materials (such as geoboards) can be helpful even with older students. From another point of view, this report relates also to teaching *heuristics*, since it shows how different *representations*—in this case, arithmetic, algebraic, and geometric—can be helpful in suggesting ways to solve problems. (Cf. also Davis (1980) and Schoenfeld (1979).)

Erlwanger, Stanley H. 1973. Benny's conception of rules and answers in IPI mathematics. *Journal of Children's Mathematical Behavior* 1 (2) (Autumn 1973): 7-26.

Shows, by a careful use of task-based interviews how students construct their own meaningful interpretations of mathematical symbols and procedures. Unfortunately — as this important study also shows — if no correct meanings are supplied by the teacher or textbook, and if the teacher fails to monitor the ideas that students are building up in the privacy of their own minds, then these ideas are quite likely to be wrong, perhaps grotesquely wrong — and to become a serious obstacle to further learning. Erlwanger's studies, together with those of Lochhead, Clement, Rosnick, and their colleagues, constituted a breakthrough in the study of how human beings think about mathematics. All students show great originality and independence in the creation of their own personal mental representations. Conscientious teachers *must* monitor carefully the growth of each student's ideas. One can no longer defend "lecturing" and "telling" as adequate forms of teaching, if such monitoring is not done.

Fennema, Elizabeth. 1981. The sex factor. In *Mathematics Education Research: Implications for the 80's*, edited by Elizabeth Fennema, 92-105. (See also Response by Grace Burton, 105-110.) Alexandria, Va.: Association for Supervision and Curriculum Development and National Council of Teachers of Mathematics.

Reviews research on the gender gap: why female students have, on the average, less success in mathematics than male students do. Do not expect a definitive answer; much about this phenomenon is still a mystery.

Freudenthal, H. 1974. Soviet research on teaching algebra at the lower grades of the elementary school. *Educational Studies in Mathematics* 5 (4) (December 1974): 391-412.

Reviews Soviet efforts to create a more effective synthesis of algebra and arithmetic, and to teach it to younger students. Somehow the Soviets always seem to have more, and deeper, discussions than most other nations on matters relating to the mathematics curriculum: what they *do* teach, what they *should* teach, what they should *change*, and so on.

Goldin, Gerald A. 1982. Mathematical language and problem solving. *Visible Language* 16 (3) (Summer 1982): 221-238.

Gives an indication of one of the ways that serious scholarly study is being applied to the teaching and learning of algebra and other mathematical subjects.

Good, Thomas L., and Douglas A. Grouws. 1981. Process-product research. In *Mathematics Education Research: Implications for the 80's*, edited by Elizabeth Fennema, 82-91. Alexandria, Va.: Association for Supervision and Curriculum Development and National Council of Teachers of Mathematics.

Grinstein, Louise S. 1981. Pascal's triangle: Some recent references from the *Mathematics Teacher*. *Mathematics Teacher* 74 (6) (September 1981): 449-450.

> Provides a short annotated bibliography of articles related to Pascal's triangle. Every student should be able to find some aspect of Pascal's triangle that will intrigue her/him.

Hannibal, Katie Reynolds. 1976. Observer report on the Madison Project's seventh grade class. *Journal of Children's Mathematical Behavior*. Supplement No. 1 (Summer 1976): 159-175.

> Describes an effective seventh-grade program that combines arithmetic, algebra, and geometry.

Harkin, Joseph B., and Gerald R. Rising. 1974. Some psychological and pedagogical aspects of mathematical symbolism. *Educational Studies in Mathematics* 5 (3) (March 1974): 255-260.

> Presents a discussion of alternative notations for variables, functions, graphs, and even numbers themselves— a matter that is of great importance in introductory algebra but rarely seems to get the attention it deserves.

Hirsch, Christian R. 1974. Pick's rule. *Mathematics Teacher* 67 (5) (May 1974): 431-434, 473.

> Shows how students can discover one of the most fascinating formulas in elementary mathematics.

Holcomb, Joan. 1980. Using geoboards in the primary grades. *Arithmetic Teacher* 27 (8) (April 1980): 22-25.

> Presents some interesting problems that can be used to increase student thoughtfulness. Although the author intended to aim at rather young children, some of the tasks she presents can be intriguing for older students, including adults. For example: How many different pentominoes are there? When shall we say that two pentominoes are "really the same"? How can we devise a *systematic* approach to counting them, so as to be sure we don't miss any and never count the same one twice?

Hoyles, Celia. 1985. What is the point of group discussion in mathematics? *Educational Studies in Mathematics* 16 (2) (May 1985): 205-214.

> Considers what can be gained by creating opportunities for students to work together in small groups during class time. This article reviews and interprets much of the relevant literature, and identifies six cognitive processes that may be developed in a useful way by having students spend less time listening to lectures and more time talking to fellow students.

Hughes, Barnabas B. 1974. Heuristic teaching in mathematics. *Educa-*

tional Studies in Mathematics 5 (3) (March 1974): 291-299.

> Presents probably the best general survey of the literature dealing with the use of *heuristics* in teaching algebra (or any other part of mathematics). This article comes close to being "must" reading for any serious teacher of mathematics (see also Schoenfeld (1979)).

Kantowski, Mary Grace. 1981. Problem solving. In *Mathematics Education Research: Implications for the 80's,* edited by Elizabeth Fennema, 111-126. Alexandria, Va.: Association for Supervision and Curriculum Development and National Council of Teachers of Mathematics.

> Reviews the research literature on the effective teaching of problem solving, including some research that highlights the importance of student creativity, and the need for teachers to avoid "squelching" student creativity.

Kilpatrick, Jeremy. 1985. Reflection and recursion. *Educational Studies in Mathematics* 16 (1) (February 1985): 1-26.

> Introduces the modern point of view in mathematics education. Some readers may find this essay difficult, but it will repay careful study and restudy, especially if one makes use of the references listed at the end.

Kimberling, Clark. 1985. Graph many functions. *Mathematics Teacher* 78 (3) (March 1985): 195-200, (4) (April 1985): 278-280, (9) (December 1985): 663.

> Shows how much some students can gain from graphing functions early in their studies (as world-famous computer scientist Donald Knuth says he did), and how computers can be used to facilitate this process.

Knapp, Thomas R. 1985. Instances of Simpson's paradox. *College Mathematics Journal* 16 (3) (June 1985): 209-211.

> Presents an intriguing but little-known property of averages that many students find highly provocative: consider two baseball players, Strong and Poore. Against right-handed pitchers, Strong has a better batting average than Poore. Against left-handed pitchers one sees the same situation—Strong again has a better batting average than Poore has. Now: who has the better batting average overall? Actually, Poore does! How is this possible? Knapp shows how.

Lesh, Richard, and Marsha Landau, eds. 1983. *Acquisition of Mathematics Concepts and Processes.* New York: Academic.

> Provides an excellent cross-section of modern scholarly studies in mathematics education, including many key ideas of introductory algebra, such as ratio and proportion, rational numbers, the use of graphs, problems of visualizing mathematical situations, and the interpretation of problem solving as a sequence of decisions and performance tasks. No list of topics, however, reveals what is most valuable about this book: its worth lies rather in the kinds of questions that it raises, the concepts used in seeking answers, and the demonstration that the

activity of teaching algebra (or other mathematics) is *itself* a subject worth thinking about in a seriously analytical way.

Madell, Rob. 1985. Children's natural processes. *Arithmetic Teacher* 32 (7) (March 1985): 20-22.

Shows how young children often take a creative approach to mathematics, sometimes even inventing their own methods for solving problems. These invented methods are frequently algebraic in nature, and may make use of negative numbers. It argues that excessively routine instructional programs can be harmful to many students.

Maor, Eli. 1980. A summer course with the TI 57 programmable calculator. *Mathematics Teacher* 73 (2) (February 1980): 99-106.

Presents a number of activities that many students should find challenging. Especially interesting is Ulam's conjecture, sometimes called the "Syracuse Problem" (p. 103).

Matz, Marilyn. 1980. Towards a computational theory of algebraic competence. *Journal of Mathematical Behavior* 3 (1) (Fall 1980): 93-166.

Presents one of the most comprehensive theories ever developed to explain how human beings think about and learn introductory algebra. A thoughtful teacher needs to have some sort of idea about "what's going on in the minds of the students." Matz's analysis can be extremely helpful. Matz is an expert in "artificial intelligence" and brings this perspective to the study of mathematics education.

Norris, Donald O. 1981. Let's put computers into the mathematics curriculum. *Mathematics Teacher* 74 (1) (January 1981): 24-26.

Shows how the use of computers can be integrated into the teaching of introductory algebra.

O'Daffer, Phares G. 1985a. Strategy spotlight: Solve a simpler problem. *Arithmetic Teacher* 32 (7) (March 1985): 34-35.

Shows how the heuristic "try to make up a simpler problem and see what you can learn from solving *it*" can be used in actual teaching situations. Heuristics are very important, and need to receive far more emphasis in teaching.

————. 1985b. Strategy spotlight: work backward. *Arithmetic Teacher* 32 (8) (April 1985): 34-35.

Shows another important heuristic: "try to solve the problem by working backwards." Most commonly used in geometry, this heuristic is also valuable in algebra, where it usually means: "think of what you'd like to see in some *later* step in the problem. Now—what should come *before* that?"

Page, David A. 1964. *Number Lines, Functions, and Fundamental*

Topics. New York: Macmillan.

Shows how key ideas of algebra can be incorporated into arithmetic.

Papert, Seymour. 1980. *Mindstorms: Children, Computers, and Powerful Ideas.* New York: Basic Books.

Presents an analysis of human mathematical thought which has played a deservedly influential role in shaping modern teaching of introductory algebra. Papert is the creator of the Logo computer-programming language, and the inventor of "Logo environments" for learning mathematics. This, too, involves a major synthesis: arithmetic, algebra, geometry, and computer-programming are treated as a single indivisible whole, not to be carved up into separate pieces. The inclusion of each part facilitates the learning of the others.

Pedersen, Katherine, Dorothy R. Bleyer, and Patricia B. Elmore. 1985. Attitudes and career interests of junior high school mathematics students: Implications for the classroom. *Arithmetic Teacher* 32 (7) (March 1985): 45-49.

Excellent introduction to the problem of gender differences in mathematical performance; suggests a few teaching ideas intended to help alleviate the situation. Also contains a useful introduction to the literature on gender differences.

Pólya, George. 1945. *How To Solve It: A New Aspect of Mathematical Method.* 1957. 2nd ed. Garden City, N.Y.: Doubleday. 1971. Reprint. Princeton, N.J.: Princeton University Press.

Presents the best-known discussion of the use and value of *heuristics* in teaching mathematics or in thinking about mathematical problems. This is the book that created the great interest in this subject. Pólya was a world-famous research mathematician who also somehow found time to work on the teaching and learning of mathematics, and to attempt to analyze the way human beings think about mathematical problems (see also Schoenfeld (1979) and Hughes (1974)).

Radatz, Hendrik. 1979. Error analysis in mathematics education. *Journal for Research in Mathematics Education* 10 (3) (May 1979): 163-172.

Presents a survey of some of the research literature on student errors. Errors are very often not random slips, but on the contrary are "symptoms of an underlying misconception," and can serve as valuable diagnostic clues for a teacher who wants to identify a student's misconceptions and correct them (which, unfortunately, can be surprisingly difficult in many cases).

Ralston, Anthony. 1984, 1985. Will discrete mathematics surpass calculus in importance? *College Mathematics Journal* 15 (5) (November 1984): 371-382; 16 (1) (January 1985): 19-21 (includes responses by other authors.)

Presents the case for including a greater emphasis on combinatorics or "discrete mathematics" in early mathematics instruction. While the intended focus is on college freshman courses (or something close to this level), the implications for earlier courses can easily be seen. Both sides of the case are argued very cogently; it is by no means clear that a shift *away* from calculus would be desirable, but the *inclusion* of more "discrete mathematics" in high-school-level courses may be indicated.

Ralston, Anthony, and Gail S. Young, eds. 1983. *The Future of College Mathematics*. New York: Springer-Verlag.

Proposes a major modification of the first two years of college mathematics (i.e., freshman and sophomore courses). The argument is that less attention should be paid to calculus (and to those topics that lead into calculus), and the new emphasis should be put on so-called "discrete mathematics". The implications for introductory algebra are that more attention should be paid to combinatorics and finite difference methods.

Risoen, John W., and Jane G. Stenzel. 1978. A truck driver looks at square roots. *Arithmetic Teacher* 26 (3) (November 1978): 44.

Reports on an actual episode of a truck driver who became interested in the operation of finding square roots, discovered a pattern that fascinated him, and went on to invent an original algorithm. This report has two points of relevance to a course in algebra: first, how can one help students find similar excitement and challenge in thinking about mathematics?; second, how can one rewrite the truck driver's work in algebraic terms and get a clearer idea of what is going on?

Roberti, Joseph V. 1980. One step further. *Mathematics Teacher* 73 (3) (March 1980): 227-230.

Shows very convincingly how algebra, analytic geometry, and the ideas of calculus fit together to give added power to students.

Roberts, Fred S. 1984. The introductory mathematics curriculum: Misleading, outdated, and unfair. *College Mathematics Journal* 15 (5) (November 1984): 383-399 (includes responses by several other authors).

Argues the case for changing the content of freshman and sophomore mathematics courses and manner in which they are taught. More attention must be paid to conceptual understanding, to reasons underlying the historical development of topics and methods, and to heuristics for guiding the selection of strategies for solving mathematical problems.

Rosnick, Peter. 1981. Some misconceptions concerning the concept of variable. *Mathematics Teacher* 74 (6) (September 1981): 418-420, 450.

Reports on one of the most important student misunderstandings in all of algebra. Many seemingly successful students are badly confused about how *variables* are used in simple equations.

———, and John Clement. 1980. Learning without understanding:

The effect of tutoring strategies on algebra misconceptions. *Journal of Mathematical Behavior* 3 (1) (Fall 1980): 3-27.

> Shows, by carefully-conducted task-based interviews, that many high-school and college students harbor extreme misconceptions about the meaning of algebraic notation. Should serve as a warning to all who teach algebra that it can be extremely harmful to focus attention too heavily on what is *written,* instead of on the *meanings* of what we write (cf. also Davis (1984)).

Schoenfeld, Alan H. 1979. Explicit heuristic training as a variable in problem-solving performance. *Journal for Research in Mathematics Education* 10 (3) (May 1979): 173-187.

> Presents what is probably the best introduction ever written to the teaching of *heuristics*: general strategies to help find something useful to do in attacking a problem for which you do not know a routine solution strategy. Reports on one of the few actual empirical studies of the effect of teaching heuristics (see also Hughes (1974) and Pólya (1957)).

―――. 1985. Making sense of "out loud" problem-solving protocols. *Journal of Mathematical Behavior* 4 (2) (October 1985): 171-191.

> Shows how a thoughtful teacher can study the way students are thinking about mathematics.

Schools Council. 1965. *Mathematics in Primary Schools.* London: Her Majesty's Stationery Office.

> Shows how key ideas of algebra can be taught and learned in elementary school.

Shumway, Richard J. 1981. Response to Weaver (1981). In *Mathematics Education Research: Implications for the 80's,* edited by Elizabeth Fennema, 169-171. Alexandria, Va.: Association for Supervision and Curriculum Development and National Council of Teachers of Mathematics.

> Argues the case for generous use of calculators in any algebra class.

Skemp, Richard R. 1978. Relational understanding and instrumental understanding. *Arithmetic Teacher* 26 (3) (November 1978): 9-15.

> Presents one of the best-known analyses of what is meant by "understanding", in algebra or in any other part of mathematics.

Sowder, Larry K. 1981. Response to Kantowski (1981). In *Mathematics Education Research: Implications for the 80's,* edited by Elizabeth Fennema, 126-130. Alexandria, Va.: Association for Supervision and Curriculum Development and National Council of Teachers of Mathematics.

> Discusses research studies that show practical ways to teach students a more powerful approach to the solution of mathematical problems. Reviews studies

that demonstrate the importance of giving students a more creative role in problem solving, such as having students propose a strategy for attacking a problem, and even having students make up some of the problems.

Stein, Sherman K., and Calvin D. Crabill. 1972. *Elementary Algebra — A Guided Inquiry.* Boston, Mass.: Houghton Mifflin.
   Presents traditional "ninth-grade algebra" in a novel and highly effective way, by focusing on certain key problems, such as maximizing the volume of a tray. At first the problem is treated as a review of arithmetic; then, as skills develop, it is treated by graphing, and finally by finding the derivative, setting it equal to zero, and solving the resulting quadratic equation. Careful trials have demonstrated the effectiveness of this text; it shows once again the value of combining algebra with other parts of mathematics, instead of dissecting it out and attempting to teach it separately, isolated from such helpful devices as graphs (and even derivatives).

Steinkamp, Marjorie W., Delwyn L. Harnisch, Herbert J. Walberg, and Shiow-Ling Tsai. 1985. Cross-national gender differences in mathematics attitude and achievement among thirteen-year-olds. *Journal of Mathematical Behavior* 4 (3) (December 1985): 259-277.
   Gives an excellent overview of studies that seek to understand why females seem to perform less well than males in mathematics. That teaching, advising, and textbooks discourage female students unnecessarily is a situation we *can* do something about — if we understand the true root causes.

Stodolsky, Susan S. 1985. Telling math: Origins of math aversion and anxiety. *Educational Psychologist* 20 (3) (Summer 1985): 125-133.

Sweller, John, and Graham A. Cooper. 1985. The use of worked examples as a substitute for problem solving in learning algebra. *Cognition and Instruction* 2 (1) (1985): 59-89.
   Presents a point of view (supported by empirical data) that seems on the surface to be diametrically opposed to nearly all of the other studies reported here. The authors argue *against* what they see as the more common forms of "problem solving" in typical classroom teaching at present, and argue instead for showing students carefully-designed solutions to certain well-chosen "type" problems. The goal is to establish certain clear ideas in the students' minds.

Thompson, Charles S., and John Van de Walle. 1985. Patterns and geometry with LOGO. *Arithmetic Teacher* 32 (7) (March 1985): 6-13.
   Shows how Logo computer materials can be used with young students. Despite the title of this article, it is directly relevant to teaching and learning *algebra*. The Logo language was originally developed by Seymour Papert for the explicit purpose of helping students to learn concepts such as *variable* and *function*, which are essential in the study of algebra.

Thompson, Patrick W. 1982. Were lions to speak, we wouldn't understand. *Journal of Mathematical Behavior* 3 (2) (Summer 1982): 147-165.

   Presents one of the clearest discussions of the modern "constructivist" interpretation of the teaching and learning of mathematics. Whereas considerable traditional thought saw "teaching mathematics" as a matter of showing, telling, and supervising drill and practice, the modern constructivist view sees students as building up, in their own minds, representations of mathematical concepts and mathematical procedures. This new view implies new expectations of appropriate teacher behaviors, stressing the importance of providing experiences from which students can synthesize these representations, and monitoring the development of the student's representations in order to avoid the kinds of misconceptions reported by Erlwanger (1973) and others.

Travers, Kenneth J., ed. 1985. *Second International Mathematics Study Summary Report for the United States.* Champaign, Ill.: Stipes Publishing Company.

   Fits the teaching and learning of algebra into a larger context of all introductory mathematics instruction in the United States, and even internationally. In most other nations, "algebra" is not separated out; a single homogenized "mathematics" is taught, wherein arithmetic, algebra, graphs, functions, analytic geometry, vectors, slope, rate-of change, and possibly other topics are included and studied *simultaneously*. One topic often supports another, and the combination is learned more easily — and more creatively — than any single piece can be learned in isolation. This valuable summary also deals with many other topics, such, as (for example) teachers' beliefs in methods of effective instruction.

Vance, Irvin E. 1981. A partridge in a pear tree, a stack of cubes, and four buckets of balls. *Mathematics Teacher* 74 (9) (December 1981): 698-703.

   Shows how many interesting counting problems relate to various algebraic ideas.

VanLehn, Kurt. 1982. Bugs are not enough: Empirical studies of bugs, impasses, and repairs in procedural skills. *Journal of Mathematical Behavior* 3 (2) (Summer 1982): 3-71.

   Shows how systematic student errors may be created as the student tries to overcome some specific intellectual obstacles. This is one of the most famous studies in the growing literature that analyzes student errors. Although the specific content of this study was arithmetic, the principles apply equally to algebra (and, indeed, have been applied to algebraic errors in the famous study by Matz (1980)).

Weaver, J. Fred. 1981. Calculators. In *Mathematics Education Research: Implications for the 80's,* edited by Elizabeth Fennema, 154-168.

Alexandria, Va.: Association for Supervision and Curriculum Development and National Council of Teachers of Mathematics.

Provides an overview of the ways that calculators can be used in the teaching of algebra, and surveys some of the more important research studies attempting to show the effect on students.

Young, Stephen C. 1982. The mental representation of geometrical knowledge. *Journal of Mathematical Behavior* 3 (2) (Summer 1982): 123-144.

Provides an outstanding example of how a teacher can study student thought processes, and make use of the results for the improvement of future teaching and learning. Although the content in this instance is more geometrical than algebraic, Young's approach can be equally valuable in algebra.

Zukav, Gary. 1979. *The Dancing Wu Li Masters: An Overview of the New Physics*. New York: Bantam.

Discusses the art of teaching complicated mathematical ideas by focusing on central concepts (see especially pp. 7-9).

7. Instruction in Geometry

DORIS W. SCHATTSCHNEIDER

Geometry is a fascinating, multifaceted subject to learn and teach. Far from being "dead," as the skeptics might choose to declare, geometry pervades all aspects of our life and deserves a prominent place in the high-school and college curriculum. Geometry stimulates and challenges mathematical thought and understanding in many ways. It embodies

- visual recognition and understanding of form
- construction and manipulative skills
- investigation of relationships
- observation and conjecture
- elementary logic and deductive proof
- generalization from simple cases to more complex
- a rich history of evolution of mathematical thought.

There is an extensive body of resources for teaching geometry at all levels. Elementary concepts of shape, measurement, model-building (blocks), and symmetry are easily and naturally learned by preschoolers — there are many toys and educational aids available for use with young children. Although a few items in the appended bibliography are suitable for use in elementary school, materials have been chosen that are appropriate for use in grades 7-12, and in college geometry courses.

The geometry curriculum is far from standard, whether judged by grade level, by school district, by text, or by instructor. The "traditional" Euclidean geometry course (geometry as a theorem-proving discipline) most often leaves students with no working knowledge of geometry at all. They are not aware that engineering, architecture, robotics, computer graphics, biology, chemistry, crystallography, and graphic design are a few of the fields in which a rich knowledge of many kinds of geometry is needed, and where there are many active researchers working on unsolved problems. In an introductory course students should learn elemental facts of shape and form, simple constraints on two and three-dimensional forms, interrelationships between forms, and some transformations of figures. The history of these ideas and their importance in both natural and man-made designs should be an integral part of the course. Definitions, axioms, and theorems should be taught, but these should follow (indeed grow out of) exploration and investigation of intuitive ideas.

The list of resources cannot hope to be complete, but it is representative of the kinds of books and other materials that should be sought out by teachers of geometry and be available to students of geometry.

BIBLIOGRAPHY

Categories of resources are as follows:

- Books
- Activities, Worksheets, Contest Problem Books
- Demonstration Aids
- Displays
- Model-Making Kits
- Visual Aids Requiring Projection
- Microcomputer Materials.

Books

Enrichment of classroom presentation, material for student investigations and projects, ideas for teaching, challenging problems, and historical background are just a few of the reasons to have a geometry library. In this list of books, general references (such as encyclopedias, dictionaries, histories), and standard texts for high-school or college geometry (a couple of "classics" excepted) have not been included. Journal articles have also not been cited. Active teachers and departments will have subscriptions to journals of the National Council of Teachers of Mathematics, the Mathematical Association of America, the Canadian

Mathematical Society, and the Association of Teachers of Mathematics (United Kingdom), as well as receive information from textbook publishers.

Book entries have been arranged in categories for easy reference. These include

- Collections, Classics, References
- Teaching
- Proof
- Constructions
- Curves and Conic Sections
- Polygons and Polyhedra
- Geometry in the Environment — Geometric Design of Nature and Humans
- Non-Euclidean and Transformation Geometry
- History
- Geometry with a Computer.

Although several books logically belong in several categories, we have listed each book only once, choosing the category that seems to be its primary emphasis. The reader may wish to check several categories for books on certain topics.

Collections, Classics, References

Aichele, Douglas B., and Melfried Olson. 1981. *Geometric Selections for Middle School Teachers (5-9)*. Washington, D.C.: National Education Association.

Altshiller-Court, Nathan. 1952. *College Geometry*. 2nd ed. New York: Barnes and Noble.
> A comprehensive text that belongs in every teacher's library as a resource book for facts and problems.

Ball, W. W. Rouse, and H. S. M. Coxeter. 1987. *Mathematical Recreations and Essays*. 13th ed. New York: Dover.
> A wonderful source of motivational material and projects. Contains two chapters on geometrical recreations: a chapter on polyhedra, and one on map-

coloring problems and various solutions to these. A great book to put in the hands of a curious student.

Beck, Anatole, Michael N. Bleicher, and Donald W. Crowe. 1969. *Excursions into Mathematics.* New York: Worth.

Excellent chapter on polyhedra – proves Euler's formula and gives several illustrations of its consequences; proves there are only eight deltahedra. Discusses platonic solids, polyhedra without diagonals, the n-dimensional cube, the 4-color problem, and the 5-color theorem. Also chapters on "What is area?" and "Exotic geometries" (non-Euclidean, finite, affine, projective). Contains many exercises and topics for projects.

Berloquin, Pierre. 1976. *One Hundred Geometric Games.* New York: Scribner's.

Coxeter, H. S. M. 1969. *Introduction to Geometry.* 2nd ed. New York: Wiley.

Coxeter's spare style makes this an excellent reference but a difficult text for college students. Subject matter gives a comprehensive overview of geometry: Euclidean, non-Euclidean, affine, and projective.

————, and Samuel L. Greitzer. 1967. *Geometry Revisited.* New Mathematical Library no. 19. Washington, D.C.: Mathematical Association of America.

A second look at several topics in geometry – can be used to supplement a high-school course, or even as the basis of a second course in geometry. Uses modern techniques such as transformations, inversive geometry, and projective geometry to recall some classical theorems and link the subject with other branches of mathematics.

Dudeney, Henry E. 1958. *Amusements in Mathematics.* New York: Dover.

Eves, Howard W. 1972. *A Survey of Geometry.* Rev. ed. Boston, Mass.: Allyn & Bacon.

An excellent source of problems. Eves believes in involving the student in problem solving and even experimenting to learn geometry. Good bibliographic references for each chapter. Chapters include: history (ancient Greek geometry), modern elementary geometry, transformations, constructions, dissections, projective geometry, non-Euclidean geometry, foundations.

Hilbert, David, and Stephan Cohn-Vossen. 1952. *Geometry and the Imagination.* Translated by P. Nemenyi. New York: Chelsea.

A classic exploration of many geometrical ideas, with clear and elementary explanation of historical topics, good illustrations, and experiments. Excellent sourcebook for topics for projects and motivational material.

Honsberger, Ross. 1973, 1976, 1985. *Mathematical Gems*. 3 vols. Dolciani Mathematical Expositions nos. 1, 2, 9. Washington, D.C.: Mathematical Association of America.

> Each of these volumes contains a few especially attractive geometry "nuggets" to illustrate interesting problems and ingenious solutions to them. Two other collections in the same vein, also edited by Honsberger and published by the MAA, are *Ingenuity in Mathematics* and *Mathematical Plums*.

Johnson, Roger A. 1929. *Modern Geometry*. New York: Houghton Mifflin. 1960. Reprint under the title *Advanced Euclidean Geometry*. New York: Dover.

> Although dated, this classic continues to be one of the most comprehensive collections of results in Euclidean geometry.

Kazarinoff, Nicholas D. 1961. *Geometric Inequalities*. New Mathematical Library no. 4. Washington, D.C.: Mathematical Association of America.

> The arithmetic-geometric mean inequality and many others; isoperimetric theorems (least measure), reflection problems, Steiner's symmetrization – all with problem-solving emphasis. Good source for projects and contests.

Ludwig, Hubert J. 1986. *An Annotated Bibliography of Articles of Interest to the Teacher and Student of Geometry Selected from The Mathematics Teacher, Volume 1 through Volume 78*. Muncie, Ind.: Ball State Technical Report no. 66.

> An excellent reference for articles on geometry published in the *Mathematics Teacher*, from its first issue (1908) through 1985. Titles are gathered by category, and each entry lists title, author, volume, date and pages, and a brief description of content. Easier to use than the index for the *Mathematics Teacher* compiled by the NCTM, this is the source to turn to for supplemental material for classroom use, student projects and discussions on teaching geometry.

Mathematics: An Introduction to its Spirit and Use; Readings from Scientific American. 1979. San Francisco, Calif.: W. H. Freeman.

> Excellent collection of expository articles with introductions by Morris Kline. Includes 11 articles on geometry, with 8 by Martin Gardner, whose topics are: geometry constructions, triangle theorems, conics, cycloid curve, curves of constant width, geometric fallacies, planar graphs, topological diversions. Also includes two survey articles by Kline on projective geometry and geometry, and a translation of L. Euler's account of the Koenigsberg bridge problem.

Posamentier, Alfred S. 1984. *Excursions in Advanced Euclidean Geometry*. Rev. ed. Menlo Park, Calif.: Addison-Wesley.

Reviews elementary Euclidean geometry, then introduces many topics not covered in the usual high-school course. Excellent for use with an honors class, or as a supplement, or even as a second course in geometry in high school or college. Topics include: concurrency of lines in a triangle, collinearity of points, symmetric points in a triangle and other triangle properties, quadrilaterals, equicircles, nine-point circle, golden section and Fibonaci numbers.

Seidenberg, Abraham, ed. 1980. *Studies in Algebraic Geometry*. MAA Studies in Mathematics no. 20. Washington, D.C.: Mathematical Association of America.

An elementary presentation of some of the most interesting results in algebraic geometry. This field, which blends algebra and geometry is usually reserved for graduate-level courses, and bright students could enjoy seeing the richness of this blend.

Steinhaus, Hugo. 1969. *Mathematical Snapshots*. 3rd ed. New York: Oxford University Press.

A wonderful collection of illustrated observations about mathematical relationships, mostly geometrical. Dissection puzzles, polyhedra and their relationships, map projections, minimal paths on a three-dimensional surface, constructions, and many more topics. The kind of book that will "hook" a curious mind to explore mathematics further.

Teaching

Berger, Emil J., ed. 1973. *NCTM Yearbook 34*.

Although some of the material in this resource volume is dated (especially the calculator and computer section), it remains a valuable reference for ideas and sources of resource material. Most of the bibliographic material is still useful, and the lists of producers and distributors of instructional aids, with some updating, are extremely helpful.

Dessart, Donald, and Marilyn Suydam. 1983. *Classroom Ideas from Research on Secondary School Mathematics*. Reston, Va.: National Council of Teachers of Mathematics.

A review of recent research; contains ideas for teaching geometry effectively, based on the research findings.

Driscoll, Mark. 1983. *Research within Reach: Secondary School Mathematics*. Reston, Va.: National Council of Teachers of Mathematics.

Research on effective teaching in response to questions asked by classroom teachers. The project was funded by the National Institute of Education and carried out by the Research and Development Interpretation Service.

Henderson, Kenneth B., ed. 1973. *NCTM Yearbook 36*.

Collection of essays on the teaching of geometry in elementary and high school and the education of teachers. These views should be contrasted with those in Lindquist (1987), the 1987 yearbook.

Kespohl, Ruth C. 1979. *Geometry Problems My Students Have Written*. Reston, Va.: National Council of Teachers of Mathematics.

Collection of problems written by high-school students can give insight into their view of problems and process of problem solving. One teacher's answer to conventional (boring, "textbook") problems—have the students write their own (together with solutions).

Kilpatrick, Jeremy, Izaak Wirszup, Edward G. Begle, and James Wilson, eds. 1970. *Problem Solving in Geometry*. Soviet Studies in the Psychology of Learning and Teaching Mathematics no. 4. Reston, Va.: National Council of Teachers of Mathematics.

————. 1971. *Development of Spatial Abilities*. Soviet Studies in the Psychology of Learning and Teaching Mathematics no. 5. Reston, Va.: National Council of Teachers of Mathematics.

Lindquist, Mary M., ed. 1987. *NCTM 1987 Yearbook*.

Collection of twenty essays on learning and teaching geometry at the elementary and secondary level. Most authors address one or more areas of concern or interest in the geometry curriculum: spatial perception, cognitive research, computer graphics, applications of geometry, computational and probabilistic geometry, problem solving, geometry for calculus readiness, geometry for high-school teachers.

Maletsky, Evan M., and Christian R. Hirsch. 1981. Activities from the *Mathematics Teacher*. Reston, Va.: National Council of Teachers of Mathematics.

Several of these activities are on topics from geometry. They include discovery lessons, puzzles, model construction.

Mathematics Teacher. 1985. Vol. 78, no. 6 (Sept. 1985). Reston, Va.: National Council of Teachers of Mathematics.

Special issue devoted to teaching geometry.

O'Daffer, Phares G., and Stanley R. Clemens. 1976. *Geometry: An Investigative Approach*. Menlo Park, Calif.: Addison-Wesley.

Text for a course in teaching geometry at elementary and secondary level, emphasizes the discovery of geometric ideas and relationships through investigations. Should be in the personal and departmental library of geometry teachers.

Pólya, George. 1945. *How to Solve It: A New Aspect of Mathematical Method*. 1957. 2nd ed. Garden City, N.Y.: Doubleday. 1971. Reprint. Princeton, N.J.: Princeton University Press.

> The teaching ideas and methodology outlined in this book, together with examples primarily chosen from geometry, are as timely today as when they were first put down in 1945.

————. [1962-1965] 1981. *Mathematical Discovery: On Understanding, Learning and Teaching Problem Solving*. 2 vols. Combined ed. New York: Wiley.

> A more careful development of the maxims for good teaching by the master teacher. Excellent examples, many chosen from geometry.

Two-Year College Mathematics Journal. 1980, 1981. Vol. 11, no. 1 (Jan. 1980), and vol. 12, no. 4 (Sept. 1981).

> Special issues on geometry—Is it alive? What should be taught?

Proof

Dubnov, Ya. S. 1963. *Mistakes in Geometric Proofs*. Boston, Mass.: D. C. Heath.

> Outlines common mistakes made in geometric proofs, analyzing the origins of the errors.

Fetisov, A. I. 1978. *Proof in Geometry*. Translated by Mark Samokhvalov. Moscow: Mir (distributed by Imported Publications).

> Written for teachers, this booklet addresses the questions most often asked by pupils (if not explicitly, implied by attitudes): What is a proof? What purpose does a proof serve? What form should a proof take? What may be accepted without proof in geometry? In answering the questions, the author gives many examples. The book is a useful source for examples and discussion of mathematical proof.

Golovina, L. I., and I. M. Yaglom. 1979. *Induction in Geometry*. Translated by Leonid Levant. Moscow: Mir (distributed by Imported Publications, Inc.).

> A collection of worked examples demonstrating the use of mathematical induction in geometric proofs. Includes summation formulas, map-coloring theorems, construction by induction, finding loci by induction, definition by induction, and induction on the number of dimensions.

Lakatos, Imre. 1976. *Proofs and Refutations: The Logic of Mathematical Discovery*. Edited by John Worrall and Elie Zahar. Cambridge, England: Cambridge University Press.

Through dialogue, a teacher and students discover proofs of Euler's formula, as well as proper formulations of conditions under which it holds. Good illustrations of subtleties of proof as well as the Socratic method of teaching.

Loomis, Elisha S. 1927. *The Pythagorean Proposition*. 1940. 2nd ed. 1968. Reprint of 2nd ed. Reston, Va.: National Council of Teachers of Mathematics.

Collection of 367 proofs of the Pythagorean theorem, classified according to method: algebraic, geometric, quaternionic, and dynamic; sources are given. Contains historical perspective on the theorem (which predated Pythagoras), bibliography, and a section on Pythagorean magic squares.

Maxwell, Edwin A. 1959. *Fallacies in Mathematics*. Cambridge, England: Cambridge University Press.

Contains examples of fallacious proofs, several of which are in geometry.

Northrop, Eugene P. 1944. *Riddles in Mathematics*. Princeton, N.J.: Princeton University Press. 1975. 2nd ed. Melbourne, Fla.: Krieger.

The "riddles" are fallacious proofs, many of which are "proofs" of geometric statements. Several of the geometry demonstrations show the danger in reliance on diagrams, as well as the necessity of accurate diagrams. Good source of examples in illustrating pitfalls to avoid.

Pottage, John. 1983. *Geometrical Investigations: Illustrating the Art of Discovery in the Mathematical Field*. Reading, Mass.: Addison-Wesley.

A dialogue in the Galilean style in which angels Salviati, Sagredo, and Simplicio discuss classic problems concerning measure. Descartes, Newton, and Euclid are among the discussants. A good way to show the rich fabric of problems and the conceptualization of solutions.

Solow, Daniel. 1984. *Reading, Writing, and Doing Mathematical Proofs: Geometry*. Palo Alto, Calif.: Dale Seymour.

A workbook that systematically presents the main ideas necessary to understand and construct proofs. The presentations are in short lessons, with follow-up exercises.

Constructions

Beard, Robert S. 1973. *Patterns in Space*. Palo Alto, Calif.: Creative.

Collection of line illustrations, facts, and tables of numerical information about polygons and polyhedra, as well as other interesting geometric forms.

Dayoub, Iris M., and Johnny W. Lott. 1977. *Geometry: Construction and Transformations*. Potomac, Md.: Dayott Associates (distributed by Spectrum).

> A collection of investigative and self-teaching exercises in geometric construction with Mira (or any see-through reflective plastic or glass plate). Covers isometries as products of reflections. A worthwhile approach to use as an alternative or supplement to ruler-and-compass constructions.

Kazarinoff, Nicholas D. 1970. *Ruler and the Round*. Boston, Mass.: Prindle, Weber & Schmidt.

> Angle trisection and circle division. Discusses the most famous impossible constructions and the algebras associated with them.

Kempe, Alfred B. [1877] 1977. *How to Draw a Straight Line*. Reprint. Reston, Va.: National Council of Teachers of Mathematics.

> Contains descriptions of linkages (linked systems of bars) that can be used to construct a straight line.

Kostoviskii, Aleksandr. 1986. *Geometrical Constructions with Compasses Only*. Translated by Janna Suslovich. Moscow: Mir (distributed by Imported Publications).

> Method of such constructions; inversions; special constructions; Steiner's circle. Thirty-six problems and solutions.

Olson, Alton T. 1975. *Mathematics Through Paper Folding*. Reston, Va.: National Council of Teachers of Mathematics.

> A "hands on" experience in discovering and demonstrating mathematical relationships.

Pohl, Victoria. 1986. *How to Enrich Geometry Using String Designs*. Reston, Va.: National Council of Teachers of Mathematics.

> Constructions of string designs on polygons and polyhedra. Step-by-step instructions, activity sheets for duplication.

Pritulenko, P.V. 1980. *Plane Figures and Sections: How to Construct Them Given Specific Conditions*. Translated by Vladimir Shokurov. Moscow: Mir (distributed by Imported Publications).

> Solutions to three-dimensional problems in construction and design.

Row, T. Sundara. 1966. *Geometric Exercises in Paper Folding*. New York: Dover.

> Constructions, proofs, dissections, and other geometric exercises can all be carried out by paper folding. A good resource for investigations and activities.

Seymour, Dale, and Reuben Schadler. *Creative Constructions*. Palo

Alto, Calif.: Creative.

> A collection of over 250 designs for ruler and compass construction. Worksheets with directions, analysis of designs, and explanation of designs.

Seymour, Dale, Linda Silvey, and Joyce Snider. 1974. *Line Designs*. Palo Alto, Calif.: Creative.

> Over 100 designs for "curve stitching" works of art.

Shaw, Sheila. 1986. *Kaleidometrics: The Art of Making Beautiful Patterns from Circles*. Stradbroke, Diss, England: Tarquin.

> Construction of grids in circles are developed into elaborate patterns.

Silvey, Linda, and Loretta Taylor. 1976. *Paper and Scissors Polygons*. Palo Alto, Calif.: Creative.

> Principles of kaleidoscopic symmetry guide the directions for cutting out lacy symmetric patterns within polygons.

Somervell, Edith L. [1906] 1975. *A Rhythmic Approach to Mathematics*. Reprint. Reston, Va.: National Council of Teachers of Mathematics.

> "String art" embodies the concept of an envelope of tangents outlining a curve. Somervell's book proposes curve stitching by children as a means to evoke the geometric instinct. Includes a wide variety of patterns.

Winter, John. *String Sculpture*. Mountain View, Calif.: Creative.

> The fundamentals of creating "string sculptures," which are based on the concept of a geometric curve or surface created by an envelope of tangent lines. Patterns and instructions included.

Curves and Conic Sections

Lawrence, J. Dennis. 1972. *A Catalog of Special Plane Curves*. New York: Dover.

> A good reference for a wide variety of curves – includes general equations for generating the curves, and illustrations of each curve for various values of the parameters. The graphics are a bit shaky ("early computer graphics"), but you can recognize the curves; with more-current computer equipment, you can use the equations to create stunning examples of almost any curve in classical analytic geometry and calculus.

Lyng, Merwin J. 1978. *Dancing Curves: A Dynamic Demonstration of Geometric Principles*. Reston, Va.: National Council of Teachers of Mathematics.

> Instructions for construction of a string model to be used with light beams

to dynamically demonstrate the creation of conic sections, lines, curves and surfaces. Includes four color slides.

Pedoe, Daniel. 1979. *Circles, A Mathematical View*. New York: Dover.

Eighty-seven pages about circles — classic theorems concerning them, their use in models of non-Euclidean geometry, isoperimetric properties, and more. A good source for projects.

Swienciki, Lawrence W. 1977. *Geometry of the Conics*. San Jose, Calif.: A. R. Davis.

A 48-page booklet devoted to the geometry of the conics.

Vasilev, Nikolai B., and V. Gutenmacher. 1980. *Straight Lines and Curves*. Translated by Anjan Kundu. Moscow: Mir (distributed by Imported Publications).

Paths traced out by moving points, locus problems, and maxima/minima problems. Over 200 problems.

Yates, Robert C. [1952] 1974. *Curves and Their Properties*. Reprint. Reston, Va.: National Council of Teachers of Mathematics.

A compendium of plane curves, which serves as an excellent quick reference. Each curve is described, illustrated, and accompanied by a few historical notes.

Polygons and Polyhedra

Barnette, David. 1984. *Map Coloring, Polyhedra and the Four Color Problem*. Dolciani Mathematical Expositions no. 8. Washington, D.C.: Mathematical Association of America.

The problem of determining the minimal number of colors to map-color any convex polyhedron or planar map has a rich history, culminating in the controversial proof in 1976 by Appel and Haken. This book outlines some of the powerful and diverse ideas that were developed in the hundred-year assault on the problem.

Critchlow, Keith. 1970. *Order in Space; A Design Source Book*. New York: Viking.

The development of polygons and polyhedra, with special attention to the question of shapes which "pack" space. Many good drawings of the regular and semi-regular solids and their duals; fold-out tables of summary information.

Cundy, H. Martyn, and A. P. Rollett. 1961. *Mathematical Models*. 2nd ed. New York: Oxford University Press.

Comprehensive book on model-making, with details of Platonic and Ar-

chimedean solids, duals, compounds, stellations, and other interesting
polyhedral forms.

Goldberg, Steven A. 1977. *Pholdit*. Hayward, Calif.: Activity Resources.

    Pictures step-by-step instructions for folding interesting polyhedron models.

Hilton, Peter, and Jean Pedersen. 1988. *Build Your Own Polyhedra*.
Palo Alto, Calif.: Addison-Wesley.

    Features several different methods of constructing polygons and polyhedra.
Includes Pedersen's technique of "braiding" polyhedra and folding strips of paper
to obtain polygonal faces.

Holden, Alan. 1971. *Shapes, Space and Symmetry*. New York: Columbia University Press.

    Filled with photographs of excellent models, this is the best book that il-
lustrates the properties of polyhedra and the relationships between polyhedra.
Models demonstrate the symmetries of polyhedra and their cross-sections; series
of models demonstrate how polyhedra can be obtained from others by dualiz-
ing, by truncation, by faceting or stellation, or by compounding.

Johnson, Donavan A. 1974. *Mathmagic with Flexagons*. Hayward,
Calif.: Activity Resources.

    The puzzle magic of flexagons always holds students' attention.

Laycock, Mary. 1984. *Bucky for Beginners*. Hayward, Calif.: Activity
Resources.

    A sequence of explorations with solid shapes and synergy — encourages stu-
dents to create space models from everyday materials.

————. *Straw Polyhedra*. Mountain View, Calif.: Creative.

    Directions for constructing "frame" polyhedra from soda straws.

Lindgren, Harry. [1964] 1972. *Recreational Problems in Geometric Dissections & How to Solve Them*. Reprint. New York: Dover.

    When (and how) can one polygon be dissected and reassembled to form
another polygon (having the same area)? This book provides fascinating
problems and solutions.

Loeb, Arthur L. 1976. *Space Structures: Their Harmony and Counter-
point*. Reading, Mass.: Addison-Wesley.

    An overview of combinatorial and algebraic constraints on geometric struc-
tures.

Lyusternik, L. A. 1966. *Convex Figures and Polyhedra*. Boston, Mass.:
D. C. Heath.

> A good introduction to some non-elementary properties of convex figures:
> central symmetry, networks and convex polyhedra (includes Cauchy's theorem).

Pearce, Peter, and Susan Pearce. 1978. *Polyhedra Primer*. New York:
Van Nostrand Reinhold.

> A starter book on polyhedra, containing more than 200 captioned drawings
> (warning: the drawings are not technically accurate). Considers symmetry,
> regular and semi-regular solids; questions of plane and space filling.

Pugh, Anthony. 1976. *Polyhedra, A Visual Approach*. Berkeley, Calif.:
University of California Press.

> Covers not only the Platonic and Archimedean solids, but all of the convex
> polyhedra with regular polygon faces and some polyhedra that pack space. Em-
> phasis on illustrations, relationships; also notes the golden ratio, and discusses
> the geodesic polyhedra of Buckminster Fuller.

Senechal, Marjorie, and George Fleck, eds. 1986. *Shaping Space: A
Polyhedral Approach*. Boston, Mass.: Birkhäuser.

> Based on lectures and workshops at an interdisciplinary conference held at
> Smith College in 1984. Contains ideas on investigating polyhedra, their proper-
> ties and importance in the environment, and hands-on projects. Excellent bibli-
> ographies.

Stewart, Bonnie M. 1970. *Adventures Among the Toroids*. 1983. 2nd
ed. Okemos, Mich.: B. M. Stewart.

> Presents a galaxy of polyhedra with "holes" (hence the name 'toroids')
> together with instructions for constructing them. Many are made up of blocks of
> easily constructed convex polyhedra with regular polygon faces.

Stonerod, David. 1982. *Puzzles in Space*. Palo Alto, Calif.: Stokes.

> Contains several good projects for constructing polyhedra and observing
> some not-so-obvious cross-sections, relationships with other polyhedra, and
> other curiosities.

Swienciki, Lawrence W. 1976. *Quadraflex Model Book*. San Jose,
Calif.: A. R. Davis.

> Step-by-step instructions to build collapsible models.

Wenninger, Magnus J. 1975. *Polyhedron Models for the Classroom*. 2nd
ed. Reston, Va.: National Council of Teachers of Mathematics.

> Directions for making a variety of polyhedron models, together with histori-
> cal notes. Contains seven removable pages of designs to be used as templates to
> make the models shown in the text.

———. 1971, 1979, 1983. *Polyhedron Models. Spherical Models. Dual Models.* 3 vols. London, England: Cambridge University Press.

Gives directions for building an enormous variety of models from paper. The first book covers all of the Platonic and Archimedean as well as many of the stellated models. The spherical models are a great challenge but illustrate the projection of polyhedra onto the face of a sphere. The dual models book complements the first book. Photos of assembled models are shown.

Wills, Herbert. 1985. *Leonardo's Dessert: No Pi.* Reston, Va.: National Council of Teachers of Mathematics.

Leonardo da Vinci's attempts to square the circle led him to discover many interesting dissections that transform curvilinear regions into rectangular regions with the same area.

Geometry in the Environment – Geometric Design of Nature and Humans

Bentley, Wilson A., and William J. Humphreys. [1931] 1962. *Snow Crystals.* Reprint. New York: Dover.

Actual photographs of hundreds of snowflakes illustrate the beauty of geometric symmetry in nature.

Beskin, Nikolai M. 1985. *Images of Geometric Solids.* Translated by Valery Barvashov. Moscow: Mir (distributed by Imported Publications).

Theory and application of the geometry of representation of three-dimensional figures on a plane surface.

Bezuszka, Stanley J., Margaret J. Kenney, and Linda Silvey. 1977. *Tessellations: The Geometry of Patterns.* Mountain View, Calif.: Creative.

Lessons and practice exercises develop the mathematics of tessellations: regular, semiregular, and demiregular tessellations, as well as non-regular polygons that tessellate.

Boles, Martha, and Rochelle Newman. 1983. *The Golden Relationship: Art, Math, Nature.* Book 1: Universal Patterns. Bradford, Mass.: Pythagorean Press.

A compendium (345 pages) of material about, or related to, the golden ratio. Includes explanations, exercises, projects, bibliographies, and copious illustrations. Chapter titles: Basic constructions, Unique relationships [giving rise to the golden ratio]; Special triangles; Dynamic rectangles; Fibonacci numbers; Spirals.

Bouleau, Charles. 1963. *The Painter's Secret Geometry: A Study of Composition in Art.* Translated by Jonathan Griffin. New York: Harcourt Brace & World. 1980. Reprint. New York: Hacker Art Books.

A comprehensive study of the use of geometry in the composition of art throughout various periods in history.

Boys, Charles V. 1959. *Soap Bubbles: Their Colours and the Forces Which Mold Them.* 3rd ed. New York: Dover.
> Soap bubbles create minimal surfaces on wire frames, and "pack" according to rules of physics and geometry. Properties of polyhedra and crystals can be investigated using soap bubbles.

Campbell, Paul J. 1988. Growth and form. Chapter 14 in *For All Practical Purposes: Introduction to Contemporary Mathematics*, edited by Lynn Arthur Steen, 270-284. New York: W. H. Freeman.
> Discusses geometric similarity, scaling of real objects, how high a mountain can be, the tension between volume and area, size and flight, keeping cool (and warm), similarity and biological growth, and logarithmic plots and allometry. (PJC & LSG)

Cook, Theodore Andrea. [1914] 1978. *The Curves of Life.* Reprint. New York: Dover.
> "The classic reference on how the golden ratio applies to spirals and helices in nature"—Martin Gardner. Cook contends the "divine proportion" is central to human art and architecture and "spirality is one of the great cosmic laws." Amply illustrated.

Critchlow, Keith. 1976. *Islamic Patterns: An Analytical and Cosmological Approach.* New York: Schocken.
> An excellent source to illustrate the ruler and compass constructions that underlie intricate repeating Islamic patterns.

Crowe, Donald W. 1986. Symmetry, Rigid Motions, and Patterns. HiMAP Module no. 4. Arlington, Mass.: COMAP. 1987. Reprint. *UMAP Journal* 8 (3): 207-236.
> Module containing text, worksheets, and transparency masters explains how the four-plane isometries generate one- and two-dimensional repeating patterns. Generous illustrations and application to the classification of patterns in an archeological site.

Dixon, Robert. 1987. *Mathographics.* Oxford: Blackwell.
> Extremely readable source for background on the use of Euclidean geometric tools, as well as on many geometric transformations that can be used to create wonderful designs by hand or by programming a computer. Richly illustrated.

Edwards, Edward B. 1967. *Pattern and Design with Dynamic Symmetry.* New York: Dover.

A good art source to show some of the designs that can result from the simple idea of constructing right triangles having an irrational hypotenuse.

Fejes Tóth, L. 1964. *Regular Figures*. New York: Pergamon.
A comprehensive treatment of symmetry in the plane and in three-space. Fejes Tóth gives the details of the classification of the plane symmetry groups and space groups, the symmetries of crystals, and much more. Contains many illustrations (line drawings and color plates) and the unique stereographic illustrations of crystals which appear three-dimensional when viewed through special glasses with red and green lenses (included).

Ghyka, Matila C. [1946] 1977. *The Geometry of Art and Life*. Reprint. New York: Dover.
Discusses geometric proportion as observed in nature and art and notes some historic figures and their contributions to the theory. Golden section is a main topic.

Grünbaum, Branko, and Geoffrey C. Shephard. 1986. *Tilings and Patterns*. New York: W.H. Freeman.
The definitive book on tilings (of the plane and other surfaces) by polygons and patterns on surfaces. Features history, development of theory and applications, solved and unsolved problems, enumerations of different kinds of tilings, careful consideration of the role of symmetry. Lavishly illustrated; an excellent source for problems and projects.

Hildebrandt, Stefan, and Anthony Tromba. 1985. *Mathematics and Optimal Form*. New York: W. H. Freeman.
Superb photos illustrate this exploration of the topic of minimal surfaces and packing of forms with special attention to their occurrence in nature.

Huntley, H. E. 1970. *The Divine Proportion: A Study in Mathematical Beauty*. New York: Dover.
A classic on the fascination of the golden section in nature and man-made environment.

Lockwood, Edward H., and Robert H. MacMillan. 1978. *Geometric Symmetry*. London, England: Cambridge University Press.
An overview of symmetric patterns and tilings in the plane. The writing is spare, and the explanations of color symmetry are confusing.

Pedoe, Daniel. 1976. *Geometry and the Liberal Arts*. 1976. New York: St. Martin's. 1983. Reprint under the title *Geometry and the Visual Arts*. New York: Dover.
Presents the story of geometry as a central force in art and architecture. Includes contributions to the understanding of geometric form and its repre-

sentation on a two-dimensional surface by Euclid, Vitruvius, Dürer, and da Vinci. Treats Cartesian and projective geometry, the construction of curves, and an excursion into consideration of higher dimensions. Highly readable and non-textbookish; a great deal about — and a good deal of — geometry can be learned here.

Ranucci, Ernest R., and J. L. Teeters. 1977. *Creating Escher-Type Drawings*. Mountain View, Calif.: Creative.

Simple directions for creating "creature" tilings that are alterations of tilings by polygons. The authors fall far short of Escher's creations, and they fail to explain the transformation geometry that makes things "work."

Rosen, Joe. 1975. *Symmetry Discovered. Concepts and Applications in Nature and Science*. New York: Cambridge University Press.

An elementary, fairly non-technical introduction to the language of symmetry as used by scientists and mathematicians and applied to various fields. Briefly covers geometric symmetry (linear, planar, spatial), other symmetry (temporal, permutations, color), approximate symmetry, symmetry in nature, and its uses in science. Good bibliography (although needs updating).

Runion, Garth E. 1972. *The Golden Section and Related Curiosa*. Glenview, Ill.: Scott, Foresman.

Details the constructions (with proof) of the golden section and regular pentagon, and explores several related topics. The best supplemental mathematical tract on the golden section.

Shubnikov, Aleksei V., and V. A. Koptsik. 1974. *Symmetry in Science and Art*. Translated by G.D. Archard. Edited by David Harker. New York: Plenum.

A comprehensive book on symmetry in the plane and in three-space, written by crystallographers and intended for an (educated) popular audience. A good book for the reference shelf.

Stevens, Peter S. 1974. *Patterns in Nature*. Boston, Mass.: Little, Brown.

A classic on the role of geometry in nature, this book was a main source for the Nova program "The Shape of Things".

———. 1981. *A Handbook of Regular Patterns: An Introduction to Symmetry in Two Dimensions*. Cambridge, Mass.: MIT Press.

An excellent compendium of symmetric patterns with explanation of the symmetries. Stevens covers "rosette," "frieze," and "wallpaper" patterns.

Thompson, D'Arcy W. 1942. *On Growth and Form*. Cambridge, England: Cambridge University Press.

A classic investigation on the nature and geometry of growth of plant and animal forms.

Vero, Radu. 1980. *Understanding Perspective*. New York: Van Nostrand Reinhold.
> A problem-oriented approach to learning the principles of correct perspective drawing. An excellent text.

de Vries, Jan Vredeman. [1604] 1968. *Perspective*. Reprint. New York: Dover.
> A collection of superb plates that illustrate the Renaissance artist's mastery of the art (and geometry) of perspective.

Weeks, Jeffrey R. 1985. *The Shape of Space: How to Visualize Surfaces and Three Dimensional Manifolds*. New York: Marcel Dekker.
> Written to fill the gap between the simplest examples of manifolds (such as the Moebius strip and the Klein bottle) and the sophisticated mathematics found in upper-level college courses.

Weyl, Hermann. 1952. *Symmetry*. Princeton, N.J.: Princeton University Press.
> A collection of essays (originally lectures) on symmetry in nature and manmade art and architecture. Weyl's writing is persuasive and not technical, yet he touches on the mathematical meaning of symmetry as it governs these forms. A classic.

Williams, Robert. [1972] 1979. *Natural Structure*. Republished as *The Geometric Foundation of Natural Structure: A Source Book of Design*. New York: Dover.
> Discusses constructions and packings that have implications for structure in nature.

Non-Euclidean and Transformation Geometry

Abbott, Edwin A. [1886] 1963. *Flatland: A Romance of Many Dimensions*. 5th ed. New York: Barnes & Noble.
> A classic fable that stretches the imagination and helps the reader to realize that geometric perception greatly depends on the relative position and dimension of the viewer! Every teacher should know this book and introduce it to students— especially in light of new interest in geometry in the fourth and higher dimensions.

Bakel'man, I. Ya. 1974. *Inversions*. Translated by Susan Williams and Joan W. Teller. Chicago, Ill.: University of Chicago Press.

An elementary introduction to the transformation of inversion in a circle.

Burger, Dionys. 1965. *Sphereland: A Fantasy About Curved Spaces and an Expanding Universe.* Translated by Cornelie J. Rheinboldt. New York: Thomas Crowell, Apollo Editions.

    A sequel to Abbot's *Flatland* [1886] (1963), this fantasy introduces its readers to the geometries of curved space.

Eccles, Frank M. 1971. *An Introduction to Transformational Geometry.* Menlo Park, Calif.: Addison Wesley.

    An elementary introduction to isometries and similitudes.

Hess, Adrien L. 1977. *Four-Dimensional Geometry—An Introduction.* Reston, Va.: National Council of Teachers of Mathematics.

    A brief introduction to the history and some of the configurations in four-dimensional geometry, with suggestions on how to study the configurations and some applications.

Lieber, Lillian R. 1944. *The Education of T. C. Mits.* New York: Norton.

    A classic fable introduces the reader to the world of non-Euclidean geometry.

Maxwell, Edwin A. 1975. *Geometry by Transformations.* Cambridge, England: Cambridge University Press.

    A readable (and usable) introduction to transformation geometry, and a text produced for the School Mathematics Project.

Meschkowski, Herbert. 1964. *Non-Euclidean Geometry.* Translated by A. Shenitzer. New York: Academic.

    An elementary introduction to non-Euclidean geometry.

Rosenfeld, Boris A., and N. D. Sergeeva. 1977. *Stereographic Projection.* Translated by Vitaly Kisin. Moscow: Mir (distributed by Imported Publications).

    Lobachevskian methods of projection with applications to astronomy and geography.

Rucker, Rudolf von Bitter. 1977. *Geometry, Relativity and the Fourth Dimension.* New York: Dover.

    Presentation of intuitive picture of four-dimensional space-time. Part of the book continues the adventures of characters of Abbot's *Flatland* [1886] (1963).

————. 1984. *The 4th Dimension: Toward a Geometry of Higher*

Reality. Boston, Mass.: Houghton Mifflin.

> A mind-stretching book, not limited to the geometric notion of the fourth dimension. Rucker explores the concept of the fourth dimension in physics, philosophy, even mysticism.

Runion, Garth E., and James R. Lockwood. 1978. *Deductive Systems: Finite and Non-Euclidean Geometries*. Reston, Va.: National Council of Teachers of Mathematics.

> Two non-Euclidean geometries are explored; such study highlights the role of axioms and deductive systems. In addition, students are made aware of geometries other than the familiar.

Smogorzhevsky, A. 1976. *Lobachevskian Geometry*. Translated by Vitaly Kisin. Moscow: Mir (distributed by Imported Publications).

> The fundamentals of Lobachevskian non-Euclidean geometry.

Yaglom, Isaak M. 1962, 1968, 1973. *Geometric Transformations*. 3 vols. Vols. 1, 2 trans. by Alan Shields, vol. 3 by Abe Shenitzer. New Mathematical Library nos. 8, 21, 24. Washington, D.C.: Mathematical Association of America.

> Geometric transformations—what they are, their properties, major theorems, constructions, and many problems (including different proofs of Euclidean theorems), together with complete solutions. Well-written, these books are very useful for a variety of teaching purposes. Vol. 1 is on Euclidean isometries, 2 on similarities, and 3 on affine and projective transformations.

Young, John W. 1930. *Projective Geometry*. Carus Monograph no. 4. Washington, D.C.: Mathematical Association of America.

> A classic book treats the most fundamental propositions of projective geometry, culminating in the theorems of Pascal and Brianchon.

History

Aaboe, Asger. 1964. *Episodes from the Early History of Mathematics*. New Mathematical Library no. 13. Washington, D.C.: Mathematical Association of America.

> Highly readable "episodes" include topics reconstructed from Euclid's Elements, from the writings of Archimedes, and from Ptolemy's Almagest.

Baumgart, John K., et al., eds. 1969. *NCTM Yearbook* 31.

> An excellent reference for several historical topics in geometry. Look here first for a capsule summary of a historical topic (such as trisection of an angle, or golden section) and list of references for more detailed information. Good source of enrichment topics and student projects.

Beckmann, Petr. 1971. *A History of Pi*. Boulder, Colo.: Golem.

Sourcebook for many discoveries concerning the number pi. Students need to learn the geometric meaning of pi and some of its rich history — most know it only as a calculator button, or a decimal constant.

Bold, Benjamin. 1969. *Famous Problems of Geometry and How to Solve Them*. New York: Dover.

Trisection of an angle, squaring of a circle, and duplication of a cube — the classic "unsolvable" problems of ancient Greece are discussed. Many attempts to solve (or explain) the problems led to parts of modern mathematics. The reader is given practice problems to develop understanding.

Carroll, Lewis (= C. L. Dodgson). 1885. *Euclid and His Modern Rivals*. 1973. Reprint. New York: Dover.

A spoof play that derides the many geometers who, over the centuries, tried to "improve" on Euclid. A unique way to learn about the "flaws" in Euclid.

Descartes, René. [1637] 1954. *The Geometry of René Descartes* (incl. facsimile of first edition 1637). Translated by David E. Smith and Marcia L. Latham. New York: Dover.

Taken for granted in almost all applications of mathematics, the coordinatization of the plane and solution of geometric problems by the use of algebraic equations was formulated by René Descartes. His contribution deserves study.

Euclid. [1926] 1956. *The Thirteen Books of Euclid's Elements*. 2nd ed. 3 vols. Translated by Thomas L. Heath. Cambridge, England: Cambridge University Press. Reprint. New York: Dover.

Going to the source (or discovering the wealth of Euclid's thirteen books) can be rewarding for student or teacher.

Federico, Pasquale J. 1982. *Descartes on Polyhedra: A Study of the* De Solidorum Elementis. New York: Springer-Verlag.

A careful translation and commentary on Descartes' "De Solidorum Elementis." Federico makes clear what Descartes did and did not prove — for example, the polyhedron formula of Euler $(v + f - e = 2)$ is *not* found here, contrary to the claims of many writers.

Friedrichs, Kurt O. 1965. *From Pythagoras to Einstein*. New Mathematical Library no. 16. Washington, D.C.: Mathematical Association of America.

A short monograph that begins with the Pythagorean theorem, and through vector geometry, discusses a variety of mathematical and physical contexts, culminating with Einstein's $E = mc^2$.

Klein, Felix. 1956. *Famous Problems of Elementary Geometry*. Translated by W. W. Berman and D. E. Smith. New York: Dover.

Gives the detailed algebraic analysis necessary to prove the impossibility of solving the "Delian problem" (of duplicating the cube) with straightedge and compasses. Part I examines the possible constructions of algebraic expressions; Part II covers transcendental numbers and the quadrature of the circle (including a proof of the transcendence of pi).

Knorr, Wilbur R. 1986. *The Ancient Tradition of Geometric Problems*. Boston, Mass.: Birkhäuser.

A scholarly work which is an excellent reference.

Lanczos, Cornelius. 1970. *Space Through the Ages*. New York: Academic.

The evolution of geometrical ideas from Pythagoras to Hilbert and Einstein.

Swetz, Frank J., and T. I. Kao. 1977. *Was Pythagoras Chinese?* Reston, Va. and State College, Pa.: National Council of Teachers of Mathematics and Pennsylvania State University.

An examination of right-triangle theory in ancient China.

Tietze, Heinrich. 1965. *Famous Problems of Mathematics*. Edited by Beatrice K. Hofstadter and Horace Komm. New York: Graylock.

Good exposition and bibliographies on the famous geometry problems: trisection of an angle, squaring the circle, constructing regular polygons, the four-color problem, non-Euclidean geometry.

van der Waerden, B. L. 1983. *Geometry and Algebra in Ancient Civilizations*. New York: Springer-Verlag.

A full comparative discussion of the geometry (and algebra) of the ancient civilizations in China, Babylonia, Egypt, and Greece. Main topics: Pythagorean triangles, area and construction problems, geometric algebra.

Yates, Robert C. [1942] 1971. *The Trisection Problem*. Reprint. Reston, Va.: National Council of Teachers of Mathematics.

Discussion of the problem, solutions by means of curves, mechanical trisectors, approximations, and "Don Quixotes."

Geometry with a Computer

Abelson, Harold, and Andrea di Sessa. 1981. *Turtle Geometry: The Computer as a Medium for Exploring Mathematics*. Cambridge, Mass.:

MIT Press.
> Excellent interaction of geometry and the microcomputer. Geometry is exploited to create graphics on the microcomputer and conversely, the use of "turtle" graphics introduces the user to a wide spectrum of geometric topics, from plane geometry to symmetry groups and topological invariants.

Billstein, Rick, Shlomo Libeskind, and Johnny W. Lott. 1985. *Problem Solving with Logo*. Menlo Park, Calif.: Addison-Wesley.
> Examples and solutions of problems that can be explored and solved using the Logo language on a microcomputer. Some problems are geometry problems.

Johnson, Jerry. *Graphics Discoveries: A Problem-Solving Approach to Color Graphics*. 2 vols. Mountain View, Calif.: Creative.
> Book I is an introduction to low-resolution graphics on the Apple II +, IIe, and IIc; Book II extends the concepts to high resolution graphics. Geometric concepts take on importance as they are utilized to produce computer graphics. Teacher's Resource Disk contains programs and solutions from both books.

Myers, Roy E. 1984. *Microcomputer Graphics*. (Separate books for the Apple and for the IBM-PC). Menlo Park, Calif.: Addison-Wesley.
> Provides the essential techniques for programming microcomputer graphics; accompanying disk provides programs from the text for creating graphics. Assumes knowledge of programming.

Moore, Margaret L. *Geometry Problems for Logo Discoveries*. Mountain View, Calif.: Creative.
> Discovery-oriented activities build deductive and inductive reasoning skills; also use geometry concepts to solve problems in Logo. Activities for use on 64K Apple II computers with either Terrapin/Krell or Apple Logo. Teacher's Resource Disk contains procedures and solutions.

Thornburg, David D. 1983. *Discovering Apple Logo: An Invitation to the Art and Pattern of Nature*. Menlo Park, Calif.: Addison-Wesley.
> Teaches programming in Logo on an Apple II computer.

Activities, Worksheets, Contest Problem Books

Investigative activities should be a major component of any geometry course. Supplemental materials in the form of worksheets and suggestions for activities are available for almost every aspect of geometry. Geometry problems are among the most easily stated and most challenging to solve, and have fascinated mathematicians from the earliest times. They also are among the most "beautiful"—surprising geometric relationships and facts abound. Such problems occur in every high-school mathematics competition and are also found in many journals. Students should be challenged to try to solve such problems — they are excellent for class activities (individually, or even better, in groups), and for mathematics clubs.

Activities and Worksheets

Amusements in Developing Geometry Skills. Chatsworth, Calif.: Opportunities for Learning.

> Two-book set (reproducible) provides practice exercises, puzzles, designs, covering a wide range of informal geometry.

Clemens, Stanley R., Phares G. O'Daffer, and T. Cooney. 1984. *Teacher's Resource Book for Geometry with Applications and Problem Solving.* Menlo Park, Calif.: Addison-Wesley.

> Over 200 pages of teaching aids for use in teaching the high-school geometry course. Although produced for use with the authors' text, it can be used with other texts.

de Cordova, Chris. 1986. *The Tessellations File.* Stradbroke, Diss, England: Tarquin.

> Thirty-two page file is a collection of regular, semi-regular and other tessellations, which are useful when teaching about symmetry and a starting point for students to create their own tessellations.

Farrell, Margaret A. 1971. *Geoboard Geometry: Teacher's Guide.* Mountain View, Calif.: Creative.

> Teacher's guide, which illustrates and describes activities with geoboards.

Foster, Allan C., Jerry J. Cummins, and Lee E. Yunker. 1984. *Merrill Geometry, Teacher's Resource Book.* Columbus, O.: Charles E. Merrill.

> Blackline masters and enrichment material.

Gawronski, Jane D., G. R. Prigge, and K. E. Vos. *Informal Geometry Activities.* Portland, Me.: J. Weston Walch.

> 50 spirit masters contain discovery activities for essential concepts in geometry. Answer key.

Hawley, Newton, and Patrick Suppes; revised by G. Gearhart and P. Rasmussen. *Key to Geometry.* 8 vols. Berkeley, Calif.: Key Curriculum Project.

> Discovery and reinforcement activities for students to learn and understand basic concepts, definitions, and constructions in plane geometry. Can be used

independently, or in conjunction with standard texts. Step-by-step instructions, questions, and review are well thought-out. Titles of books: Book 1: Lines and Segments; 2: Circles; 3: Constructions; 4: Perpendiculars; 5: Squares and Rectangles; 6: Angles; 7: Perpendiculars and Parallels, Chords and Tangents, Circles; 8: Triangles, Parallel Lines, Similar Polygons.

Hirsch, Christian R., M. A. Norton, D. O. Coblentz, A. J. Samide, and H. L. Schoen. 1984. *Resource Book, Blackline Masters for Scott, Foresman Geometry*. 2nd ed. Glenview, Ill.: Scott, Foresman.
> Contains 13 enrichment activities and 18 blackline masters suitable for making copies or overhead visual masters. (Supplementary exercises and scrambled proof activities are keyed to the text, but other materials may be used with any text.) Topics include: polygonal games, taxi-distance, angles and circles, Pick's theorem, geometry in sports, geometric probability, Einthoven's triangle, symmetry groups, regular polyhedra, latitude and longitude.

Jacobs, Harold R. 1986. *Geometry*. 2nd ed. *Teacher's Guide and Transparency Masters*. New York: W.H. Freeman.
> Extensive collection of blackline masters.

Joint Committee of the Mathematical Association of America and National Council of Teachers of Mathematics. 1980. *A Sourcebook for Applications of School Mathematics*. Reston, Va.: National Council of Teachers of Mathematics.
> A collection of realistic problems which show the recognition and use of mathematics. Includes answers and an annotated bibliography.

Jurgensen, Ray C., et al. 1988. *Houghton Mifflin Geometry, Resource Book*. New York: Houghton Mifflin.
> Blackline masters for practice, testing, review.

Kutepov, Aleksandr, and Anatoli Rubanov. 1975. *Problems in Geometry*. Translated by Oleg Meshkov. Translation edited by Leonid Levant. Moscow: Mir (distributed by Imported Publications).
> Problems (1351 of them) and answers in plane and solid geometry for technical schools and colleges.

Laycock, Mary, and William T. Stokes. *Math Activity Worksheet Masters*. Mountain View, Calif.: Creative.
> Blackline masters for various geometry activities.

Luckas, Mary. *Challenging Problems in Geometry*. Portland, Me.: J. Weston Walch.
> Fifty worksheets (spirit or photocopy masters) challenge students to apply

known concepts in creative ways. Detailed solutions provided.

Lund, Charles. 1980. *Dot Paper Geometry — With or Without a Geo-board*. New Rochelle, N.Y.: Cuisenaire.

Students may work directly on dot paper provided in the workbook, or use geoboards to solve the problems.

Nichols, Eugene D., M. Edwards, E. Garland, S. Hoffman, A. Mamary, and W. Palmer. 1986. *Holt Geometry, Teacher's Resource Package*. New York: Holt, Rinehart & Winston.

O'Daffer, Phares G., and Stanley L. Clemens. 1976. *Laboratory Investigations in Geometry*. Menlo Park, Calif.: Addison-Wesley.

Over 120 investigations and hands-on activities to encourage students to discover relationships, properties, and theorems. Can supplement any text. Topics: puzzles and dissections, polygons and symmetry (including geoboard use and special properties of triangles), tessellations, polyhedra, reflections (including work with Mira).

Palmaccio, Richard J. *Problems in Analytic Geometry*. Portland, Me.: J. Weston Walch.

Twenty-four worksheets (spirit or photocopy masters) provide illustrated problems of realistic applications of analytic geometry; emphasize problem-solving skill and integration of related concepts. Detailed solutions.

Posamentier, Alfred S., and G. Sheridan. 1982. *Math Motivators! Investigations in Geometry*. Menlo Park, Calif.: Addison-Wesley.

Over 30 lesson-length investigations, each with reproducible student worksheet and accompanying teacher's notes. Topics include: constructions, problems of antiquity, post-Euclidean theorems, non-Euclidean geometries (taxicab, projective, spherical), solid geometry, geometric applications, geometric fallacies, circles related to a triangle. Can supplement any text; teacher notes give useful advice as to when and how to best introduce an activity.

Smart, Margaret A., and Mary Laycock. 1982. *Focus on Geometry*. Hayward, Calif.: Activity Resources.

A collection of elementary, "hands on" activities to discover and formulate rules for finding area of plane figures, surface area, and volume of solids.

Stokes, William T. 1978. *Gems of Geometry*. Rev. ed. Palo Alto, Calif.: Stokes (distributed by Activity Resources).

Collection of lessons has fine graphics to teach topics such as constructions, angle measuring, Pythagorean theorem.

Walch, J. Weston. *Confidence-Building Geometry Problems. Amusing Problems in Geometry*. Portland, Me.: J. Weston Walch.

> Two sets of 24 worksheets (spirit or photocopy masters) show practical uses of geometry, provide clever word problems and unusual proofs. Answer key.

Wiltshire, Alan. *The Geometrics File*. Stradbroke, Diss, England: Tarquin.

> Eighty-page file of construction activities, which may be duplicated for students. Encourages students to develop original patterns.

Contest Problem Books

Alexanderson, Gerald L., Alexander P. Hillman, Leonard F. Klosinski, and David Logothetti. 1985. *The Santa Clara Silver Anniversary Contest Book*. Palo Alto, Calif.: Dale Seymour.

Alexanderson, Gerald L., Leonard F. Klosinski, and Loren C. Larson, comps. 1986. *The William Lowell Putnam Mathematics Competition (1965-1984)*. Washington, D.C.: Mathematical Association of America.

> For Putnam examinations for years 1938-1964 see Gleason et al. (1980).

Artino, Ralph A., Anthony M. Gaglioni, and Neil Shell, comps. 1983. *Contest Problem Book IV*. New Mathematical Library no. 29. Washington, D.C.: Mathematical Association of America.

Barry, Donald, and J. Richard Lux. *The Phillips Academy Prize Examinations in Mathematics*. Palo Alto, Calif.: Dale Seymour.

Brousseau, Brother Alfred. 1972. *St. Mary's College Mathematics Contest Problems*. Mountain View, Calif.: Creative.

Fisher, Lyle, Bill Kennedy, and William Medigovich. 1984. *The Brother Alfred Brousseau Problem-Solving and Mathematics Competition*. 2 vols. Palo Alto, Calif.: Dale Seymour.

Gleason, Andrew M., R. E. Greenwood and L. M. Kelly, comps. 1980. *The William Lowell Putnam Mathematical Competition: Problems and Solutions: 1938-1964*. Washington, D.C.: Mathematical Association of America.

> For Putnam examinations for 1965-1984, see Alexanderson et al. (1986).

Greitzer, Samuel L., comp. 1978. *International Mathematical Olympiads, 1959-1977*. New Mathematical Library no. 27. Washington, D.C.: Mathematical Association of America.

Klamkin, Murray S., comp. 1986. *International Mathematical Olympiads, 1978-1985 and Forty Supplementary Problems*. New Mathematical Library no. 31. Washington, D.C.: Mathematical Association of America.
    Greitzer (1978) covers earlier years.

Salkind, Charles T., comp. 1961, 1966. *Contest Problem Book I, II*. New Mathematical Library nos. 5, 17. Washington, D.C.: Mathematical Association of America.

──────, and James M. Earl, comps. 1973. *Contest Problem Book III*. New Mathematical Library no. 25. Washington, D.C.: Mathematical Association of America.

Saul, Mark, G. Kessler, S. Krilov, and L. Zimmerman. 1986. *The New York City Contest Problem Book*. Palo Alto, Calif.: Dale Seymour.

Demonstration Aids

Geometry demands the use of demonstration aids both by the teacher and by the student. Aids are invaluable in visually and/or tactically demonstrating facts, constructions, definitions, concepts and proofs. ("I SEE and I understand.")

Some of these aids are readily available from any educational supply house or art and drafting materials supplier; others are more special and available from only one or two distributors. For this reason, we have not listed individual items. Instead, we discuss the types of items that are useful and indicate which distributors carry the more special items. Many of the special items are expensive and teachers may wish to have students build some of the demonstration aids as special projects.

Key to Distributors: Activity Resources = AR; Carolina Biological Supply Co. = CB; Creative Publications = CP; Cuisenaire = C; Dick Blick = DB; Delta Education = DE; Dale Seymour = DS; Gamco = Ga; Geyer = Ge; Lano = L; Spectrum = S.

Blackboard Aids (CB, CP, DE, Ga, Ge, L)

Colored chalk can emphasize special parts of a diagram and make constructions and arguments easier to follow.

Grids (Cartesian, polar, 3-D, isometric) etched on blackboard panels, or perforated stencils to create such grids using chalkdust, ensure accurate sketching of diagrams and encourage students to use the same care. A graph liner holds 19 pieces of chalk equispaced, so that in two strokes a graph grid can be drawn.

Construction tools should be used to demonstrate to students their proper use (and limitations) and to insure accuracy of constructions. These include: blackboard compass, straightedge (yard/meter stick), protractor (semi-circular, circular, or a special "gravity protractor" which combines straightedge, T-square, ruler, protractor, and angle-finder), T-square, triangle, ellipse and parabola makers, pantograph, polygon shapes (to trace around).

Overhead Projector Aids (CP, Ga, Ge, L)

Colored pens (water-based ink for transparency acetate, such as Vis-a-vis or 3M) give vivid diagrams that are easy to follow.

Preprepared transparencies containing graph grids, diagrams, demonstrations, etc., are available in ready-to-use form. More often, they are in the form of "blackline masters" (in teacher resource collections) which are copyright free and of good quality to make transparencies using a heat-sensitive copying machine (such as Thermofax) which "burns" a smudgeproof permanent copy of the diagram into clear acetate.

Continuous roll *clear acetate* (or a supply of clear individual sheets) makes possible the enhancement of preprepared transparencies (slip the prepared transparency under the clear sheet and make diagrams or emphasis marks with colored pens on the top clear sheet). Concepts of transformation geometry are strikingly demonstrated using two transparencies containing exactly the same figure (but with one of them outlined in color). The top sheet overlays the second (which is anchored so that it does not move) so that the figures are superimposed; and then the top sheet can be rotated, shifted, or turned over to demonstrate the action of a transformation and the final position of the transformed figure in relation to its original position.

Construction tools especially for use on the overhead projector make possible accurate constructions and sketches. These include the Circle Master Compass (with plastic center locator), clear plastic protractors and straight edges, templates and polygon shapes to trace.

Colored acetate can be used effectively in many ways on the overhead projector. Shapes can be cut from sheets of (different colored) acetate and then used to demonstrate the action of isometries using superposition. In addition, properties of line symmetry and even constructions using paper folding can be demonstrated with colored acetate using the overhead projector. The acetate creases easily, and the fold lines are clearly visible under projection. Colored overlays (strips) can highlight important statements or diagrams on a preprepared clear acetate transparency, just as this technique is used in modern texts.

Transparent models, either clear or colored, can be projected using the overhead projector. Plastic geoboards, models demonstrating certain theorems and other geometric relationships, polygons and other shapes are available. Some three-dimensional models can also be projected — by changing the focus of the projector, the image on the screen seems to travel through the model, showing its changing cross-sections.

Construction and Drawing Aids (C, CB, CP, DB, DE, DS, Ga, Ge, S)

Grids of every variety for graphing (lines, dots, various coordinate systems, various scales) are available in tablets and notebooks, activity books, in collections of blackline masters for duplicating, and as rubber stamps. Poster-sized grids for use on an easel can be used for class demonstrations. Bristol board (Tara) is also available with imprinted rectangular grid; this is excellent material to use in the layout and construction of polyhedra.

Construction and drawing tools for individual use are available in inexpensive form as well as drafting quality. These include: compasses (of which there are safety varieties without sharp points — e.g., the Triman compass), protractors (half-circle, full-circle, and some with rotating arm), rulers (with and without markings), T-square, parallel rule, triangles, templates with polygon and other shapes, ellipse and parabola makers, pantograph.

Mirrors, either glass or plastic, fully reflective (one-way) or semitransparent (two-way) are useful in creating constructions as well as testing drawings for symmetry. Unbreakable plastic mirrors are found in educational supply houses (Mira is a trade name of a ruby plexiglass two-way mirror) and some plastics and model stores; plate glass mirrors (one- and two-way) may be gotten at any glass supply house. Constructions exploiting the properties of reflections (transformation geometry) can be carried out with two-way mirrors; two-way mirrors can be placed on a design to test if it has line symmetry; hinged mirrors can be used to create regular polygons and kaleidoscopic designs.

Manipulatives and Demonstration Models

A wide variety of commercially produced manipulatives and fully assembled models are available to demonstrate geometric concepts, definitions, constructions, relationships, formulas and theorems. Although some of the models are expensive, they are sturdy and encourage "hands-on" demonstration of geometric properties that are not immediately obvious.

Geoboards, with pegs arranged in a square lattice, equilateral triangular lattice, or a circular lattice, can be a very effective way to teach many geometric concepts (e.g., shapes, similarity, area, perimeter) and illustrate theorems (e.g., Pythagorean theorem, various area theorems, including Pick's theorem). They can be purchased in a variety of sizes (even transparent for projection), or easily made, and the stretched rubber-band figures provide an active (and fast) alternative to drawing polygons on dot graph paper. Numerous books and activity packets are available from the suppliers of geoboards. (C, CP, DE, S)

Tiles in a variety of polygon and puzzle shapes are available and can be used to demonstrate shapes, congruence, similarity, properties of symmetry, tilings of rectangles or of the plane (with copies of a single tile or with several different shapes), symmetric colorings of tilings by sets of tiles, and transformation of shapes having the same area. Excellent for use in problem solving and in understanding properties of dissections and tiling. Some varieties are transparent colored for use on the overhead projector. Readily available commercial sets of tiles are: Tangrams, SuperTangrams, Pentominoes, Pattern Blocks, Wheeler's Design Tiles. There are many activity books available for use with these sets of tiles. (AR, C, CP, DE, S)

Plastic models, both clear and colored, of plane figures and of various geometric solids (polyhedra, prisms, cones, spheres and hemispheres, cylinders) are designed to demonstrate a variety of properties and relationships. Some show cross-sections; some show axes, altitudes, or diagonals; some are designed to be filled with liquid or sand to demonstrate volume; some have hinged faces to open out flat and demonstrate surface area; some contain inscribed solids (configuration of Archimedes, Dandelin's cone, dual polyhedra); some dissect into two or more pieces (cones, spheres, liter block). (DE, Ga, Ge, L)

Slated models of sphere and cone can be marked with chalk. (Ge)

Wood models of geometric solids (polyhedra, prisms, sphere, cone, ellipsoid) are beautiful to see and handle. (C, CP, DE, S)

Adjustable models of plane figures demonstrate properties and theorems: triangles, quadrilaterals, parallels with transversal; adjustable figures (angles, chords, tangents, triangles, quadrilaterals) inscribed in a circle; adjustable cevians in a triangle (medians, angle bisectors, altitudes). All have built-in protractors to demonstrate angle relationships. (Ge)

Formula and theorem demonstrators give visual "proof" of facts: the Pythagorean theorem; determining pi; binomial and trinomial squares and cubes; area of a trapezoid. (Ge, L)

Displays

Attractive displays in classrooms, hallways, or display cases can catch student's attention and generate interest and curiosity. Students should be encouraged to create display material, through original posters, photographs, designs and models, or to find it in advertisements or art prints. Several excellent display items are also available from distributors.

Brandes, Louis Grant. Introduction to Optical Illusions. Portland, Me.: J. Weston Walch.

Thirty-two posters, 8-1/2 x 11 inches in size, illustrate seven major types of optical illusions, from simple to complex, and build awareness of symmetry and visual representation.

Geometry Posters. (CP)

Excellent poster sets for displaying uses of geometry and geometry facts. Five "Circles" posters; Six "String Art" posters (Peter Catranides); Eight "Math in Architecture" posters; Three "Tessellation" posters (J. Teeters); Twelve "Earthshapes" posters (Joseph N. Portney).

Kirk, James. Environmental Geometry. (AR)

Sixteen photographs of "patterns of geometry" in nature and the environment.

Leapfrog Posters. Distributed by Tarquin.

Colorful posters show the beauty of geometric design: Islamic designs, circle packings, fractals, maze, spiral tiling, great dodecahedron, spiral squares, diagonals of 23- and 24-gons.

Lowell, Stephen S. Optical Illusions in Life. Portland, Maine: J. Weston Walch.

Eighteen posters, 11 x 14 inches in size, show in photos and drawings the optical illusions that occur in nature, art, architecture, design.

Math Around Us. (CP)

Six sets of colorful posters illustrate geometry in art and nature: seashells, butterflies, patterns in nature, quilt patterns, stained glass tessellations, gems and minerals. Some have accompanying books.

National Council of Teachers of Mathematics. 1984. Calendars for the Calculating. Reston, Va.: National Council of Teachers of Mathematics.

Nine calendars, one for each school month, with date (but not day) can be used each year — there is a problem, puzzle, or historical note for each day. Many of the problems are geometric.

Polyhedra poster. Stradbroke, Diss, England: Tarquin.

Nineteen different polyhedra in color; 84 x 60 cm poster can be cut into four strips 21 x 60 cm and displayed as a frieze .

Schadler, Reuben. Geometry Problems: One Step Beyond. (DS)

Twenty-four "problem of the week" challenges for high-school geometry, together with problem book (75 reproducible problems) and solutions. These are "think" problems, rather than the usual drill.

Wenninger, Magnus J., and Dale G. Seymour. Polyhedra Posters. (DS)

Two large posters colorfully depict the Platonic and Archimedean solids as well as many compounds.

Model-Making Kits

Geometry in our world is more three-dimensional than two, and students enjoy the construction and exploration of three-dimensional shapes. After completing basic straightedge and compass constructions, the construction of regular polygons leads naturally to the construction of polyhedra, either from individual polygons or from connected nets of polygons. Bristol board is best for these constructions.

Directions for construction of an extraordinary variety of polyhedra can be found in books listed in the bibliography (under "Polygons and Polyhedra" and "Activities and Worksheets"). There is also a large selection of model kits available from which models can be built out of card stock, from plastic, from rods, and from wood.

Baracs, Janos. Poly-Kit. Quebec, Canada: Modulo Éditeur.

Sixty sheets of cardboard with 20 figures per sheet die-cut. After bending the scored tabs, a wide variety of polyhedra can be assembled; all Platonic, Archimedean, several duals, some space-filling solids, and numerous others with regular polygon faces or rhombic faces. Rubber bands in notched tabs join faces; easy assembly and disassembly of the polyhedra encourages exploration. Instruction booklet with accurate drawings of the polyhedra—for each, several orthogonal projections and a Schlegel diagram.

D-Stix. Spokane, Wash.: Geodestix.

Plastic rods (color-coded for length) and multipronged plastic connectors make building various "frame" models easy.

Gamepuzzles. Pasadena, Md.: Kadon Enterprises.

A challenging collection of geometric games and puzzles. Includes blocks of pentominoes (five joined squares, called "quints") and hexominoes (six joined squares) and pentacubes (five joined cubes, called "superquints"), as well as other unusual cutout puzzle pieces which tile in numerous ways.

Jenkins, Gerald, and Magdalen Bear. 1986. Tarquin Polyhedra. 3 vols. Stradbroke, Diss, England: Tarquin.

Three separate models to cut and assemble: 1. The sixth stellation of the icosahedron, 2. The compound of five cubes, 3. The final stellation of the icosahedron.

———. 1986. The Tarquin Globe. Stradbroke, Diss, England: Tarquin.

A cut and assemble polyhedral globe, with trapezoidal facets. Folds are at 30-degree intervals of both latitude and longitude. Good for exploring geometry of the globe; includes minibook, stand, and suggested activities.

Jenkins, Gerald, and A. Wild. 1985. Make Shapes—Mathematical Models. 3 vols. Stradbroke, Diss, England: Tarquin. (DS).

Contain nets of various models, ready to score, cut, and assemble. Models can also be decorated. Book 1 has 19 models, book 2 has 8 larger and more intricate models, and book 3 has 3 large models.

———. The Mathematical Curiosities Series. 1985, 1986. 3 vols. Stradbroke, Diss, England: Tarquin. (DS).

Nets of models ready to score, cut, and assemble. Each book contains nine models, each with a descriptive card about the model; the cards become a minibook for the assembled models. Models have curious properties—some rotate, some twist or unfold, some fit together in strange ways.

Minimath projects: string design kits, polyhedron kits. Chicago, Ill.: Minimath Projects.

String design kits include numbered cards, directions, needle and thread. Circle, hexagon, and square designs of various sizes. Polyhedron kits contain nets of models on colored cards and directions. Platonic solids, plus three stellated solids.

Orbit material. (S)

Color-coded (for length) plastic straws are joined using pronged joints (some of which are rigid, others flexible) to create frame models of polyhedra.

Pedersen, Jean J., and Kent A. Pedersen. [1973] 1985. Geometric Playthings. Reprint. Los Angeles, Calif.: Price, Stern & Sloan.

Contains colored patterns of the eight deltahedra to cut out, score, and assemble.

Polydrons. St. Louis, Mo.: Polydron USA. (C)

Extremely sturdy plastic polygons with snap-together hinges. Using the equilateral triangles, squares and pentagons, many polyhedra can be built.

Rhombics. "Rhomblocks" and other wooden blocks and puzzles. Watertown, Mass.: Rhombics.

Beautiful wooden blocks that are a dissection of the rhombic dodecahedron can be combined to form many structures and packings. Also available are magnetized blocks and wooden puzzles, including the Soma cube. Teacher booklet, "Rhomblocks: Geometric Blocks for Discovery," includes patterns for the various polyhedral blocks to be made from paper and suggestions for activities.

Schattschneider, Doris W., and Wallace Walker. 1977. *M. C. Escher Kaleidocycles.*. New York: Ballantine. Reprint. 1982. Stradbroke, Diss, England: Tarquin. Reprint. 1987. Corte Madera, Calif.: Pomegranate Artbooks. (DS).

Seventeen colorful models decorated with designs by M. C. Escher, ready to score, cut, and assemble. Accompanied by a monograph describing the models and how geometry of several kinds was used in creating them. Twelve of the models (called *kaleidocycles*) are tight linkages of tetrahedra in a loop, which turn through the center hole; designs on the models continue to match while the models are rotated into new positions.

Smart, Margaret A., and Mary Laycock. Create a Cube. (AR)

A book of patterns and instructions for filling a cube 24 different ways. Reproducible activity pages; includes exercises, teacher suggestions, bibliography.

Smith, A. G. 1986. *Cut and Assemble 3-D Geometrical Shapes*. New York: Dover.

> Ten models in color to cut and assemble: the 5 Platonic solids, inter-penetrating tetrahedra and cubes, two stellations of the dodecahedron and trapezohedron.

Symmetrics Model Kits. Atkinson, N.H.: Symmetrics.

> These polystyrene model kits are the most accurate and durable available. Kits for all of the Platonic solids, many Archimedean solids, some compounds and several stellated solids. Precision-cast, the faces can be glued accurately and the models used to demonstrate basic properties of polyhedra, including duality and stellation. The plastic faces can be marked with water-base ink and wiped clean.

Visual Aids Requiring Projection

Overhead transparencies, slides, filmstrips, films and videotapes can all enrich the visual understanding of geometric concepts. Films are not listed here (see Chapter 20, Films/Videotapes). More than 60 films that touch on a wide variety of geometric topics are listed in Schneider (1980). Teachers and students can benefit from class projects that produce over-head transparencies or slides or even videotapes illustrating geometric ideas. We list several commercially-available items.

Overhead Projector Transparencies

Analytic Geometry; Conics. (Ga)

> Eleven transparencies review analytic geometry concepts; twelve transparencies on conics contain lessons and have accompanying questions; some transparencies have overlays.

Geometry. United Transparencies. (Educational Audio Visual)

> A set of 44 transparencies, each of which is a static film for the overhead projector, presenting the main concepts and diagrams for a course in plane geometry. Includes model proofs.

Slides and Filmstrips

Cabisco Mathematics. Seeing Geometry. Burlington, N.C.: Carolina Biological Supply.

> Color filmstrip with narrative cassette that examines ways in which geometric objects occur in the creations of nature and of humans.

Concepts of Geometry. (Ga)

Thirty filmstrips and cassettes, nine worksheets; self-instruction. Topics: The Protractor, Geometric Constructions, Basic Figures of Geometry, Concepts of Perimeter/Area, Concepts of Volume.

Fundamentals of Geometry (Series I & II). 1977. New York: Harper & Row Media.

Each module consists of a collection of slides or a filmstrip, teacher's guide, library kit and worksheet. Series I has five modules: Points, Lines and Planes; Angles; Triangles; Polygons; Area and Volume. Series II has four geometry modules: Similarities and Proportions; Circles; Constructions; Analytic Geometry.

Geometry. 1977. (Ga)

Set of 40 filmstrips and cassettes contain lessons that are step-by-step development of a topic, followed by practice problems. Topics: Basics, Parallel Lines, Similar Polygons, Congruent Triangles, The Right Triangle, The Circle, Quadrilaterals, Area and Volume.

Geometry 500. 1969. New York: Harcourt Brace Jovanovich.

Eight carousel trays of color slides that can be projected on the blackboard and used for illustration, for teaching relationships and theorems. Teacher's handbook and pictorial index of all slides. Topics: Assumptions, Induction and Deduction, Logic and Proof, Congruent Triangles, Parallels and Coordinates, Parallelograms and Inequalities, Circles and Spheres, Locus, Similar Polygons, Pythagorean Theorem, Polygons and Area, Trigonometry, Area and Volume.

Geometry in our World. 1986. Reston, Va.: National Council of Teachers of Mathematics.

A series of slides, with instructional guide, which illustrates geometry in natural and man-made environment. A selection by NCTM's Educational Materials Committee from slides submitted by teachers and others.

Metropolitan Museum of Art. 1979. The Mathematics of Islamic Art. Reston, Va.: National Council of Teachers of Mathematics.

Packet of 20 color slides from the MMA collection of Islamic art, together with transparency, illustrates how the intricate geometric designs which are the hallmark of Islamic art are based on straightedge and compass construction. An excellent unit to illustrate the use of geometry to create art.

Plane Geometry. Chicago, Ill.: Eye Gate Media.

Nine captioned filmstrips deal with elementary concepts in plane geometry. Provision for student discussion; also, review frames. Topics: Introduction and Angle Definitions, Triangles, The Polygon Family (Quadrilaterals), Circles and Tangents, Sets and Reasoning, Locus, Area, Coordinate Geometry I: Introduction, Coordinate Geometry II: Slope.

Videotapes

Bronowski, Jacob. 1974. The Music of the Spheres. The Ascent of Man Series. New York: Time-Life Multimedia.

Color videotape (or 16mm film) in which Bronowski shows some of the great geometric achievements in history—how people tried to understand nature through geometry and used geometry to achieve some monumental works of art and architecture. 52 min.

COMAP. 1987. Mathematics of Size, Shape and Growth. For All Practical Purposes Series. Wilmette, Ill.: Annenberg/CPB Collection.

Five half-hour videotapes, each accompanied by a study guide and together accompanied a textbook entitled *For All Practical Purposes*, edited by L. A. Steen (New York: W. H. Freeman, 1988). Designed as part of a television course on PBS, these modules may be used individually to supplement geometry courses. Titles of the videotapes: Size, Shape and Growth Overview; The Size of Things; Measuring Without a Telescope; Measuring With a Telescope; Linear and Exponential Growth.

Landscape of Geometry. Dallas, Tex.: TV Ontario.

A series of eight 15-minute videotapes (plus teacher's guide/student workbook) illustrating applications of geometry at the junior-high level. Hosted by David Stringer, programs combine animation with live action to show transformation geometry in everyday use. Titles: The Shape of Things; It's Rude to Point; Lines that Cross; Lines that Don't Cross; Up, Down, Sideways; Trussworthy; Cracking Up; The Range of Change.

The Shape of Things. 1985. NOVA series. New York: Time-Life.

Marvelous photography that shows the recurrence of a few basic geometric forms in nature. Polygon, sphere, spiral, fractal, meander—all are shown in various manifestations. What is missing in this 60-minute film is any real attempt to explain the geometry and the possible reasons for their occurrence.

Microcomputer Materials

Computers can be used as an exciting and active investigative tool in learning geometry. The desire to produce wonderful graphics motivates students to learn the necessary rudiments of graphing, of transformations, and of the geometric constraints of the programming language or machine they use. The Logo language is especially suited to elementary geometric investigations. The literature on computer graphics and on problem solving with computers is large (and growing exponentially); we have listed just a few "classics."

There are many commercial graphics software packages available (their titles usually contain one of the words "draw," "paint," "design," or "graph"); these can be used successfully for demonstration and investigation if the teacher takes the time to learn the capabilities of the program and then provides appropriate problems to be solved. Most educational software developers have concentrated their energies on producing "courseware," a new name for the computerized version of the (deservedly) defunct "teaching machine" of more than twenty years ago. The student is patiently (and relentlessly) guided (prodded) through presentation of a topic, drill exercises, and tests, until "mastery" is achieved. Few students will be "turned on" by these programs.

A few developers of software have chosen to produce programs that exploit the speed and (relative) accuracy of the computer (especially with regard to graphics) to minimize the drudgery of checking numerous cases of a geometric construction or conjecture. These programs quickly "construct" desired figures and encourage exploration and testing of conjectures. Armed with a wide variety of figures that point to the truth of a general statement, the investigator can then attempt to provide a proof. As both hardware and software for microcomputers increase in sophistication, more of this kind of program, whose aim is computer-aided investigation, rather than drill, should be forthcoming, for both two- and three-dimensional Euclidean, as well as non-Euclidean geometry.

Baskin, B., E. Friedland, F.J. Napolitano, A. Piekut, R. Piekut, and D.R. Thomas. BEST Instructional Module: Geometry. Stony Brook, N.Y.: Krell Software.

> Elementary tutorial on nine areas of geometry: introduction, points and lines, angles, triangles, polygons, circles, solid figures, symmetry (reflection only), UFO quiz. Apple II.

Chap, A., and D. Sidewater. Scott Foresman Geometry Courseware. Glenview, Ill.: Scott, Foresman (developed by Computer Age Education.)

> Eight packages, each consisting of a program diskette, teacher's guide, student worksheets, record forms, and teaching suggestions (key to use with all major geometry texts). Programs are tutorials and drills. Eight titles: Angles of Triangles and Polygons; Congruent Triangles; More on Congruent Triangles; Quadrilaterals; Parallel Lines; Similarity; The Pythagorean Theorem; Circles— Angles, Arcs and Segments.

Dylan, Jason A. Geometry Alive! Freeport, N.Y.: Educational Activities.

> Three disks, each providing definitions and practice exercises; management system. Topics: Geometry Fundamentals, Areas of Triangles, Quadrilaterals and Circles. Apple II 48K.

Finzer, W.F., J.E. Gutierrez, and D. Resek. 1984. Math Worlds: Exploring Mathematics with Computers. Austin, Tex.: Sterling Swift.

Two units of this seven-unit interactive program utilize a program called "Turtleworks," in which students can experiment with polygons and angles and explore symmetry. Apple 32K, Pet 16K, IBM 128K, Acorn 32K, Commodore 64.

Geoboard Geometry and Measurement. (C).

Replaces a "real" geoboard and rubberbands with a display of a geoboard on which students can "draw" the figures and answer questions. The real thing is more fun and doesn't require directions from a computer!

Geometric Constructions. Port Chester, N.Y.: Microcomputer Workshops.

Practice the six basic constructions on a screen using "compass and straightedge." Why any student should do this on a computer rather than use the actual instruments and a piece of paper is inexplicable. Apple II + 48K.

Geometry. Bloomington, Minn.: Control Data.

Fifteen modules cover all topics in basic high-school geometry course. Tutorial practice and review, divided into 45 lessons. Instructional disks and instructor's guide. Apple II +, IIe, IBM-PC.

Geometry Concepts. Ventura.

Tutorial to teach terms, concepts and formulas in geometry. Includes a figure-recognition game, data-retrieval option, quiz utility and construction demonstration utility. Teacher's notes. Apple 48K.

Geometry I: Planely Simple. MicroLearn, division of MicroLab.

Tutorial program for elementary concepts: lines, angles, triangles, quadrilaterals, polygons, measurement. Apple II 48K, IBM-PC/PCjr, Commodore 64K.

Geometry III: Introductory Concepts and Proofs. MicroLearn, division of MicroLab.

Tutorial uses algebraic problem-solving techniques. IBM-PC.

Geometry Series. 4 disks. Educational Courseware.

Provides explanations, with graphics, practice examples and cumulative tests to help students master geometry skills. Titles: Elements of Geometry, Angles and Intersecting Lines; Parallel Lines and Triangles; Polygons, Congruent Triangles, Area/Perimeter; Ratios and Right Triangles. User's manual and worksheets. Disks may be purchased individually. Apple 48K.

Geometry with Logo. San Jose, Calif.: Metier.

Practice and demonstration problems using trigonometric functions. IBM-PC.

Houghton Mifflin Geometry. Computer activities and microcomputer diskette. Boston, Mass.: Houghton Mifflin.

Courseware to supplement text. Duplicating masters, diskette. Tutorial, plus students learn to write and modify programs. Apple II, IBM-PC, TRS-80 Model II or IV.

Kimberling, Clark. Euclid. Evansville, Ind.: University of Evansville Press.

A geometry program which, in single strokes, performs all Euclidean constructions as well as produces (with easy instruction) polygons, circumcircles, incircles, excircles, and conic sections which "fit" given data. Several figures can be drawn on the screen and points of intersection computed. A powerful aid in demonstration and exploration of Euclidean geometry. Manual. IBM-PC 256K (DOS 2.1 graphics adapter).

Logic Workout. Novato, Calif.: Avant-Garde.

Presents nine basic proof patterns in geometry as well as the concept of congruence. Exercises. Apple 48K, Commodore 64.

Merrill Geometry. Microcomputer supplement. Columbus, O.: Charles E. Merrill.

Interactive disc for skill practice, review and reinforcement. Apple II+, IIe, IIc.

Miller, John. Descartes' Delight. Stony Brook, N.Y.: Krell Software.

Interactive; explores the world of graphs and teaches user to write programs in special language. For use in analytic geometry. Apple 48K.

PLATO Geometry. Bloomington, Minn.: Control Data.

Fifteen modules, each with a disk and instructional guide, covers a complete geometry course. Can be used individually or as a complete series for supplemental or remedial instruction. IBM-PC, Apple II+.

Practical Geometry Series. Bridgeport, Conn.: Intellectual Software.

Six disks, each with management system, with tutorials and drills on topics in geometry. Titles of disks: Lines and Angles; Triangles; Circles; Quadrilaterals, Polygons and Solid Geometry; Theorems and Proofs of Theorems. Apple II 48K.

Proofs and Properties: A First Step into Plane Geometry. Micro Power & Light.

Simple properties (Euclid's common notions), recognition of geometric shapes, scrambled proofs to put in correct order. Apple II 32K with Applesoft.

Pythagorean Proofs. Micro Power & Light.

Proofs of the Pythagorean Theorem by Legendre, Bézout, Garfield, Euclid, Pythagoras, and ancient Chinese. Includes history of each proof, display of construction, and rationale for each proof. Apple II 48K.

Schwartz, Judah, and Michal Yerushalmy. The Geometric Presupposer. Pleasantville, N.Y.: Sunburst Communications.

Interactive software designed for elementary and middle school students to familiarize them with basic geometric concepts and constructions: properties of geometric shapes, elements and the relationships between them. Teacher guide. Apple II + 64K, IIe, IIc.

———. 1985. The Geometric Supposer. Pleasantville, N.Y.: Sunburst Communications.

Interactive microcomputer software allows students to test geometric hypotheses by quickly testing several cases. Two disks: Triangles and Quadrilaterals. On each, user may "construct" a triangle (quadrilateral) using given properties, or request a randomly chosen triangle. On the figure, additional constructions (medians, midpoints, angle bisectors, etc.) can be made, and from the figure, the student may hypothesize or verify a conjecture. Fine use of the computer for investigation! Teacher guide; training videotape. Apple II + 64K, IIe, IIc.

Sensei Geometry. 1986. San Rafael, Calif.: Broderbund Software.

Two disks cover the classic curriculum; includes over 350 problems and extensive practice with proofs. Interactive animation gives many examples to "test" a theorem before proving it.

Symmetry. Albion.

Program allows students to create patterns with reflection or rotation symmetry. Apple II 48K.

Thompson, Patrick W. Motions (A Microworld for Transformation Geometry). West Lafayette, Ind.: Cosine.

A "microworld" environment to investigate isometries on a microcomputer. Uses Logo: includes comprehensive workbook and set of transparency masters. Provides over 100 problems (some with solutions) that actively involve the student. Topics: Get Acquainted, Investigations, Combining Motions, Symmetries of Plane Figures, General Motions.

8. Instruction in Precalculus

PETER J. HILTON

It is common ground that students are today not well prepared for core college calculus courses. Some argue that this provides an additional reason for putting the emphasis, at the precollege level, on courses in discrete mathematics, reinforcing the argument based on the view that this, in any case, is now the most important and most applicable part of mathematics.

I will not discuss this latter view here (but see Ralston and Young (1983), Hilton (1984)). However, in considering the proper nature of precalculus instruction, I will put forward two related propositions which, if accepted, invalidate the argument that we can circumvent the problem of imperfect articulation between secondary and college mathematics by concentrating on discrete mathematics; I can only hope that the reader does not take the view that my championing these propositions also invalidates my right to speak at all on the topic of this essay.

First, then, I claim that

- *the learning of calculus imposes no particular prerequisites on the precalculus curriculum*;

and, second, I claim that, in devising a coherent secondary mathematics curriculum,

- *no great distinction needs to be made between the student contemplating a college calculus course and other students.*

I take it to be obvious that these propositions do imply that we cannot escape from our present difficulties merely by dethroning the calculus. But are the propositions themselves correct? I believe they are, since they derive from the nature of mathematics itself. Mathematics is a system of thought, incorporating but transcending a well-adapted language. It is not a set of skills, though its practice requires skill. It is not a set of separate disciplines, but a single unity comprising many interrelated areas of study. Thus what matters is that a student learn to think mathematically and *any* significant part of mathematics can be used as the vehicle to convey the necessary understanding and thinking ability. Conversely, no part of mathematics, however seemingly appropriate, can prepare the student really to understand the calculus, *if it is taught simply as a set of isolated skills to be retained by the exercise of undiscriminating memory.* This style of instruction — and learning — can continue to give the illusion of success through the first two college years. Then comes the student's cruel awakening to the realization that no real mathematics has yet been learned and, therefore, none can be used. It is usually too late then to change; and the student may well become embittered.

I would happily undertake to teach the calculus to any student who understood the mathematics of the rational number system and had some geometric intuition, whether or not that student had great familiarity with algebraic manipulations. A student who had received a genuine *education* in mathematics would have many advantages over the student who had merely received a technical training; not the least of these advantages would be the blessed gift of "knowing what one does not know" — a key to good education.

This is my most important point, and I am grateful for this opportunity to make it. But, having made it, I do now owe it to the reader to discuss what choices I would, in fact, make if I had the assurance that genuine mathematical education was taking place at the secondary level and would take place in the subsequent college calculus course, too. Clearly the following are desirable ingredients of a precalculus course. (For an appropriate textbook, see Hilton and Pedersen (198x)).

An appropriate role for applications. The student should be convinced not only of the power of mathematics to solve problems but also of its usefulness. Thus genuine applications, *of interest to the student at the student's level of development,* should feature in a well-designed precalculus course. The precise role of applications is a topic in itself within the general purview of a discussion on precollege mathematics instruction, so we will go no deeper into this important issue here beyond remarking that it is unnecessary, and perhaps even undesirable, that all the real-world problems considered during a course should be capable of being solved with the help of the mathematical tools at the student's disposal.

We now turn to questions of mathematical content.

Algebra

There should be an ability to execute significant algebraic manipulations and to understand their significance. There should be a familiarity with the behavior of quadratic polynomials in one variable (not merely with a formula for solving a quadratic equation); this should include the properties of parabolas and facts about the maximum or minimum of a quadratic polynomial.

Functions

There should be familiarity with the qualitative features of the graphical representation of a function of one variable, and with functions as mathematical objects of study to which mathematical operations may be applied. It is very important that the concept of equality of functions should be understood and not confused with the notion of equations. The exponential function and natural logarithm should be understood, in their own right and as inverse functions; and the trigonometric functions (especially sine and cosine) should be regarded as functions of a real variable. An intuitive notion of continuity should have been presented and studied in simple special cases; in fact, the intuitive notion of continuity is far more easily grasped for functions from two variables to two variables than for functions from one variable to one variable.

Geometry

I do not recommend axiomatics, nor, indeed, a heavy dose of Euclidean geometry as currently administered. But students should be able to think geometrically (in two and three dimensions) and should know how to prove geometrical statements both synthetically and analytically. Of supreme importance are the concept of similarity of geometrical figures and the analytical geometry of straight lines and circles in the plane. The role of algebra in answering genuinely geometrical questions should be clear to our students — to be distinguished from the current role of coordinate geometry as a thin excuse for doing some dull algebra.

The Real Number System

Of outstanding importance to the precalculus student is the understanding of the real number system with its several structures. First must come the rational number system (the minimal requirement for any such student, as already mentioned), both as an algebraic system and as a topological space with its standard topology. Thus, of course, the continuity of the algebraic operations should be understood and appreciated. The order relation should also be explicitly recognized, along with its relation to the other structures in the rationals. It is critical here that, in passing from the integers to the rationals one not only changes the algebraic properties but also the nature of the order relation. The inadequacy (more technically, the incompleteness) of the rationals should be demonstrated geometrically and the rationals should be completed to the reals, probably by means of infinite decimals. This would require an intuitive understanding of limits of sequences, especially in order to present the operations of addition and multiplication on the reals.

The term "real" used in describing the real numbers is quite ludicrous and the confusion is compounded by using the terms "imaginary" and "complex" in connection with the extension of the reals to the field of complex numbers. Real numbers are obviously a figment, albeit a sublime figment, of the human imagination. They are thus just as imaginary as the imaginary numbers; indeed, the properties of the reals are in many respects more complex than those of the complex numbers. (A function of a complex variable, differentiable in a domain, is analytic there – no such simple, beautiful situation obtains in the reals.)

It is very important to demystify the nature of real numbers – and, preferably, also complex numbers – before the student embarks on the calculus. Of course, this demystification will have a geometrical flavor; but an additional, and crucial, element is imported into the process through the hand-calculator and the computer. First, it must be understood that "calculator arithmetic" is not the same as "human arithmetic." We humans talk of the *field* of real numbers; irrational numbers have no real-world existence but, when adjoined to the rational numbers, they produce a number system with beautiful properties. The machine rejects irrational numbers; but the arithmetic of its simplified number system has many awkward and ugly features. Our students must understand the role of the computer in mathematics and, in particular, the trade-off involved in passing between the world of the mind and the world of the machine.

Finally, I would make a plea for presenting to all students at the secondary level a clear, if intuitive, notion of *rate of change*. It must be understood that change, or flux, is the natural state of the universe, and that the principal role of mathematics in the real world is to model that state of flux, just as the principal role of science is to explain, anticipate and ultimately influence that flux. At this elementary level, a presentation of these crucial ideas might well begin with a discussion of the meaning of "average speed." Our everyday language (say English) suggests that we only understand "average speed" if we understand the words "average" (in its adjectival sense) and "speed." In fact, this is quite wrong—the notion of "average speed," meaning "total distance traveled divided by total time taken," is much easier to comprehend than either of the notions "average" or "speed." Indeed, it is illuminating to present "average speed" both as a special case and as an extension of the usual notion of "average"; and then to present "speed" as a limiting case of "average speed."

Certainly one is led inevitably to consider the function concept here in a more profound light. The true meaning of a *variable* is elucidated; and the distinction between a genuine variable and the x's and y's of elementary algebra becomes apparent. For the latter are, almost always, merely numbers which cannot yet be specified or which do not need to be specified. They are rarely genuinely variable.

I rest my case. Above all, we must teach our students to think, qualitatively and quantitatively, if they are to be able to reason within mathematics, to understand it, and, hence, to *do* it. We have no need of human robots today!

REFERENCES

Hilton, Peter. 1984. Review of Ralston and Young (1983). *American Mathematical Monthly* 91 (7) (August-September 1984): 452-455.

————, and Jean Pedersen. 198x. *Bridging the Gap*. Reading, Mass.: Addison-Wesley.

Ralston, Anthony, and Gail S. Young, eds. 1983. *The Future of College Mathematics*. New York: Springer-Verlag.

BIBLIOGRAPHY

STEPHEN F. WEST

Sources are listed under the categories

- Precalculus,
- Algebra, Geometry, and Trigonometry.

Precalculus

Bailey, Donald F. 1971. *Prerequisites for Calculus*. Tarrytown, N.Y.: Bogden & Quigley.

> Represents a textbook for students lacking the manipulative skills for calculus. Mathematical topics include sets, numbers, exponents, relations, functions and graphs. One chapter contains a non-standard presentation of trigonometric functions.

Barbasso, Salvatore, and John Impagliazzo. 1977. *Precalculus, A Functional Approach with Applications*. New York: Harcourt Brace Jovanovich.

> Can be used by students in a non-calculus, applications oriented field of study. Textual material is a good blend of theory and application. Chapters contain numerous problems as well as calculator exercises.

Barnett, Raymond A. 1985. *Functions and Graphs: A Precalculus Course*. New York: McGraw-Hill.

> Represents an extremely readable precalculus text which emphasizes functions and graphs. Chapters contain over 4000 exercises including calculator applications. Related texts by the same author include *College Algebra*, 3rd ed., *College Algebra and Trigonometry*, 3rd ed., and *College Algebra and Trigonometry with Analytic Geometry*.

Connelly, James F., and Robert A. Fratangelo. 1975. *Precalculus Mathematics, A Functional Approach*. New York: Macmillan.

> Presents a unified discussion of algebra, trigonometry, and analytic geometry with the concept of function as the central theme.

Costello, John J., Spenser O. Gowdy, and Agnes M. Rash. 1981. *Finite Mathematics with Applications*. New York: Harcourt Brace Jovanovich.

> Presents the noncalculus aspects of mathematical modeling. Topics include functions and graphs, vectors, matrices, linear programming, probability and statistics.

Dolciani, Mary P., E. F. Beckenbach, A. J. Donnelly, R. C. Jurgensen, and W. Wooton. 1964. *Modern Introductory Analysis.* Boston, Mass.: Houghton Mifflin.

> Represents an older but well-written textbook in an integrated format. Chapters contain numerous graded exercises, reading lists, and historical biographies. Mathematical topics include vectors, matrices, probability, and solid geometry, in addition to the standard precalculus topics.

Elich, J., and C. J. Elich. 1982. *Precalculus with Calculator Applications.* Menlo Park, Calif.: Addison-Wesley.

> Contains the standard precalculus topics with a large number of calculator activities integrated throughout. An appendix includes a detailed treatment of computation with approximate numbers.

Fisher, Robert C., and Allen D. Ziebur. 1982. *Integrated Algebra, Trigonometry and Analytic Geometry.* Englewood Cliffs, N.J.: Prentice-Hall.

> Represents a highly-successful precalculus text that makes extensive use of the hand-held calculator. Mathematical topics are standard precalculus topics plus chapters on theory of equations, geometric trigonometry, and analytic geometry.

Flanders, Harley. 1972. Analysis of calculus problems. *Mathematics Teacher* 65 (1) (January 1972): 9-12.

> Suggests a method for selecting topics and placing emphasis in courses for precalculus mathematics students.

Fleenor, Charles R., Merrill E. Shanks, and Charles F. Brumfiel. 1968. *The Elementary Functions.* Menlo Park, Calif.: Addison-Wesley.

> Discusses those functions that are differentiated and integrated in calculus. Special attention is paid to analytic geometry and graphing.

Forbes, M. P. 1973. *Elementary Functions: Backdrop for the Calculus.* New York: Macmillan.

> Uses a function oriented approach to the standard precalculus topics. A "things to think about" section at the end of each chapter provides motivation for further study.

Gade, Edward, III, and John Oman. 1984. *Math-Graph.* New York: Macmillan.

> Contains a software package of fourteen programs for Apple II computers. Intended for any class where graphical representations of functions will enhance learning.

Hart, William L. 1971. *Preparation for Calculus.* Scranton, Pa.: Intext Educational Publishers.

> Contains the standard precalculus topics as well as a substantial review of elementary mathematics and a detailed treatment of conic sections and analytic geometry. This textbook should serve as a good sourcebook for problems.

Harvey, John G. 1978. Precalculus mathematics: A look through the big end of the telescope. *Mathematics Teacher* 71 (1) (January 1978): 22-28.

> Provides a look at the content and emphasis in current calculus courses. The article also provides a list of performance objectives for precalculus mathematics.

Horner, Donald R. 1969. *Pre-Calculus: Elementary Functions and Relations.* New York: Holt, Rinehart & Winston.

> Uses real valued functions as a unifying concept to develop the standard precalculus topics. Appendices deal with logic and the real number system. Chapters contain review exercises and quizzes.

Howes, V. E. 1967. *Pre-Calculus Mathematics, Functions and Relations.* New York: Wiley.

> Programmed textbook which can be used to review the elementary functions, essential for the study of calculus.

Iglewicz, Boris, and Judith Stoyle. 1973. *An Introduction to Mathematical Reasoning.* New York: Macmillan.

> Contains an introduction to logic, mathematical reasoning and methods of mathematical proof. Mathematical content is at a level accessible to the average high-school student.

Knight, Ronald A., and William E. Hoff. 1969. *Introduction to the Elementary Functions.* Belmont, Calif.: Dickenson.

> Contains a thorough discussion of the elementary functions necessary for the study of calculus. The last chapter contains an introduction to functions of two variables.

Kolman, Bernard, and Arnold Shapiro. 1984. *Precalculus: Functions and Graphs.* New York: Academic Press.

> Employs an informal function-oriented approach to precalculus mathematics, with an additional feature being numerous "warnings" pointing out incorrect practices commonly found in homework and exams.

Larson, Roland E., and Robert P. Hostetler. 1985. *Precalculus.* Lexington, Mass.: D.C. Heath.

Last in a series of four texts on precalculus mathematics; contains extensive calculator exercises with a special emphasis on the algebra of calculus.

Leithold, Louis. 1985. *Before Calculus: Functions, Graphs, and Analytic Geometry.* New York: Harper & Row.

Contains numerous examples and illustrations stressing both theoretical and computational aspects of the subject. Exercises are numerous, varied in scope, and contain many applications. Function is the unifying concept and mathematical topics range from equations and inequalities to series and sequences.

Lial, Margaret L., and Charles D. Miller. 1973. *Precalculus Mathematics.* Glenview, Ill.: Scott, Foresman.

Represents the standard precalculus topics and in addition, matrices, and combinatorics. This text is designed for the student who has only one introductory algebra course.

Lockwood, Edward H. 1961. *A Book of Curves.* London, England: Cambridge University Press.

Contains descriptions of plane curves, conic sections, and spirals. Appropriate for honors students in secondary school and undergraduate school.

Lorch, Edgar R. 1973. *Precalculus: Fundamentals of Mathematical Analysis.* New York: Norton.

Contains mathematically-precise and often rigorous presentations of the standard precalculus topics. Chapters contain a large number of exercises with many non-traditional applications.

Maurer, Stephen B. 1974. Functional equations in secondary mathematics. *Mathematics Teacher* 67 (4) (April 1974): 293-298.

Presents a different look at functions via functional equations and demonstrates a method for integrating seemingly-unrelated topics.

Meserve, Bruce E., A. J. Pettofrezzo, and D. T. Meserve. 1970. *Principles of Advanced Mathematics.* New York: Random House.

Contains many useful precalculus topics and can be used as a reference source for teachers in both secondary schools and two-year colleges. Numerous graded exercises, self tests and chapter tests are provided. Mathematical topics include sets, probability, number systems, circular functions, special functions, sequences, series, vectors, and matrices.

Munem, Mustafa A., and James P. Yizze. 1984. *Precalculus: Functions and Graphs*, 4th ed. New York: Worth.

Presents clear and accessible development of vectors and theory of equations in addition to the standard precalculus topics. Each chapter provides a large number of exercises and applications.

Niven, Ivan M. 1961. *Numbers: Rational and Irrational.* New Mathematical Library no. 1. New York: L. W. Singer. Available through Mathematical Association of America.

> Represents a detailed development of the real number system presented at a level of understanding accessible to high-school students and laymen.

Payne, Michael N. 1977. *Pre-Calculus Mathematics.* Philadelphia, Pa.: W. B. Saunders.

> Contains standard precalculus topics in student-oriented format. Many examples which stress geometrical and physical intuition are integrated throughout the text.

Pownall, Malcolm W. 1983. *Functions and Graphs: Calculus Preparatory Mathematics.* Englewood Cliffs, N.J.: Prentice-Hall.

> Contains the standard precalculus topics in addition to sections on limits, continuity, extrema, and a detailed exposition on the composition of functions.

Saunders, Hal. 1980. "When are we ever gonna have to use this?" *Mathematics Teacher* 73 (1) (January 1980): 7-16.

> Represents the author's response to students' questions regarding the relevance of mathematics. Tables provide a source for applications of precalculus mathematics.

School Mathematics Study Group. 1960. *Elementary Functions.* New Haven, Conn.: Yale University Press.

> Represents the recommendations of the commission on mathematics of CEEB. The central theme is the study of functions and is intended as a one-semester course for grade 12. Chapters contain a large number of problems.

Sobel, Max A., and Norbert Lerner. 1983. *Algebra and Trigonometry: A Pre-Calculus Approach.* 2nd ed. Englewood Cliffs, N.J.: Prentice-Hall.

> Skills oriented text that provides an extensive review of the fundamentals of algebra; strong emphasis on graphing.

Stockton, Doris S. 1978. *Essential Precalculus.* Boston, Mass.: Houghton Mifflin.

> Represents the third in a series of precalculus mathematics texts (others being *Essential Algebra*, and *Essential Algebra and Trigonometry*.) An emphasis is placed on manipulations in a review of algebra and an introduction to elementary functions.

Swartz, Clifford E. 1973. *Used Math for the First Two Years of College Science.* Englewood Cliffs, N.J.: Prentice-Hall.

Assumes exposure to most of precalculus mathematics and serves as a reference and a reminder to the usefulness of mathematics. Topics include simple functions of applied mathematics, dimensional analysis, geometry, vectors, complex numbers, systems of equations, and quadratic and higher-order equations.

Yaqub, A. 1975. *Elementary Functions*. Boston, Mass.: Houghton Mifflin.

Contains the standard precalculus topics as recommended by CUPM. Chapters contain a large number of illustrative examples and a good selection of graded exercises.

Yates, Robert C. 1974. *Curves and Their Properties*. Reston, Va.: National Council of Teachers of Mathematics.

Contains detailed descriptions of plane curves and conic sections and their properties.

Zlot, William L. 1985. On the importance of the function concept in mathematics. *New York State Mathematics Teachers' Journal* 35 (1): 16-20.

Presents examples of the application of functions for teaching the concept to juniors and seniors in high school.

Algebra, Geometry, and Trigonometry

Ayres, Frank Jr. 1954. *Theory and Problems of Plane and Spherical Trigonometry*. Schaum's Outline Series. New York: McGraw-Hill.

Contains 680 solved problems and more than 300 supplemental problems and answers. Textual material is minimized. Mathematical topics include circular functions, logarithmic/trigonometric solutions of triangles, identities, trigonometric equations, solid geometry and spherical trigonometry.

Bogart, Kenneth P. 1977. *The Functions of Algebra and Trigonometry*. Boston, Mass.: Houghton Mifflin.

Develops the properties of all the standard elementary functions for students with one year of elementary algebra and geometry. The initial chapter is a review of elementary algebra. Other chapters contain sections on linear programming, rational functions, sequences, series, progressions, and permutations and combinations.

Ellis, Robert, and Denny Gulick. 1984. *Fundamentals of College Algebra and Trigonometry*. New York: Harcourt Brace Jovanovich.

Covers the standard algebra and trigonometric topics using geometric explanations and motivation where appropriate. Each chapter begins with an application indicating the relevance of the topic. Calculator exercises are included.

Foerster, Paul A. 1977. *Trigonometry: Functions and Applications.* Menlo Park, Calif.: Addison-Wesley.

Contains both theory and applications in a fundamental approach to trigonometry. Textual material assumes prerequisites of high-school geometry and intermediate algebra. Exercises contain calculator- and computer-oriented problems.

Fraser, Marshall. 1978. *College Algebra and Trigonometry, A Functions Approach.* Menlo Park, Calif.: Benjamin/Cummings.

Presents the standard algebraic and trigonometric topics using functions and graphing as the unifying theme. The initial chapter is a self study review, subsequent chapters contain calculator and historical exercises in addition to numerous problems.

Hauck, William. 1968. *Trigonometry Review Manual.* New York: McGraw-Hill.

Represents a programmed text intended as a review of traditional topics found in high-school trigonometry. Mathematical topics include interpolation, solving right triangles, identities, and circular functions.

Heineman, E. Richard. 1979. *Plane Trigonometry.* 5th ed. New York: McGraw-Hill.

Contains standard trigonometric topics plus logarithms, graphical methods and complex numbers. The use of hand-held calculators is integrated throughout.

Hirsch, C. R., and H. L. Schoen. 1985. *Trigonometry and Its Applications.* New York: McGraw-Hill.

Contains a mathematically sound treatment of the standard topics in plane trigonometry with a good balance between analytic and numerical work. Also contains (micro)computer applications.

Keedy, Mervin L., A. Griswold, J. F. Schacht, and A. Mamary. 1968. *Algebra and Trigonometry.* New York: Holt, Rinehart & Winston.

Contains a thoroughly-integrated treatment of algebra and trigonometry, and can be used as a reference source for teachers of intermediate algebra and trigonometry. Chapters contain numerous exercises.

Kindle, Joseph H. 1950. *Theory and Problems of Plane and Solid Analytic Geometry.* Schaum's Outline Series. New York: McGraw-Hill.

Contains 345 solved problems and 910 supplementary problems. Topics include conic sections, transformation of coordinates, polar coordinates, and solid analytic geometry. A good sourcebook for problems to supplement courses in precalculus and calculus.

Larson, Loren C. 1979. *Algebra and Trigonometry Refresher for Calculus Students*. San Francisco, Calif.: W. H. Freeman.
Supplemental textbook organized in a fashion that allows the necessary review of algebra and trigonometry to be spread throughout the entire calculus course. A unique table of contents contains diagnostic questions that enable the reader to determine areas of weakness.

Levy, Lawrence S. 1983. *Trigonometry with Calculators*. New York: Macmillan.
Presents a detailed investigation of standard trigonometric topics supplemented by a regular use of calculators. A chapter is devoted to trigonometry and complex numbers.

Lial, Margaret L., and Charles D. Miller. 1978. *Algebra and Trigonometry*. Glenview, Ill.: Scott, Foresman.
Contains the standard topics from intermediate algebra and trigonometry. The first three chapters provide a review of elementary algebra with diagnostic pretests.

Nanney, J. Louis, and John L. Cable. 1980. *Algebra and Trigonometry, A Skills Approach*. Boston, Mass.: Allyn and Bacon.
Contains the standard precalculus topics. Textual material is minimized and rigor is progressive. Chapters contain "cautions" to help in avoiding common student difficulties. The use of the calculator is discussed and encouraged.

Rees, Paul K., Fred W. Sparks, and Charles S. Rees. 1985. *College Algebra*. 9th ed. New York: McGraw-Hill.
A classic in college algebra that has been in print for over forty years. Includes standard college algebra topics plus progressions and annuities, induction, permutations, combinations and probability.

Rich, Barnett. 1963. *Principles and Problems of Plane Geometry*. Schaum's Outline Series. New York: McGraw-Hill.
Provides a brief review of topics in plane geometry in addition to in excess of 800 solved problems.

Riddle, Douglas F. 1982. *Analytic Geometry*. 3rd ed. Belmont, Calif.: Wadsworth.
Requires a sound background in algebra and trigonometry. Mathematical topics include, plane geometry, vectors, transformation of coordinates, transcendental curves, polar coordinates and solid geometry.

Spiegel, Murray R. 1968. *Mathematical Handbook of Formulas and Tables*. Schaum's Outline Series. New York: McGraw-Hill.

Willerding, Margaret F. 1975. *College Algebra and Trigonometry*. 2nd ed. New York: Wiley.

Contains the standard topics in intermediate algebra and trigonometry in addition to sections on determinants, theory of equations, and combinatorics. Trigonometry is well-developed.

9. Instruction in Calculus

ROSS L. FINNEY

Calculus is the mathematics of motion and change. Where there is motion or growth, where variable forces are at work producing acceleration, calculus is the right mathematical tool to apply.

Calculus is a gateway to nearly all fields of higher mathematics. In addition, it is used to predict the orbits of earth satellites, to design inertial navigation systems, cyclotrons, and radar systems, to explore problems of space travel, to test theories about ocean currents and the dynamics of the atmosphere. It is applied increasingly to solve problems in biology, business, economics, linguistics, medicine, political science, psychology, and robotics. Calculus is so widely used that almost every professional field employs it in some way.

Student enrollments in calculus have been increasing. The number of high schools presenting candidates for Advanced Placement examinations in calculus has increased from 2,000 to more than 4,000 during the past ten years. More than 40,000 students took the examinations in May 1985. The trend has been much the same in two-year colleges, with enrollments of 46,000 in 1966, 69,000 in 1970, 76,000 in 1975, and 91,000 in 1980. It is expected that because of pressure for career preparation, these trends will continue in coming years. It is no surprise, therefore, that student enrollments in calculus are increasing and that calculus courses are under pressure to include more effective instructional materials.

Calculus teachers bear an educational burden that is now heavier than in past years. Not only must they teach the concepts of calculus, already no small task, but they also must be able to acquaint students with ways in which calculus is used in other fields. Thus they must introduce students to mathematical modeling — a process of constructing a mathematical system that behaves the same way as a real-world phenomenon or process. This mathematical system, called a model, is analyzed for new mathematical relationships that are then given physical interpretations, with the goal of learning more about the observed phenomenon. Modeling is one of the chief ways by which scientists gain understanding of reality.

Fortunately, new printed materials and microcomputer programs are available to help teachers meet the new demands for instruction in calculus and its applications. Many of these new resources have been prepared for the students themselves to use. None of them require special previous experience on the part of either teacher or student, and all fit naturally into the present curriculum.

For teachers especially, there is a journal devoted to professional applications of undergraduate mathematics that frequently describes applications of calculus, articles by Ralph P. Boas on what is important to focus on when you teach calculus (and what is not), and a fine book by Morris Kline that gives an historical perspective to calculus by showing its role in the development of mathematical thought from ancient to modern times. There is even a recent book on mistakes and how to find them (good for everyone) and there is some good television footage on calculus and mathematical modeling of whose potential you will want to be aware. A number of fine Apple and IBM microcomputer programs on calculus topics are available for individual and classroom use.

BIBLIOGRAPHY

The bibliography is subdivided into:
- UMAP Modules
- Book and Periodical Literature
- Microcomputer Programs
- Television Programs.

UMAP Modules

The UMAP Modules are lesson-length booklets. Each is self-contained except for the mathematical prerequisites listed at the beginning, and each requires no previous acquaintance with the field of application. Each contains exercises (with answers), and usually there is a sample exam (with answers) that readers can use to test their understanding. These modules are all written for students to work through on their own, although a teacher can use information from them in lectures as well.

Approaches to use of these modules can vary. For example, when I am ready to introduce students to calculus applications, I spend five minutes in class discussing the specific application; if it is, say, the measurement of cardiac output, I say what cardiac output is and why one wants to measure it. I then assign the unit and some of its calculus-based exercises as homework. Two or three units a semester add to the interest and credibility of a course.

The following is a partial listing of the UMAP Modules that use calculus.

Calter, Paul. 1977. Graphical and Numerical Solution of Differential Equations. Units 81-83.

Prerequisite knowledge: differentiation and integration of simple rational, logarithmic, and exponential functions; calculation of moment of a force about a point (only for hacksaw application).

Describes an experiment for modeling a light filter's behavior, models a beam with a hacksaw blade, and gives counts for the number of fish entering and leaving a pond. Each model leads to an elementary differential equation that is solved either by looking at an associated tangent field or by applying Euler's method.

Cameron, David H., Frank R. Giordano, and Maurice D. Weir. 1983. Modeling Using the Derivative: Numerical and Analytic Solutions. Unit 625.

Prerequisite knowledge: calculus of exponential and logarithmic functions.

Reviews the derivative as physical rate of change and as a geometric slope. The physical interpretation leads to first-order initial-value problems. The geometric interpretation is used to uncover Euler's method for approximating the numerical values of the solution functions. Analytic solutions are found by separation of variables. Applications are relevant to the biological and social sciences, the physical and environmental sciences, and engineering.

Cannon, Raymond J. 1980. Recognition of Problems Solved by Exponential Functions. Unit 84. Reprinted in *UMAP Modules 1977-1979: Tools for Teaching*, 77-95. Boston: Birkhäuser, 1981.

Prerequisite knowledge: interpretations of derivatives as rates of change and tangent slopes.

Written for students in a single-semester calculus course or in the first semester of a standard calculus sequence. Introduces the equation $y' = ky$ to describe proportionate rates of change. Studies properties characteristic of the graphs of exponential functions and describes features shared by word problems whose solutions involve exponential functions. Applications come from the biological, behavioral, and social sciences. Subsequent units by the same author (Units 85-88), written for the same audience, discuss exponential change, numerical approximations to $y = e^x$, and solutions of word problems.

Casstevens, Thomas W. 1981. Exponential Models of Legislative Turnover. Unit 296. Reprinted in UMAP *Modules 1981: Tools for Teaching*, 61-77. Boston: Birkhäuser, 1982.

Prerequisite knowledge: arithmetic of exponential functions.

In any legislative body the number of legislators who serve continuously from a given starting point decreases exponentially with time. This observation can be used to forecast the number of legislators who will survive an election, to speculate on what might have happened had a postponed election not been postponed, and to disclose the effects of secret purges. It is of particular interest to compare the decay constants for legislative bodies in different countries. Except for the development of the model $dM(t)/dt = -cM(t)$, which is integrated to produce the equation $M = M_0 e^{-ct}$, no calculus is required here.

Fink, A. M. 1980. Kepler's Laws and the Inverse Square Law. Unit 473. Reprinted in UMAP *Modules 1981: Tools for Teaching*, 149-173. Boston: Birkhäuser, 1982.

Prerequisite knowledge: vector differentiation; computation of area in polar coordinates.

Shows how Kepler's empirical laws of planetary motion follow from the inverse square law of gravitation. Also shows how the inverse square law follows from Kepler's laws. The resulting formulas are applied to modern-day satellites and used to estimate the masses of the earth and sun.

Greenwell, Raymond N. 1983. Whales and Krill: A Mathematical Model. Unit 610. UMAP *Journal* 3 (2): 165-183. Reprinted in UMAP *Modules 1982: Tools for Teaching*, 43-61. COMAP, 1983.

Prerequisite knowledge: maximum-minimum problems, differentiation and integration techniques.

Uses a system of elementary differential equations to model a predator-prey system of whales and krill. The system is not readily solvable because the equations are not linear, but useful inferences are drawn from a study of the system's equilibrium points. Introduces the notion of maximum sustainable yield and leads readers to draw conclusions about fishing strategies.

Horelick, Brindell, and Sinan Koont. 1979. Measuring Cardiac Output. Unit 71. UMAP *Journal* 0 (0): 15-32. Reprinted in UMAP *Modules 1977-1979: Tools for Teaching*, 333-351. Boston: Birkhäuser, 1981.

Prerequisite knowledge: Riemann sums; trapezoidal and Simpson rules.

Cardiac output is the amount of blood the heart pumps in one minute. The unit develops a formula for computing cardiac output from measurements of the concentration of a dye injected into the blood stream.

———. 1979. Radioactive Chains: Parents and Daughters. Unit 234.

Prerequisite knowledge: logarithmic and exponential functions; use of the first and second derivatives in graphing.

Three radioactive chains account for all naturally-occurring radioactive substances beyond thallium in the periodic table. Sets up equations for calculating the amounts of the substances in a radioactive chain; discusses states of equilibrium between substances and their predecessors.

————. 1979. Pi is Irrational. Unit 240. Reprinted in *UMAP Modules 1977-1979: Tools for Teaching*, 401-419. Boston: Birkhäuser, 1981.

Prerequisite knowledge: the binomial theorem; differentiation and integration of rational and trigonometric functions; the fundamental theorem of calculus; integration by parts; mathematical induction.

Defines rational and irrational numbers, discusses their decimal representations, and moves directly to a self-contained proof of pi's irrationality.

————. 1979. Buffon's Needle Experiment. Unit 242. Reprinted in *UMAP Modules 1977-1979: Tools for Teaching*, 443-467. Boston: Birkhäuser, 1981.

Prerequisite knowledge: definition of definite integral.

Describes Buffon's needle experiment for obtaining numerical approximations to pi. This self-contained presentation introduces enough probability for readers to understand the statement, "The probability that the needle will cross the line is $2/\pi$" and is devoted to the proof of this result. Includes a brief discussion of a computer simulation of the experiment together with a short computer program.

————. 1980. Prescribing Safe and Effective Dosage. Unit 72. Reprinted in *UMAP Modules 1977-1979: Tools for Teaching*, 353-380. Boston: Birkhäuser, 1981.

Prerequisite knowledge: integration of $C'(t) = kC(t)$; summation of geometric progressions.

Concentration of a medicine in the blood stream needs to be high enough to be effective and low enough to be safe. How do you schedule the administration of a medicine to be sure that its presence is both safe and effective? Decay of the medicine's concentration in the blood is assumed to be exponential and readers use this assumption to determine how to keep the concentration between given upper and lower bounds.

————, and Sheldon F. Gottlieb. 1980. Modeling the Nervous System: Reaction Time and the Central Nervous System. Unit 67. Reprinted in *UMAP Modules 1977-1979: Tools for Teaching*, 283-306. Boston: Birkhäuser, 1981.

Prerequisite knowledge: the derivative as a rate of change; integration of du/u.

Presents a mathematical model of the process by which the central nervous system reacts to a stimulus. Compares predictions of the model with experimental data. Draws various conclusions from the model about reaction time; compares different assumptions about the relationship between the intensity of an external stimulus and the intensity of the corresponding excitation of the nervous system.

Insel, Arnold J. 1983. Atmospheric Pressure in Relation to Height and Temperature. Unit 426.

Prerequisite knowledge: calculus of logarithmic and exponential functions.

Applies theory of ideal gases to derive a function relating atmospheric pressure to temperature and altitude. This formula is then used to obtain conditions for atmospheric instability, thus describing a role that calculus can play in constructing a mathematical model of the atmosphere.

Peressini, Anthony. 1981. The Shape of the Surface of a Rotating Liquid. Unit 507.

Prerequisite knowledge: first-semester calculus; algebra of vectors in the plane.

When a vertical cylinder containing a fluid is rotated about its axis at a constant velocity, the surface of the fluid assumes the shape of a paraboloid of revolution. An analysis of the forces on the particles of the liquid explains why.

Rheinboldt, Werner C. 1981. Algorithms for Finding Zeros of Functions. Unit 264. *UMAP Journal* 2 (1): 43-72. Reprinted in *UMAP Modules 1981: Tools for Teaching*, 471-500. Boston: Birkhäuser, 1982.

Prerequisite knowledge: acquaintance with the statements of the mean value and intermediate value theorems; differentiation of elementary functions; absolute value notation.

Discusses methods for approximating the numerical values of zeros of functions. Discusses strong points and limitations of the bisection method, the secant method, and Newton's method. Presents a hybrid algorithm that combines the best features of the bisection and secant methods. Also discusses rates of convergence and some pitfalls of numerical computation.

Schoenfeld, Alan H. 1980. Integration: Getting It All Together. Units 203-205. Reprinted in *UMAP Modules 1977-1979: Tools for Teaching*, 587-679. Separate solutions manual available.

Prerequisite knowledge: familiarity with standard substitutions, partial fractions, and integration by parts..

Presents a strategy for solving integration problems in three steps: simplify, classify, and modify. Comparison testing has shown the strategy to be quick and effective.

Sherbert, Donald R. 1981. The .6 Rule for Industrial Costs. Unit 508. *UMAP Journal* 2 (2): 45-55. Reprinted in *UMAP Modules 1981: Tools for Teaching*, 637-666. Boston: Birkhäuser, 1982.

Prerequisite knowledge: elementary differential calculus.

Before management increases the capacity of a manufacturing plant, it tries to project the relation between the increases in labor, raw materials, and equipment and the resulting output of finished goods. This unit examines a rule of thumb used in the chemical industry for relating capacity to equipment cost.

Tuchinsky, Philip M. 1978. Mercator's World Map and the Calculus. Unit 206. Reprinted in *UMAP Modules 1977-1979: Tools for Teaching*, 677-727. Boston: Birkhäuser, 1981.

Prerequisite knowledge: integral calculus.

In 1569 Nicolas Mercator published a map on which every course of constant compass heading appeared as a straight line. With this map, a navigator could draw a straight line from a departure point to a destination point and read from the line a course of constant compass heading for the voyage. To create the map, Mercator needed to space the parallels of latitude according to the integral of the secant function — a century before this integral was known! Tuchinsky discusses the history of the map and the history of the development of the integral of the secant. He then applies the integral to determine the spacing of the lines of latitude on the Mercator maps in use today.

————. 1979. The Human Cough. Unit 211. Reprinted in *UMAP Modules 1980: Tools for Teaching*, 581-593. Boston: Birkhäuser, 1981.

Prerequisite knowledge: maximum-minimum theory.

Our windpipes contract during a cough in a way that maximizes the velocity of the air in the pipes. A mathematical model for this behavior is developed here; the amount of contraction required is predicted. The development uses the formula for Poiseuille's law at one point, but no previous experience with the formula is required. The velocity is expressed as a function of the radius of the windpipe. Its maximum is found by setting the derivative equal to zero.

Wagon, Stanley. 1980. Evaluating Definite Integrals on a Computer: Theory and Practice. Unit 432.

Prerequisite knowledge: definition of a definite integral; trapezoidal rule; Romberg's method.

Shows how to estimate the value of a definite single integral by implementing the trapezoidal rule and Romberg's method on a computer or programmable calculator. Develops/discusses two methods and error control. Readers are encouraged to develop computer programs. Programming experience is helpful but not necessary.

Whitley, Thurmon W. 1979. Five Applications of Max-Min Theory from Calculus. Unit 341. Reprinted in *UMAP Modules 1980: Tools for Teaching*, 617-648. Boston: Birkhäuser, 1981.

Prerequisite knowledge: maximum-minimum theory.

Application topics include minimum cost, maximum profit, minimum surface area of a honeycomb cell, arterial branching, and the travel time of light.

————. 1981. Some Applications of Exponential and Logarithmic Functions. Unit 444.

Prerequisite knowledge: differentiation and integration of logarithmic and exponential functions; infinite limits; l'Hospital's rule; integration by partial fractions.

Topics included here are carbon-14 dating; the infusion of glucose into a patient's body; population changes of organisms that compete amongst themselves or with other species.

Wilde, Carroll O. 1978. The Contraction Mapping Principle. Unit 326. Reprinted in *UMAP Modules 1981: Tools for Teaching*, 713-746. Boston: Birkhäuser, 1982.

Corequisite knowledge: Newton's method.

Set your calculator for radian measure, enter a one, and press the cosine key repeatedly. The display eventually converges to .7390851332 ..., a fixed point of the cosine function. This illustrates the solution of the equation $\cos x = x$ by Picard's method, an iterative method. This method is presented here and applied to the solution of a variety of physical problems. The unit also provides a context in which to study or review inverses of functions before the introduction of transcendental functions. If the Picard method does not work on f it is likely to work on the inverse function f^{-1}, which has the same fixed points. This module requires somewhat more mathematical maturity than other UMAP Modules, thus entailing greater teacher explanation initially.

Book and Periodical Literature

Apostol, Tom M. 1967-1969. *Calculus*. 2 vols. 2nd ed. Waltham, Mass.: Blaisdell.

Still in print. Most accessible of the more advanced works on calculus, and one of the most readable.

———, Hubert E. Chrestenson, C. Stanley Ogilvy, Donald E. Richmond, and N. James Schoonmaker, eds. 1969. *Selected Papers on Calculus*. Raymond W. Brink Selected Mathematical papers no. 2. Washington, D.C.: Mathematical Association of America.

A collection of articles from the *American Mathematical Monthly* and *Mathematics Magazine* that provide suggestions for instruction in calculus.

Boas, Ralph P. 1971. Calculus as an experimental science. *American Mathematical Monthly* 78 (6) (June-July 1971): 664-667. Reprinted in *Two-Year College Mathematics Journal* 2 (1971): 36-39.

Discusses what is worth proving in a beginning calculus course, and what isn't. Just as no beginning course in an experimental science would attempt to reproduce all the experiments on which the science is founded, no beginning calculus course should present all of the proofs on which the calculus is founded. Teachers of calculus would do well to follow the lead of experimental scientists in this respect. Give proofs when they are easy and justify unexpected things, omit tedious and difficult proofs, especially those of plausible things. Give easy proofs under simplified assumptions rather than complicated proofs under general hypotheses. Give correct statements, but not necessarily the most general ones you know. After giving this and other good advice, the author shows how it applies to some of the topics in calculus.

————. 1981. Who needs those mean-value theorems, anyway? *Two-Year College Mathematics Journal* 12 (3) (June 1981): 178-181.

Refers to the theorem that if f is differentiable then $f(b) - f(a) = (b-a)f'(c)$, where c is some value between a and b. We usually do not know anything more about c than this statement tells us, which is that c exists. While we can sometimes satisfy our curiosity about the value of c, the importance of the theorem lies elsewhere, in the estimates that can be obtained from the inequality $(b - a) \min f'(x) \leq f(b) - f(a) \leq (b - a) \max f'(x)$.

The article indicates what some of these estimates are.

————.1985. Inverse functions. *College Mathematics Journal* 16 (1) (January 1985): 42-47.

The article begins, "I still remember — after more than half a century — how puzzled I was at first by inverse functions, especially by the notation and the method of getting the graph. If anybody ever told me why the graph of $y = x^{1/2}$ is the reflection of the graph of $y = x^2$ in a 45° line, it didn't sink in. To this day there are textbooks that expect students to think that it is so obvious as to need no explanation." Addressed to both students and teachers, this article is the clearest presentation of the subject I have seen so far.

Calinger, Ronald, ed. 1982. *Classics of Mathematics*. Oak Park, Ill.: Moore. Review: *American Mathematical Monthly* 92 (8) (October 1985): 601-603.

Presents selections (all in English translation) from the writings of mathematicians from classical antiquity through the early twentieth century. Includes Proclus on geometers, Aristotle on the irrationality of the square root of 2, Claudius Ptolemy on sines of angles, John Napier on logarithms, Johann Kepler on integration, and Pierre de Fermat on maxima and minima. Also includes articles by such mathematicians as Brook Taylor, Colin Maclaurin, Isaac Newton, Leonhard Euler, Augustin-Louis Cauchy, Karl Weierstrass, Joseph Fourier, and Henri Lebesgue.

Cipra, Barry. 1983. *Misteaks ... and How to Find Them Before the Teacher Does*. Cambridge, Mass.: Birkhäuser.

Short, fun, and entertaining; the chapters do not have to be read in any particular order. Each contains good advice about how to tell when your calculations have gone wrong and what to do about it. What fudging does, says Chapter 2, is turn an obviously wrong answer into something that might be correct: not a bad strategy. Upon confronting a new and suspicious formula, try relating it to things you know are true (this from Chapter 5). Before you calculate, advises

Chapter 8, think about what kind of answer to expect. It will help in the early detection of absurdity (and many entertaining absurdities there are, too, in the exercises).

Douglas, Ronald G., ed. 1987. *Toward a Lean and Lively Calculus, Report of the Conference/Workshop to Develop Curriculum and Teaching Methods for Calculus at the College Level.* MAA Notes no. 6. Washington, D.C.: Mathematical Association of America.

Giordano, Frank R., and Maurice D. Weir. 1985. *A First Course in Mathematical Modeling.* Monterey, Calif.: Brooks/Cole.

Giordano and Weir's book deals with the modeling process and indicates some of the roles that calculus plays in modeling motion and change in the world. The book is self-contained and written for beginners.

Grinstein, Louise S., and Brenda Michaels, eds. 1977. *Calculus: Readings from the Mathematics Teacher.* Reston, Va.: National Council of Teachers of Mathematics.

Presents a collection of articles representing suggestions for instruction in calculus. Topics dealt with include historical and pedagogical overviews, functions, limits, differentiation, integration, numerical methods, series, and applications. (SFW)

Kline, Morris. 1972. *Mathematical Thought from Ancient to Modern Times.* New York: Oxford University Press.

Treats the major mathematical creations and developments from ancient times through the first decades of the twentieth century. Almost every mathematical subject is treated in historical perspective; calculus is a major actor in a beautiful pageant.

Ralston, Anthony. 1984-1985. Will discrete mathematics surpass calculus in importance? *College Mathematics Journal* 15 (5) (November 1984): 371-382; 16 (1) (January 1985): 19-21.

Includes responses by others.

Smith, David A. 1984. *Interface: Calculus and the Computer.* 2nd ed. Philadelphia, Pa.: Saunders.

Deals with the relationship of computing to calculus and calculus instruction. A pleasure to read; the ideas in it will enrich any calculus course. Contains student projects, class activities, historical notes, discussions, and exercises that will provide insight into calculus and into what one can and cannot achieve through computation.

Swann, Howard, and John Johnson. 1975. *Prof. E. McSquared's Orig-*

inal, Fantastic and Highly Edifying Calculus Primer. 2 vols. Los Altos, Calif.: William Kaufmann. Review: *MATYC Journal* 15 (3) (Fall 1981): 226.

A readable and sometimes humorous introduction to differential calculus through the eyes of Prof. E. McSquare and a host of cartoon characters. Mathematical topics covered include functions, limits, and derivatives. (SFW)

Microcomputer Programs

Bell, Ian, Jon Davis, and Steve Rice. *Calculus-Pad*, Kingston, Ontario: Queen's University.

For IBM microcomputers.

Burgmeier, James, and Larry Kost. *Exploration Programs in Calculus (EPIC).* Englewood Cliffs, N.J.: Prentice-Hall.

For IBM microcomputers.

Finney, Ross L., Dale Hoffman, Judah Schwartz, and Carroll O. Wilde. 1984. *The Calculus Toolkit.* Reading, Mass.: Addison-Wesley. Review: *Mathematics and Computer Education* 19 (2) (Spring 1985): 137-140.

For Apple II series and IBM microcomputers.

————. *The Calculus Student's Toolkit.* Reading, Mass.: Addison-Wesley.

A first-semester subset of The Calculus Toolkit.

Flanders, Harley. *Micro-Calc.* New York: W. H. Freeman.

For Apple and IBM microcomputers.

Fraleigh, John, and Lewis Pakula. 1985. *Exploring Calculus with the IBM-PC.* Reading, Mass.: Addison-Wesley.

For IBM microcomputers.

muMATH/muSIMP. Bellevue, Wa.: Microsoft.

Package capable of *symbolic* algebra and calculus.

Television Programs

Models in the Mind. 1978. Program 1 of the series *Dimensions in Science.* Dallas, Tex.: TV Ontario.

Contains dynamic footage of processes and activities that are so compelling that we find ourselves seeking mathematical explanations of what we see. Flight, fluid flow, computer simulations of turbulence, wheels, spirals, conic sections, solar reflectors, bubbles crowding together, lava formations, falling bridges, moving galaxies, and whistles from speeding trains are only a few of the phenomena that tempt us to make mathematical models. The modeling activity takes place in the classroom, however, guided by a booklet that accompanies the half-hour tape. While no mathematics per se is on the tape, there are excellent images to motivate mathematical modeling.

The Law of Falling Bodies. Program 2 of the series *Mechanical Universe*. Pasadena, Calif.: California Institute of Technology.

One of a series of half-hour programs that constitute a calculus-based introductory physics course. Explores the phenomenon that in a vacuum all bodies fall with the same constant acceleration. Looks first at historical, precalculus explanations of free fall, then studies the phenomenon of free fall near the surface of the earth and derives the familiar equations $a = 32$, $v = 32\,t$, and $s = 16\,t^2$. Well worth students' time.

10. Instruction in Statistics and Probability

ANN E. WATKINS

There is no subject with a worse public image than statistics. The language and literature are filled with references to its perfidy (as cited in Bibby (1983)):

> In earlier times, they had no statistics, and so they had to fall back on lies.
> —Stephen Leacock

> Statistics are like loose women; once you get them you can do anything you want with them. —Walt Michaels of the New York Jets

> I believe dreams sooner than statistics. —William Saroyan

> There are three kinds of lies: lies, damned lies, and statistics.
> —attributed to Benjamin Disraeli by Mark Twain

> Statistics can be used to support anything—especially statisticians.
> —Franklin P. Jones

Added to this skeptical view by the general public that statistics are numbers obtained in some devious manner and then manipulated to support a preconceived and prejudiced position, the student of statistics typically believes that the subject consists of formulas that are almost impossible to understand; it is boring, hard, and a torture to learn:

> I have reached the point where I can only express the inarticulate, taste food without taste, smell whiffs of the past, read statistical books and sleep in uncomfortable positions. —Zelda Fitzgerald

And yet, it is undisputed that statistical literacy should be a fundamental goal of schooling:

> Statistical thinking will one day be as necessary for efficient citizenship as the ability to read and write.   — H. G. Wells

> The most important questions of life are, for the most part, really only problems of probability.   — Pierre Simon, Marquis de Laplace

> Elementary statistics and probability should now be considered fundamental for all high-school students.   — National Science Board Commission on Precollege Education in Mathematics, Science, and Technology, 1983

As a response to this schizophrenic view of statistics, the teaching of statistics and probability is currently undergoing a quiet and long-needed revision. The most basic change is the adoption by many states and districts of guidelines that mandate an early introduction to statistics and probability for all students. For example, the 1980 New York State framework, *Mathematics K-6: A Recommended Program for Elementary Schools* recommends exploring chance events in kindergarten and gathering and recording data in first grade. The 1985 California mathematics framework says that students must have the opportunity to begin developing their understanding of probability and statistics in kindergarten.

These frameworks reflect a growing recognition that, not only is an understanding of statistics and probability important in our world of lotteries and public opinion polls, but that, as with calculus, many years of preparation are necessary before a student is sophisticated enough for the typical college-level course. The teaching of statistics and probability will no longer be limited largely to colleges.

A second basic change is in the nature of the introductory statistics course that is offered in colleges and high schools. In colleges the course was traditionally for students majoring in a field such as psychology, but now it is frequently a general education requirement. The typical high-school course, although taken by very few students, was similar to the college course. These courses are changing so that they are more "statistical" and less "mathematical." For example, the binomial distribution was traditionally developed in class by teaching students about combinations and the addition and multiplication rules of probability. A modern course is more likely to first generate the binomial distribution through repeated sampling from a given population (Travers et al. 1985).

The characteristics of a modern statistics course are:

Emphasis on the conceptual rather than the computational.
The typical elementary statistics textbook has been accused of being a "cookbook"; that is, students are given a mathematical recipe for different statistical situations. This approach enables students to work exercises that require plugging numbers into formulas, but does not help them build a solid basis of statistical understanding. A new generation of textbooks and courses is more concerned with students learning, say, the proper use of confidence intervals and the logic behind them, rather than just how to construct them (see, e.g., Moore 1985; Freedman, et al. 1978; and Landwehr et al. 1986).

Introduction to fewer statistical tests, but in more depth.
Instead of doing endless variations of, say, the *t*-test (paired samples, small sample size, standard deviation known, standard deviation unknown, etc.), modern courses concentrate on the most basic hypothesis-testing situations and examine them in more detail.

A recognition that mathematical probability is not a necessary prerequisite to statistics.
Research is showing what teachers have known all along: probability is a very difficult subject to learn. Many of people's intuitive concepts are incorrect — witness all of the so-called paradoxes in probability. Consequently, teachers are backing away from the mathematical formula approach to probability. There is an increased emphasis on experiment and on simulation in order to build probabilistic intuition. For interesting discussions of the difficulty people have with probabilistic reasoning, see Hope and Kelly (1983), Shaughnessy (1981), and Kahneman et al. (1982).

Real data as the foundation of teaching statistics.
The use of contrived, hypothetical data is no longer necessary when every student has a calculator. It is the use of real data that gives legitimacy to a statistics course. When data are interesting and important to the students, the students' involvement in the course increases proportionately.

A new emphasis on data analysis.
Data analysis is the display and contemplation of data in order to find patterns in them and to generate hypotheses about them. All data should be analyzed using data analysis techniques before being subjected to the usual hypothesis testing/ estimation types of procedures.
Teachers of modern statistics courses believe that these techniques

and this philosophy should be part of the student's knowledge. Students are being asked to look at a set of data, organize it, summarize it, and write a description of its important features.

The emergence of data analysis as the first step in statistics is due in part to the renaissance of statistical graphics in the world of professional statisticians. This trend was begun by John Tukey, who invented some useful new graphs such as the stem-and-leaf plot (Velleman and Hoaglin 1981).

Student projects.

Many teachers ask their students to do a project as part of the course. This involves defining a problem, collecting data, analyzing the data, and writing a report.

Introduction to robust and resistant techniques.

Robust statistics are those that do not give misleading results when basic assumptions are not met. For example, rank sum tests can be used instead of t-tests when it cannot be assumed that the data come from a population that is normally distributed.

Resistant statistics are those that are resistant to outliers; that is, several extremely large or small values do not affect them very much. The median is considered resistant to outliers; the mean isn't.

Use of the computer.

The computer is used in many ways in the modern statistics class. Statistical programs such as Minitab make hand computation of analysis of variance and correlation coefficients unnecessary. Advanced graphics aid in data analysis. Computer-aided instruction is available for elementary concept development. Although few in number and mostly developed locally by teachers, classroom demonstration programs on topics such as the central limit theorem are being used. Finally, the use of the computer has made simulation a viable approach in the teaching of probability and in statistical topics such as constructing sampling distributions.

The emergence of statistics as a basic part of the mathematics curriculum provides teachers with both our greatest challenge and our greatest potential source of satisfaction. We are generally not trained in the teaching of statistics and do not yet have the materials we need. However, a modern statistics course generates more student excitement and provides more lasting benefit to our students than any other mathematics course we teach.

REFERENCES

Bibby, John. 1983. *Quotes, Damned Quotes, and* .... Halifax, England: Demast Books.

Freedman, David, Robert Pisani, and Roger Purves. 1978. *Statistics.* New York: Norton.

Hope, Jack A., and Ivan W. Kelly. 1983. Common difficulties with probabilistic reasoning. *Mathematics Teacher* 76 (8) (November 1983): 565-570.

Kahneman, Daniel, Paul Slovic, and Amos Tversky, eds. 1982. *Judgment Under Uncertainty: Heuristics and Biases.* Cambridge, England: Cambridge University Press.

Landwehr, James M., Jim Swift, and Ann E. Watkins. 1986. *Exploring Surveys and Information from Samples.* Quantitative Literacy Project. American Statistical Association-National Council of Teachers of Mathematics Joint Committee on the Curriculum in Statistics and Probability. Palo Alto, Calif.: Dale Seymour.

Moore, David S. 1985. *Statistics: Concepts and Controversies.* 2nd ed. New York: W. H. Freeman.

Shaughnessy, J. Michael. 1981. Misconceptions of probability: From systematic errors to systematic experiments and decisions. In *NCTM Yearbook 1981*, 90-100.

Travers, Kenneth J., et al. 1985. *Using Statistics.* Menlo Park, Calif.: Addison-Wesley.

Velleman, Paul F., and David C. Hoaglin. 1981. *Applications, Basics, and Computing of Exploratory Data Analysis.* Boston, Mass.: Duxbury.

BIBLIOGRAPHY

Bibliographic entries are listed under the categories of
- High-School Textbooks
- Notable College Textbooks
- Supplementary Materials for Student Use
- Sources of Ideas for Classroom Lessons
- Enrichment Reading for Students & Teachers
- Background Reading for Teachers
- Computer Software
- Sources of Data
- Newsletters and Journals.

High-School Textbooks

The dearth of appropriate textbooks has been the major problem confronting the secondary teacher of statistics. Most of the existing textbooks were written many years ago and they subordinate statistics to the axiomatic-set theory approach to probability. Consequently, many high-school teachers use books written for college.

Newmark, Joseph. 1983. *Statistics and Probability in Modern Life*. 3rd ed. Philadelphia, Pa.: Saunders.

> As this college-style textbook is widely used by high-school teachers, there have been several curriculum guides written for it. A 201-page manual that includes a course outline, suggested time schedule, notes about the lessons, suggested assignments, tests, and quizzes can be ordered from the Curriculum Research and Development Group at the University of Hawaii in Honolulu.

Travers, Kenneth J., et al. 1985. *Using Statistics*. Menlo Park, Calif.: Addison-Wesley.

> The first major book published specifically for the high school in many years, this textbook is not a watered-down college text. It contains many innovative features, such as the use of simulation and experiment, that will give students an intuitive but solid introduction to statistics. Students will be interested in the (occasional) real data. For example, students will compare the number of admissions to the emergency room of a Virginia mental health clinic during times when the moon was full to times when the moon was not full.

Notable College Textbooks

There exist at least fifty textbooks written for an introductory college statistics course with an algebra prerequisite. The vast majority of these books are practically indistinguishable from one another. They promote the so-called "cookbook" approach to statistics by stressing computation and not interpretation. There is a growing realization that this approach is not viable in an age when computers can handle the computation and when statistical literacy is required of every citizen. The textbooks listed below all emphasize understanding of statistical concepts; all use real data; and all reject the idea that formal probability is the best road to statistics.

Freedman, David, Robert Pisani, and Roger Purves. 1978. *Statistics*. New York: Norton.

> Every teacher should own this book. It has had an enormous impact on statistical education. There are very few formulas in the book and very little probability. However, students are introduced to statistical reasoning in great depth. An example of a representative exercise is: If women always married men who were five years older, what would the correlation between their ages be? Explain.

Koopmans, Lambert H. 1981. *An Introduction to Contemporary Statistics*. Boston, Mass.: Duxbury.

> Similar to Mosteller, et al. (1983) in style and intent, this textbook is a more sophisticated introduction to statistics and data-analysis techniques.

Mosteller, Frederick, Stephen E. Fienberg, and Robert E. K. Rourke. 1983. *Beginning Statistics with Data Analysis*. Reading, Mass.: Addison-Wesley,

> This textbook is distinguished primarily by its intriguing sets of genuine data (Are Olympics judges biased towards competitors from their own country?) and by inclusion of data-analysis techniques (such as breaking the entries of a table into the grand mean plus row effect plus column effect plus residual).

Nemenyi, Peter, et al. 1977. *Statistics from Scratch*. San Francisco, Calif.: Holden-Day.

> Confidence intervals in Chapter III? How is this possible? This text does it by beginning with nonparametric statistics. Students are introduced to confidence intervals by this problem: You have a basket containing 500 tickets, each marked with a person's age. If you draw two tickets, what is the probability the median age of all tickets is between the two ages you drew? More-traditional topics are brought in later.

Noether, Gottfried E. 1976. *Introduction to Statistics: A Nonparametric Approach*. 2nd ed. Boston, Mass.: Houghton Mifflin.

> As the title suggests, this textbook also uses nonparametric methods to illustrate statistical ideas. This approach enables the student to skip most of the usual material on descriptive statistics, probability, means and variances of random variables, and normal distribution theory, in order to get rapidly to estimation and hypothesis testing.

Smith, Gary. 1985. *Statistical Reasoning*. Boston, Mass.: Allyn and Bacon.

> The chapter titles of this textbook are the same as in most other introductory books, but this is where the similarity ends. The author has done a terrific job of finding real-life data and quotations from the media to illustrate his points. Although students are asked to perform routine computations, the emphasis of the text and the exercises is on statistical reasoning.

Supplementary Materials for Student Use

Agnew, Jeanne L., and Marvin S. Keener, eds. 1981. *Catalogue of Industry Related Problems for Mathematics Students*. Stillwater, Okla.: Department of Mathematics, Oklahoma State University.

> A catalog is available which lists each problem, its source, general level, the mathematical prerequisites, price (minimal), and a summary. The class time required for each problem varies from one hour to five weeks. Each problem is written by an expert and is based on a real-world experience. Many are statistical in nature, such as "Radar failures in a group of air bases," in which students are asked to determine if the differences in the number of radar failures at different bases can be attributed to chance.

American Statistical Association — National Council of Teachers of Mathematics Joint Committee on the Curriculum in Statistics and Probability. 1986. Quantitative Literacy Project. Four booklets: *Exploring Data* by James M. Landwehr, and Ann E. Watkins. *Exploring Probability* by Claire M. Newman, Thomas E. Obremski, and Richard L. Scheaffer. *The Art and Techniques of Simulation* by Mrdulla Gnanadesikan, Richard L. Scheaffer, and Jim Swift. *Exploring Surveys and Information from Samples* by James M. Landwehr, Jim Swift, and Ann E. Watkins. Palo Alto, Calif.: Dale Seymour.

> As the result of a National Science Foundation grant, these four booklets have been extensively field-tested. They consist of short explanatory material followed by student worksheets. A teacher's guide accompanies each one.
>
> The first booklet, *Exploring Data*, is a guide to data analysis and includes techniques such as stem-and-leaf plots, box plots, and scatter plots. Students are

asked to make the plots, but the emphasis is on analyzing them. Students answer the question, "What can we see from the plot that we couldn't see before?" Real data of interest to teenagers appear in every worksheet.

The second booklet, *Exploring Probability*, begins at the basic level of coin flipping and so is suitable for early junior high school.

The third booklet, *The Art and Techniques of Simulation*, introduces students to this powerful method of solving probability problems that are too difficult for them to do analytically.

The fourth booklet, *Exploring Surveys and Information from Samples*, is an introduction to confidence intervals and methods of taking samples. Confidence intervals are constructed by means of simulation, not by formulas. Again, real data from surveys such as the Gallup poll are used throughout.

Baum, Paul, and Ernest M. Scheuer. 1976. *Statistics Made Relevant: A Casebook of Real Life Examples*. New York: Wiley.

This casebook contains forty-eight articles and advertisements of a statistical nature. Each is followed by a series of questions that help students evaluate the statistical reasoning in the article. Although the articles are now aging, this book provides a model of how teachers can use the media as a source of statistical lessons.

Consortium for Mathematics and its Applications (COMAP). UMAP Modules.

A catalog of the modules is available from COMAP. These are self-contained lessons in the applications of mathematics and statistics. As an example, one of the more than 30 modules in probability and statistics, "An application of EDA to the 1980 New York City Marathon," uses both exploratory and standard methods of data analysis to determine the factors upon which a runner's speed depends.

Hoffer, Alan. 1978. *Statistics and Information Organization*. Palo Alto, Calif.: Creative.

This excellent set of materials has four sections: classroom materials, content for teachers, didactics, and teaching emphases, plus an annotated bibliography. It is the largest single source of reproducible classroom materials (over 500 pages) for the junior high school. The materials for students introduce topics from many disciplines and are activity oriented.

Larsen, Richard J., and Donna Fox Stroup. 1976. *Statistics in the Real World: A Book of Examples*. New York: Macmillan.

This supplementary textbook is similar to Baum and Scheuer (1976), although the data here came primarily from articles in professional journals. For example, students are given data from the *Journal of Nervous and Mental Diseases* in order to test if men have nightmares as often as women.

Mosteller, Frederick, et al., eds. 1973. *Statistics by Example*. Reading,

Mass.: Addison-Wesley.

> The four volumes in this series, *Exploring Data, Weighing Chances, Detecting Patterns,* and *Finding Models,* each contain twelve to fourteen actual statistical problems together with discussions and exercises for students.

National Council of Teachers of Mathematics. 1979. *Organizing Data and Dealing with Uncertainty.* Reston, Va.: National Council of Teachers of Mathematics.

> This booklet contains fifty-one pages of reproducible student worksheets for grades 5 through 8. The first section, "Organizing data," gives students the opportunity to collect their own data on, say, class birthdays, and then to construct frequency tables and scatter plots. The second section, "Dealing with uncertainty," is an introduction to empirical probability through coin flipping and dice rolling experiments.

Shulte, Albert P., and Stuart A. Choate. 1977. *What Are My Chances?* Books A and B. Palo Alto, Calif.: Creative.

> Each booklet contains over seventy reproducible student worksheets with solutions for the teacher. Concepts covered include listing outcomes, the meaning of probability, the law of large numbers, combinations and permutations, the multiplication principle, mutually exclusive events, and conditional probability.

Sources of Ideas for Classroom Lessons

Armstrong, Richard D., and Pamela Pedersen, eds. 1982. *Probability and Statistics.* Scranton, Pa.: Harper & Row.

> Although this nicely-illustrated 128-page booklet is part of the Comprehensive School Mathematics Program's elementary school curriculum, most of the eight papers describe lessons that would work well in secondary schools and two-year colleges. For example, one article is on Pascal's triangle and its use in investigating probability problems through a combinatorial approach.

Bibby, John. 1983. *Quotes, Damned Quotes, and* . . . . . Halifax, England: Demast Books.

> All of the quotes at the beginning of this article were taken from this pamphlet. It contains hundreds of quotes, verse, and cartoons about statistics and probability.

College Curriculum Support Project. Data User Services Division, Bureau of the Census, Washington, D.C. 20233.

> The College Curriculum Support Project has several publications, such as the *CCSP High School Supplement* and *Census '80: Projects for Students,* on how the census is conducted and how census data are used. Teachers may wish to add their names to the mailing list in order to receive announcements of publications.

Shulte, Albert P. and James R. Smart, eds. *NCTM Yearbook 1981.*

The thirty articles in this yearbook discuss existing courses and programs, classroom activities, teaching and learning specific topics, applications, statistical inference, simulation, and using computers. In addition, there is a bibliography and list of possible student projects.

Teaching About U.S. Population Trends! 1981. Washington, D.C.: Population Reference Bureau.

This package contains a wall chart full of data for each state from the 1980 census. Four accompanying ditto masters with blind answers require students to use the wall chart to find such things as the state with the greatest percentage of its land in farms. A copy of the newsletter *Interchange* is also included, which provides further information and lesson ideas.

Visiting Lecturer Program in Statistics.

Sponsored by the leading statistical societies in the United States and Canada, statisticians visit college and high-school classrooms to discuss topics ranging from the central limit theorem to careers in statistics. Contact Jon R. Kettenring, Bell Communications Research, Room 2A-331, 435 South Street, Morristown, NJ 07960-1961.

Woodrow Wilson National Fellowship Foundation Institute on High School Mathematics. 1984. *Focus on Statistics.* Princeton, N.J.: Woodrow Wilson Institute.

This 470-page book was written by high-school teachers who attended a month-long institute on statistics in the summer of 1984. It is the largest source of ideas for lessons at the high-school level. As well as having many descriptions of exciting classroom lessons. it contains everything from a review of statistical programs available for the Apple computer to a guide for structuring project work.

Enrichment Reading for Students and Teachers

Brook, Richard J., Gregory C. Arnold, Thomas H. Hassard, and Robert M. Pringle. 1986. *The Fascination of Statistics.* New York: Dekker.

A good introduction to advanced statistical techniques such as factor analysis, cluster analysis, and multidimensional scaling, as well as to more-familiar aspects of statistics such as experimental design, estimation, and hypothesis testing. Contains 30 readable chapters by different authors. Each chapter begins with a real problem (How could the theory of evolution be disproved?, for example) and then describes the appropriate statistical technique.

Campbell, Stephen K. 1974. *Flaws and Fallacies in Statistical Thinking.* Rev. printing. Englewood Cliffs, N.J.: Prentice-Hall.

Amusing look at the ways statistics can be distorted, complete with real-life examples. Chapters include Cheating charts, Accommodating averages, Ignoring dispersion, and Improper comparisons.

Careers in Statistics. 1987. Rev. ed. Washington, D.C.: American Statistical Association.

This booklet contains the information that a student interested in a career in statistics should know: examples of interesting statistical problems, descriptions of possible jobs, expected salaries, and educational requirements. Also included is a list of the U.S. and Canadian schools that offer degrees in statistics.

Gubbins, S., D.A. Rhoades, and D. Vere-Jones. 1982. *Statistics at Work: A Handbook of Statistical Studies for the Use of Teachers and Students.* Wellington, New Zealand: New Zealand Statistical Association.

This 112-page booklet is intended to give high-school teachers ideas for lessons involving practical applications of statistics. It contains eleven case studies, each of which is a real-life problem with data, statistical analysis, and exercises. Sample titles include, "An industrial sampling problem" and "How to calculate your earthquake risk." It is similar to Tanur et al. (1978) but written at a lower level.

Haack, Dennis G. 1979. *Statistical Literacy: A Guide to Interpretation.* Boston, Mass.: Duxbury.

Without much computation or many formulas, this book introduces the major ideas of statistics. It could be used as a textbook for an introductory course. There are especially interesting chapters on epidemiology, sample surveys, and index numbers.

Hollander, Myles, and Frank Proschan. 1984. *The Statistical Exorcist: Dispelling Statistics Anxiety.* New York: Dekker.

This entertaining 247-page book consists of 26 vignettes on making decisions, sampling, learning from data, and estimating probabilities. It is a compendium of familiar examples such as the *Literary Digest* pool, the birthday problem, and the 1970 draft lottery, as well as newer ones such as monitoring a nuclear reactor, statistical control charts, and the capture-recapture method. Wonderful source for lecture notes!

Hooke, Robert. 1983. *How to Tell the Liars from the Statisticians.* New York: Dekker.

In seventy-six succinct essays, this lively book shows us the effects of statistical reasoning and its misuse on our lives. Discussed are college entrance exams, television ratings, and the statement that "90% of the cars we've made are still on the road," among many other topics.

Huff, Darrell. 1954. *How to Lie with Statistics.* New York: Norton.

No bibliography would be complete without this book, the original one that gave statistics its bad name. The examples of lying graphs and biased samples make as entertaining reading today as they did thirty years ago.

Mathematics at Work in Society Project (MAWIS). 1981. Washington D.C.: Mathematical Association of America.

Four 20-minute video cassettes produced by John Jobe and a 32-page booklet, "Opening Career Doors," by James R. Choike, are available free of charge for teacher reproduction. One of the videotapes, "An actuary — What's that?," shows an actuary describing the mathematics needed for work in a large life insurance company.

Moore, David S. 1985. *Statistics: Concepts and Controversies.* 2nd ed. New York: W. H. Freeman.

The best of the "statistical literacy" books. A wide range of examples taken from real experiments and surveys is discussed. The sections on experimental ethics are particularly noteworthy. The exercises require reflection and insight.

Niven, Ivan M. 1965. *Mathematics of Choice: How to Count without Counting.* New Mathematical Library no. 15. Washington, D.C.: Mathematical Association of America.

One of a series of books written for talented high-school students. It includes chapters on permutations and combinations, binomial coefficients, probability, partitions of an integer, generating polynomials, and mathematical induction.

Packel, Edward W. 1981. *The Mathematics of Games and Gambling.* New Mathematical Library no. 28. Washington, D.C.: Mathematical Association of America.

Excellent introduction to the elementary mathematics necessary for the analysis of games and gambling. Games analyzed include craps, roulette, Keno, blackjack, backgammon, poker, bridge, state lotteries, and horse racing. There is also a chapter on elementary game theory and one on the history of gambling. Most chapters have exercises.

Runyon, Richard P. 1977. *Winning with Statistics: A Painless First Look at Numbers, Ratios, Percentages, Means, and Inference.* Reading, Mass.: Addison-Wesley.

Introduces many of the major concepts of statistics through entertaining stories, such as "The standard deviation is not a sexual perversion." Many parts are similar to an up-to-date Huff (1954).

Statistics as a Career: Women at Work. 1983. Washington, D.C.: American Statistical Association.

This brochure was designed to introduce high-school and college students to the career opportunities in statistics and to encourage women to enter the field. It includes pictures and job descriptions of six women statisticians.

Statistics: The Mathematics of Choice and Chance. Wilmette, Ill.: Annenberg/CPB Collection.

> Consists of five high-quality half-hour programs on videocassette: Statistics Overview, Collecting Data, Organizing Data, Probability, and Confidence Intervals. They are part of a series of 26 programs presented as a television course, *For All Practical Purposes: An Introduction to Contemporary Mathematics.* A study guide is available, as well as a textbook of the same title as the film series, edited by L. A. Steen (New York: W. H. Freeman, 1987).

Tanur, Judith M., et al., eds. 1978. *Statistics: A Guide to the Unknown.* 2nd ed. Monterey, Calif.: Brooks/Cole.

> This very popular book is a series of 46 essays on important applications of probability and statistics in the fields of biology, politics, sociology, and the physical world. It successfully tries to undo the impression of statistics given by Huff (1954) by showing students the positive contributions statistics has made to society.

What Is a Survey? Washington, D.C.: American Statistical Association.

> This 32-page booklet can be read by high-school students. It contains information on types and characteristics of surveys, designing and conducting a survey, sources of errors, and using the results of a survey.

Zeisel, Hans. 1985. *Say It with Figures.* 6th ed. New York: Harper & Row.

> The first edition of *Say It with Figures* was published in 1947. Written in a clear, easy-to-read style that requires very little previous knowledge, it has become a standard in the field of social statistics. The first part of the book is on how to present numbers in tables. For example, if a two-way frequency table is to be converted to percentages, how should it be done? Other sections review indices (what is the best way to measure the batting performance of baseball players?), how to handle "don't knows" in surveys, regression analysis, experimental evidence, and the panel (a group of individuals that serves as a continuous source of information).
>
> This book is fun to read and is a good introduction to the kinds of statistical problems that social scientists deal with.

Background Reading for Teachers

Box, George E. P., William G. Hunter, and J. Stuart Hunter. 1978. *Statistics for Experimenters: An Introduction to Design, Data Analysis. and Model Building.* New York: Wiley.

> Textbook for research workers with sections on comparing two treatments, comparing more than two treatments, measuring the effects of variables (factorial design), and regression analysis.

Chambers, John M., et al. 1983. *Graphical Methods for Data Analysis.* Belmont, Calif.: Wadsworth International Group.

> This is not a book about how to use graphics to communicate information to the public; the techniques of data analysis presented here are designed to display data so that the structure may be observed by researchers. Methods discussed include box plots, smoothing, quantile-quantile plots, and plotting multivariate data.

Cleveland, William S. 1985. *The Elements of Graphing Data.* Monterey, Calif.: Wadsworth.

> This easy-to-understand book describes powerful graphical methods and principles for showing the structure of scientific and technical data. These methods are the current state-of-the-art tools of the applied statistician. Students should be familiar with them, for, as the author says, "An infusion of this graphical methodology into science and technology will raise the effectiveness of data analysis just as confidence intervals and hypothesis tests did decades ago."

David, Florence N. 1962. *Games, Gods and Gambling.* New York: Hafner.

> Traces the history of probability and statistical ideas up to the Newtonian era. Includes, for example, a discussion of the Fermat-Pascal correspondence, with translated copies of the letters.

Ehrenberg, A. S. C. 1982. *A Primer in Data Reduction: An Introductory Statistics Textbook.* New York: Wiley.

> This easy-to-read book emphasizes methods of summarizing and organizing data. It contains a unique section on communicating data through tables, graphs, and words.

Feller, William. 1968. *An Introduction to Probability Theory and Its Applications.* 3rd ed. New York: Wiley.

> This is the classic textbook on probability. It contains wonderful exercises and examples.

Folks, J. Leroy. 1981. *Ideas of Statistics.* New York: Wiley.

> Presents the great ideas of statistics from a historical point of view. It begins with a discussion of the census mentioned in the Old Testament and ends with the twentieth-century method of discriminant function analysis. Contains information about such things as the Fisher-Pearson controversy that are hard to find elsewhere.

Grey, D. R., et al. 1983. *Proceedings of the First International Conference on Teaching Statistics.* Sheffield. England: The University Press.

> The First International Conference on Teaching Statistics was held at the University of Sheffield in August 1982. This two-volume set contains articles on

all aspects of teaching statistics by leading statistical educators from around the world.

Kahneman, Daniel, Paul Slovic, and Amos Tversky, eds. 1982. *Judgment Under Uncertainty: Heuristics and Biases.* Cambridge, England: Cambridge University Press.

> Contains thirty-five articles on how people make probabilistic judgments. Much of the research on the fallacies in people's intuitive judgments will be a revelation to teachers.

Larsen, Richard J., and Morris L. Marx. 1986. *An Introduction to Mathematical Statistics and its Applications.* 2nd ed. Englewood Cliffs, N.J.: Prentice-Hall.

> The most fun to read of the mathematical (calculus-based) statistics books. Historical anecdotes and data from real experiments and surveys make this textbook particularly interesting reading for teachers who want an introduction to the mathematical theory of statistics.

Quality Productivity Training Network (formerly Transformation of American Industry). A training project of the American Association of Community and Junior Colleges and the American Society for Quality Control.

> This project trains community-college instructors so that they will be able to assist local industries in improving quality and productivity. Video and print materials are available. Contact Carole Hannan, Jackson Community College, Jackson, MI 49201.
>
> Statistical quality control is being touted as the salvation of American industry. Teachers of statistics can learn more about it from this project or from the textbooks listed below:
>
> Ishikawa, K. 1976. *A Guide to Quality Control.* Milwaukee, Wis.: American Society for Quality Control.
>
> Juran, Joseph M., ed. 1974. *Quality Control Handbook.* New York: McGraw-Hill.
>
> Western Electric. 1958. *Statistical Quality Control Handbook.* 2nd ed. Indianapolis, Ind.: Western Electric Co.

Sullivan, John L., ed. Quantitative Applications in the Social Sciences. Beverly Hills, Calif.: Sage.

> A series of about fifty inexpensive paperback booklets (average length 88 pages) for students and teachers who want a short, nontechnical overview of one area of statistics. Sample titles include *Exploratory Data Analysis*, *Introduction to Survey Sampling*, and *Applied Regression: An Introduction*.

Tufte, Edward R. 1983. *The Visual Display of Quantitative Information.* Cheshire, Conn.: Graphics.

A leader in the renaissance in statistical graphics. It discusses the principles necessary to achieve graphical excellence and has an unmatched selection of the best statistical graphics ever drawn.

Velleman, Paul F., and David C. Hoaglin. 1981. *Applications, Basics, and Computing of Exploratory Data Analysis*. Boston, Mass.: Duxbury.

This is the most readable explanation of John Tukey's methods of exploratory data analysis. (Tukey's own book, *Exploratory Data Analysis* (1977) is very difficult reading for the non-specialist.) Topics include stem-and-leaf displays, letter-value displays, box plots, resistant lines, smoothing, median polish, and rootograms. The book contains listings of BASIC and FORTRAN programs and discusses the use of Minitab. The programs are available from CONDUIT.

Williams, William H. 1978. *A Sampler on Sampling*. New York: Wiley.

This is a nontechnical introduction to the procedures and pitfalls of taking surveys.

Youden, W. J. 1984. *Experimentation and Measurement*. Washington, D.C.: U.S. Department of Commerce, National Bureau of Standards. Available from the U.S. Government Printing Office.

This inexpensive booklet is a classic introduction to measurement error.

Computer Software

Due to the rapid changes in both hardware and software, it is impossible to provide an up-to-date list of statistics programs. There is still very little software available for either classroom demonstration purposes or for computer-aided instruction in elementary statistics and probability. One of the least expensive packages is listed below. There are, however, many software packages that perform statistical analyses. The most popular of these is Minitab.

Minitab. Available from Minitab, Inc., 215 Pond Laboratory, University Park, PA 16802.

Minitab is a statistical computing system that can serve as an aid to students in introductory statistics classes. It is available for the IBM-PC and other computers running the MS-DOS operating systems. The Fundamental Module contains the most commonly used procedures such as plots, histograms, descriptive statistics, simple and multiple regression, analysis of variance, non-parametrics, cross-tabulation, and random data generation.

Sets, Probability, and Statistics: The Mathematics of Insurance. Available from Order Fulfillment, American Council of Life Insurance, 1850

K Street, N.W., Washington, D.C. 20006-2284.

The four disks in this package contain easy-to-use programs that correspond closely to the lessons in an accompanying booklet. Students are shown how probability and statistics are used in the life insurance business in mortality tables, compound interest, and figuring premiums. Students can perform the computations needed using a built-in calculator. Permission is given for instructors to duplicate the disks for classroom use.

Sources of Data

It is the use of real data that brings both zest and credibility to a statistics class. The sources listed below all contain data that can be used when teaching graphical and descriptive statistics.

Consumer Reports magazine

The *Gallup Reporter* magazine (gives the latest survey results and has discussions of methodology)

Historical Statistics of the United States, Colonial Times to 1970 (available from the U.S. Government Printing Office)

Statistical Abstract of the United States (available from the U.S. Government Printing Office)

USA Today newspaper

World Statistics in Brief (this and other collections of world statistics are available from United Nations Publications, Room DC2-853, New York, NY 10017)

Newsletters and Journals

This short bibliography does not list any individual articles from journals, as there are dozens and dozens of good ones. Consequently, it is well worth a teacher's time to look through back issues of journals and newsletters as

- *American Statistician*
- *College Mathematics Journal*
- *International Statistical Education Newsletter*

- *Mathematics Teacher*
- *Random News*
- *Statistics Teacher Network Newsletter*
- *Teaching Statistics.*

For publication information on these, see Chapter 20, Resources.

11. Instruction in Discrete Mathematics

BETTYE ANNE CASE

A year course sequence called *discrete mathematics* includes topics important for students to learn before studying theoretical computer science courses. The discrete mathematics taught in the first or second year of a baccalaureate program has no calculus or programming prerequisite and is different from, although it shares some topics with, both finite mathematics courses on the lower undergraduate level and discrete structures courses on the upper level. The course is important for all majors in mathematical sciences. As the course becomes more uniform and its usefulness more apparent, more interest may be shown by non-computer engineering disciplines and the physical sciences. Just as less-theoretical calculus courses for management and technology majors have become common, courses may exist that utilize some of the techniques of the discrete mathematics sequence but which are less mathematically demanding. Such courses, or the many possibilities for inclusion of discrete mathematics topics in other courses, are not discussed here. The last section of the bibliography includes some general references.

Although there is much discussion of teaching discrete mathematics at the two-year college level (e.g., Albers et al. 1985), currently the number of institutions and students involved in such courses in these institutions is small (but growing) when compared with calculus sequence enrollments. High schools and preparatory schools may attempt to teach discrete mathematics courses, just as they have added calculus almost routinely to the senior-year curriculum. (As a university faculty member directing mathematics advisement and placement and observing student difficulties in a university discrete mathematics course, this writer feels such a course addition would be unwise were it to be made at the expense of background topics needed for calculus and discrete mathematics and the intangible "mathematical maturity" essential for success in all future courses.)

After briefly chronicling the development of the teaching of discrete mathematics courses in baccalaureate programs, describing the courses, giving evidence of their introduction into two-year baccalaureate parallel programs, and discussing experiences including some from this writer's institution with a two-year college, this chapter will conclude with recommendations concerning background material that should be mastered prior to a student's beginning a discrete mathematics sequence.

The topics and their applications, that appear in discrete mathematics sequences (but all of which are not likely to be found in any one such sequence) are:

- sets, functions, relations and the number system
- formal logic and the nature of proof
- induction and recursion
- graphs and trees
- combinatorics
- abstract algebraic structures and algorithmic linear algebra.

This content is not essentially new material. Students receiving a baccalaureate degree in computer science in past years were eventually taught most of it in some form. Anthony Ralston, a former president of the Association of Computing Machinery, first focused mathematicians' attention on computer science students' acute need for early coverage of discrete mathematics topics not found in the traditional finite mathematics, statistics, or calculus service courses (Ralston 1981). Then, twenty-nine scientists, including twenty-four mathematicians concerned about the need to strengthen the first two years of college mathematics, met at Williams College for a conference funded by the Alfred P. Sloan Foundation. Participants agreed on the need for change in the lower division curriculum to include content identified as *discrete* mathematics, for mathematics as well as computer science students (Ralston and Young 1983).

There was general respect for this content as good mathematics but a diversity of philosophies and delivery modes were propounded. In particular, there was much discussion of both "integrated" calculus/discrete mathematics courses and a "two separate sequences" model. (Ralston and Young 1983, 243-260) In the months that followed, the call for adding content to an already full curriculum led some mathematicians to an unfortunate "calculus vs. discrete" mentality. Productive efforts to implement ideas from the Williams conference were enhanced by the funding (again by the Sloan Foundation) of six projects to develop two-sequence and integrated lower-division curriculum models that would include adequate discrete mathematics topics.

The Mathematical Association of America's Committee on Discrete Mathematics in the First Two Years was established to investigate the concerns expressed in the Williams conference report, to examine the various efforts to include discrete mathematics topics, and to monitor the six funded experimental projects. The committee issued a preliminary report at the end of 1984 (Committee ... 1984), and concluded its work in 1986 (Committee ... 1986). This committee of seven members, chaired by Martha Siegel, includes Ralston among the three members who are computer science faculty. The needs of computer science students, as perceived by the computer science professional and research organizations, were carefully considered by the committee. The discrete mathematics sequence is consistent with the recommendations of the Association of Computing Machinery and the Institute of Electrical and Electronics Engineers. (The data processing organization, Data Processing Managers Association, has no suggested mathematics requirement, indicating a quite different degree program from those in the mathematical, physical, engineering, and computer sciences supported by the discrete mathematics sequence.)

The Committee's Preliminary Report points out that it is not so much the particular content that is important but how the course is taught. Students should be "solving problems, writing proofs, constructing truth tables, manipulating symbols in Boolean algebra, deciding when, if and how to use induction, recursion, proof by contradiction, etc. And their efforts should be corrected" (Committee ... 1984, 8). The textbooks that have appeared so far at the elementary level (see Bibliography) require a rather careful and sophisticated mathematical approach to the topics. Certainly the course must support an upper-division curriculum with a degree of mathematical development that will allow the better baccalaureate graduates to pursue graduate work successfully.

The differences in delivery modes for the discrete mathematics content recommended at the Williams conference carried over into the six Sloan-funded projects. Of those, Colby College and Florida State University proposed a two-sequence model for calculus and discrete mathematics, to be taken in either order or concurrently. Montclair State College also proposed a two-sequence model, but the discrete mathematics was placed first "to defer the rigors of calculus until students are better prepared and more mature" (Committee ... 1984, 15). On the other hand, the St. Olaf College project, also with separate discrete mathematics and calculus semesters, requires a semester of calculus before the discrete mathematics, to give both the content and maturity St. Olaf faculty feel are necessary for this type of discrete mathematics sequence. (The subsequent experience at Florida State University supports the St. Olaf contention that the demands on the student beginning discrete mathematics are certainly not less than those of the calculus sequence, and probably are greater.) The only one of the projects to propose true topic integration was that of the University of Denver, which also indicated availability of parallel traditional sequences. The panel's final report, and a more extensive report by each project, give results of the projects (Committee ... 1986, Ralston 1988).

Since the discrete mathematics sequence appears to add two courses to the lower division mathematics requirements for affected majors, it is appropriate to consider possible omissions. Although a few colleges have a two-semester calculus sequence that includes multivariate calculus, there is no consensus as yet as to the omissions or changes from the more traditional three-semester development. The Committee made no recommendations for such changes. Some students may therefore need five semesters of mathematics classified as "first two years' material." The Committee also addressed the matter of which faculty — mathematics or computer science — should teach discrete mathematics courses. Although discrete structures courses are often taught in the junior or senior year by computer science faculty, the Committee felt that mathematics should be taught by the mathematics department and presented a course that it expects will be taught by mathematicians (Committee ... 1984, 4-5).

Until recently there were no texts in discrete mathematics intended for students at an adequately elementary level of background and mathematical maturity. The bibliography comments on four texts that may meet the needs of departments searching for a text which presumes only a (strong) college algebra background. (Johnsonbaugh 1984; Kolman and Busby 1984; Mott et al. 1986; Ross and Wright 1985.) New texts, some related to the Sloan-funded projects, are appearing. One example is Hillman et al. (1987), an impressive volume that should be compared with those four. Much care is needed in text selection. This should include working through examples and problems from selected sections rather than simply overall examination. Two somewhat more advanced texts are used at some schools (Liu 1977; Tucker 1984). While some of the titles of these texts contain the phrase "for computer scientists," there is not much difference in topics or approach between those that do and those that don't.

The Sloan project at Florida State University included among its activities the introduction of the first-semester discrete mathematics course at a community college in the same city as the university conducting the project. There was no significant difference between the course at the two institutions, nor in the success of the enrolled students. The community-college instructor also taught the course at the university as an adjunct instructor (Hoffmann and Case 1988). In the long run the success of discrete mathematics courses in two-year colleges will be measured by the same yardstick already used for the calculus sequence: articulation success of students in baccalaureate programs (Case and Goldstein 1985). Gordon (1985) and Case and Goldstein (1985) discuss the relative importance of the topics, their inclusion in the current curriculum, and inclusion in baccalaureate programs of discrete mathematics, but do not detail any experiences from two-year colleges.

The problems of fitting discrete mathematics courses into the curriculum for mathematical sciences majors are formidable if there is no decrease planned, e.g., in the calculus sequence. Large universities will probably add them at least as service courses and as electives or optional courses for mathematics majors. It is likely that two-year colleges will be similarly forced to meet the articulation needs of their students by adding discrete mathematics. Smaller four-year colleges may have the hardest time with this curriculum addition.

The Committee's Preliminary Report remarks at length on the preparation needed by a student before a discrete mathematics course, suggesting more emphasis on formal and informal proof in geometry courses. Concerning the current "precalculus" courses in college the committee notes: "It is not obvious that courses ordinarily taught to mathematically deficient first year students to prepare them for the calculus would also prepare them for this course." Relative to high-school preparation, increased use of algorithmic thinking in problem solving and revived emphasis on formal and informal proof in geometry courses are suggested (Committee ... 1984, 10).

In a study relating background and success in Discrete Mathematics I, it was found that students who had taken only precalculus courses that omitted certain traditional college algebra topics did not do as well as those whose courses had included these topics (Case 1988). These topics are those "end topics" often included in a chapter titled "Sequences and Series" and include: careful treatment of mathematical induction; the binomial theorem; infinite sequences and summation notation; arithmetic and geometric sequences; permutations and combinations; probability. Also included in the course taken by the more-successful students were a few class hours of instruction about symbolic logic. These topics are sometimes omitted or not well-taught in the high schools, often being neglected in favor of beginning study of the calculus. High-school students who have adequate mathematical abilities to succeed in computer science, engineering, or the mathematical or physical sciences would profit from a curriculum that both reclaims some currently omitted topics and also affords increased practice opportunities on proof and problem-solving techniques.

REFERENCES

Albers, Donald J., Stephen B. Rodi, and Ann Watkins, eds. 1985. *New Directions in Two-Year College Mathematics*. New York: Springer-Verlag.

Case, Bettye Anne. 1988. Background and performance of 1700 students in discrete mathematics, 1982-1985, The Florida State University. In Ralston (1988).

————, and Jerome A. Goldstein. 1985. Coordinating curriculum in two-year colleges with baccalaureate institutions. In Albers (1985), 439-454.

Committee on Discrete Mathematics in the First Two Years. 1984, 1986. *Preliminary Report. Report.* Washington, D.C.: Mathematical Association of America.

Gordon, Sheldon. 1985. Discrete topics in the undergraduate curriculum: How big a step should we take? In Albers (1985), 225-241.

Hillman, Abraham P., Gerald L. Alexanderson, and Richard M. Grassl. 1987. *Discrete and Combinatorial Mathematics*. San Francisco, Calif.: Dellen (Macmillan).

Hoffman, J., and Bettye A. Case. 1988. Discrete Mathematics I at Tallahassee Community College. In Ralston (1988).

Johnsonbaugh, Richard. 1984. *Discrete Mathematics*. New York:

Macmillan.

Kolman, Bernard, and Robert C. Busby. 1984. *Discrete Mathematical Structures for Computer Science*. Englewood Cliffs, N.J.: Prentice-Hall.

Liu, C.L. 1977. *Elements of Discrete Mathematics*. New York: McGraw-Hill.

Mott, J., A. Kandel, and T. Baker. 1986. *Discrete Mathematics for Computer Scientists and Mathematicians*. 2nd ed. Reston, Va.: Reston (Prentice-Hall).

Ralston, Anthony. 1981. Computer science, mathematics, and the undergraduate curriculum in both. *American Mathematical Monthly* 88 (7) (1981): 472-485.

————, ed. 1988. *The Six-College Sloan Foundation Program in Mathematics*. MAA Notes Series. Washington, D.C.: Mathematical Association of America.

————, and Gail Young. 1983. *The Future of College Mathematics*. Springer-Verlag.

Ross, K., and C. Wright. 1985. *A First Course in Discrete Mathematics*. Englewood Cliffs, N.J.: Prentice-Hall.

Tucker, Alan. 1984. *Applied Combinatorics*. 2nd ed. New York: Wiley.

BIBLIOGRAPHY

Annotated listings are restricted to those directly concerning the type of courses described in the first paragraphs of this chapter. The annotated listings follow alphabetically within the categories:
- Descriptive and Philosophical
- Elementary Textbooks
- Advanced Textbooks and References.

Descriptive and Philosophical

Albers, Donald J., Stephen B. Rodi, and Ann Watkins, eds. 1985. *New Directions in Two-Year College Mathematics.* New York: Springer-Verlag.
Includes papers by individuals invited to participate at a conference of the same title at Menlo College. Related papers are grouped and a helpfully edited version of the discussion that followed is included.

Committee on Discrete Mathematics in the First Two Years. 1984, 1986. *Preliminary Report. Report.* Washington, D.C.: Mathematical Association of America.
See text for descriptions of these reports.

Hilton, Peter J. 1982. The emphasis on applied mathematics today and its implications for the mathematics curriculum. In *New Directions in Applied Mathematics.* Edited by Peter J. Hilton and Gail S. Young, 155-163. New York: Springer-Verlag.
This paper is concerned with the training of mathematicians. The problems dealing with entering students having inadequate preparation, and the philosophies of the last part of the article, are universal.

Maurer, Stephen B. 1984. Two meanings of algorithmic mathematics. *Mathematics Teacher* 77 (6) (September 1984): 430-435.
Distinguishes between the use of the term "algorithmic mathematics" as rote learning or simply the performing of algorithms (which Maurer calls the traditional meaning) and as the creation of algorithms and their use for solving problems and developing theorems (called by Maurer the contemporary meaning).

———. 1985. The algorithmic way of life is best. *College Mathematics Journal.* 16 (1) (January 1985): 2-18.
Written as a "bait" article at the invitation of the editor of the Journal and submitted to well-known invited respondents. A "response" is included written by Maurer after all the invited respondents had submitted opinion pieces. The title of the original piece, and those of the respondents, give a good indication of the content:
Douglas, R.G. One needs more than the algorithmic approach.
Korte, Bernhard. Algorithmic mathematics versus dialectic mathematics.
Hilton, Peter J. Algorithms are not enough.
Renz, Peter. The path to hell.
Smorynski, Craig. The need for abstraction.
Hammersley, J.M. Three algorithmic exercises.
Halmos, Paul R. Pure thought is better yet.

Ralston, Anthony. 1981. Computer science, mathematics, and the undergraduate curriculum in both. *American Mathematical Monthly* 88

(7) (August-September 1981): 472-485.

Published in a journal widely read by research and university mathematicians, as well as those primarily interested in college teaching, the article was intended to and did receive wide discussion.

————. 1984-1985. Will discrete mathematics surpass calculus in importance? *College Mathematics Journal* 15 (5) (November 1984): 371-382; 16 (1) (January 1985): 19-21.

Another provocative article with nature of the responses indicated by their titles (see Maurer 1985). Responses are:
MacLane, Saunders. Calculus is a discipline.
Wagner, Daniel H. Calculus versus discrete mathematics in OR applications.
Hilton, Peter J. The need for coherence and unity.
Woodriff, R.L. A distinctly discrete indiscretion.
Kleitman, Daniel J. Calculus defended.
Lax, Peter D. In praise of calculus.

————, ed. 1988. *The Six-College Sloan Foundation Program in Mathematics*. MAA Notes Series. Washington, D.C.: Mathematical Association of America.

Describes the results of each of the six Sloan-funded projects involving discrete mathematics in the first two years.

Ralston, Anthony, and Gail Young. 1983. *The Future of College Mathematics: Proceedings of a Conference/Workshop on the First Two Years of College Mathematics*. New York: Springer-Verlag.

Contains the papers presented at the Sloan-funded conference at Williams College; several of these focus on the need for discrete mathematics taught in the first two years. Some discussion from the conference is included. At the end of the volume, the results of two workshops are presented—one assigned to develop a unified curriculum integrating topics from discrete mathematics and calculus in the same courses, and the other presenting a more-traditional approach to the calculus material (with omissions and comparisons) and description of a discrete mathematics sequence to be added.

Roberts, Fred S. 1984. The introductory mathematics curriculum: Misleading, outdated, and unfair. *College Mathematics Journal* 15 (5) (November 1984): 383-399.

Another provocative article with responses:
Lucas, William F. Discrete mathematics courses have constituents besides computer scientists.
Hamming, R.W. Calculus and discrete mathematics.
Tall, David. Continuous mathematics and discrete computing are complementary, not alternatives.
Davis, Robert B. It's not what you do, it's how you do it.
Ellis, Wade Jr. Teaching is mathematics, too.

Thompson, Patrick W. Issues of content versus method.
Mason, John. A need for better role models and attitudes.
Guy, Richard K. How can we learn in an up-to-date and fair fashion?

Rung, Donald C., moderator. 1983. Session titled "Freshman Mathematics." *Notices of the American Mathematical Society* 30 (2) (March 1983): 166-171.

Reports on an unusual session. The American Mathematical Society is generally considered the research-oriented mathematical organization, and it does not often have sessions of this type. This one was organized the winter following the Williams Conference and continues the same sort of discussion as in Ralston and Young, 1983. The panelists at this session were: Peter D. Lax, Anthony Ralston, R.O. Wells Jr., and Gail S. Young. Wells summarizes his discussion: "One of the important roles of mathematics in our society is not only the ability to solve problems, but the ability to invent languages in which you can express problems."

Tucker, Alan C., ed. 1981. *Recommendations for a General Mathematical Sciences Program.*" CUPM Report. Washington, D.C.: Mathematical Association of America.

Includes recommendations for various concentrations in the mathematical sciences, with topical inclusion and emphasis for courses described. The report states the need for mathematics majors to understand some of the content in the discrete mathematics courses described in this chapter, but does not prescribe the early sequence for mathematics majors.

Varansi, Murali R., and Oscar N. Garcia. 1985. Discrete mathematics for computer science. *Potentials* 1 (February 1985): 16-17.

Discusses mathematical topics needed for computer science, and the two broad streams of discrete mathematics needed: concepts of modern algebra (applied to sequential machines and computer system design) and graphs and trees (applied to data structures and algorithms). The approach implied by the article does not require the early sequence dealt with in this chapter, but discussion with the first author indicates that he does feel the early sequence is the preferable time for most of the material to be taught and in fact that his school is instituting the requirement.

Elementary Textbooks

Four textbooks suitable for discrete mathematics courses in the first two college years have been examined closely by this writer. Two excellent earlier textbooks that may be suitable for strong students in an early sequence are Liu (1977) and Tucker (1984). Tucker, as indicated by the title *Applied Combinatorics*, has heavy emphasis there. Both, as appropriate at an upper level, do not devote a lot of space to logic and foundations material. Liu has material on Boolean algebras; Tucker does not. Tucker does assume that students know calculus already. We list four elementary textbooks and follow with a comparative discussion.

Johnsonbaugh, Richard. 1984. *Discrete Mathematics*. New York: Macmillan. (Denoted *J*.)

Kolman, Bernard, and Robert C. Busby. 1984. *Discrete Mathematical Structures for Computer Science*. Englewood Cliffs, N.J.: Prentice-Hall. (Denoted *KB*.)

Mott, Joe L., Abraham Kandel, and Theodore P. Baker. 1986. *Discrete Mathematics for Computer Scientists and Mathematicians*. 2nd ed. Reston, Va.: Reston. (Denoted *MKB*.)

Ross, Kenneth A., and Charles R.B. Wright. 1985. *A First Course in Discrete Mathematics*. Englewood Cliffs, N.J.: Prentice-Hall. (Denoted *RW*.)

It is perhaps of passing interest that three of these books — *KB*, *MKB*, *RW* — are available through the same distributing publisher (though *MKB* was produced with other editors). The "slant" on these books which is given by this publisher's representatives could unduly influence the choice among them. This writer urges that all four (and other comparable texts), together with the supplementary materials available with each, be carefully compared before adoption, with local needs in mind.

The size of *MKB* correctly implies an inclusiveness of topics and emphases which allows instructor choice in presenting the material, and also a lot of explanation for the student reader. (The flip side of this big advantage is the often quoted "students are turned off by too much reading.") A quick comparison of the coverage of these texts on several essential topics:

Logic and Foundations: There is careful handling in *MKB* and *RW*. *KB* provides an appendix of 15 pages but Johnsonbaugh only mentions logic in passing.

Combinatorics: *KB* has very light coverage — about five pages; *RW* has comprehensive coverage, but does not devote as much explanation as *MKB*; *J* has some coverage.

Graph Theory: All authors devote considerable coverage; there is some difference in choice of topics, probably due as much to author preferences as to future applications. *KB* devotes the lightest coverage of the four to this topic. *MKB* devotes a chapter to the content and algorithms of Network Flows. *RW* considers other graph algorithms.

Algebraic Systems: *KB* has extensive abstract algebra coverage, and *RW* includes group theory, omitted in the other two. All mention Boolean algebras, though *KB* has fewer applications.

Recurrence Relations: There is development in Chapter 3 of *MKB*, with supporting background in Chapter 1. Not much attention is given this topic in *KB* and *RW*.

Advanced Textbooks and References

None of the materials below are judged suitable for a course in discrete mathematics at an early level (before calculus or programming experience). They are listed for the convenience of instructors of discrete mathematics courses.

Berztiss, Alfs. 1975. *Data Structures Theory and Practice*. 2nd ed. New York: Academic.

Bobrow, Leonard S., and Michael A. Arbib. 1974. *Discrete Mathematics*. Philadelphia, Pa.: Saunders.

Bogart, Kenneth P. 1983. *Introductory Combinatorics*. Marshfield, Mass.: Pitman.

Brualdi, Richard A. 1977. *Introductory Combinatorics*. New York: North Holland.

Even, Shimon. 1979. *Graph Algorithms*. Potomac, Md.: Computer Science Press.

Gersting, Judith L. 1982. *Mathematical Structures for Computer Science*. San Francisco: W. H. Freeman. Review: *American Mathematical Monthly* 91 (6) (June-July 1984): 379-381.

Gill, A. 1975. *Modern Algebra and Applications to Computer Science*. New York: McGraw-Hill.

Harary, Frank. 1969. *Graph Theory*. Reading, Mass.: Addison-Wesley.

HiMAP and UMAP Modules.
    Write COMAP (60 Lowell St., Arlington, MA 02184) for catalog, which features a number of modules on discrete mathematics.

Knuth, Donald E. 1968-   . *The Art of Computer Programming*. 3 vols. Vol. 1: *Fundamental Algorithms*. 2nd ed. 1973. Vol. 2: *Semi Numerical Algorithms*. 2nd ed. 1981. Vol. 3: *Sorting and Searching*. 1973. Reading, Mass.: Addison-Wesley.

Levy, Leon S. 1980. *Discrete Structures of Computer Science*. New York: Wiley.

Lipschutz, Seymour. 1976. *Theory and Problems of Discrete Mathematics*. Schaum's Outline Series. New York: McGraw-Hill.

————. 1982. *Theory and Problems of Essential Computer Mathematics*. Schaum's Outline Series. New York: McGraw-Hill.

Liu, Chung Laung. 1977. *Elements of Discrete Mathematics*. New York: McGraw-Hill.

Prather, Ronald E. 1976. *Discrete Mathematical Structures for Computer Science*. Boston, Mass.: Houghton Mifflin.

Preparata, Franco P., and Raymond T. Yeh. 1973. *Introduction to Discrete Structures*. Reading, Mass.: Addison-Wesley.

Riordan, John. 1980. *An Introduction to Combinatorial Analysis*. Princeton, N.J.: Princeton University Press.

Roberts, Fred S. 1976. *Discrete Mathematical Models, with Applications to Social, Biological, and Environmental Problems*. Englewood Cliffs, N.J.: Prentice-Hall.

Stanat, Donald F., and David F. McAllister. 1977. *Discrete Mathematics in Computer Science*. Englewood Cliffs, N.J.: Prentice-Hall.

Stone, Harold. 1973. *Discrete Mathematical Structures and Their Application*. Chicago, Ill.: Science Research Associates.

Tremblay, Jean-Paul, and Ram Manohar. 1975. *Discrete Mathematical Structures with Applications to Computer Science*. New York: McGraw-Hill.

Tucker, Alan. 1984. *Applied Combinatorics*. 2nd ed. New York: Wiley.

Wand, Mitchell. 1980. *Induction, Recursion, and Programming*. New York: North Holland.

12. Choosing Computers and Software

R. S. CUNNINGHAM

New teaching technologies didn't start with the computer. Twenty-five years ago the teaching machine was the "new wave" in educational technology. It failed to have any real impact: I have not seen (or missed) mine in years. Will the personal computer as a teaching tool be similarly dead twenty-five years from now? A comparison readily shows that it will not.

Recall that the teaching machine used a roll or workbook of printed material containing three types of sheets: questions, answers, and explanations. A single question was posed, the student answered it and turned to the answer page to compare his or her answer with those presented, and the student was given the page number of an explanation page. If the answer was correct, the explanation reinforced the correct response: if it was an error, the explanation described the mistake and gave a quick tutorial on the material. A lesson consisted of a number of these questions, and a topic contained several lessons.

This technology served a single user in a very limited way. It had no demonstration capability, provided very limited responsiveness, had only canned explanations in the printed text, and offered no other modes of operation beyond the question-answer-explanation cycle. This kind of "programmed instruction" stifled creative learning; and though the machines were quite inexpensive, no one was interested in writing materials for them. They died from a lack of interest, educational effectiveness, and materials.

Personal computers offer a radically different set of teaching capabilities. These include animation, graphics, and color (to attract and hold students' attention); flexible ways to generate unique problem sets and respond flexibly to student answers; record-keeping (to keep track of students' progress); usability by individuals, small groups, or whole classes in a number of ways; and the opportunity to encourage creativity and intellectual play. These wider capabilities have led individuals and publishers to invest a great deal of time and resources in developing software. I am aware of over 280 software packages from more than 125 publishers, all devoted to teaching high-school or college mathematics. So there is no lack of materials or interest, and these factors fuel the fire of educational computing quite brightly.

One of the real strengths of twentieth-century education is the diversity of approaches educators can bring to each subject. Adding computer-based materials to a course will strengthen this diversity. It will surely change the nature of that course, since the instructor will have to answer questions about the computers, schedule time on them, and integrate the computer-based materials into class discussions. It takes extra work to do this, although neither teachers nor students need learn to program the computer unless they want to do so. All the materials described in the bibliography run without programming.

When deciding to use computer-based materials in mathematics teaching, the teacher must decide how to use the computer. The decision involves two questions: (1) Do you want to have individuals, small groups, or the whole class use a single computer? and (2) Will the whole class work at the same pace, will the pace vary but include standard exercises in prescribed order, or will the student be free to exercise any part of the software according to his or her own interests or needs? The two choices are intertwined, but the answers will be largely determined by what the students are expected to get from their computer experience.

Let us consider five options among the many possible and see what the choices might be. A teacher can use the computer for:

- review,
- drill-and-practice,
- exploring mathematical ideas,
- going beyond classwork with faster students or as a reward, and
- giving classroom demonstrations.

The distinction between review and drill-and-practice is mostly in learning goals; drill-and-practice is a way to consolidate new skills, while review goes over material that has already been learned in order to refresh concepts and skills.

Computer-based materials used for review can fit any of the groupings: individual work, small-group study, or whole-class review. Individual work requires either a large number of computers or a way to schedule students on shared computers. If everyone is to use the computer, then clearly a number of computers must be available. However, if students needing individualized review are to use the computers, then scheduling computers is probably best, since students can use individual materials as the need arises. If a whole class is to use review materials at the same level, it may be most useful to have groups of two to four students working at each computer, since they can reinforce each other's learning. Alternatively, whole-class review under the teacher's direction can be done with a central monitor system. Review software differs from drill-and-practice software in offering explanation, diagrams, or stepped examples instead of simply a set of practice problems.

Although drill-and-practice materials may be used in small groups or for a whole class, they are usually designed for individual study. Here the key is to find software whose problems fit the course topics as well as the class pace. It is also important that the programs not require constant teacher supervision. The selected software should provide each student with a unique set of problems so that the work is truly individual. A laboratory, where students can come to check out the software and work on their own, is probably the best way to handle individual study. Such study is essentially computer-based homework, and can be done during class time if the class allows a variety of individual activities.

Mathematical explorations require unstructured software that leaves students free to enjoy intellectual play. This software includes function or surface graphers, equation solvers, and exact-arithmetic mathematics systems. Students can also investigate mathematics by programming solution algorithms for a number of different kinds of problems. There is an interesting gap in the available software here; there seems to be no software beyond elementary-school levels that uses any form of manipulatives. A teacher who uses such physical devices in teaching might find a market for software that simulates them.

Using computers to enrich the educational program for students who move quickly through regular material is one of the oldest educational computer applications. Students can work individually or together, exploring a topic outside normal class topics or using an alternate approach to familiar ideas. Game-format programs can be a good choice here: some of them will take two or even four players: good if there are more students than computers, but watch out for the noise!

Whole-class computer demonstrations are effective for describing graphing and other graphic-based topics, adding variety to presentations of standard materials, shortcutting calculations to focus on setting up problems, or generally setting up an "intelligent overhead projector." The useful "computer slide show" stores several graphic screens on a disk and displays them one at a time; it may be built into another program or purchased separately.

Beyond student use, teachers can use computers to ease several mechanical problems in teaching. Electronic spreadsheets or special gradebook programs can update each student's progress without laborious hand calculations. Several publishers are selling test-bank software with textbooks. Some programs make exercise sets. Graphic screens can be made into handouts or illustrations. Computer slide shows can help illustrate discussions. The commonplace word processor can greatly reduce the time needed to write tests, handouts, and letters. Computers can reduce drudgery and let teachers devote more of their time to teaching.

What kind of computer set-up should be considered for use with mathematics courses? Two configurations are possible in a dedicated laboratory--a number of computers (perhaps of different brands) each operating independently, or several computers operating from a single shared file server (often called a "network"). This kind of laboratory is usually associated with courses in computer programming, however, and is difficult to schedule for a range of mathematics courses. A better approach probably is to try to have an unscheduled laboratory that can accommodate students from a range of courses and can be used for individual work. Such an approach is usually more successful in colleges than in high schools; a mathematics department serious about using computers should set up its own computer laboratory.

Outside the formal laboratory, there are two smaller options for a single classroom: a small set of computers constantly available for individual or small-group work, or a single computer with one or two large monitors so everyone can see its output clearly. Of course, this latter could be built from a class computer by adding monitors. This configuration is tempting in a department with only a few classes using the computers, but could mean a lot of computers if a number of classrooms are so equipped; the formal laboratory may be better there.

The choice of which computer to use for teaching mathematics is not as complicated as it might seem. There are only two computers available with a wide range of mathematics software: the Apple II and the IBM PC (together with its close MS-DOS cousins). By topic, the number of commercial packages available for each, and for all other personal computers together, is shown in Figure 12.1 below. Any other computer will need to have its own programs written, which can be a very long-range job and is really not recommended.

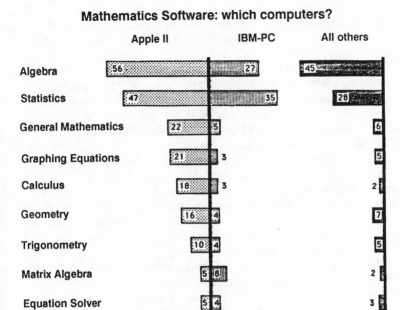

Figure 12.1

For most topics, there is more software for the Apple than for the IBM; but the raw count is somewhat misleading, since much of the IBM-oriented material is newer. Secondary-level software is much more widely available for the Apple, but college materials are moving toward the IBM while remaining strong on the Apple. Note that any good educational software for the IBM will require graphics adaptors and color monitors to get the best results. The Apple II is certainly not dead for education; it is very much alive and dominates the education market. The question of an 8-bit processor (the Apple II) vs. a 16-bit processor (the IBM-PC) is not germane for teaching needs, since most educational computing is limited by student interaction. Educational systems are not yet sophisticated enough to need large disks and memories and fast processors, except for exact mathematics systems and some statistics. The future of educational computing, however, may lie with systems like the Apple Macintosh which offer extremely easy interaction and more computing power than either the Apple II or the IBM-PC. There are some mathematics packages coming onto the market for the Macintosh that seem very interesting.

Let us consider the costs of the computer facilities we are discussing. We assume that you will use the Apple II, the IBM-PC, or a PC look-alike. An Apple can be bought with high-quality color monitor, dual disks, and 128K memory for about $1250; an IBM-PC computer with color monitor and color graphics card, dual disks, and 256K memory runs about $2200; and an IBM cousin will be somewhere in between. These prices include current educational discounts. A good range of software for each station can cost as much as $400 per machine. Thus a complete 15-station laboratory with two printers and software would cost between $30,000 and $45,000. This amount can often be obtained by grants, donations, fund-raisers, or special state or local funds.

Along with the purchase costs of the computers, it is necessary to consider the costs to maintain the equipment and facilities. Facility renovation and maintenance vary so widely that we cannot say more, except to suggest that they not be overlooked in developing laboratories. Equipment maintenance is more consistent. It is possible to take out maintenance contracts on equipment: my experience is that such contracts typically cost about 1% of the original equipment cost per month (so a $1500 computer should cost about $15 per month for a contract). However, if a skilled staff is available to perform maintenance, this cost may be reduced. David Sealey, who manages personal computer clusters at the University of Iowa, quotes figures of $13 per month for an IBM-PC, $12 for an Apple IIe, $13.50 for a 512K Macintosh, $5.50 for a color monitor, and $2.50 to $5 for a printer. Since Iowa operates on a break-even basis and does in-house maintenance whenever possible, this should give a good idea of what costs may be expected.

One feature of software that must be considered is copy protection. Some publishers copy-protect disks to prevent widespread copying of their software. Technically and legally, the purchaser of a piece of software is allowed to use it on one single computer. It cannot be used on two computers at once, be put on a file server for several computers, or be copied to give a copy to someone else. Special site licenses or network licenses may be available for the software you want; however, be sure to ask. This perceived need for security (which may or may not be real) can cause a problem for teachers. Any disk that students use has a pretty limited life. If that disk is the only copy of the program, the program is lost when the disk goes. When possible, buy copyable software (but don't abuse the contract); when not, be sure to investigate the ease of getting replacements. In the worst case, when the software is copy-protected and replacements are not easy and cheap, use disk-copying software to create backups (this is expressly permitted by law) — and store the originals in a safe place. But don't abuse the backups as extra copies.

The accompanying annotated bibliography describes the high points and low points of individual pieces of software for several mathematical topics. It attempts to give a cross-section of as many different kinds of materials as possible. I hope that these comments will give some concrete guidance in evaluating the many pieces of software that are not included.

The most important consideration in evaluating software is the same as for any other educational materials: it must be educationally sound and fit the teaching style and class content of its intended course. Beyond that, look for as many of the following points as possible:

- Does it make real use of the computer, or is it just a teaching-machine page-turner?

- Does it make sound use of graphics, color, animation, and other techniques to make attractive and attention-holding presentations?

- Can the student control the pace and level of the presentations?

- Does the software communicate in real mathematical notation?

- Do you get good diagnostics and response for errors, including diagnoses of student problems?

- Are the presentations consistent and at appropriate levels?

- Can it be used in several places and in several ways in the curriculum?

- Are there good materials, such as manuals and on-line help, to help the class understand and use the software?

- Is the cost reasonable?

On the other hand, it is fairly easy to say what is *not* wanted: software that is dull, clumsy, inaccurate, feels wrong, or is pedagogically unsound.

When one is starting in with mathematical software and is still awkward with a computer, it is hard to have confidence in one's own judgment. There are several places to get help, including reviews and others' experience. Journals or newsletters containing software reviews include the *College Mathematics Journal*, *Mathematics Teacher*, the EPIE Institute's *Educational Software Selector*, *Hands On!* from Technical Education Research Centers, the *Digest of Software Reviews: Education*, the IEEE Computer Society *Education Newsletter*, or the *CIMSE Newsletter* (Computers in Mathematics and Science Education). Another approach is to go to conferences such as NECC (National Educational Computer Conference), AEDS (Association for Educational Data Systems), ADCIS (Association for Development of Computer-Based Instructional Systems), or state or regional educational computing organizations. Their conference proceedings are also useful. Talk to friends or colleagues who have more computer experience, or consult nearby colleges or universities. In my own experience, CONDUIT and MECC produce consistently high quality materials for colleges and secondary schools, respectively, and educational publishers are getting more experience and producing better software.

Advertisements and announcements in magazines and journals can be helpful in learning about available software: *T.H.E. Journal*, *Byte*, and *Personal Computing* are reliable and easily obtained sources. Be careful of advertisements: vendors' claims are not always accurate. When a program looks useful, get a demonstration disk or examination copy so it can be tried in its intended course. Individual styles differ markedly, and it is not possible to be really sure a program will work otherwise.

While the computer has taken some time to become established as an important tool in teaching mathematics, it has now clearly reached that point. Programs are available to support many different points of view on most topics. Packages are becoming as sound and as polished as other educational materials. Costs of both computers and software are becoming much more reasonable. With the diversity of approach that computers add to the classroom, it is no longer necessary to defend a decision to add some computer-based materials to a mathematics curriculum.

Implementing a decision to add computing to mathematics courses is much the same as implementing any other decision requiring the commitment of resources. A case must be prepared, support gathered (often from off-campus sources), and the people who commit budgets must be persuaded that this is an important educational step. Developing a full computer capability can take some time. Be prepared to work patiently to achieve it and use partial facilities for some time as it is developed. My experience, and that of an increasing number of others, is that the results are worth the effort.

BIBLIOGRAPHY

The following listings describe software with which the author is familiar and which seems to be generally useful for teaching. They cover only a fraction of the software on the market, but their descriptions indicate their strengths (and their weaknesses) and may be taken as a practical guide to evaluating other programs. Some available software has been omitted because it is known to be weak, but more was left out because it was not personally known or because the topic was already adequately covered.

The bibliographic entries are listed by topic:

- Algebra
- Calculus
- General Mathematics
- Geometry
- Matrix Algebra
- Statistics
- Symbolic Mathematics
- Trigonometry.

Information on the publishers can be found in Chapter 20, Resources. A more exhaustive, but noncritical, software list is found in Cunningham and Smith (1986, 1987).

The author would like to thank the reviewers for the _College Mathematics Journal_, whose reviews helped in preparing several of these listings. The reviews and the reviewers are listed following the Bibliography.

Algebra

Algebra Arcade by Dennis Mick et al. Brooks/Cole, $49.95; Apple II, IBM-PC, and Commodore 64.

> Arcade-style game in which "Algebroids" are placed randomly on a grid and the player/student gives equations whose graphs hit as many of the Algebroids as possible. Nicely packaged with good color, graphics, and animation. A wide range of algebraic and trigonometric functions can be used. The usable functions, and many other features, can be chosen by the instructor to make this package work from high-school algebra to college algebra and precalculus. While the

package is not deep, it is motivating and can add variety and interest to a course. (Hirschfelder 1987)

Algebra Drill and Practice I, II by R. C. Detmer and C. W. Smullen. CONDUIT. $125 each; Apple II, IBM-PC.

For college-level intermediate algebra, upper-level high-school algebra, or college precalculus. The authors provide very flexible user interaction, well beyond most educational software. Answers may be given in several forms, exponents are shown in true superscript, graphics are used where appropriate, problems are generated randomly, and syntax errors (as opposed to mathematical errors) are diagnosed and pointed out. On the other hand, example solutions are given completely instead of in stepwise chunks. A good choice for drill-and-practice work. A third package in this series, by Detmer and Wells, is also available. (Rossi 1985)

Algebra I. Prentice-Hall. $79.95: Apple II, IBM-PC, Atari, and Commodore 64.

One of three packages for high-school algebra, dealing with set concepts and notation, and number systems. Its format is shared with the *Geometry* package described below, including a very good user interface with color and animation. Mostly a terminology, review, and quiz package, at least as good as most other software at this level. However, it shares the common faults of somewhat primitive range of presentation, error diagnosis, test feedback, and response handling. On the other hand, it allows the student to move easily among the programs, ask for test, or see the contents of the disk at any time. This makes it useful for review, which is probably its best application. The other two packages cover equations, formulas, graphs, and simple equations (Algebra II) and radicals, quadratics, matrices, and complex numbers (Algebra III).

Algebra Word Problems. Queue. $49.95: Apple II, Macintosh.

Word problems are terrifying for beginning students. This program takes students through several kinds of word problems step by step, and should help them see the patterns of successful problem solving. It is less flexible for more proficient students, since it insists on following a set solution pattern without skipping steps, so it will be most useful at beginning levels. The Macintosh version is largely translated from the Apple II and does not use all the Macintosh capability: this practice is fairly common with early Mac software and does not reduce its teaching potential. Those Mac features that are used generally work well.

Electronic Blackboard for Algebra by Richard O'Farrell et al. Brooks/Cole, $95; Apple II.

This package is one of a set including the *Electronic Blackboard for Trigonometry*, described below. It makes effective and interesting use of graphics to teach and reinforce algebra concepts at both high-school and college level. Covers coordinate systems, lines, polynomials and factoring, conic sections, exponentials, and inequalities. Topics are presented in three modes: *display* mode gives demonstrations, _interactive_ mode allows experimentation, and (when present) _target_ mode has the student determine parameters to match a given graph. The manual is very good. A useful tool for class presentations or individual exploration. (Brown 1986)

Electronic Study Guide for Precalculus Algebra by Robert C. Steinbach and David A. Lundsford. COMPress, $275; Apple II.

An algebra review and practice package for self-paced individual use. It is a computer-based version of printed study guides. This is, in fact, a computerized "back of the book": a problem is presented for the student to work on paper, and then the answer is presented. Some of the computer's abilities are used to enhance the presentations, but such use is inconsistent. The package might be a useful supplement to an algebra course, but at the price we suggest getting a demonstration first. (Bookman and Smith 1985)

Graphing Equations by Sharon Dugdale and David Kibbey. CONDUIT, $60; Apple II.

Graphs of functions and equations are an important part of high-school and college algebra courses: "Equation Plotter" in this package covers just that. Other functions include graph matching and two games which manipulate graphs. One game, "Green Globs," is the parent of the _Algebra Arcade_ program above. A nice addition to beginning algebra courses. (Smith 1987)

Interpreting Graphs by Sharon Dugdale and David Kibbey. CONDUIT; $45; Apple II.

Contains two unique programs introducing students to graphs. "Relating Graphs to Events" helps students relate the shape of graphs to everyday events, and "Escape" introduces graph coordinates and graph reading in a game setting. An excellent, flexible piece of software with many high-school and some college applications. (Dye and Tolbert 1984)

Word Problems for Algebra by Marjorie A. Fitting. Metier, $49.95; Apple II and IBM-PC.

This differs from all the other programs in this bibliography in that it is not intended for the student, but for the instructor. It randomly generates word problems (with their solutions) to be printed for class use. These problems cover several steps to prepare students for word problem processes, culminating in actual small "Stories for Solution" — i.e., word problems. While this program does nothing that teachers haven't done for themselves for years, it produces a range of problems of uniform quality with reasonable solutions, without a lot of effort on the instructor's part. This kind of tool is very promising.

Calculus

ARBPLOT by Austin R. Brown and Mark Harris. CONDUIT. $125;

Apple II.

Graphics-oriented package for the single-variable calculus course, including preliminary and follow-up material. An excellent tool for graphing (rectangular, polar, and parametric), conics, epsilon-delta concepts, sequences and series, tangent lines, the mean value theorem, derivatives, root finding, integration, arc length, and differential equations. It has an excellent instructor's manual. Overall, a powerful package at a reasonable price, which can add much to students' understanding of the calculus. (Leinbach 1984)

The Calculus Toolkit by Ross L. Finney et al. Addison-Wesley, $350; Apple II.

Probably the most complete calculus package for the computer. *The Calculus Toolkit* can be used for precalculus through single- and multiple-variable calculus to other upper-division courses. While expensive, it is extremely well done. Graphics are used when appropriate, interactive sequences with the student are well thought-out, graphic displays can be saved to a disk or organized into a "slide show" for class presentations, and the manual is carefully planned and pedagogically sound. If you can afford it, this is an excellent teaching tool. A limited subset has been released as *The Calculus Student's Toolkit* at $19.95. (Leinbach 1986)

Interactive Experiments in Calculus by Frank Wattenberg and Martin Wattenberg. Prentice-Hall, $29.95; Apple II.

This program is designed for learning by doing. Its experiments include the bisection method of finding zeros, several methods of approximating integrals, applications of integrals, graphing functions and their series, and graphing slope fields and solution curves for initial value problems. Can be used for numerical assignments or to explore a number of ideas in calculus. For example, one can zoom in on the graph of a function to see the behavior of differentiable and nondifferentiable functions. The manual is helpful and the package is worth the price. (Abram, forthcoming)

Mathematics Volume 4 — Advanced. MECC, $49; Apple II.

MECC's most advanced mathematics package for upper-level algebra or AP Calculus in high school. It may also be used in college precalculus, finite mathematics, calculus, or linear algebra courses. Programs include graphing, limits, numerical integration, matrix operations, row reduction, linear programming, and least-squares fits. The programs are well-documented and are easy to use as calculation tools, allowing a class to deal with problems of a realistic and interesting size. (Abram 1987)

Surfaces for Multivariate Calculus by Roy E. Myers. CONDUIT, $65; Apple II.

Together with *SURFACE* of the same price, source, and computer, this is an excellent program for examining functions of two variables through their graphs. "Surface Construction," in particular, allows the user to specify a function, X- and Y-ranges, scaling factor, and viewpoint; the function's graph is then drawn as a 2-D projection of the gridded surface with obscured parts omitted. The package is well-designed and polished, performing a limited function very well instead of trying for too much and compromising on quality. Excellent for either student use or demonstrations. (Herman 1984)

General Mathematics

Estimation. MECC. $36; Apple II.

Developing skills in estimation is one way to approach the problem of "number sense" in students. This package integrates computer demonstrations, classroom activities and materials, and simple immediate-mode computer operations to help students develop estimation skills. Its operation is simpler than most programs in this bibliography but is entirely appropriate to its topic and should be effective.

Interpreting Graphs by Sharon Dugdale and David Kibbey. CONDUIT; $45; Apple II.

See annotation under Algebra above.

Mathematics Volume 1 – Graphing, Logic, and Equations. MECC, $46; Apple II.

Straightforward algebra and graphing programs as well as several games in logic, coordinate systems, and angles. Can be used at several points in a general mathematics class. Since the package has such a wide range of programs, the instructor will have to decide which to use and when to use them; but the handouts in the manual will help integrate them into the course.

Mathematics Volume 3 – Geometry. MECC, $45; Apple II.

This package concentrates on geometric shapes and their perimeters and areas. The programs are easy to use, with informative discussions and good practice problems. The manual includes a number of handout masters for class use. A good package for measurement geometry in general mathematics, but too elementary for a real geometry course.

Problem Solving in Everyday Math. MCE, $165; Apple II.

This package focuses on problems found in normal living involving the elementary operations of addition, subtraction, multiplication, and division, as well as more general problems having several steps. It also has an introduction to solving general word problems. Some effort is made on presenting problems at appropriate reading levels, with the teacher being able to choose from a low of second-grade level to a high of about sixth-grade level. The speed of screen printing and the detail level of the problem presentations can also be set. Low-resolution graphics in color are used effectively to hold student attention. These are useful programs for early high-school students who are struggling with real world problems, probably in a general mathematics course.

TK! Solver. Software Arts, $399; MS-DOS, Apple II. Macintosh, TRS-80 Model 4, IBM-PC, and DEC Rainbow.

There are two parts to solving any word problem: setting up the problem's formulas from the problem statement, and solving those formulas mathematically. *TK! Solver* does formula solving, freeing the student to concentrate on expressing word problems in formulas. Any collection of formulas may be used, with any of the variables' values given, and the program will carry out the solution if one is possible. The help facility and documentation are quite good. In spite of the price – *TK! Solver* is really designed for use outside the classroom – this is a good way to bring real-world problems into class. (Carter 1985)

Geometry

The Geometric Supposer: Triangles by Judah Schwartz and Michal Yerushalmy. Sunburst, $99; Apple II.

One of a three-part series, to include also *Quadrilaterals* and *The Pre-Supposer*. This package realizes a great deal of the computer's potential to help students explore the relationships underlying mathematics; indeed, it has allowed a high-school student to discover previously unknown geometric relationships. Because of its remarkable learning potential, its ease of use, and its manual with an emphasis on helping the teacher make the most of the program, this package should be part of any high-school geometry course. It is also recommended for methods courses for secondary mathematics teachers. (Kunkle and Leinbach 1987)

Geometry. Prentice-Hall, $79.95; Apple II, IBM-PC, Atari, and Commodore 64.

This package shares the operations of *Algebra I*, described above. It covers measurement geometry, terminology and elementary postulates, standard figures, right triangles, and space geometry, and would be useful for review and supplement on these topics. It does not have any material on logic and proofs.

Geometry with Logo by Peter Singleton. Metier, $49.95; Apple II.

A unique introduction to points, lines, rays, angles, planes, parallelism, and congruences. The program discusses each topic and then explores it using LOGO. The discussions are well-done, and the error handling is instructive. A good program for beginning a geometry course.

Matrix Algebra

Linear Algebra Computer Companion by Gareth Williams and Donna Williams. Allyn & Bacon, $35; Apple II.

A matrix manipulation package that provides a number of useful tools for a linear algebra course. The options include matrix arithmetic, transformations and reductions, Gram-Schmidt orthogonalization, eigenproblems, simplex and

Markov operations, applications (digraphs, electrical networks, relativity), and graphics. The operations are sound and accurate, and can be stepped through for instruction as well as computed completely for results. The programs could stand to be rewritten for newer microcomputers, since they use 40 columns and somewhat primitive interaction.

Mathematics Volume 4 — Advanced. MECC, $49; Apple II.
See annotation under Calculus above.

Statistics

Exploring Statistics with the IBM PC by David P. Doane. Addison-Wesley, $39.95; IBM-PC.

Very good computer support for a full-year course in statistics. As with any successful statistics package, data can be entered in disk files for testing and manipulation in several ways. The programs allow data description and transformation, hypothesis tests, regressions, time series, and various probability operations. An excellent feature of this package is the large data set provided, which can be used for many examples. The programs provide some useful line-printer graphing, but no real graphics, probably because the IBM PC makes graphics an extra-cost option.

The Graphing Companion for General Statistics by R. S. Cunningham. CONDUIT, $125 (est.); Apple II and IBM-PC.

Statistical computations once formed the main component of the general statistics course and students' intuitive understanding of statistics suffered in comparison. The introduction of numerical computation removed much of the hand calculation and allowed the emphasis to shift to realistic (and sometimes real) data analysis. *The Graphing Companion,* on the other hand, uses graphics to help build and reinforce intuition. It contains laboratory activities keyed to topics in most general statistics courses, from probability and data exploration, through standard hypothesis tests on means, to nonparametric tests. It can be a useful supplement for general statistics courses.

NWA Statpak. Northwest Analytical, $350 ($279 for Macintosh); MS-DOS, CP/M, and Macintosh.

This is a standard microcomputer statistics package. It runs on a wide variety of inexpensive computers, with an impressive range of functions. These include a large set of single-variable statistics, many regression and correlation computations, a number of probability and distribution functions, several means tests, chi-square analyses, and nonparametric statistics, a number of ANOVA tests, extensive data manipulations, and others. The package illustrates a trait common to large systems that use diskettes: the user must set up "work disks" containing a boot system, BASIC, a logical group of programs, and data files. This is not difficult and does not impede the use of the programs. Instructors who like to teach statistical algorithms can do so, since the programs are distributed in source code.

SPSS/PC. SPSS, Inc., $795; IBM-PC (320K, 8087 recommended).

BMDPC. BMDP Statistical Software, $450 up; IBM-PC (640K, hard disk, 8087).

SPSS and BMDP have been standard mainframe statistical programs for years. High-end microcomputers have now caught up to serious statistical needs, and these packages take full advantage of that fact. Both use the familiar command language of their mainframe counterparts, so no re-learning need be done to use them. Possibly the most important reason to consider these PC-based systems, though, is the cost of running the mainframe versions, which make heavy demands on these expensive computers. The PC versions can take this load off your mainframe or can provide these standard systems if a mainframe is not available.

Visual Statistics by B. J. Korites. Kern, $65; Apple II, IBM-PC, and Zenith Z-100.

These programs emphasize the visualization of data, including plotting data, histograms, and doing linear regressions. Data can be stored and retrieved via diskettes. This package does a generally good job on this somewhat limited topic, and could be used at the high-school level to familiarize student with data concepts. The Apple version is somewhat less powerful and thus less useful than the others.

Symbolic Mathematics

muMATH. Microsoft, $225; Apple II (CP/M) and MS-DOS.

Exact symbolic mathematics has been under development for over ten years but has yet to make the mark it deserves in mathematics education. *muMATH* is the only symbolic mathematics program on microcomputers. It is not trivial to use, as it takes time to learn the command language, but it provides an exciting range of applications across arithmetic, algebra, matrices, single and multiple variable calculus, and differential equations. Such programs can add exploration, discovery, and algorithmic approaches to mathematics. Mathematics may be much richer when these programs are used to focus our teaching on real mathematics and reduce our need to emphasize rote operations.

Trigonometry

Discovery Learning in Trigonometry by John C. Kelly. CONDUIT, $75; Apple II.

This supports discovery learning by helping the student experiment with trigonometric functions and their graphs and relationships. A worthwhile supplement to a trigonometry, analysis, or precalculus course that uses discovery learning techniques. The programs and User's Guide are quite good, but the instructor will need to give additional support to ensure their successful use. (Schmalzreid 1984)

Electronic Blackboard for Trigonometry by Richard O'Farrell et al. Brooks/Cole, $50; Apple II.

> Similar to the *Electronic Blackboard for Algebra* described above, this covers angle measurement and function graphing. Not as useful as its algebra counterpart because of its more limited scope, but can support parts of a trigonometry or precalculus course. (Brown 1986)

Electronic Study Guide for Trigonometry by Robert C. Steinbach and David A. Lundsford. COMPress, $275; Apple II.

> Like the *Electronic Study Guide for Precalculus Algebra*, this can supplement other materials for individual student study. It includes trigonometric function definitions, basic identities, polar coordinates, rectangular and polar graphing, inverse functions, vectors, and complex numbers. It contains a few errors and inconsistent difficulty levels, however, and the instructor should compensate for these rough spots. As with the algebra version, a demonstration is recommended. (Clarke 1986)

REFERENCES

All references are to the *College Mathematics Journal*.

Abram, Thomas J. 1987. 18 (1) (January 1987): 67-68.

Abram, Thomas J., forthcoming.

Bookman, Jack, and David A. Smith. 1985. 16 (3) (June 1985): 218-221.

Brown, Judith R. 1986. 17 (4) (September 1986): 358-359.

Carter, Thomas J. 1985. 16 (5) (November 1985): 414-415.

Clarke, Judith L. 1986. 17 (2) (March 1986): 182-183.

Cunningham, R.S., and David A. Smith. 1986, 1987. A mathematics software database. 17 (3) (May 1986): 255-266. A mathematics software database update. 18 (3) (May 1987): 242-247.

Dye, Jackie, and Pat Tolbert. 1984. 15(4) (September 1984): 343.

Herman, Eugene A. 1984. 15 (1) (January 1984): 65-66.

Hirschfelder, Rosemary. 1987. 18 (2) (March 1987): 158-159.

Kunkle, Dan, and L. Carl Leinbach. 1987. 18 (1) (January 1987): 66.

Leinbach, L. Carl. 1984. 15 (2) (March 1984): 160-162.

Leinbach, L. Carl. 1986. 17 (1) (January 1986): 90.

Rossi, Donald E. 1985. 16 (3) (June 1985): 222.

Schmalzreid, Cynthia. 1984. 15 (3) (June 1984): 263-264.

Smith, Carol M. 1987. 18 (5) (November 1987): 423.

13. Recreational Mathematics

BONNIE AVERBACH and ORIN CHEIN

$\mathbf{M}$athematical puzzles and games have been tantalizing and exciting men and women of all ages and backgrounds for many centuries. The Rhind Papyrus shows that more than 3,500 years ago people in Egypt considered problems such as the following:

> Mass, its two thirds, its one half, its one seventh, its whole, it makes 33.

Today we might be amused by the quaint way in which the problem is stated; but there are indications that problems of this type were of interest not just as a means of diversion, but rather for specific applications and as a tool for training the mind.

Problems such as the example above might be included in the realm of "recreational mathematics," a term that is difficult to define precisely but which incudes puzzles, games, and problems whose primary purpose is to challenge the intellect, usually more for the fun of it rather than because the solutions will have practical applications or will have value in furthering the mainstream of research in mathematics.

Through the years many collections of recreational problems have appeared. From the Greek anthology of Metrodorus (c. 500) to the recent books and articles of Martin Gardner (see Bibliography), the field of recreational mathematics has provided not only a source of diversion but also a means to stimulate and develop our ability to think analytically and to solve problems.

There can be little argument that the development of this ability in our students should be among the primary goals of education. And it is our belief that recreational mathematics provides an effective vehicle for aiding this development. Success at becoming a good problem solver can only come about as a result of experience gained by working on problems — problems that are not merely a rote application of a particular mathematical fact or technique taught in a given lecture but that require some creativity on the part of the solver. Problems of recreational mathematics are usually ideal in this regard. Most recreational problems are easily stated and their solutions do not require extensive knowledge in any particular area. What they do require is a certain amount of ingenuity and imagination — traits that are necessary for solving any kind of problem (mathematical or otherwise) that a student might encounter in life. As a result, we believe that mathematical recreations deserve a place in the mathematics curriculum.

There are two different ways in which this can be accomplished — by incorporating recreational material into existing courses, or by creating at least one new course. In our opinion both approaches should be attempted.

The fact that recreational problems do not require any specific background and that they need not be strongly course-related makes it easy to weave them into any curriculum. Many textbooks currently in use in elementary schools have already taken the first step toward incorporating material of this type by including "problems for thought" or some similar concept at the end of most units of the text. These problems are not always directly related to the drill exercises of the unit; they just challenge the student to think. For example,

> Kim, Pete, and Nancy are the pitcher, the catcher, and the first baseman (although not necessarily in that order) for the Eastern Little League Midgets baseball team. The first baseman and Nancy are siblings and live at 315 Elm Street. Pete is left handed and is the catcher's next door neighbor. The Midgets only have right-handed pitchers. What position does each child play?

The elementary-school teacher may make use of problems such as this, or of mathematical games to help develop the student's reasoning abilities. For example, the following game might be introduced at any level once the children have mastered the basic multiplication tables.

> Place 19 pencils (or matchsticks, or pieces of chalk) on the desk and tell the class to remove one or two of them. Then you (the teacher) remove one or two; then the class does; then you do; and so on. Whoever leaves the opponent without a move wins.

After playing the game a few times, many students will realize that the outcome of the game is determined once only a few pencils remain: The player to leave 3 sticks is the eventual winner. Ask the class: "When can a player be sure that she will win?" After the "3 pencils left" answer is clear to the class, play the game again. Ask, "What will happen if a player leaves 4 or 5 pencils after his turn?" After the answer becomes clear, ask, "What if 6 pencils remain?" Play some more. Soon many students will have mastered the game. Have them elucidate the winning strategy. (Leave multiples of 3.) Then play the game over again, this time starting with 24 pencils instead of 19. Again lead the class to a solution.

Tell the class that you are going to play the game again tomorrow, but that players will be given the option of choosing 1, 2, or 3 pencils at a turn. For homework, the students should try to work out a winning strategy.

Such experiences introduce the students to the process of mathematical discovery and help develop their thinking ability.

Playing games and solving recreational puzzles seem reasonable enough for the elementary school student, but what relevance does this approach have for higher-level education? The fact is that even many adults are intrigued by such problems and get a great deal of satisfaction out of solving them. Why else is it that so many newspapers have puzzle sections and that magazines such as *Scientific American* and *Discover* have columns on mathematical mind-bogglers and recreations? At any level, a well-chosen problem can challenge us to strain our minds to strive for the solution; and discussing the solution to such a problem with others can help us learn to organize our thinking processes and to become better problem solvers.

With this in mind, it is not unreasonable to attempt to incorporate material of this type into existing courses at the secondary or even college level. It is easier to do this with some subjects than it is with others, considering that the syllabus is sometimes already quite crowded. But, when time does permit, remember that it is not essential that the added material be tied directly to the main subject matter of the course. On the other hand, many recreational topics would fit very nicely into traditional courses.

Some examples follow of topics that might be incorporated into the traditional curriculum. The bibliography at the end of the chapter lists a variety of sources in which many other suitable topics may be found.

Algebra is probably the course in which it is easiest to incorporate recreational type material. In fact, many of the "verbal problems" already included in the syllabus are of a recreational nature. Standard problems of this type may be augmented by such thought-provoking challenges as the famous fly problem:

> Two driverless trains, 65 miles apart, are rushing toward each other on the same track, at speeds of 60 miles per hour and 70 miles per hour respectively. A fly starts from the front of the 60 mph train and flies toward the other. When the

fly reaches the other train, the fly turns around and flies back to the first train. Then the fly turns around and flies back to the second; and so on. Assuming that the fly maintains a constant speed of 110 miles per hour and that it loses no time when changing direction, how far will the fly fly before it is crushed when the trains collide?

In dealing with verbal problems, emphasis should be placed on how to translate the English sentences of the problem into appropriate equations. Most college students still have a great deal of difficulty with this aspect of problem solving.

Another type of recreational problem that is especially appropriate for an algebra course is the algebraic "self-working" card trick (see Fulves 1976). The success of tricks of this type (which can be quite intriguing) depends not upon the sleight of hand of any magician, but rather purely on the mathematics of the situation. For example, give an ordinary 52-card deck to a student and issue the following instructions:

Shuffle the deck. Now, while my back is turned, turn over the top card. If it is a picture card, return it to the middle of the pack and repeat the procedure. Continue doing this until you obtain a card numbered between one (ace) and ten. Place this card face up on the table and, beginning with the next number, start counting quietly to yourself until you reach twelve. With each count, take one card from the deck and place it face up on the pile that you are creating. When you reach twelve, turn the pile over so that the cards are face down with the card you originally selected on top. Thus, for example, if you originally turned up a nine, place a card on top of the nine and silently count "ten"; then place another card and count "eleven"; then another card and count "twelve"; then turn the pile over. When you have completed the first pile, create a new pile in the same manner. Continue creating piles until too few cards remain to complete a new pile. Give these remaining cards to me.

Turn around, take a look at the number of (face down) piles and predict the sum of the top cards of these piles. (Your prediction should be the number of unused cards plus thirteen times four less than the number of piles.) Have the student verify that the prediction is correct.

The learning experience comes from having the students try, for homework, to figure out how the trick works. Some hints such as "How many cards would a pile contain if the first card were a six? What if it were a seven?" might be worthwhile if you think the class needs them.

There are many tricks of this nature that can be quite impressive. You might dedicate several different classes throughout the year to performing and subsequently to discussing such tricks, or you might keep a deck of cards handy and, whenever time permits at the end of another lesson, perform a trick to be discussed when the next opportunity arises.

Other recreational topics that might be appropriate for an algebra class are cryptarithmetic problems and Diophantine equations. Included in the former category are such alphametic problems as the well-known SEND + MORE = MONEY (in which different letters represent different digits, the same letter representing the same digit throughout), as well as such cryptic problems as

$$
\begin{array}{r}
{*}{*}3{*} \\
\times \quad {*}{*}{*} \\
\hline
{*}{*}{*}0{*} \\
{*}{*}{*}7{*} \\
{*}23{*} \\
\hline
{*}4{*}{*}{*}5{*}
\end{array}
$$

in which some of the digits are missing. In each case, the task is to restore the original numbers.

Diophantine equations are equations for which the solutions must be integers (often, positive integers). Such equations arise in problems in much the same way that ordinary linear equations do, but in Diophantine problems there are usually fewer equations than there are unknowns. It is only by virtue of the fact that the solutions must be positive integers that we are able to arrive at a unique solution (or a small number of solutions). The following is an example of a problem that leads to a Diophantine equation:

> One month ago, a used car salesman purchased a number (fewer than 50) of very old and battered cars for $89 each. He has sold some of them for $225 each and has already made a profit (total sales price minus total outlay for all cars purchased) or $2,327. How many of the cars that he purchased remain?

Although the solution of problems such as this can often be found by trial and error, discussion of these problems provides an ideal opportunity to introduce some topics (divisibility, prime numbers, the Euclidean algorithm, congruence) from elementary number theory, which, in turn, lead to other interesting problems.

Geometry offers a somewhat more limited choice of relevant recreational topics. The books of Sam Loyd (1959) and H. E. Dudeney (1954) contain some interesting geometry puzzles. Tangrams and other dissection problems can help develop the student's ability to visualize and reason. If time is available, a small excursion into graph or network theory might be very appropriate for a geometry class. Starting with a problem such as

Can Figure 13.1 be drawn without lifting your pencil from the paper and without retracing any edge?

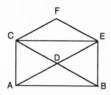

Figure 13.1

you can lead students to the development of mathematical structure. They will quickly appreciate the need for definitions and will see how theorems are first discovered intuitively and then given rigorous proof. Graph theory then lends itself to the solution of many different recreational puzzles such as the knight's tour of the chessboard and the colored cubes problem that was marketed a number of years ago under the name Instant Insanity.

Other games that could be connected peripherally with a geometry course are games in which symmetry plays a role in the solution – either because certain positions are symmetrical to each other and therefore equivalent or else because symmetry is an integral part of the winning strategy. In addition, games played in three dimensions can help develop the student's ability to visualize.

A course in finite mathematics, discrete mathematics, or probability might discuss the analysis of games of chance like Craps and might also include a variety of counting problems such as the following:

> Given six colors, in how many different ways is it possible to color the faces of a cube so that each face is solidly colored with one of the six given colors? (Two colorings of the cube are considered to be the same if one can be rotated to give the other.)

Problems such as this can teach the student how to conduct a careful case-by-case analysis, making sure that each possibility is counted exactly once.

Developing a computer program to carry out such an analysis would be a worthwhile project for students in a course in computer programming. Thus, counting problems might be considered in such courses, as might strictly determined games (that is, finite chance-free two-person games of perfect information). Students might be asked to program the computer to play reasonably simple two-person games, like tic-tac-toe; or, in more advanced courses the students could attempt to program the computer to analyze a game by means of a case analysis.

In all of these situations, the primary goal is to get the students to think and to learn how to become better problem solvers. This would also be the goal of a separate course in recreational mathematics. (We already offer such a course at Temple University as do a number of colleges.) At the college level such a course offers an excellent alternative to the usual "liberal arts mathematics" course that so many freshmen and sophomores take to satisfy their school's mathematics requirement. Learning to think analytically and to become a better problem solver is likely to provide a much greater payoff in a student's continuing education and later life than is the introductory knowledge of a few limited mathematical topics. (As a matter of fact, the course we offer covers some of the same topics discussed in more traditional courses, but the emphasis is on thinking and problem solving.)

As mentioned above, a number of colleges in the U.S. and in Canada already offer such courses. While we would like to see more colleges do so, we are also advocating the introduction of such a course in the senior year of high school. We do not think that this course would be right for all students. Those who are bright and well-motivated and who enjoy mathematics would really profit from the experience. Most of the students who currently take a fourth year of high-school mathematics fall into this category. Fourth-year courses like calculus, discrete mathematics, and finite mathematics are certainly beneficial, but we feel that the one that we propose would be even more so. We have found that students who take such a course are often stimulated to want to learn more mathematics, and they are better prepared to do so.

The course might last for one semester and be taken during the first half of the senior year, or it might be a full year course which might (but need not) be combined with an introduction to computer programming. Classroom time should be a mixture of lecture and problem solving. Lectures should discuss techniques of problem solving and present the mathematical background necessary to attack problems in new mathematical areas. It is important that students spend time trying to solve problems, both as individuals and as part of a group. It is also important that they learn to present their solutions, both in writing and orally, in a well-organized and convincing manner. Problems should be assigned regularly as homework, and solutions should be presented and constructively criticized. Sometimes the class as a whole should attempt to attack a problem or analyze a game.

Topics to be covered in the course could include any of those mentioned above as well as many others that can be found in the various sources in the bibliography. The course we offer usually begins with a discussion of some general techniques of problem solving as it is applied to matching problems and general logic problems. A more formal discussion of logic and related problems is then followed by some of the following topics: algebra, number theory, number bases, cryptarithmetic, graph theory, probability, strictly determined two-person games, and solitaire manipulative games and puzzles. Time does not permit us to do all of these in a 56-hour, 14-week semester, so we must be somewhat selective. In a high-school course (whether full or half year), more time would be available and possibly all of these could be covered.

Strictly determined games are one of the topics which we most enjoy including in the course. For homework, students are asked to analyze games of this type, to determine which player (the first or second to move) has a winning strategy, and to find that strategy if possible. After a game has been analyzed, it is sometimes instructive to see how slight modifications in the rules can result in interesting variations which require a totally new analysis. Occasionally, the class may be divided into competing teams when playing some of these games. Team discussions and strategy sessions can be an instructive experience.

A full-year course of the type we are proposing might be combined with a course in computer programming. Some class sessions would be devoted to the various problem solving activities suggested above, while others would be concerned with programming. As more advanced programming techniques are developed, programming skills can be applied to play and analyze games, to solve a variety of more difficult problems such as cryptarithmic problems that require a great deal of trial and error, or to develop probabilistic simulations, such as throwing dice.

When we first started teaching our course in recreational mathematics, we relied on a selection of problem books as the required texts. This proved to be unsatisfactory, as these books are not organized for that purpose and they usually do little to explain new mathematical ideas. For this reason, we wrote our own text (Averbach and Chein 1980), which is intended for the level and the audience suggested above. Other books which might be used for the purpose are Jacobs (1970) for a lower-level class and Beck et al. (1969) for a more advanced one. Neither of the latter two specifically deals with recreational mathematics or with techniques of problem solving, but both contain many interesting topics and challenging problems which could be used. Any of these texts could be supplemented by problems chosen from other sources like those contained in the bibliography below.

REFERENCES

Averbach, Bonnie, and Orin Chein. 1980. *Mathematics: Problem Solving Through Recreational Mathematics*. San Francisco, Calif.: W. H. Freeman.

Beck, Anatole, Michael N. Bleicher, and Donald W. Crowe. 1969. *Excursions into Mathematics*. New York: Worth.

Dudeney, Henry E. 1954. *536 Puzzles and Curious Problems*. New York: Scribner's.

Fulves, Karl. 1976. *Self Working Card Tricks*. New York: Dover.

Jacobs, Harold R. 1970. *Mathematics: A Human Endeavor*. San Francisco, Calif.: W. H. Freeman.

Loyd, Samuel. 1959. *Best Mathematical Puzzles of Sam Loyd*. Edited by Martin Gardner. New York: Dover.

BIBLIOGRAPHY

This bibliography, which is by no means exhaustive, includes materials of five types
- Bibliographic Works (which primarily contain lists of other recreational materials, by topic)
- Textbooks
- Resource Materials (which may include self-contained essays and/or historical information on recreational topics)
- Problem Collections
- Journals with regular columns on puzzles, games, or other recreational matter.

Bibliographic Works

Schaaf, William L. 1970-1978. *A Bibliography of Recreational Mathematics*. 4 vols. Reston, Va.: National Council of Teachers of Mathematics.
Extensive bibliography, listed by topic, of recreational materials appearing through 1978.

————. 1983-   . Vestpocket bibliographies, nos. 1- . *Journal of Recreational Mathematics* 16 (1983-1984) and following.
An update to the four volumes listed above, running to a dozen installments through 1987.

Textbooks

Averbach, Bonnie, and Orin Chein. 1980. *Mathematics: Problem Solving through Recreational Mathematics*. San Francisco, Calif.: W. H. Freeman.
Text geared to teaching the reader how to approach problem solving in general. It also could serve as a resource book for teachers, containing as it does a large number of recreational problems arranged by topic, in the areas of general reasoning, logic, algebra, number theory, cryptarithmetic and number bases, graph theory, strictly determined games, and manipulative puzzles. Each chapter includes a discussion of the mathematical concepts and a variety of problems and puzzles in the area. A solutions manual is available for teachers. Most appropriate for students from the eleventh grade through the third year of college.

Beck, Anatole, Michael N. Bleicher, and Donald W. Crowe. 1969. *Excursions into Mathematics*. New York: Worth.
Contains discussions of a variety of topics, not all recreational in nature, from the fields of geometry, topology, graph theory, number theory, and strictly determined games. Most appropriate for use at the second-year college level or beyond.

Berlekamp, Elwyn R., John H. Conway, and Richard K. Guy. 1982. *Winning Ways for Your Mathematical Plays*. New York: Academic.
Deals with an approach to analyze and play a wide variety of mathematical games. Although its use does not require any specific background, it is most appropriate for the mathematically-sophisticated student at the third-year college level or above.

Jacobs, Harold R. 1970. *Mathematics: A Human Endeavor*. San Francisco, Calif.: W. H. Freeman.
Contains elementary mathematical discussions on a variety of topics, not all

recreational in nature (although the book does have a recreational flavor), including logic, geometry, topology, and probability. Most appropriate for students in the third or fourth year of high school. A solutions manual is available for the instructor.

Stein, Sherman K. 1963. _Mathematics: The Man-Made Universe._ San Francisco, Calif.: W. H. Freeman.
Contains mathematical discussions of a variety of topics from the fields of number theory, geometry, probability, topology, as well as a number of manipulative puzzles. Most appropriate for use at the second-year college level or beyond.

Resource Materials

Ball, W. W. Rouse, and H. S. M. Coxeter. 1987. _Mathematical Recreations and Essays._ 13th ed. New York: Dover.
A collection of short essays on recreational topics, most of which are of an arithmetic, geometric, or graph-theoretic nature or else involve some game or manipulative puzzle.

Beiler, Albert H. 1964. _Recreations in the Theory of Numbers — The Queen of Mathematics Entertains._ New York: Dover.
Contains a discussion of number theoretic concepts and problems, many of which are of a recreational nature.

Frey, Alexander H., Jr., and David Singmaster. 1982. _Handbook of Cubik Math._ London: Enslow.
A solution of the Rubik's cube puzzle and a discussion of the underlying mathematical structure.

Fulves, Karl. 1976. _Self-Working Card Tricks._ New York: Dover.
A collection of self-working card tricks, many of which can be explained on the basis of mathematical principles.

Gardner, Martin. 1959. _The Scientific American Book of Mathematical Puzzles and Diversions._ New York: Simon & Schuster.

———. 1961. _The Second Scientific American Book of Mathematical Puzzles and Diversions._ New York: Simon & Schuster.

———. 1966. _New Mathematical Diversions from Scientific American._ New York: Simon & Schuster. Reprint. 1983. Chicago: University of Chicago Press.

————. 1967. *The Numerology of Dr. Matrix.* New York: Scribner's.

————. 1969. *The Unexpected Hanging and Other Mathematical Diversions.* New York: Simon & Schuster.

————. 1971. *Martin Gardner's Sixth Book of Mathematical Games from Scientific American.* San Francisco, Calif.: W. H. Freeman. Reprint under the title *Martin Gardner's Sixth Book of Mathematical Diversions from Scientific American.* 1983. Chicago, Ill.: University of Chicago Press.

————. 1975. *Mathematical Carnival.* New York: Knopf.

————. 1976. *The Incredible Dr. Matrix.* New York: Scribner's.

————. 1977. *Mathematical Magic Show.* New York: Knopf.

————. 1979. *Mathematical Circus.* New York: Knopf.

————. 1983. *Wheels, Life and Other Mathematical Amusements.* New York: W. H. Freeman.

————. 1986. *Knotted Doughnuts and Other Mathematical Entertainments.* New York: W. H. Freeman.

————. 1987. *Time Travel and Other Mathematical Bewilderments.* New York: W. H. Freeman.

————. 1987. *Riddles of the Sphinx and Other Mathematical Puzzle Tales.* New Mathematical Library no. 32. Washington, D.C.: Mathematical Association of America.

> Each of the above books by Martin Gardner is a collection of self-contained essays based upon material that appeared in his "Mathematical Games" column in *Scientific American.* Each chapter deals with some recreational topics selected from a wide range of areas. Discussions usually include the relevant mathematical considerations.

Hunter, James A. H., and Joseph S. Madachy. 1975. *Mathematical Diversions.* New York: Dover.

> Contains puzzles and essays on a number of topics including paradoxes, number theory, topology, geometry, cryptarithmetic, probability, and logic.

Kasner, Edward, and James Newman. 1962. *Mathematics and the Im-*

agination. New York: Simon & Schuster.
> Contains discussions of a number of topics, not all recreational, including numbers, geometry, topology, paradoxes, probability, and calculus.

Klarner, David A., ed. 1981. *The Mathematical Gardner.* Boston, Mass.: Prindle, Weber, & Schmidt.
> Consists of essays on games, geometry, and other topics. Although no particular background is necessary, the book is most appropriate for a reader with some mathematical sophistication.

Kraitchik, Maurice. 1953. *Mathematical Recreations.* 2nd ed. New York: Dover.
> A collection of problems with excellent commentary and mathematical discussion. Topics include logic, arithmetic, geometry, algebra, combinatorics, probability, and games.

Krulik, Stephen, and Jesse A. Rudnick. 1980. *Problem Solving: A Handbook for Teachers.* Boston: Allyn & Bacon.
> Discusses how to approach problem solving and includes a collection of problems and games that are designed to help teach problem-solving techniques.

Lindgren, Harry. 1972. *Recreational Problems in Geometric Dissections & How to Solve Them.* New York: Dover.
> Presents a discussion of methods of geometric dissection and related problems.

Madachy, Joseph S. 1966. *Mathematics on Vacation.* New York: Scribner's.
> Contains discussions of a variety of recreational topics including geometric dissections and constructions, numbers, and cryptarithmetic.

Pólya, George. 1945. *How to Solve It: a New Aspect Of Mathematical Method.* 1957. 2nd ed. Garden City, N.Y.: Doubleday. 1971 Reprint. Princeton, N.J.: Princeton University Press.
> Presents a discussion of techniques of problem solving. For the most part, the problems considered are not recreational in nature.

Rademacher, Hans, and Otto Toeplitz. 1957. *Enjoyment of Mathematics: Selections from Mathematics for the Amateur.* Translated by Herbert Zuckerman. Princeton, N.J.: Princeton University Press.
> Discusses a number of topics in number theory, geometry, and topology. Most appropriate for advanced college students.

Schuh, Frederik. 1968. *The Master Book of Mathematical Recreations.*

Translated by F. Göbel. Translation edited by T. H. O'Beirne. New York:
Dover.

Contains discussions of a number of recreational topics including methods
of solving problems, games, number systems and related problems, probability,
number theory puzzles, and problems related to networks and to mechanics.

Schwartz, B. L. 1968. *Mathematical Solitaires and Games*. Farmingdale, N.Y.: Baywood.

Discusses a number of mathematical games and manipulative puzzles and
how they may be analyzed.

Singmaster, David. 1980. *Notes on Rubik's Magic Cube*. London:
Mathematical Sciences and Computing Polytechnic of the South Bank.

A solution of the Rubik's cube puzzle and a discussion of the underlying
mathematical structure.

Problem Collections

The books listed in this section consist primarily of collections of
problems and puzzles on a variety of recreational topics. Although some
of these books concentrate on problems in one particular area (which is
usually clear from the book title), most contain a miscellany of problems,
some of which are arranged at random, others by topic. Almost all of these
books contain answers to the problems, and most also contain solutions.

Bakst, Aaron. 1965. *Mathematical Puzzles and Pastimes*. 2nd ed.
Princeton, N.J.: Van Nostrand.

Contains recreational problems in arithmetic, geometry, and trigonometry.

Carroll, Lewis (= C. L. Dodgson). 1958. *Mathematical Recreations of
Lewis Carroll*. Vol. I: *Symbolic Logic* and *The Game of Logic*: Vol. II: *Pil-
low Problems* and *A Tangled Tale*. New York: Dover.

Logic problems.

Degrazia, Joseph. 1954. *Math is Fun*. New York: Emerson.

Miscellaneous problems.

Dudeney, Henry E. 1954. *536 Puzzles and Curious Problems*. New
York: Scribner's.

Miscellaneous problems.

————. 1958. *Canterbury Puzzles and Other Curious Problems*. 4th ed.

New York: Dover.
  Miscellaneous problems.

———. 1970. *Amusements in Mathematics*. New York: Dover.
  Miscellaneous problems.

Dunn, Angela, ed. 1980. *Mathematical Bafflers*. Rev. ed. New York: Dover.
  Miscellaneous problems.

———. 1983. *Second Book of Mathematical Bafflers*. New York: Dover.
  Miscellaneous problems.

Emmet, Eric R. 1977. *Puzzles for Pleasure*. Buchanan, N.Y.: Emerson.
  Miscellaneous problems.

———. 1978. *Brain Puzzler's Delight*. Buchanan, N.Y.: Emerson.
  Miscellaneous problems.

Friedland, Aaron J. 1970. *Puzzles in Math and Logic: 100 New Recreations*. New York: Dover.
  Miscellaneous problems.

Gardner, Martin. 1956. *Mathematics, Magic & Mystery*. New York: Dover.
  A collection of tricks and puzzles that are of mathematical interest.

———. 1961. *Mathematical Puzzles*. New York: Harper & Row.
  Miscellaneous problems.

———. 1978. *Aha! Aha! Insight*. San Francisco, Calif.: W. H. Freeman.
  Coextensive with a set of film strips dealing with a variety of mathematical problems concerning numbers, logic, geometry, combinatorics, and procedural routine, as well as with a variety of word problems.

———. 1982. *Aha! Gotcha: Paradoxes to Puzzle and Delight*. San Francisco, Calif.: W. H. Freeman.
  A collection of number, logic, geometry, probability and statistics puzzles and paradoxes.

Graham, L. A. 1959. *Ingenious Mathematical Problems and Methods*.

New York: Dover.
> A collection of miscellaneous problems having clever elegant solutions.

————. 1968. *The Surprise Attack in Mathematical Problems*. New York: Dover.
> A collection of miscellaneous problems for which unexpected approaches lead to clever solutions.

Greenblatt, M. H. 1965. *Mathematical Entertainments, A Collection of Illuminating Puzzles, New and Old*. New York: Crowell.
> Miscellaneous problems.

Greenes, Carole E., Rika Spurgin, and Justine M. Dombrowski. 1977. *Problem-Mathics: Mathematical Challenge Problems with Solution Strategies*. Palo Alto, Calif.: Creative.
> Presents problems in the areas of arithmetic, geometry, algebra, number theory and logic and discusses techniques for solving them.

Heath, Royal V. 1953. *Mathemagic: Magic, Puzzles, and Games with Numbers*. New York: Dover.
> Miscellaneous puzzles, games, and magic tricks related to mathematics.

Hunter, James A. H. 1965. *Fun with Figures*. New York: Dover.
> Miscellaneous puzzles involving numbers.

————. 1966. *More Fun with Figures*. New York: Dover.
> Miscellaneous puzzles involving numbers.

————. 1976. *Mathematical Brain-Teasers*. New York: Dover.
> Miscellaneous problems.

————. 1980. *Challenging Mathematical Teasers*. New York: Dover.
> Miscellaneous problems.

Knitzer, Carol A. 1983. *Making Mathematics Fun!* West Nyack, N.Y.: Parker.
> Contains problems in arithmetic and geometry for elementary school students.

Kordemsky, Boris A. 1982. *Moscow Puzzles: Three Hundred Fifty-Nine Mathematical Recreations*. New York: Scribner's.
> Miscellaneous problems.

Loyd, Samuel. 1959. *Best Mathematical Puzzles of Sam Loyd*. Edited by Martin Gardner. New York: Dover.
Miscellaneous problems.

————. 1960. *More Mathematical Puzzles of Sam Loyd*. Edited by Martin Gardner. New York: Dover.
Miscellaneous problems.

Meyer, Jerome S. 1956. *Puzzle Quiz and Stunt Fun*. New York: Dover.
Miscellaneous problems.

Mosteller, F. 1965. *Fifty Challenging Problems in Probability*. Reading, Mass.: Addison-Wesley.
Problems in probability.

Mott-Smith, Geoffrey. 1954. *Mathematical Puzzles for Beginners and Enthusiasts*. 2nd ed. New York: Dover.
Miscellaneous problems.

O'Beirne, T. H. 1965. *Puzzles and Paradoxes*. New York: Oxford University Press. Reprint under the title *Puzzles and Paradoxes: Fascinating Excursions in Recreational Mathematics*. 1984. New York: Dover.
Miscellaneous problems.

Patton, T. 1968. *Card Tricks Anyone Can Do*. New York: Castle Books.
A collection of card tricks, some of which are mathematical in nature.

Phillips, Hubert C. 1961. *My Best Puzzles in Mathematics*. New York: Dover.
Logic and general reasoning problems.

————. 1961. *My Best Puzzles in Logic and Reasoning*. New York: Dover.
Logic and general reasoning problems.

Read, Ronald C. 1965. *Tangrams — 330 Puzzles*. New York: Dover.
Tangram problems (geometric dissection).

Silverman, David L. 1971. *Your Move*. New York: McGraw-Hill.
Problems relating to what move you should make in a given game situation.

Summers, George J. 1968. *New Puzzles in Logical Deduction*. New York.

Logic and general reasoning problems.

————. 1972. *Test Your Logic: 50 Puzzles in Deductive Reasoning.* New York: Dover.

Logic and general reasoning problems.

Trigg, Charles W. 1967. *Mathematical Quickies.* New York: McGraw-Hill. Reprint. 1985. *Mathematical Quickies: 270 Stimulating Problems with Solutions.* New York: Dover.

Miscellaneous problems and puzzles which can be solved quickly if approached from the proper perspective.

Wylie, C. R. Jr. 1957. *101 Puzzles in Thought and Logic.* New York: Dover.

Logic and general reasoning problems.

Journals

For pertinent material, including articles of interest and problems, readers should consult current and back issues of

- *American Mathematical Monthly*
- *College Mathematics Journal*
- *Discover Magazine*
- *Games Magazine*
- *Journal of Recreational Mathematics*
- *Mathematical Gazette*
- *Mathematics Magazine*
- *Mathematics Teacher*
- *Scientific American*
- *Technology Review.*

For publication information, see Chapter 20, Resources.

14. Applications of Mathematics

JAMES R. CHOIKE

$\mathbf{M}$athematics is a valuable tool to discover and describe the actions of nature and mankind. In partnership with other disciplines, such as the physical, biological, social, engineering, management, and computer sciences, it can assist society in human endeavors; used in this way, it becomes applied mathematics.

All too often, the early years of students' study of mathematics are mostly taken up with disjointed topics and drill-and-practice activities, which — they are told — are needed to make them ready for the applications of mathematics to real-world and important problems. How long must students wait until they begin to see the fruits of their mathematical studies? Even if they are patient, or good with mathematics, or both, they may wait many years before they see honest and inspiring applications of mathematics. How long they wait depends upon how willing their teachers are to present good examples of applied mathematics. Usually in the four- to five-year period devoted to the study of algebra I, algebra II, plane geometry, trigonometry, and precalculus mathematics, the efforts of mathematics students are directed principally to drill-and-practice over a collection of mathematical facts and skills. Some of these topics are taken up again and again; each time they are presented as if for the first time. Examples of such topics are factoring polynomials, the quadratic formula, the equation of a line, and solving simultaneous linear equations. Young people become bored with practice and rehearsal. When the preparation for the big game or the great performance continues endlessly, and the game or performance never seems to come, is it any wonder that the players lose interest and drop out?

To keep their interest in mathematics, students must be shown more of the *real* applications of mathematics. They must be presented early in their training with the notion of a mathematical model. For most students, and people in general, the triumphs of mathematics are its applications. These applications are found in every discipline: in the physical sciences, in the biological sciences, in business, in social sciences, in short, every-where, even in mathematics itself. An application of mathematics occurs whenever mathematics is a means to obtaining an answer to a question or problem.

The standard examples presented by most textbooks of applications of mathematics are "word problems," sometimes called "story problems." How real are they? Often they are not examples of applications of mathematics; they are merely exercises to give students practice and drill in mastering the art of translating a problem stated in words to a problem expressed in mathematics. Consider the following typical example:

> A farmer had chickens and rabbits. In all, he had 50 heads and 120 legs. How many chickens and how many rabbits did he have?

This problem is not totally worthless. It does afford students the chance to convert the word problem into the mathematical form

$$\begin{aligned} x + y &= 50 \\ 2x + 4y &= 120 \end{aligned}$$

and to solve it, learning that the farmer had 40 chickens and 10 rabbits. But this activity cannot be called an application of mathematics. After all, a farmer would know the livestock, or else could merely go to the barn and count.

When students are fed a continual and exclusive diet of such lifeless drill-and-practice problems, they become undernourished and uninterested. Students need to be shown enriched and real examples of mathematics in action at all levels, from the moment they begin algebra. Students also need the opportunity to work with and do applied mathematics. Some will be able to do it better than others. But the more chances students are given to try their hand at mathematics to which they can relate, the more likely they will be able to do it better. Even if they choose not to make mathematics a part of their adult professional careers, at least they will appreciate mathematics for what it can do.

I will list some examples of mathematics in action that add some spice to the drill-and-practice routine.

Early in a first course in algebra students are introduced to the concept of a variable. This is a deep and subtle concept for these students, and a good teacher covers the ground slowly and clearly so that all will understand. A typical problem is:

Given $S = 8x + 2y + 5$. Find S when
(a) $x = 2, y = 1$; (b) $x = 2, y = 2$; (c) $x = 4, y = 3$.

The basic concept to be practiced is the concept of "substitution for variables." Students need this practice. But why not also, as a treat, give them the equation

$$S = 0.8w + 0.13h - 1.03$$

and explain that the equation is a mathematical model for the surface area of an eighth- or ninth-grader's skin as a function of the student's weight, w, in pounds, and height, h, in inches. The surface area, S, is expressed in square feet. Students can substitute their own dimensions to compute their own surface area. An instructor could even suggest for homework that each student cut out and paste together from old newspapers a rectangular sheet with the same flat area as the surface area of the student's body. Would students enjoy this exercise? Try it and see.

The surface area equation is not frivolous, either. It is valuable in the area of health and the prescribing of an effective, yet safe, dosage of medicine to children. What fraction of an adult dosage should a child receive? Some methods are based on a child's age (check any aspirin bottle). But the best method takes into account, not the age, but the child's height and weight, or surface area. Thus, *this* is the applied setting (Choike 1981).

Notice how students can be introduced to the important concept of a mathematical model. Loosely speaking, a mathematical model is a mathematical description for a phenomenon, observed or occurring, in the physical world. The reader may be interested to know that the surface area equation is a Taylor polynomial approximation to a more exact expression for human surface area (Routh 1971). The latter is

$$S = 10.59w^{0.425}h^{0.725}$$

In this form the formula is too complicated to give to beginning algebra students. However, a complicated mathematical model can often be brought to the students' level by appropriate use of approximation techniques that are a part of the college background of most mathematics teachers. This is one example of how the advanced mathematics courses taken in college can aid secondary-school teachers of mathematics in their own classrooms.

   Some important topics presented to students of algebra and geometry
are ratio, proportion, and properties of geometric figures such as the triangle and the circle. As an example to motivate students to learn these
concepts, I offer the impressive calculation that the Greek mathematician
Eratosthenes (275-194 B.C.) gave for the circumference of the earth,
about 1,500 years before Columbus. This is one of many examples that
can be found in sources on the history of mathematics, examples that are
real applications of mathematics and often have an interesting story to
boot.
   Eratosthenes began with the observation that at noon of the summer
solstice, the sun was directly overhead. This fact he determined by observing that there were no shadows cast at the bottom of a deep well in the
city of Syene. At the same time, in the city of Alexandria, located due
north of Syene, the angle between the direction of the sun and the
straight-up direction was measured to be 1/50th of 360°. Figure 14.1
illustrates the measurements that were taken.
   In Figure 14.1, S denotes Syene and A denotes Alexandria. The angle
α represents the angle that was measured at Alexandria.

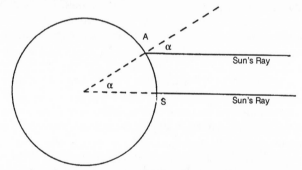

Figure 14.1. Eratosthenes' Measurements.

   Because of the great distance between the earth and the sun, Eratosthenes assumed that the sun's rays strike the earth in parallel rays. Hence,
the angle α that was measured at Alexandria is equal to the angle at the
center of the earth (assumed to be a sphere). This angle α is also the angle
that subtends the arc AS. Eratosthenes reasoned further that since α was
measured to be 1/50th of 360°, the arc AS subtended by α must be 1/50th
of the total circumference. The measurement of the earth's circumference can be accomplished once the length of the arc AS is known. As
it happened, the distance between Syene and Alexandria was known to

be 5,000 stadia (a stadium was a unit of measure used in Greek times, with 1 stadium = 515 feet approximately), from the camel trains that used this well-traveled trade route. Therefore, according to Eratosthenes, since the length of the arc AS is 5000 stadia and since also the arc AS is 1/50th of the total circumference, the circumference of the earth is

50(5,000) = 250,000 stadia.

Eratosthenes' estimate in feet and miles is

250,000 (515) = 128,750,000 feet $\doteq$ 24,400 miles.

The amazing feature of Eratosthenes' computation is its accuracy. Although the earth is not quite a sphere, its average radius is 3,958.89 miles. Hence its circumference is

2π(3,958.89) = 24,874 miles.

Eratosthenes' estimate is off by less than 500 miles, or 2%.

Eratosthenes made clever use of the sun and mathematics to estimate the earth's circumference. Now it is time to challenge your students to a problem that has a similar solution. Does your school have a flagpole or other tall landmark? Their problem is to find the height of the flagpole. As a hint, tell them to wait for a sunny day and to remember Eratosthenes.

The last example I present is one that exemplifies the notion of a mathematical model and illustrates the importance of the trigonometric functions. The values of the trigonometric functions sine and cosine are to be seen in two different settings. In the setting of the geometry of triangles, they represent ratios of sides of a right triangle relative to one of the triangle's acute angles. Utilizing this setting, the problem of finding the height of the flagpole can be solved through trigonometry by merely measuring the shadow cast by the flagpole and the angle of elevation to the top of the flagpole, measured from the tip of its shadow.

However, the trigonometric functions can also be defined in the setting of motion, periodic motion, around a circle. Such motion abounds in nature. The most obvious examples are the seasons of the year and the hours of the day. Students will enjoy having a fairly accurate mathematical model for computing the hours of sunlight in their hometown for a given date of the year. Of course, the mathematical model most certainly must involve the trigonometric functions! Here is the model.

Let h denote the number of hours of sunlight, λ denote the latitude in degrees of a point on the earth (e.g., the latitude of a student's hometown), ω_1 denote the angular velocity of the earth's rotation on its axis ($\omega_1 = 360$ degrees/24 hours = 15 degrees/hour), ω_2 denote the angular velocity of the earth around the sun ($\omega_2 = 360$ degrees/365 days = 0.986 degrees/day), and t denote the time measured in number of days since the vernal equinox (March 21). If i denotes the angle of inclination of the earth's axis of rotation relative to the plane of its orbit, then

$$h = (180° + 2\theta)/15$$

where θ is the angle between -90° and 90° that satisfies

$$\sin \theta = C/\sqrt{A^2 + B^2}$$

$$A = \cos \lambda \cos \omega_2 t$$
$$B = \cos \lambda \sin \omega_2 t \cos i$$
$$C = \sin \lambda \sin \omega_2 t \sin i.$$

In the case of the earth, $i = 23.55°$ and

$$A = \cos \lambda \cos \omega_2 t$$
$$B = 0.9167 \cos \lambda \sin \omega_2 t$$
$$C = 0.3995 \sin \lambda \sin \omega_2 t.$$

This mathematical model is surprisingly accurate, even though it is based on a number of simplifying assumptions. The model assumes a spherical earth, circular orbit of the earth about the sun with uniform angular velocity, no refraction of the sunlight by the earth's atmosphere, and a point-mass sun (Choike 1984).

As you can see, the above mathematical model is very trigonometric and offers students of trigonometry an application they will find interesting once they are encouraged to work with it. For example, the latitude for their local vicinity can usually be obtained from a nearby airport. Latitudes for various locations throughout the world can be found in a good world almanac, available in most libraries. A more challenging question is to solve for the latitude in the Northern Hemisphere above which full days of darkness and full days of sunlight are possible. The answer can be obtained by solving the equation

$$C/\sqrt{A^2 + B^2} = 1$$

with the values above substituted for A, B, and C, to find λ. This value for λ is 66.5° N in the Northern Hemisphere, the latitude of the Arctic Circle (Choike 1984).

An activity to follow up the hours-of-sunlight model is to have your students try their hand at constructing a model for a periodic natural phenomenon. After all, students practice mathematics so that (as most teachers frequently tell them) they will be ready to use it when called upon. Why have them wait? Let us get them involved *now* with using their mathematics. Ask them to construct a mathematical model that gives a reasonable approximation to the average daily temperature for their local vicinity (Lando and Lando 1977; McCloskey 1981). This is an applied problem. It has no unique solution (if each student does this problem independently, each may present you with a different model). Part of the problem is to obtain the data (a local weather station or newsroom may help here). Finally, because of the periodic nature of the problem, trigonometric functions come in handy.

I have given three examples to illustrate how real applications of mathematics can liven up the classroom and motivate topics under discussion. These examples are by no means unique. There is a vast literature of such appropriate examples at all levels of instruction just waiting to be used. It does require from the instructor the time, initiative, and spirit to find these examples, and also prepare them for the students' appetite.

An excellent annotated bibliography on applications of mathematics appeared in the NCTM *1979 Yearbook*. A similar bibliography, which should be viewed as a supplement to that yearbook, follows.

REFERENCES

Choike, James R. 1981. *Opening Career Doors*. MAWIS Project. Washington, D.C.: Mathematical Association of America.

————. 1984. *A Path to Applied Mathematics: Hours of Daylight*. TEAM Project. Washington, D.C.: Mathematical Association of America.

Lando, Barbara M., and Clifton A. Lando. 1977. Is the graph of temperature variation a sine curve? An application for trigonometry classes. *Mathematics Teacher* 70 (6) (September 1977): 538-540.

McCloskey, John W. 1981. A model for atmospheric temperature. *UMAP Journal* 2 (4) (1981): 5-12.

Routh, Joseph I. 1971. *Mathematical Preparation for Laboratory Technicians*. Philadelphia, Pa.: Saunders.

BIBLIOGRAPHY

Bibliographic entries are listed under the categories:
- General References
- Multi-Media Materials
- Books
- Articles in Journals.

General References

Agnew, Jeanne L., and Marvin S. Keener, eds. 1981. *Catalogue of Industry Related Problems for Mathematics Students*. Stillwater, Okla.: Department of Mathematics, Oklahoma State University.

> A collection of over 50 problems of applied mathematics from industry written for classroom use. Problems range in difficulty from secondary level to senior college level. Catalogue may be obtained by writing to the editors.

Joint Committee of the Mathematical Association of America and the National Council of Teachers of Mathematics. 1980. *A Sourcebook for Applications of School Mathematics*. Reston, Va.: National Council of Teachers of Mathematics.

> Vast collection of applied problems using arithmetic, algebra, geometry, trigonometry, logarithms, and probability. Also has some project problems and an extensive annotated bibliography on applied mathematics.

Sharron, Sidney, and Robert E. Reys, eds. 1979. *NCTM 1979 Yearbook*.

> Presents a collection of essays on applications of mathematics for classroom use at all grade levels, with an excellent annotated bibliography.

UMAP Modules.

These are lesson-length booklets from which students may learn applications of mathematics to a variety of fields. They are ideal as supplements to existing courses and texts, from secondary-level through college-level mathematics. Selected UMAP Modules are published in the UMAP Journal and in the annual collections UMAP Modules: Tools for Teaching. A catalog is available from the publisher, COMAP, Inc. (60 Lowell St., Arlington, MA 02174).The following sample of titles indicates the range of applications of mathematics found in the UMAP Modules:

Population Growth and the Logistic Curve. Unit 68.
The Digestive Process of Sheep. Unit 69.
Prescribing Safe and Effective Dosage. Unit 72.
Mercator's World Map. Unit 206.
Management of a Buffalo Herd. Unit 207.
The Human Cough. Unit 211.
Price Discrimination and Consumer Surplus. Unit 294.
Public Support for Presidents. Unit 299.
The Geometry of the Arms Race. Unit 311.
Genetic Counseling. Unit 456.

Multi-Media Materials

Applications in Mathematics (AIM) Project. 1986-1988. Washington, D.C.: Mathematical Association of America.

Collection of six modules. Each module includes a resource booklet with Student Book and Teacher Book bound together, by Jeanne L. Agnew; a three-segment video on the problem, problem preparation, and a solution, by John Jobe; and software for Apple II computers. The six topics are:

A Backwater Curve for the Windsor Locks Canal. 1986. Uses algebra and geometry to discover the answer to "What upstream level is required to deliver 1,500 cu. ft. of water at the downstream end?"

Pricing Auto Insurance. 1986. Balances income and costs to create an equation that, when solved, will determine the fair price of auto insurance for males 16-19 or females 16-19.

Testing Surface Antennas. 1986. Uses algebra and trigonometry to perform one part of the testing of a new invention.

Routing Telephone Service. 1987. Students investigate some choices required in automatic routing of 800 service and display these in a decision tree.

Capturing a Satellite. 1988. The astronaut leaves the space shuttle in the manned maneuvering unit to capture the satellite. What is the optimum targeting to use the least propellant?

Volcanic Eruption Fallout. 1988. Mt. St. Augustine, Alaska, is located along a major air route. The problem involves using observed data to study ash cloud hazard.

The AIM materials are available from the Mathematical Association of America free of charge. They are specifically designed for high-school students in grades 9-12. Each learning module is based on an industry-related applied mathematics problem that can be solved using high-school mathematics. The

Student Resource Books contain needed background and a statement of the problem. The Teacher Resource Books contain detailed solutions of the central problems, suggestions for use of the materials, and a selection of additional problems for further exploration. Each video is twenty minutes in length and consists of an on-site interview with the industrial mathematician who supplied the problem.

The Electoral College System. 1984. Stillwater, Okla.: College of Arts and Sciences, Oklahoma State University.

Booklet of teacher resource materials and 15-minute video. Contains a description of the electoral college system, a collection of exercises on the electoral college system, hints, and solutions. This material is appropriate for secondary-school social studies and algebra students.

Mathematics at Work in Society (MAWIS) Project. 1981. Washington, D.C.: Mathematical Association of America.

Booklet:Choike, James R. *Opening Career Doors*. Presents career information on over eighty different careers, and also presents over 75 realistic examples and exercises illustrating how mathematics is used in these careers.

Video:There are four 20-minute video cassettes produced by John Jobe.

An Actuary—What's That? Looks at mathematics needed in the insurance business.

Mathematics in Space. Looks at mathematics needed at NASA to prepare space flights.

Mathematics: The Language of Research. An applied mathematician at Bell Labs describes her work.

Mathematics: Where Will I Ever Use It? A high-school teacher talks about her career, as well as other mathematics-dependent careers.

The MAWIS materials are available from the Mathematical Association of America free of charge. They are appropriate for students of grades eight and above.

Teaching Experiential Applied Mathematics (TEAM) Project. 1984-1985. Washington, D.C.: Mathematical Association of America.

Collection of six modules. Each module includes a booklet with Student Book and Teacher Book bound together, by James R. Choike; a two-segment video on the problem and a solution, by John Jobe; and software for Apple computers, where appropriate. The six topics are:

Hours of Daylight. 1984. For a given date, determine the amount of time a particular location on a planet spends in sunlight.

Highway Slope Design. 1984. Determine the smooth parabolic transition between two straight roads with different grades.

Aircraft Sidestep Maneuver. 1984. Determine the path of an airplane while it is rolling to make the transition from a straight line path to a circular path.

Satellite Communications Subsystem. 1985. Given the failure rates of tube amplifiers, determine if the proposed communications subsystem design on a satellite meets contractual reliability requirements.

Loan Insurance Analysis. 1985. Determine the combination of whole-life and

decreasing term insurance which will cover a loan and yield a minimum premium.
The Statue of Liberty. 1985. Find the amount of deflection at various points on the main head arch of the Statue of Liberty when external forces are applied.

The TEAM materials are available from the Mathematical Association of America free of charge. They were specifically designed for college mathematics students, but all are adaptable to high-school mathematics students.

Books

Aaboe, Asger. 1964. *Episodes from the Early History of Mathematics.* New Mathematical Library no. 13. Washington, D.C.: Mathematical Association of America.

Discusses the contributions and progress made by the ancients in mathematics.

Bender, Edward A. 1978. *An Introduction to Mathematical Modeling.* New York: Wiley.

Contains many applications of mathematics with the emphasis on mathematical modeling.

Bowden, Leon. 1984. *The Role of Mathematics in Science.* Washington, D.C.: Mathematical Association of America.

Discusses mechanics, population growth, probability, optics, and the application of matrices to the theory of relativity.

Brams, Steven J., William F. Lucas, and Philip D. Straffin, Jr., eds. 1983. *Political and Related Models.* Modules in Applied Mathematics, vol. 2. New York: Springer-Verlag.

Volume 2 of a 4-volume series on case studies in applied mathematics. Most topics are for college-level students, but there are some that can be adapted for secondary-level students.

Braun, Martin. 1983. *Differential Equations and Their Applications: An Introduction to Applied Mathematics.* 3rd ed. New York: Springer-Verlag.

A textbook for a college-level introductory course in differential equations that contains many fascinating applications.

————, C.S. Coleman, and D.A. Drew, eds. 1983. *Differential Equation Models.* Modules in Applied Mathematics, vol. 1. New York: Springer-Verlag.

Volume 1 of a 4-volume series on case studies in applied mathematics. Most topics are for college-level students, but there are some that can be adapted for secondary-level students.

Edwards, Charles H., Jr., and David E. Penney. 1982. *Calculus and Analytic Geometry*. Englewood Cliffs, N.J.: Prentice-Hall.

> Introductory calculus textbook that presents many applications of mathematics.

Eves, Howard W. 1982. *Great Moments in Mathematics Before 1650*. Dolciani Mathematical Expositions no. 5. Washington, D.C.: Mathematical Association of America.

> Presents twenty-three descriptions of important developments and outstanding achievements in mathematics from antiquity to 1650.

————. 1982. *Great Moments in Mathematics After 1650*. Dolciani Mathematical Expositions no. 7. Washington, D.C.: Mathematical Association of America.

> Presents twenty descriptions of outstanding events in mathematics after 1650.

————. 1983. *An Introduction to the History of Mathematics*. 5th ed. New York: Saunders College Publishing.

> Excellent resource for historical applications of mathematics. Also contains many problems and projects that are interesting and accessible to students.

Friedrichs, Kurt O. 1965. *From Pythagoras to Einstein*. New Mathematical Library no. 16. Washington, D.C.: Mathematical Association of America.

> Discusses the Pythagorean formula and basic facts of vector geometry in a variety of mathematical and physical settings leading to Einstein's $E = mc^2$.

Goldstein, Larry J., David C. Lay, and David I. Schneider. 1987. *Calculus and Its Applications*. 4th ed. Englewood Cliffs, N.J.: Prentice-Hall.

> An introductory calculus textbook that presents many applications of mathematics. It contains a useful "Index of Applications."

Goldstein, Larry J., and David I. Schneider. 1980. *Finite Mathematics and its Applications*. Englewood Cliffs, N.J.: Prentice-Hall.

> An introductory textbook on finite mathematics which presents many applications. It contains a useful "Index of Applications."

Kastner, Bernice. 1978. *Applications of Secondary School Mathematics*. Reston, Va.: National Council of Teachers of Mathematics.

> Discusses many applications of mathematics which use the mathematics covered in secondary school.

Lucas, William F., Fred S. Roberts, and Robert M. Thrall, eds. 1983. _Discrete and System Models._ Modules in Applied Mathematics, vol. 3. New York: Springer-Verlag.

> Volume 3 of a 4-volume series on case studies in applied mathematics. Most topics are for college-level students, but there are some that can be adapted for secondary-level students.

Marcus-Roberts, H., and Maynard Thompson, eds. 1983. _Life Science Models._ Modules in Applied Mathematics, vol. 4. New York: Springer-Verlag.

> Volume 4 of a 4-volume series on case studies in applied mathematics. Most topics are for college-level students, but there are some that can be adapted for secondary-level students.

Simmons, George F. 1985. _Calculus with Analytic Geometry._ New York: McGraw-Hill.

> An introductory calculus textbook that presents many applications. It contains in an appendix a number of essays dealing with applications and the history of mathematics.

Taub, Abraham H., ed. 1971. _Studies in Applied Mathematics._ Washington, D.C.: Mathematical Association of America.

> Presents application of mathematics to the physical sciences.

Thomas, George B., Jr., and Ross L. Finney. 1988. _Calculus and Analytic Geometry._ 7th ed. Reading, Mass.: Addison-Wesley.

> Standard college-level introductory text to calculus which contains numerous applications of mathematics.

Articles in Journals

Agnew, Jeanne L., and Marvin S. Keener. 1980. A case-study course in applied mathematics using regional industries. _American Mathematical Monthly_ 87 (1) (January 1980): 55-59.

> Discusses an applied mathematics course based on giving students problems actually encountered in industry.

Anderson, Bill D., and John F. Lamb, Jr. 1981. The mathematical aspects of a lunar shuttle landing. _Mathematics Teacher_ 74 (7) (October 1981): 549-553.

> Simple algebra is used to describe a simulation for a shuttle landing on the moon.

Austin, Joe D. 1982. Overbooking airline flights. *Mathematics Teacher* 75 (3) (March 1982): 221-223.

> Looks at the problem: how many reservations should be accepted for a flight by an airline company which must make assumptions, such as some people with reservations will not show up, etc.? Problem is solved using elementary probability theory.

Birman, Gracida S., and Katsumi Nomizu. 1984. Trigonometry in Lorentzian geometry. *American Mathematical Monthly* 91 (9) (November 1984): 543-549.

> Develops trigonometry, the science of lengths and angles pertaining to triangles, in Lorentzian geometry, the geometry appropriate for the special theory of relativity.

Boas, Ralph P. 1980, 1981. Snowfalls and elephants, pop bottles and pi. *Two-Year College Mathematics Journal* 11 (2) (March 1980): 82-89. Reprint. *Mathematics Teacher* 74 (1) (January 1981): 49-55. Revised from an article in *Arts and Sciences* (Northwestern University) 2 (1) (1979).

> An entertaining article about probability, expected value, and infinite series applied to topics of the title.

Brams, Steven J., and Philip D. Straffin, Jr. 1979. Prisoner's dilemma and professional sports drafts. *American Mathematical Monthly* 86 (2) (February 1979): 80-88.

> Discusses game theoretic paradoxes similar to the prisoner's dilemma that arise in the sports draft system.

Carr, Karen D. 1978. A common cents approach to mathematics. *Arithmetic Teacher* 26 (2) (October 1978): 14-15.

> Presents suggestions for conducting a classroom activity based upon managing a household budget.

Choike, James R. 1980. The pentagram and the discovery of an irrational number. *Two-Year College Mathematics Journal* 11 (5) (November 1980): 312-316.

> Story and details of the discovery of an irrational number, believed to have been made by the young Pythagorean Hippasus.

Chosid, Leo. 1981. Compounding energy savings. *Two-Year College Mathematics Journal* 12 (1) (January 1981): 56-57.

> Illustrates that combining percentages involves compounding, not adding.

Czepiel, James, and Edward Esty. 1980. Mathematics in the newspaper. *Mathematics Teacher* 73 (8) (November 1980): 582-586.

Authors classified the mathematical content of articles that appeared on the front page of the *New York Times* over a four-month period. The results of their survey are presented.

Di Carlucci, Joseph. 1979. Earthquakes and Venn diagrams. *Mathematics Teacher* 72 (6) (September 1979): 428-433.

Presents a lesson that illustrates how Venn diagrams and the intersection of sets can help to pinpoint the origin of an earthquake.

Donaghey, Robert, and Warren Gordon. 1980. An investment approach to geometric series. *Two-Year College Mathematics Journal* 11 (2) (March 1980): 120-121.

Shows the connection between a geometric series and annuities.

Fawcett, George. 1981. Camera calculations. *Mathematics Teacher* 74 (5) (May 1981): 366-367.

Discusses f-stop, area, ratios, and photography.

Franklin, Joel. 1983. Mathematical methods of economics. *American Mathematical Monthly* 90 (4) (April 1983): 229-244.

Examines the developments that have taken place in economics and in mathematics from work done combining the two areas.

Gallian, Joseph A. 1981. An optimal football strategy. *Two-Year College Mathematics Journal* 12 (5) (November 1981): 330-331.

Trailing by 14 points, should a college football team go for a two-point or a one-point conversion after their next touchdown?

Gibson, Edwin C., and Jane B. Gibson. 1982. "I can see clearly now" (Another look at Norman windows). *Mathematics Teacher* 75 (8) (November 1982): 694-696, 719.

Presents modifications to a standard calculus problem on Norman windows. Solutions also presented.

Graening, Jay. 1982. The geometry of tennis. *Mathematics Teacher* 75 (8) (November 1982): 658-663.

Elementary plane geometry and algebra are used to analyze and formulate tennis playing strategy.

Harmeyer, Kathleen M. 1982. Flying in algebra class. *Mathematics Teacher* 75 (3) (March 1982): 224-226.

Presents simple algebraic formulas for determining temperatures at various altitudes and line of sight view from an altitude.

Harris, Whitney S., Jr. 1983. The corner reflector. *Mathematics Teacher* 76 (2) (February 1983): 92-95.

> Describes a corner reflector, its use by the Apollo astronauts, and its relationship to geometry and elementary vector algebra.

Henningsen, Jacqueline. 1984. An activity for predicting performances in the 1984 Summer Olympics. *Mathematics Teacher* 77 (5) (May 1984): 338-341.

> Presents an introductory look at regression analysis (least squares linear approximation) of past Olympic performances to predict 1984 performances. Has suggested student activities, problems, and projects.

Hilton, Peter. 1984. Cryptanalysis in World War II and mathematics education. *Mathematics Teacher* 77 (7) (October 1984): 548-552.

> Author recalls the role of mathematics and mathematicians in breaking down German and Japanese codes during World War II. Also presents reminiscences of the mathematician Alan Turing.

Iannone, Michael A. 1983. Round robin schedules. *Mathematics Teacher* 76 (3) (March 1983): 194-195.

> Congruences and modulo arithmetic are applied to create a round robin tournament schedule. Presents a Basic microcomputer program.

Jamski, William D. 1981. Spherical geodesics. *Mathematics Teacher* 74 (3) (March 1981): 227-228, 236.

> Discusses the distance along great-circle routes of a sphere.

————. 1983. Slam dunks, free throws, and problem solving. *Arithmetic Teacher* 30 (5) (January 1983): 34

> A partial basketball box-score is given and students are asked to complete it from information supplied.

Jech, Thomas. 1983. The ranking of incomplete tournaments: A mathematician's guide to popular sports. *American Mathematical Monthly* 90 (4) (April 1983): 246-266.

> Uses mathematics, mostly linear algebra, to show that there is a solution to ranking teams according to their records even when their playing schedules are not identical.

Jeffery, Neil J. 1980. Mathematics in photography. *Mathematics Teacher* 73 (9) (December 1980): 657-662.

> Illustrates topics of geometry, trigonometry, ratio, geometric sequence, exponents, and harmonic mean with photography.

Kluepfel, Charles. 1981. When are logarithms used? _Mathematics Teacher_ 74 (4) (April 1981): 250-253.
> Logarithms are applied to banking, astronomy, noise control, music, photography, and a popular game.

Knill, George. 1980. Cloud height at night. _Mathematics Teacher_ 73 (7) (October 1980): 508-510.
> Describes how cloud height at night is determined aided by trigonometry. Gives some problems with answers.

———. 1980. Fingerprints and fractions. _Mathematics Teacher_ 73 (8) (November 1980): 608-609.
> Describes how fractions are used to classify fingerprints.

———. 1980. Marketing records. _Mathematics Teacher_ 73 (9) (December 1980): 687-688.
> Discusses how record companies determine the retail price of a record in order to recover production expenses, pay salaries, and show a profit.

———. 1980. The telephone rate grid. _Mathematics Teacher_ 73 (6) (September 1980): 454-456.
> Illustrates the use of the distance formula between two points in a plane by the telephone company to determine long distance charges.

———. 1981. Baseball and the midway. _Mathematics Teacher_ 74 (4) (April 1981): 286-287.
> Two separate applications are presented: one from baseball concerning the frequency of games won in a big run-scoring inning, and one from the carnival game of fish-in-a-pond.

———. 1981. International Standard Book Numbers. _Mathematics Teacher_ 74 (1) (January 1981): 47-48.
> Describes the ISBN (number assigned to each published book) and the check digit that is built into it. See also Tuchinsky (1985).

———. 1981. Mathematics in forensic science. _Mathematics Teacher_ 74 (2) (February 1981): 125, 149.
> Describes how one can calculate the physical dimensions of a victim from the lengths of certain bones.

———. 1981. Relative velocity: Vectors with a difference. _Mathematics Teacher_ 74 (3) (March 1981): 209-211.
> Describes how to find the ground speed and track of an airplane by means of the technique of subtracting vectors.

Knill, George, and George Fawcett. 1981. Estimating the size of wildlife populations. *Mathematics Teacher* 74 (7) (October 1981): 548, 571.

> Describes a method based on probability, random selection, and tagging to determine a wildlife population.

————. 1981. Skid marks estimate speed. *Mathematics Teacher* 74 (9) (December 1981): 722-724.

> Presents a formula, a nomograph, and problems to determine speed from skid marks.

Krause, Eugene F. 1982. Central-point problems. *Mathematics Teacher* 75 (3) (March 1982): 198-202.

> Presents a mathematical solution to selected problems of the type: Find the best place for a meeting when distance is a consideration.

————. 1982. Some applications of the circumference formula. *Mathematics Teacher* 75 (5) (May 1982): 369-377.

> Presents applications in the settings of foot races, slot-car races, and railroads.

Kullman, David E. 1981. Math is where you find it. *School Science and Mathematics* 81 (1) (January 1981): 42-50.

> Surveys a number of everyday situations where mathematics is applied and presents an extensive bibliography for further reading.

Kunkle, Dan, and Charles I. Burch, Jr. 1984. Modeling growth — A discrete approach. *Mathematics Teacher* 77 (4) (April 1984): 266-268.

> Presents the concept of a discrete model using an example for population growth, based on the simple recursive formula $X_n = aX_{n-1}$.

Leyden, Michael B. 1981. A funny thing happened to me while waiting for a hamburger. *School Science and Mathematics* 81 (4) (April 1981): 347-348.

> Uses counting principles to discuss the number of different selections for condiments one can choose for a hamburger.

Litwiller, Bonnie H., and David R. Duncan. 1979. Vectors, velocities, and variations. *School Science and Mathematics* 79 (1) (January 1979): 41-44.

> Considers problems in which an automobile drives up an inclined ramp to jump a gap.

————. 1982. The effect of ineligible voters on election results: A

probabilistic analysis. *School Science and Mathematics* 82 (7) (November 1982): 587-592.
> Solves for the probability of a reversal of election results given that the participation of ineligible voters is deleted from an election tally.

Maor, Eli. 1979. What is there so mathematical about music? *Mathematics Teacher* 72 (6) (September 1979): 414-422.
> Excellent introduction to and survey of the connection between mathematics and music.

Nash, David H. 1985. Differential equations and the Battle of Trafalgar. *College Mathematics Journal* 16 (2) (March 1985): 98-102.
> Presents a mathematical analysis of the British strategy in the Battle of Trafalgar.

O'Shea, Thomas. 1979. Geometric transformations and musical composition. *Mathematics Teacher* 72 (7) (October 1979): 523-528.
> Shows how musical compositions can be analyzed by transformation geometry.

Palmaccio, Richard J. 1983. Shipboard weather observation. *Mathematics Teacher* 76 (3) (March 1983): 165-169.
> Applies elementary vector algebra to discover how wind velocity can be determined on a moving ship.

Parzynski, William R. 1984. The geometry of microwave antennas. *Mathematics Teacher* 77 (4) (April 1984): 294-296.
> Shows how the parabola and the hyperbola and their properties are used in microwave antennas.

Perham, Arnold E., and Bernadette H. Perham. 1979. Applications revisited. *Mathematics Teacher* 72 (8) (November 1979): 584-588.
> Reports on how a one-semester course in applications of mathematics can be given at the secondary level.

Reesink, Carole J. 1982. Geomegy or geolotry: What happens when geology visits geometry class? *Mathematics Teacher* 75 (6) (September 1982): 454-461.
> Excellent survey of three-dimensional geometry and polyhedra applied to the study of minerals and crystals.

Riley, James E., and Ruth A. Meyer. 1981. Transportation—A rich source of "story problems." *Mathematics Teacher* 74 (3) (March 1981): 180-183, 240.

Illustrates how arithmetic and common sense can be combined to solve a number of problems related to planning a bus trip.

Roberts, William J. 1984. Honeycomb geometry: Applied mathematics in nature. *Mathematics Teacher* 77 (3) (March 1984): 188-190.

Shows that the hexagonal pattern of a honeycomb maximizes the enclosed region while minimizing the wax needed for construction.

Ruppel, Elizabeth. 1982. Business formulas as Cartesian curves. *Mathematics Teacher* 75 (5) (May 1982): 398-403.

Contains a list of standard business problems involving simple and compound interest, together with their graphical solutions.

Sacco, William, and Clifford W. Sloyer. 1984. An application of the distance formula to medical science. *Mathematics Teacher* 77 (1) (January 1984): 27-29.

Four physiological/biochemical variables provide physicians with crucial information on a patient in intensive care. The distance formula provides a quantitative medical index of these four variables.

Saunders, Hal. 1980. When are we ever gonna have to use this? *Mathematics Teacher* 73 (1) (January 1980): 7-16.

Gives a table that summarizes what topics of mathematics are actually used in various careers. Also presents a number of applied word problems in various career settings.

Schwartzman, Steven. 1983. On population and resources. *Mathematics Teacher* 76 (8) (November 1983): 605-608.

Presents charts and background on the most-densely and least-densely populated countries, followed by 5 questions, with solutions, related to issues of space, standard of living, etc.

Shirley, Lawrence. 1982. 2/3 of 19. *Mathematics Teacher* 75 (7) (October 1982): 540-541.

Describes the crucial role played in the politics of a country by simple arithmetic.

Smith, David A. 1979. A seminar in mathematical model-building. *American Mathematical Monthly* 86 (9) (November 1979): 777-783.

Discusses a model-building course in applied mathematics in which each student must be involved in a modeling term project. Examples of projects are given.

Soler, Francisco de P., and Richard E. Schuster. 1982. Compound growth and related situations: A problem-solving approach. *Mathematics Teacher* 75 (8) (November 1982): 640-644.

> Presents the topic of compound growth, emphasizing the areas of lending, borrowing, and investing. Exercises for students (with solutions) are also presented.

Sterrett, Andrew. 1980. Electing a president in a three-candidate race. *Mathematics Teacher* 73 (8) (November 1980): 635.

> Simple algebra is applied to the electoral college system to analyze a three-candidate race thrown into the U.S. House of Representatives.

Sullivan, John J. 1982. Apportionment — a decennial problem. *Mathematics Teacher* 75 (1) (January 1982): 20-25.

> Describes several methods of apportioning seats in the U.S. House of Representatives that involve arithmetic and algebra.

Thuente, David J. 1982. Chain letters: A poor investment unless .... *Two-Year College Mathematics Journal* 13 (1) (January 1982): 28-35.

> Examines chain letters by means of counting arguments and probability and proves a theorem on optimal position in a chain-letter network.

Tuchinsky, Philip M. 1985. International Standard Book Numbers. *UMAP Journal* 6 (1): 41-54.

> See Knill (1981, "International ..."); Tuchinsky gives far more detail, including exercises. (PJC & LSG)

Vest, Floyd. 1979. Secondary school mathematics from the EPA Gas Mileage Guide. *Mathematics Teacher* 72 (1) (January 1979): 10-14.

> Elementary algebra is applied to practical situations involving fuel economy.

————. 1981. Speed of the earth. *Arithmetic Teacher* 29 (4) (December 1981): 32-33.

> Uses the formula for the circumference of a circle and speed = distance/time to compute the speed of the earth in space.

————. 1982. Bodies falling with air resistance: Computer simulation. *School Science and Mathematics* 82 (6) (October 1982): 506-510.

> Presents two models for a body falling with air resistance: air resistance is proportional to the velocity, or to the square of the velocity, of a falling body.

von Kaenel, Pierre A. 1981. An excursion in applied mathematics. *School Science and Mathematics* 81 (4) (April 1982): 327-331.

> Presents a case history of the motivation and discovery of a theoretical mathematical result in the aerospace industry.

Wagner, Clifford H. 1979. Determining fuel consumption — An exercise in applied mathematics. *Mathematics Teacher* 72 (2) (February 1979): 134-136.

> Raises and solves the consumer question: Should one purchase car A with average mileage, or car B with superior mileage but costing $500 more?

Wang, C.Y. 1979. Mathematics in biomedicine. *American Mathematical Monthly* 86 (6) (June-July 1979): 498-502.

> Surveys the history and the successes of mathematicians working in the area of biomedicine.

Wapner, Leonard M. 1984. Modeling with difference equations: Two examples. *Mathematics Teacher* 77 (2) (February 1984): 136-140.

> Presents an introduction to the topic of difference equations. The examples presented are a predator-prey population model and the Richardson arms race model. Both models involve a simultaneous system of two difference equations.

Wayment, Stanley G. 1980. Another question of interest. *Two-Year College Mathematics Journal* 11 (4) (September 1980): 252-254.

> States and solves a problem dealing with the repayment in equal monthly installments of a loan in which different amounts are borrowed at different times.

Williams, Gareth. 1982. Mathematics in archaeology. *Two-Year College Mathematics Journal* 13 (1) (January 1982): 56-58.

> Illustrates how archaeologists use linear algebra to obtain information about the contents and temporal ordering of graves.

Woodward, Ernest and Thomas Hamel. 1979. Calculator lessons involving population, inflation, and energy. *Mathematics Teacher* 72 (6) (September 1979): 450-457.

> The "rule of 72" is a simple arithmetic approximation for the doubling time of amounts that are compounded at a rate annually. The authors describe lessons that help students discover this rule in various settings.

15. The Slow Learner

FRANK DEMANA

The single most important recent development affecting the education of exceptional children was Public Law 94-142, the Education for All Handicapped Children Act of 1975 (Abeson and Zettel 1977). Prior to PL 94-142 the formal education of exceptional children was the sole responsibility of special educators; if schools were unwilling or unable to handle such children, parents had to keep them home or send them to special schools. In spite of smaller classes, special curricula, and specially-trained teachers, most research evidence showed that the academic and social gains of exceptional children in special settings tended to be no better than those in regular classrooms. One of the first to point this out was Lloyd M. Dunn, who claimed that many of the past and present practices in special education were morally and educationally wrong (Dunn 1968). The law now requires exceptional children to be educated in regular classrooms to the maximum extent possible. Federal courts still adhere to the least restrictive environment guidelines for education of exceptional children, suggested by Chambers (1976).

Considerable elaboration would be needed to define the encompassing term "exceptional child," as these children have been the object of studies in psychology, sociology, physiology, medicine, and education. We refer the reader to Kirk and Gallagher (1979) for a more-detailed description of the exceptional child. This chapter will use the following specific definitions given by the American Association on Mental Deficiency (Grossman 1983). *Slow learners* are children with social and academic behavior less than usual age-level standards, individuals who function between mental retardation and average intelligence (IQ's between 90 and 110). *Mental retardation* refers to significantly subaverage general intellectual functioning (IQ approximately 70 or below), existing concurrently with deficits in adaptive behavior, and manifested during the developmental period (between birth and the 18th birthday). *Adaptive behavior* is the effectiveness or degree with which individuals meet the standards of personal independence and social responsibility expected for age and cultural group.

Slow learners are neither mentally retarded nor learning disabled. Learning disabilities are defined in PL 94-142 as referring to children who exhibit a disorder in basic psychological processes involved in understanding or using spoken or written language, including conditions that have been referred to as perceptual handicaps, brain injury, minimal brain dysfunction, dyslexia, developmental aphasia, etc. Slow learners may exhibit some of the characteristics of the learning disabled; they may be deficient in academic achievement, have information-processing problems and/or attention problems, be hyperactive, have uneven patterns of learning performance, and have difficulties in social relationships.

Identification of slow learners is a difficult process. Research evidence questions the validity of assessment instruments and shows many to be culturally biased. Valencia and Rankin (1985) found many items on the McCarthy Scales of Children's Abilities to be biased against the Spanish-language group. Lindsey and Armstrong (1984) found significant differences on subtests of three tests that were designed to measure the same area of achievement. Ysseldyke and Thurlow (1984) present compelling empirically-based arguments for questioning standard psychometric approaches to assessment practices in special education.

Slow learners are sometimes classified as learning disabled if they are not mentally retarded. Howe and Keele (1982) claimed that slow learners are being reclassified as "mildly handicapped" to make them eligible for special education funds and programs. Shepard et al. (1983) showed that fewer than half of the students identified as learning disabled had characteristics that are associated in federal law and professional literature with the definitions of learning disabilities. The U.S. Department of Education 1984 report to Congress on the implementation of PL 94-142 (U.S. Department of Education 1984) stated that the learning disabled population had grown by 119% since 1976-1977, but the rate of growth appeared to be slowing due to increased efforts by states to assure that children are not erroneously classified. Greenburg (1984) gave a favorable review of this report and indicated that progress was being made toward achievement of the stated purposes of PL 94-142. However, Gerber (1984) gave a critical review of this report, claiming it fails to alert Congress that students who are difficult to teach and manage appear to be at significant risk of erroneous classification and inequitable treatment. This risk is due in part to variability in identification and referral procedures across states and local districts.

Once exceptional children are properly identified, PL 94-142 requires mainstreaming of as many of these children as possible into regular class-rooms. Madden and Slavin have reviewed research on academic and social outcomes of mainstreaming students with mild handicaps (Madden and Slavin 1983). They include research on the effects of placing these students in full-time special education classes, part-time regular classes with resource support, and full-time regular classes. Research favors placement in regular classes using individualized instruction or supplemented by well-designed resource programs for the achievement, self-esteem, behavior, and emotional adjustment of academically-handicapped students. They found few consistent benefits of full-time special education classes. Salend (1984) offers several guidelines for developing and implementing effective mainstreaming programs. Borg and Ascione (1982) describe their inservice program to help teachers develop effective classroom management skills for mainstreamed class-rooms. Schneider and Byrne (1984) report on newly mainstreamed students from special classes. They found that students who had spent one to two years in special classes were rated as having more acceptable classroom behavior than those who were enrolled for shorter or longer periods of time.

Slow learners have special needs calling for different styles of teaching. They are likely to have poor self-images as learners and as persons. Academic failure leads to frustration, which in turn leads to lack of confidence and a feeling of hopelessness when presented with new material. Glennon (1981) discusses the need for a theory of instruction for slow learners and writes about five of the variables essential to an instructional psychology: a knowledge of the mathematics itself, sources of the curriculum, sources of the teacher's methodology, sources of motivation, and consolidation of learning. Collins (1972) recommends that teachers adopt a style that counteracts the learned behavior that little is expected from these students. Fennell (1984) describes how to use a diagnostic--prescriptive or goal-referenced instructional model to plan, implement, and evaluate an individualized education program for each student. Slavin and Karweit (1984) found support for the instructional effectiveness of teamwork. Travers et al. (1971) give suggestions for teaching low achievers, plus an extensive bibliography. Walker (1980) provides forty references for use of computers with exceptional children in secondary school. Newfield and McElyea (1983) present evidence to show that grouping leads to improved achievement and attitude toward subject matter for students in regular and remedial English and mathematics classes. Readers might be interested in provisions for slow learners in foreign countries reported in Baker and Griffith (1983), Clunies-Ross and

Wimhurst (1984), and Marble (1980).

There is growing evidence that emphasis on problem solving is an effective strategy for building confidence and achievement in slow learners. Leitzel and Osborne (1985) describe a numerical problem solving approach to algebra and geometry that has been very successful with college-bound high-school seniors who were weak in mathematics. They showed that students can learn enough mathematics to reopen career options and reduce the amount of time and investment required in their college programs. The College Entrance Examination Board recommends bridging the gap between college preparatory courses and dead-end courses such as general mathematics with a new course called Computational Problem Solving. This course would be designed to provide interesting and challenging applications of arithmetic, statistics, and computing to real-world problems and make use of calculators and computers (Herbert 1985).

At the college level the slow learner will be found in remedial and developmental courses as well as in courses geared to deal with "mathematics anxiety." Many colleges provide facilities to diagnose and help students with learning disabilities. Learning disabled students will appear both in remedial and nonremedial courses. College teachers must be prepared to deal with all types of special adults.

There has been considerable research to identify variables that will predict slow learner success in mathematics. Fulkerson, Galassi, and Galassi (1984) report on a failure of cognitive theory to predict performance of mathematics-anxious students. Clute (1984) provides information on how teaching style influences performance of mathematics-anxious students. Eldersveld (1983) identified variables that predict success and failure in developmental mathematics in two-year colleges. He found that numerical skills, instructional method, age, self-assessment of mathematical knowledge, and attitude toward mathematics were discriminating variables. Ervin et al. (1984) used high-school grade point average and scores on national tests to predict academic performance.

The 1980 report of the Mathematical Association of America committee on improving remediation efforts in college (Committee ... 1981) produced a list of characteristics of effective remedial programs. Strong emphasis on problem solving and involving students with demanding problems are among the characteristics shared by successful remediation programs. The numerical problem solving course (Demana and Leitzel 1984) reported on by Leitzel and Osborne (1985) is also used successfully as a remedial mathematics course for college freshmen. Chisko (1985) describes a successful format for developmental mathematics that stresses problem solving. It appears that problem solving has a major role to play in successful programs for slow learners.

Polloway and Smith (1983) state that much of the initial work in special education was with the slow learner. The formation of learning disabilities as a separate field and severely handicapped as a distinct area have been major factors in the decline of interest in the slow learner. We need to renew our efforts with the slow learner. These new efforts should use computational problem solving at all levels. Courses will need to be developed for both preservice and inservice teachers in the use of computational problem solving methods.

Far fewer students who enter college needing remedial work graduate than nonremedial students, even in the most successful programs. The high-school program in Leitzel and Osborne (1985) gives convincing evidence that the most effective way to reduce the need for remediation in college is to accomplish the remediation in high school. The high-school remediation problem can in turn be reduced by using the same approach with students in the 7th and 8th grades as well as in the pre-algebra course. This approach will ensure that students are adequately prepared for college-preparatory mathematics courses when they take them.

College teachers, high-school teachers, elementary-school teachers, and administrators need to work together with those responsible for preparing teachers, to develop programs that are effective for all children, including exceptional children. If we work together using all our problem solving skills, then no problem is too difficult to solve.

BIBLIOGRAPHY

Abeson, Alan, and Jeffrey Zettel. 1977. The end of the quiet revolution: The Education of All Handicapped Children Act of 1975. *Exceptional Children* 44 (2) (October 1977): 114-128.

> Describes the provisions and implications of PL 94-142, which represents the standards that have been laid down by the courts, legislatures, and other policy bodies of the U.S. for the education of all handicapped children.

Baker, Colin, and Catherine Lloyd Griffith. 1983. Provision of materials and tests for Welsh-speaking pupils with learning difficulties: A national survey. *Educational Research* 25 (1) (February 1983): 60-70.

> Report of a British survey of teachers' needs with respect to children with learning difficulties.

Belmont, Ira, and Lillian Belmont. 1980. Is the slow learner in the classroom learning disabled? *Journal of Learning Disabilities* 13 (9) (November 1980): 32-35.
    Suggests that a developmental view of slow learners in the classroom reveals most of them not learning disabled.

Borg, Walter R., and Frank R. Ascione. 1982. Classroom management in elementary mainstreaming classrooms. *Journal of Educational Psychology* 74 (1) (February 1982): 85-95.
    Describes an inservice program designed to help teachers develop classroom management skills and strategies for mainstreaming classrooms. The program leads to significant increases in pupil on-task behavior and significant decreases in deviant pupil behavior.

Chambers, D. 1976. Right to the least restrictive alternative. In *The Mentally Retarded Citizen and the Law*, edited by Michael Kindred et al. New York: Free Press.
    Gives guidelines for education of the mentally retarded citizen.

Chisko, Ann M. 1985. Developmental math: Problem solving and survival. *Mathematics Teacher* 78 (8) (November 1985): 592-596.
    Describes a format for developmental mathematics that stresses three areas: developing a positive attitude toward mathematics, encouraging activeness on the part of the students, and providing survival skills for nondevelopmental courses that encourage the practice of problem solving and analytic skills. Of students enrolling, 79% are successful in this course; and of these, 94% complete the next course with a grade of C or better. These figures compare with 55% and 75%, respectively, with the old format.

Clunies-Ross, Louise, and Shirley Wimhurst. 1984. The right balance: Provision for slow learners in secondary schools. *Educational Research* 26 (1) (February 1984): 14-23.
    The report of this major NFER research project is the result of a British national survey and a series of school-based case studies of the ways schools in England provide for slow learners. Implications for curriculum, staffing, teacher training and inservice education are drawn from the study.

Clute, Pamela S. 1984. Mathematics anxiety, instructional method, and achievement in a survey course in college mathematics. *Journal for Research in Mathematics Education* 15 (1) (January 1984): 50-58.
    Found that students with a high level of mathematics anxiety had significantly lower achievement than students with low anxiety. Those with high anxiety benefited more from an expository approach and those with low anxiety from a discovery approach.

Collins, Elizabeth A. 1972. Teaching styles (secondary school). In *NCTM Yearbook 35*, 163-181.

Suggests that the primary task of secondary school teachers of slow learners is to adopt the teaching style that has the greatest potential for counteracting the learned behavior that little is expected from these students.

Committee on Improving Remediation Efforts in the Colleges, Mathematical Association of America. 1981. Report, July 1980. *American Mathematical Monthly* 88 (3) (March 1981): 230-233.

Gives characteristics of effective remedial programs and answers some frequently raised questions about remediation programs.

Cornelius, Michael, ed. 1982. *Teaching Mathematics*. New York: Nichols Publishing. Columbus, O.: ERIC/SMEAC. ERIC: ED 226962.

A collection of 10 papers that aims to provide teachers at all levels with ideas on a number of important aspects of mathematics education, including slow learners.

Demana, Franklin D., and Joan R. Leitzel. 1984. *Transition to College Mathematics*. Reading, Mass.: Addison-Wesley.

Developed for high-school college-bound seniors with weak mathematics skills and also for college remedial mathematics students.

Dunn, Lloyd M. 1968. Special education for the mildly retarded—is much of it justifiable? *Exceptional Children* 35 (1) (September 1968): 5-22.

Claims that many of the past and present practices are morally and educationally wrong. Traditional classifying labels used in special education produce negative effects.

Eisenberg, Leon. 1963-1964. Strengths of the inner-city child. *Baltimore Bulletin of Education* 41 (2) (1963-1964): 10-16.

Points out that it is important not to confuse difference with defect. We should build upon the strengths of the children.

Eisenberg, Theodore. 1981. Remedial mathematics and open admissions. *School Science and Mathematics* 81 (4) (April 1981): 341-346.

Reports that only 20% to 40% of the students in a remedial course will take another mathematics course—and almost half will fail.

Eldersveld, Paul J. 1983. Factors related to success and failure in developmental mathematics in the community college. *Community/Junior College Quarterly of Research and Practice* 7 (2) (January-March 1983):

161-174.

> Identified variables that were related to success and failure in developmental mathematics in eight Illinois community colleges. A discriminant analysis identified the following variables as discriminators: numerical skills, instructional method, age, self-assessment of mathematical knowledge, and attitude towards mathematics.

Ervin, Leroy, Mark C. Hogrebe, Patricia L. Dwinell, and Isadore Newman. 1984. Comparison of the prediction of academic performance for college developmental students and regularly admitted students. *Psychological Reports* 54 (1) (February 1984): 319-327.

> Compared the accuracy of high-school grade point average and Scholastic Aptitude Test scores in predicting freshman grade point average for Developmental Studies freshman and regularly-admitted freshman.

Fennell, Francis. 1984. Mainstreaming and the mathematics classroom. *Arithmetic Teacher* 32 (3) (November 1984): 22-27.

> Describes how to use a diagnostic-prescriptive or goal-referenced instructional model to plan, implement, and evaluate an individualized education program for each handicapped pupil.

Finkelstein, Harry. 1980. *Math for Survival*. Columbus, O.: ERIC/ SMEAC ERIC: ED 183390.

> Describes a course developed to present arithmetic topics to slow learners and learning disabled students in secondary schools.

Frary, Robert B., and Jeanne L. Ling. 1983. A factor-analytic study of mathematics anxiety. *Educational and Psychological Measurement* 43 (4) (Winter 1983): 985-993.

> Reports that scores on four of five mathematics attitude scales were strongly related to a single underlying attitude toward mathematics. Correlates of mathematics anxiety are noted.

Fulkerson, Katherine F., John P. Galassi, and Merna D. Galassi. 1984. Relation between cognitions and performance in math anxious students; A failure of cognitive theory. *Journal of Counseling Psychology* 31 (3) (July 1984): 376-382.

> Found that second-step cognitive variables (including review of information, strategic calculations, conclusions) accounted for a significant amount of variance in solving problems, beyond that of first-step cognitions (attention, self-facilitation, irrelevancies, self-inhibition).

Gelzheiser, Lynn M. 1984. Generalization from categorical memory tasks to prose by learning disabled adolescents. *Journal of Educational*

Psychology 76 (6) (December 1984): 1128-1138.
> Reports on the effectiveness of extensive direct instruction by learning disabled subjects.

Gerber, Michael M. 1984. The Department of Education's Sixth Annual Report to Congress on PL 94-142: Is Congress getting the full story? *Exceptional Children* 51 (3) (November 1984): 209-224.
> Gives a critical review of the report, with implications for both policy and special education research needed.

Gilhool, Thomas K. 1973. Education: An inalienable right. *Exceptional Children* 39 (8) (May 1973): 597-609.
> Describes litigation, which is literally "busting out all over."

Glennon, Vincent J., ed. 1981. *The Mathematical Education of Exceptional Children and Youth: An Interdisciplinary Approach.* Professional Reference Series no. 2. Reston, Va.: National Council of Teachers of Mathematics.
> Intended as a reference for the general classroom teacher, special educator, school psychologist and counselor, and preservice and inservice teacher.

Greenburg, David E. 1984. The 1984 Annual Report to Congress: Are we better off? *Exceptional Children* 51 (3) (November 1984): 203-207.
> Gives a favorable review of this report and indicates progress toward achievement of the stated purposes of PL 94-142.

Grossman, Herbert J., ed. 1983. *Classification in Mental Retardation.* Washington, D.C.: American Association on Mental Deficiency.
> Gives classification and terminology used in mental retardation. Contains an extensive glossary of terms used in the field. Is consistent with the International Classification of Diseases-9 (ICD-9) of the World Health Organization and the American Psychiatric Association's Diagnostic and Statistical Manual-III (DSM-III).

Haigh, Gerald. 1977. *Teaching Slow Learners.* London: Temple Smith.
> Reports on slow learning pupils in Great Britain. Looks at the notion of the slow learner from various angles. Claims failure may result as much from the institution as from the person who is having to cope with it.

Herbert, James, ed. 1985. *Academic Preparation in Mathematics.* New York: College Entrance Examination Board.
> Provides some assistance to teachers who would like to help students enter college with the kind of preparation in mathematics they need to be successful.

Herman, Maureen L. 1983. Hopeless in math? It's too soon to say. *Mathematics Teacher* 76 (7) (October 1983): 515-524.
    Gives suggestions and references for classroom activities for remedial high-school mathematics classes.

Hogrebe, Mark C., Leroy Ervin, Patricia L. Dwinell, and Isadore Newman. 1983. The moderating effects of gender and race in predicting the academic performance of college developmental students. *Educational and Psychological Measurement* 43 (2) (Summer 1983): 523-530.
    Examines the moderating influence of gender and race on the accuracy of high-school grades and College Board Scholastic Aptitude (SAT) scores in predicting the academic performance of developmental students.

Howe, Clifford E., and Larry X. Keele. 1982. Responsibility for the mildly handicapped: A proposal for change. *Executive Review* (University of Iowa) (March 1982). Columbus, O.: ERIC/SMEAC. ERIC: ED 217539.
    Reports that the number of handicapped school students in Iowa is increasing even as total enrollments decline, probably because slow learners are being reclassified as "mildly handicapped" to make them eligible for special education funds and programs. Recommends responsibilities be shifted to local school administrators.

Ivarie, Judith, Dorothea Hogue, and Andrew R. Brulle. 1984. An investigation of mainstream teacher time spent with students labeled learning disabled. *Exceptional Children* 51 (2) (October 1984): 142-149.
    Shows that both elementary and secondary teachers do not spend significantly more time assisting students labeled as learning disabled.

Kirk, Samuel A., and James J. Gallagher. 1979. *Educating Exceptional Children.* 3rd ed. Boston, Mass.: Houghton Mifflin.
    Can be used as an introductory text for those who will work with exceptional children.

Kulik, Chen-Lin C., and James A. Kulik. 1982. Effects of ability grouping on secondary school students: A meta-analysis of evaluation findings. *American Educational Research Journal* 19 (3) (Fall 1982): 415-428.
    Showed that ability grouping produced near-zero effects on average and below-average students, but clear effects for high-ability students.

Leinhardt, Gaea, Andrea Mar Seewald, and Naomi Zigmond. 1982. Sex and race differences in learning disabilities classrooms. *Journal of Educational Psychology* 74 (6) (December 1982): 835-843.
    Investigated whether or not difference by sex or race occurred in placement, teacher contacts, assignment practices, and student learning behaviors in learn-

ing disabilities classrooms. Results suggest a need to increase vigilance in LD placement procedures. It appears that special education teachers are ignoring race and sex in the instructional aspects of their teaching.

Leitzel, Joan, and Alan Osborne. 1985. Mathematical alternatives for college preparatory students. In *NCTM 1985 Yearbook*, 150-165.

Describes a numerical problem solving approach to algebra and geometry that has successfully remediated college intending high-school seniors who were weak in mathematics. A college mathematics placement exam is used to identify these students. Gives strong evidence that students who are college bound but have had difficulty in learning mathematics can learn enough mathematics to reopen career options.

Lilly, M. Stephen. 1979. *Children with Exceptional Needs: A Survey of Special Education.* New York: Holt, Rinehart & Winston.

Lindsey, Jimmy D., and Stephen W. Armstrong. 1984. Performance of EMR and learning-disabled students on the Brigance, Peabody, and Wide Range achievement tests. *American Journal of Mental Deficiency* 89 (September 1984): 197-201.

Found significant differences on the subtests of three tests that were designed to measure the same area of achievement when administered to mildly mentally retarded and the learning-disabled. Claims test correlations between achievement tests are typically reported and drawn from scores obtained primarily from regular student performance.

Lowry, William C., ed. 1972. *NCTM Yearbook 35* .

Provides information about and ideas for teaching the slow learner in mathematics.

Madden, Nancy A., and Robert E. Slavin. 1983. Mainstreaming students with mild handicaps: Academic and social outcomes." *Review of Educational Research* 53 (4) (Winter 1983): 519-569.

Reviews research on the effects of placing students with mild handicaps in full-time special education classes, part-time regular classes with resource support, and full-time regular classes. Also reviews research on the effects of programs designed to improve the achievement, social-emotional adjustment, and social acceptance of academically handicapped students by their nonhandicapped classmates. Research shows few consistent benefits of full-time special education on any important outcomes, and favors placement in regular classes using individualized instruction or supplemented by well-designed resource programs for the achievement, self-esteem, behavior, and emotional adjustment of academically-handicapped students.

Marble, W. O. Jr. 1980. An evaluation of the professional develop-

ment sequence on "The Slow Learner in the Secondary School." Burnaby
School District (British Columbia), February 1980. Columbus, O.: ERIC/
SMEAC. ERIC: ED 209274.

> Investigated whether "The Slow Learner in the Secondary School" program
> had any impact on the educational environment of the slower learners in Bur-
> naby. Positive shift in attitude of regular teachers during the program was statisti-
> cally significant.

Matulis, Robert S. 1981. A bibliography of articles on the teaching of
mathematics in special education. *Arithmetic Teacher* 28 (7) (March
1981): 53-56.

> Covers articles most of which were written between 1970 and 1980. The ar-
> ticles are grouped by specific topics, characteristics of special students, and
> methods of assessing students' abilities and capabilities.

Mesinger, John F. 1985. Commentary on "A Rationale for the Merger
of Special and Regular Education" or, Is it now time for the lamb to lie
down with the lion? *Exceptional Children* 51 (6) (April 1985): 510-512.

> Claims the unification of regular and special education proposed by Bel-
> mont and Belmont (1980) will be more inefficient than the current system be-
> cause it would require more specialized personnel than we now have.

Newfield, John, and Virginia B. McElyea. 1983. Achievement and attitudinal differences among students in regular, remedial, and advanced
classes. *Journal of Experimental Education* 52 (1) (Fall 1983): 47-56.

> Shows grouping leads to improved achievement and attitude toward subject
> matter for students in regular and remedial English and mathematics classes for
> sophomores and seniors.

Polloway, Edward A., and J. David Smith. 1983. Changes in mild mental retardation: Population, programs, and perspectives. *Exceptional Children* 50 (2) (October 1983): 149-159.

> States that much of the initial work in the field of special education focused
> on individuals served under the label *educable mentally retarded (EMR)* or *mild-
> ly retarded*. The formation of learning disabilities as a separate field and the recog-
> nition of severely handicapped as a distinct area have been major factors in the
> decline of the interest in the study of EMR.

Russell, Tommy, Larry DuRand Brunson, and Cynthia Ann Bryant.
1984. Effects of verbal-mediated modeling on concrete-operational reasoning for a sample of ESN children. *Psychology in the Schools* 21 (4) (October 1984): 504-511.

> Effect on verbal-mediated modeling was shown to be positive on transfer to
> a criterion-referenced paper/pencil task.

Salend, Spencer J. 1984. Factors contributing to the development of successful mainstreaming programs. *Exceptional Children* 50 (5) (February 1984): 409-416.

Offers several guidelines for developing and implementing effective mainstreaming programs.

Sapp, Gary L., Brad S. Chissom, and William O. Horton. 1984. An investigation of the ability of selected instruments to discriminate areas of exceptional class designation. *Psychology in the Schools* 21 (2) (April 1984): 258-263.

Indicates that both the LD (learning disabled) and the EH (emotionally handicapped) differed significantly from the EMR (educable mentally retarded) group, and that classification results for all groups are inadequate.

Schneider, Barry H., and Barbara M. Byrne. 1984. Predictors of successful transition from self-contained special education to regular class settings. *Psychology in the Schools* 21 (3) (July 1984): 375-380.

Investigated 129 newly-mainstreamed learning disabled, emotionally disturbed, and mildly developmentally disabled pupils. Pupils who had spent one to two years in special classes were rated as having more acceptable classroom behavior than those who were enrolled for shorter or longer periods of time. Teachers generally were satisfied with pupils' progress.

Semmel, Melvyn I., ed. 1984. Special Issue: Special Education. *Educational Psychologist* 19 (3) (Summer 1984).

Devoted to topics concerned with referral, assessment, and placement of handicapped children in special education.

Shepard, Lorrie A., Mary Lee Smith, and Carol P. Vojir. 1983. Characteristics of pupils identified as learning disabled. *American Educational Research Journal* 20 (3) (Fall 1983): 309-331.

Showed that fewer than half the sample (800) had characteristics that are associated in federal law and professional literature with the definitions of learning disabilities.

Sherman, Julia. 1979. Predicting mathematics performance in high school girls and boys. *Journal of Educational Psychology* 71 (2) (April 1979): 242-249.

Used multiple regression to show that ninth-grade scores significantly predicted performance one to three years later. Spatial visualization was an important variable, significantly predicting geometry grades for girls but not for boys. Aside from mathematics achievement, spatial visualization was the only other variable with a significant weight in predicting mathematical problem solving scores for girls over a three-year period.

Silon, Ellen L., and Susan Harter. 1985. Assessment of perceived competence, motivational orientation, and anxiety in segregated and mainstreamed educable mentally retarded children. *Journal of Educational Psychology* 77 (2) (April 1985): 217-230.
> Examined whether instruments designed to tap the self-system in normal-IQ children could be used with retarded pupils. Failure to find differences between mainstreamed and self-contained pupils was attributed to the social comparison groups used.

Slavin, Robert E., and Nancy L. Karweit. 1984. Mastery learning and student teams: A factorial experiment in urban general mathematics classes. *American Educational Research Journal* 21 (4) (Winter 1984): 725-736.
> Found support for the instructional effectiveness of team work and team reward but not for mastery of learning components in grade 9.

Slavin, Robert E., Nancy A. Madden, and Marshall Leavey. 1984. Effects of cooperative learning and individualized instruction on mainstreamed students. *Exceptional Children* 50 (5) (February 1984): 434-443.
> Showed positive effects on mainstreamed academically-handicapped students of an instruction method in mathematics that combined cooperative learning with individualized instruction.

Stainback, William, and Susan Stainback. 1984. A rationale for the merger of special and regular education. *Exceptional Children* 51 (2) (October 1984): 102-111.
> Provides a rationale for the merger of special and regular education, based on the premises that instructional needs of students do not warrant the operation of a dual system, and operating a dual system is inefficient.

Suydam, Marilyn N. 1984. What research says: Helping low-achieving students in mathematics. *School Science and Mathematics* 84 (5) (May-June 1984): 437-441.
> Gives guidelines from research with low achievers for grades K-12. Thirty-two references focus on children who are having difficulty learning mathematics because of intelligence, motivation, or disability.

Travers, Kenneth J., John W. LeDuc, and Garth E. Runion. 1971. Teaching resources for low-achieving mathematics classes. Columbus, O.: ERIC/SMEAC. ERIC: ED 053980.
> Gives suggestions for teaching low achievers and an extensive bibliography.

U.S. Department of Education. 1984. Sixth Annual Report to Congress on the Implementation of Public Law 94-142: The Education for All Handicapped Children Act. *Exceptional Children* 51 (3) (November 1984): 199-202.

Valencia, Richard R., and Richard J. Rankin. 1985. Evidence of content bias on the McCarthy Scales with Mexican American children: Implications for test translation and nonbiased assessment. *Journal of Educational Psychology* 77 (2) (April 1985): 197-207.

Investigated content bias of McCarthy Scales of Children's Abilities (MSCA). Of the 157 MSCA items examined, 23 were found to be biased—the vast majority against the Spanish language group.

Walker, Robert J. 1980. An update on computers in the classroom. Columbus, O.: ERIC/SMEAC. ERIC: ED 203849.

Gives forty references for use of computers with learning and physically handicapped students in secondary school.

White, William F., and Wanda D. Bigham. 1983. Increase of college retention by an information systems approach to instruction. *Psychological Reports* 52 (1) (February 1983): 306.

Reports attrition of freshmen at Morehead State University (North Dakota) went from 60% to 24% with this system. Significant increases in further retention were also obtained.

Williams, Paul D. 1983. Discovery learning in remedial mathematics: Multiple-choice versus written generalization. *Mathematics and Computer Education* 17 (3) (Fall 1983): 171-177.

Found no significant difference in achievement or attitudes for students given instruction with differing discovery methods.

Ysseldyke, James E., and Martha L. Thurlow. 1984. Assessment practices in special education: Adequacy and appropriateness. *Educational Psychologist* 19 (3) (Summer 1984): 123-136.

Presents compelling empirically-based arguments for questioning standard psychometric approaches to assessment practices in special education.

Zeddies, Melvin L. 1981. Creativity in general mathematics. *Mathematics Teacher* 74 (3) (March 1981): 187-189.

Reports on the creative efforts of two students in a general mathematics class.

16. Teaching the Gifted in Mathematics

MARK E. SAUL

Fire and Ice

Strange anomaly:
the flame of intuition
frozen in rigor.
— Katharine O'Brien (1981)

What Is Mathematical Talent?

The process of creating mathematics can be described as that of using highly formal language to communicate deep insights.

Learning mathematics involves penetrating the hard surface to get at the intuitions captured. The ultimate skill which the student of mathematics must acquire is to be able to use formalism and intuition equally well, so that each aids the other in creating new results or integrating older ones.

When we say that a student is gifted in mathematics, we are saying that he or she is adept at manipulating symbols while keeping track of the meanings being expressed.

The Curriculum: What Do We Teach the Gifted Student?

Most of our teaching of mathematics tends to be on a formal level. On the lowest level, it is an accomplishment to be able to manipulate symbols according to fixed rules. For example, a mastery of the algorithms of arithmetic shows that the student can perform the same operation, even though the numbers may vary.

The successful student of the subject, however, must know more. He or she must understand the motivation behind the formal symbolic manipulation. The arithmetic student, for instance, must be able to interpret the results of the algorithm. Is the new answer larger or smaller? What does it represent in terms of sharing a pie or the motion of a ship?

This second level of achievement is one which most of our students are capable of, in varying degrees. Gifted students must be urged to a higher level. They must be given the chance to create their own formal systems, or to relate existing systems to new situations.

As an example of this level of achievement, consider the following problem:

> Mary has two skirts and three blouses. How many different outfits can she wear?

Almost any third grader knows that $2 \times 3 = 6$. But it is the rare third-grade student who can relate this fact to Mary's outfits.

In planning curricula for the gifted mathematics student, we are faced with a basic dichotomy, that stems from the two fundamental aspects of mathematics.

We can expose the student to new formal systems and accelerate the process of integrating these systems. Or we can use the formal facility already developed and stretch the student's ability to use the knowledge he or she has already acquired.

The Curriculum: Deeper or Further?

This is the dichotomy faced by the teacher of gifted students in any subject area and on any grade level. In mathematics, the terms "deeper" and "further" have quite specific meanings.

To go further means, typically, to look at the next chapter of the textbook, to go on to the next syllabus, to prepare for the next examination. There are several reasons to choose this path. The material is readily available to the teacher. Students can often use the same text they have been working from. In most cases, standard examinations are readily available, so evaluation of the program is easy. Administrators have no trouble describing the program and accounting for time spent. And students can say that they are studying thus-and-such a topic, which is usually studied in a higher grade.

To go deeper is frequently more difficult. It is not easy to amass materials. Evaluation and accountability are often troublesome. And students sometimes have a problem enjoying their success if they don't have a label for their new level of achievement.

For these reasons, it is only for our best students that we make the extra effort to go deeper rather than further. A deeper study of the existing subject is the daily bread of the working mathematician. Historically, new fields of mathematics generally have not opened up until they became necessary. These milestones are achieved only after much progress at a painfully slower rate.

The problems of choosing deeper study, rather than further study, are worth solving.

Some Examples of Curriculum

What should a teacher do with gifted students of elementary algebra? To go further means to go faster. The material is there, the tests are easy to construct, and anyone can see what is being accomplished. But going faster means that a class will be split into separate tracks. It means that accelerated students will be bored later on. Most of these students could read the text themselves and absorb much of the material without a teacher's help.

Going deeper has different benefits. For instance, students who can solve simple linear equations with real numbers (a typical goal of the first few months of algebra) could be asked to solve the same equations in Z_{12} or Z_7 (arithmetic systems with 12 and 7 numbers, respectively). Working in these number systems, the students will find different meanings for the same symbols and be forced to think more about the meaning of the symbols they are manipulating. This can be done by individualizing instruction, without risking a total reorganization of the curriculum. When the next topic is presented, such as simultaneous equations or quadratic equations, the gifted students will be ready to rejoin the other students in learning the new techniques.

In a geometry class, going further would mean doing more complex congruence proofs or proving new theorems. Going deeper might mean exploring analogies in space geometry or developing intuitive conjectures about the figure being studied. This can be done without stressing formal proof, which the students can construct on their own.

In a precalculus course, going further would mean introducing epsilon-delta proofs and beginning to explore the concepts of limit and continuity. Going deeper might involve an intuitive discussion of these concepts. For instance, introductory calculus texts rarely discuss the notion of limit of a sequence. But this concept is much more intuitive than the limit of a function and offers an easy way to explore advanced concepts.

This last example is in some ways the best. The most promising material for talented students is material which forces them to use their intuition and prepares the mind for the formalism to come later.

The Method: How Do We Teach the Gifted?

In teaching most students, our job is to structure the subject matter so that the students can assimilate and use the material quickly. This process is easier in mathematics than in most other areas: our subject expresses itself naturally in structured form.

But this ease of structure is also a danger. For in structuring the material, we are limiting it. For example, the essence of a coordinate system is a one-to-one correspondence between points on a plane and ordered pairs of real numbers. The typical classroom or textbook development, however, gives only one way to achieve this correspondence (the Cartesian way) and only one way to express it (ordered pairs with x first and y second). Students learn a lot from this structured development. They learn the notation (i.e., that "x always comes first"). They can recognize when to apply the method (e.g., in "graphing equations"). For many students this much is an achievement.

For the gifted student, however, it is a limitation. There are many ways of creating the desired one-to-one correspondence. Gifted students will certainly need to use polar and oblique coordinate systems fairly often and fairly soon after their initial exposure to the ideas. They will be using coordinate systems in physics where the variables are not x and y, and may not even be in alphabetical order. Most important, they will need to be able to choose a coordinate system themselves. That is, they will need to see a coordinate system as a way of imposing an order on certain "natural" objects, rather than as an object of study in itself.

In teaching the gifted, our own preconceptions work against us. We must give gifted students enough of our own ideas to stimulate their own imaginations. We must explain enough of our own habits of thought to let them communicate their ideas. Aside from this, we should interfere as little as possible.

For example, in introducing coordinate systems, it would certainly be appropriate to show gifted students a variety of ways of naming points on the plane. After this introduction, the teacher can go through the usual development, with rectangular axes and coordinates labelled (x, y). After the students achieve a facility with the formalism, the teacher can go back and give less-structured examples. Some of these might be problems in which students themselves impose a coordinate system on a given situation. Alternatively, students could be given a situation in which two variables, labelled with arbitrary letters, can be "pictured" on a coordinate plane. Other possibilities for study are finite coordinate systems, or coordinate systems for surfaces with unusual topologies.

The teacher of gifted students must form a stockpile of such examples. They are not easy to come by. It is a hopeless task to try to invent all of them oneself. The mass market, catering as it does to the average student, does not offer much. The bibliography below consists largely of sources for such material.

The Classroom Scene

Most of our teaching methods are geared to the average student. We ask questions in order to elicit certain answers. We give paradigmatic problems that soon turn into textbook exercises. We develop one strand of curriculum at a time.

In teaching gifted students, we must let go of many of these pedagogical habits. Our questioning must be more open-ended. We must leave larger gaps between our problems and student exercises. We must interweave and synthesize different areas of the curriculum.

Many teachers of the gifted have found it useful to relinquish control of the classroom to the students. They give few developmental lessons and fewer lectures. The classroom turns into a workshop, with groups of students working on problems together. The teacher keeps order, "grounds" the discussion, and offers assistance in tight spots.

There is a bonus for the teacher in this method. When students work together in groups, the teacher can unobtrusively observe their thought patterns by listening in. A teacher with the proper respect for our ignorance of the processes of creative thinking can learn much in this situation.

Many teachers who have tried these less formal methods have also tried them with less gifted students. In some ways, the thought patterns of all students are similar: otherwise, no one would be able to talk about "teaching" problem solving. If presented with suitable material, average students can sometimes also begin to develop it for themselves and acquire skills that we think of as gifts.

REFERENCES

O'Brien, Katharine. 1981. Three haiku: What is mathematics? *American Mathematical Monthly* 88 (8) (October 1981): 626.

BIBLIOGRAPHY

Bibliographic entries are listed under the categories
- Problem Solving
- Classics
- General References
- Problem Books
- Number Theory
- Discrete Mathematics
- Geometry
- Algebra
- Analysis
- Recreational Mathematics
- Computer Science
- History
- Pedagogy.

Problem Solving

This title is used for a burgeoning area of psychological literature. Most of this material is not closely related to classroom activities. The books cited below discuss problem solving specifically as related to the teaching of mathematics.

Hadamard, Jacques S. 1954. *An Essay on the Psychology of Invention in the Mathematical Field*. New York: Dover.
  A great mathematician gives his ideas. Some are insightful, others obvious.

Hlavaty, Julius H., ed. 1963. NCTM *Yearbook 27*.

Ideas and experiences from teachers in the field, specifically for the elementary level.

Krulik, Stephen, and Robert Reys, eds. 1980. *NCTM 1980 Yearbook*.
A collection of articles from research and from the field.

Larson, Loren C. 1983. *Problem Solving through Problems*. New York: Springer-Verlag.
Advanced problems, many with solutions. The author has taken a step toward classifying the problems according to problem solving techniques. This is a difficult task, and the results are mixed. The material, however, is excellent, and the attempt worthwhile. Most problems are rather difficult.

Melzak, Z.A. 1983. *Bypasses: A Simple Approach to Complexity*. New York: Wiley.
An investigation into the thought patterns behind mathematical discovery. Much sound mathematics and some interesting insights are mixed with a dash of poetry and even mysticism. Many topics treated are rather advanced.

Pólya, George. 1945. *How to Solve It: A New Aspect of Mathematical Method*. 1957. 2nd ed. Garden City, N.Y.: Doubleday. 1971. Reprint. Princeton, N.J.: Princeton University Press.
A popular introduction to the art of mathematical problem solving, by a master of the art. Challenging problems and clever solutions are presented, together with discussion and motivation. It is all done with pleasant old-world humor and a delightful style.

⸻. 1954. *Mathematics and Plausible Reasoning*. Vol. 1: *Induction and Analogy in Mathematics*. Vol. 2: *Patterns of Plausible Inference*. Princeton, N.J.: Princeton University Press.
A deeper probe into the processes of mathematical creativity. Examples are drawn from the author's own important work, as well as the work of Euler, Bernoulli, and other good company.

⸻. [1962-1965] 1981. *Mathematical Discovery: On Understanding, Learning, and Teaching Problem Solving*. 2 vols. Combined ed. New York: Wiley.
More examples of the motivation behind the facade of mathematics. These two volumes complete Pólya's "Pentateuch" in problem solving.

Rubinstein, Moshe F. 1975. *Patterns of Problem Solving*. Englewood Cliffs, N.J.: Prentice-Hall.
An interdisciplinary approach, blending mathematics and psychology. The marriage is not always a happy one, but the book does serve to stimulate thought along these lines.

Wickelgren, Wayne A. 1974. *How to Solve Problems: Elements of a Theory of Problems and Problem Solving.* San Francisco: W. H. Freeman.
    Starting with mathematical material, the author strives to generalize the processes of problem solving so that they will apply to other areas as well.

Classics

These are all-time best sellers, in modern editions. They were originally written as texts, however, they lack modern shortcuts, current emphases, and — most important — exercises and problems. George Pólya, among others, has shown us how we can use these sources to motivate the thought processes of our students.

Archimedes. 1897, 1912. *The Works of Archimedes with the Method of Archimedes.* Translated by Thomas L. Heath. Cambridge, England: Cambridge University Press. Reprint. New York: Dover.
    The most modern of the ancients. Our students often find themselves in his shoes, facing a problem which would be routine with more advanced methods, but which demands the utmost ingenuity if the solver is restricted to simple tools.

Euclid. [1926] 1956. *The Thirteen Books of Euclid's Elements.* 2nd ed. 3 vols. Translated by Thomas L. Heath. Cambridge, England: Cambridge University Press. Reprint. New York: Dover.
    The model for curriculum for the past 2,000 years. Some of Euclid's methods are outmoded, but all are worthy of study and imitation. The number-theoretic books are particularly rich in material for motivated discovery.

Gauss, Carl Friedrich. 1966. *Disquisitiones Arithmeticae.* Translated by A. A. Clarke. New Haven: Yale University Press. Reprint with translation revised by William C. Waterhouse. 1986. New York: Springer-Verlag.
    Accessible material which affords a sampling of the methods of a fertile mind. The work of Gauss can be described as the single greatest influence on the shape of modern mathematics.

Heath, Thomas L. [1910] 1964. *Diophantus of Alexandria: A Study in the History of Greek Algebra.* 2nd ed. Cambridge, England: Cambridge University Press. Reprint. New York: Dover.
    Some excellent insights into solution of equations in integers, from the creator of the subject. Our students have a lot to learn from his bag of tricks. The intuitive approach taken is well-suited to classroom exploration.

General References

These books touch on a variety of mathematical topics. Most of them are the work of accomplished mathematicians who had something to say to the general public. They are invaluable to the student who wants to know something about an advanced topic but is not ready to master it. Such an investigation serves to whet the appetite for more serious study.

Halmos, Paul R. 1970. How to write mathematics. *Enseignement Mathématique* (16): 123-152. 1973. Reprinted in *How to Write Mathematics*, by Norman E. Steenrod et al.,19-48. Providence, R.I.: American Mathematical Society. 1983. Reprinted in P. R. Halmos, *Selecta: Expository Writing*, 157-186. New York: Springer-Verlag.

> A much-neglected topic. Here a skilled mathematician and communicator gives his ideas. Since few others have done this, this work can stimulate thought on this important subject.

Newman, James R., ed. 1956. *The World of Mathematics*. 4 vols. New York: Simon & Schuster.

> Resources for students and teachers. Articles and references are sorted by topic, indexed, and reprinted. The emphasis is on good writing and clear exposition.

Problem Books

These can serve as departure points for enrichment topics. Problems, many with solutions, are presented in different areas and on different levels.

Artino, Ralph A., Anthony M. Gaglione, and Neil Shell, comps. 1983. *The Contest Problem Book IV*. New Mathematical Library no. 29. Washington, D.C.: Mathematical Association of America.

> Collected problems from the annual high-school contest, with solutions. These problems, contributed mostly by working mathematicians, reflect on every aspect of the field. See also Salkind (1961, 1966) and Salkind and Earl (1973).

Barry, Donald and J. Richard Lux. 1984. *The Phillips Academy Prize Examinations in Mathematics*. Palo Alto, Calif.: Dale Seymour.

> Problems ranging from simple short answer types to complex proofs. Extended solutions.

Brousseau, Brother Alfred. 1972. *St. Mary's College Mathematics Contest Problems*. Mountain View, Calif.: Creative.

Exciting long-answer type problems that make for good class discussion. Two levels of contests are included (grades 7-9 and 10-12).

Charosh, Mannis, comp. 1965. *Mathematical Challenges.* Washington, D.C.: National Council of Teachers of Mathematics.

Problems from the *Mathematics Student Journal,* all worthy of reprint and discussion.

Conrad, Steven R., and Daniel Flegler. 1986. *The 1st High School Math League Problem Book: Contests for Students in Grades 9-12.* Manhasset, N.Y.: Steven R. Conrad (Box 1090, Manhasset, NY 11030).

Contains thirty actual and complete regional contests, with detailed solutions, and problems rated by difficulty. (PJC & LSG)

Greitzer, Samuel L., comp. 1978. *International Mathematical Olympiads 1959-1977.* New Mathematical Library no. 27. Washington, D.C.: Mathematical Association of America.

The top of the line in contest problems. These are very difficult, and can easily motivate in-depth exploration of advanced topics. Klamkin (1986) covers later years.

Hill, Thomas, comp. 1974. *Mathematical Challenges II, Plus Six.* Washington, D.C.: National Council of Teachers of Mathematics.

More problems from the *Mathematics Student Journal.* They will repay discussion and exploration, rather than rapid solution.

Honsberger, Ross. 1973, 1976, 1985. *Mathematical Gems.* 3 vols. Dolciani Mathematical Expositions nos. 1, 2, 9. Washington, D.C.: Mathematical Association of America.

————. 1978. *Mathematical Morsels.* Dolciani Mathematical Expositions no. 3. Washington, D.C.: Mathematical Association of America.

————. 1979. *Mathematical Plums.* Dolciani Mathematical Expositions no. 4. Washington, D.C.: Mathematical Association of America.

Collections of essays on mathematical themes. Each shows another facet of mathematical exploration. Many include exercises and solutions.

Klamkin, Murray S., comp. 1986. *International Mathematical Olympiads, 1978-1985 and Forty Supplementary Problems.* New Mathematical Library no. 31. Washington, D.C.: Mathematical Association of America.

Greitzer (1978) covers earlier years.

Pólya, George, and Jeremy Kilpatrick. 1974. *The Stanford Mathematics Problem Book.* New York: Teachers College Press.

The master at work. A series of contests, consisting of three problems on three different levels. Problems are open-ended and invite discovery and creativity.

Rapaport, Elvira, trans. 1963. *Hungarian Problem Book* I, II. New Mathematical Library nos. 11, 12. Washington, D.C.: Mathematical Association of America.

More difficult problems. The solutions include extensive background material, making these problems particularly suitable for classroom use.

Salkind, Charles T., comp. 1961, 1966. *The Contest Problem Book* I, II. New Mathematical Library nos. 5, 17. Washington, D.C.: Mathematical Association of America.

————, and James M. Earl, comps. 1973. *The Contest Problem Book* III. New Mathematical Library no. 25. Washington, D.C.: Mathematical Association of America.

Problems, together with solutions, from the annual national high-school contest (1950-1983). See also Artino et al. (1983).

Saul, Mark, G. Kessler, S. Krilov, and L. Zimmerman. 1986. *The New York City Problems Book*. Palo Alto, Calif.: Dale Seymour.

Short-answer problems, from simple to very difficult. Includes solutions, extensive bibliography, and an appendix of useful results.

Shklarsky, David O., N.N. Chentzov, and I.M. Yaglom. 1962. *The USSR Olympiad Problem Book: Selected Problems and Theorems of Elementary Mathematics*. Revised and edited by Irving Sussman. Translated by John Maykovich. San Francisco, Calif.: W. H. Freeman.

Clever problems and solutions, many of which require little or no background.

————. 1979. *Selected Problems and Theorems in Elementary Mathematics*. Moscow: Mir (distributed by Imported Publications).

Trigg, Charles W. 1967. *Mathematical Quickies*. New York: McGraw-Hill. 1985. Reprint. *Mathematical Quickies: 270 Stimulating Problems with Solutions*. New York: Dover.

Quick and amusing problems, originally from *Mathematics Magazine*. Useful as discussion starters in the classroom.

Yaglom, A.M., and I.M. Yaglom. 1964-1967. *Challenging Mathematical Problems with Elementary Solutions*. 2 vols. Translated by James McCawley, Jr. Revised and edited by Basil Gordon. San Francisco, Calif.:

Holden-Day.

> A virtuoso display of ingenuity at work on results that are otherwise inaccessible, except to professionals or graduate students.

Number Theory

Many topics in number theory can be explored by students with no other mathematical background. Some of them can be pursued on a purely arithmetic level. Others demand more experience. In either case, the field provides excellent practice for ingenuity and intuition.

Dudley, Underwood. 1978. *Elementary Number Theory*. 2nd ed. San Francisco, Calif.: W. H. Freeman.

> Among the best expository texts available. Excellent problems and clear discussion.

Hardy, Godfrey H., and E.M. Wright. 1980. *An Introduction to the Theory of Numbers*. 5th ed. Oxford, England: Oxford University Press.

> Encyclopedic and didactic, but contains tools for an advanced student.

Sierpinski, Waclaw. 1970. *250 Problems in Elementary Number Theory*. New York: Elsevier.

> Intriguing problems, mostly with solutions. Sierpinski was a master number theoretician, and his writing clearly shows the joy and pride he took in his work.

Vinogradov, Ivan M. 1954. *Elements of Number Theory*. New York: Dover.

> A brief text, whose best feature is the many worked problems presented. The elegant exposition complements the creative use of the material made in the problems.

Discrete Mathematics

With the advent of the computer age, this topic is becoming more and more salient in modern research. Many problems have become quite important which once seemed trivial or not worthy of investigation. This is quite fortunate, as it affords students the chance to make a meaningful contribution with very little mathematical background.

Niven, Ivan M. 1965. *Mathematics of Choice: How to Count Without Counting*. New Mathematical Library no. 15. Washington, D.C.: Mathematical Association of America.

Elegant and complete elementary treatment. Problems and exercises range from very simple applications of principles discussed to those demanding much thought and invention.

Sahni, Sartaj. 1981. *Concepts in Discrete Mathematics*. Fridley, Minn.: Camelot.

A well-written and well-organized text that can be read without being studied. Presents several topics whose importance is just emerging.

Geometry

Once a mainstay of the curriculum, this subject is being taught in completely new ways. Some of the classical results may now be treated as advanced topics, while others can be reached more simply with modern methods.

Altshiller-Court, Nathan. 1927. *College Geometry*. New York: Johnson. 1952. 2nd ed., under the title *College Geometry: An Introduction to the Modern Geometry of the Triangle and the Circle*. New York: Barnes and Noble.

All the important basic relationships that concern the triangle and the circle, approached in a classic synthetic manner. Many problems presented without solution. While ignoring more modern methods, such as vectors, transformations, and particularly analytic geometry, this presentation shows the power and often the elegance of the older forms.

Coxeter, H.S.M. 1969. *Introduction to Geometry*. 2nd ed. New York: Wiley.

A master discusses his favorite topics. Many advanced topics approached from an elementary base.

Golovina, L.I., and I.M. Yaglom. 1979. *Induction in Geometry*. Translated by Leonid Levant. Moscow: Mir (distributed by Imported Publications).

A topic often neglected. This source makes the connection between discrete mathematics and elementary geometry. Thought-provoking examples will stimulate and challenge the student.

Hilbert, David, and Stephan Cohn-Vossen. 1952. *Geometry and the Imagination*. Translated by Peter Nemenyi. New York: Chelsea.

Among the great mathematical books of the modern era, this is Hilbert's legacy to those of us who are not professional research mathematicians. Each chapter opens the reader's eyes to hidden complexities in seemingly simple mathematical objects. Chapters on the conic sections and projective geometry are particularly stimulating.

Kazarinoff, Nicholas D. 1961. *Geometric Inequalities*. New Mathematical Library no. 4. Washington, D.C.: Mathematical Association of America.

> An elementary but complete introduction to the subject. It points out many connections between geometry and algebra, raising questions that are avoided in the usual metric development of geometry.

Yaglom, Isaak M. 1962, 1968, 1973. *Geometric Transformations*. 3 vols. Vol. 1, 2 translated by Alan Shields, vol. 3 by Abe Shenitzer. New Mathematical Library nos. 8, 21, 24. Washington, D.C.: Mathematical Association of America.

> The author starts with simple facts drawn from the classical Euclidean development and leads the reader to the transformational point of view of Felix Klein. Problems take the place of examples in a more conventional textbook. In most cases, solutions by transformation provide a great simplification over possible synthetic solutions, convincing even the most skeptical of the power and beauty of transformational methods.

Algebra

The transition from arithmetic to algebra is usually the student's first important exposure to the powerful methods of generalization in mathematics. Since most students gain a degree of control of this tool relatively early, it offers a good field for exploration.

Beckenbach, Edwin F., and Richard Bellman. 1961. *An Introduction to Inequalities*. New Mathematical Library no. 3. Washington, D.C.: Mathematical Association of America.

> Starts with very simple results, but works up to the classical inequalities, such as Cauchy's inequality, the triangle inequality, the arithmetic-geometric mean inequality. Includes fascinating exercises and excursions into related areas of mathematics.

Chrystal, George. 1959. *Algebra: An Elementary Textbook for the Higher Classes of Secondary Schools and for Colleges*. 6th ed. 2 vols. New York: Chelsea.

> An encyclopedia of algebraic techniques. Originally published in the 1800s, this book summarizes the development of the "old" algebra, which was generalized and streamlined in the next century.

Hall, Henry S., and Samuel R. Knight. 1957. *Higher Algebra*. London:

Macmillan.
> A classic, containing "every trick in the book." This was originally a text for British universities, so the style is somewhat old-fashioned and some of the exercises are antiquated. The mathematics, however, endures.

Kretchmar, Vasilii A. 1974. *A Problem Book in Algebra*. Translated by Victor Shiffer. Translation edited by Leonid Levant. Moscow: Mir (distributed by Imported Publications).
> Olympiad-style problems, classified by subject area. Clear and complete solutions. Many problems can be solved using elementary methods, but they can also be used to motivate more advanced techniques.

Analysis

Even if the student "knows" elementary calculus, there are advanced topics, particularly in topology or transfinite arithmetic, which are quite accessible.

Beckenbach, Edwin F., and Richard Bellman. 1961. *An Introduction to Inequalities*. New Mathematical Library no. 3. Washington, D.C.: Mathematical Association of America.
> A solid introduction to the subject. Inequalities are very important in analysis, and substantial results can be achieved by a novice. Students can contrive clever arguments to support results that are neither trivial nor obvious.

Mandelbrot, Benoit B. 1982. *The Fractal Geometry of Nature*. San Francisco, Calif.: W. H. Freeman.
> Modern analysis, old-fashioned geometry, and computer science. An important researcher offers some of his ideas in accessible form. Mandelbrot's fractals are finding a place in current mathematical thought.

Niven, Ivan. 1961. *Numbers, Rational and Irrational*. New Mathematical Library no. 1. New York: L. W. Singer. Available through Mathematical Association of America.
> A simply-written introduction to the deeper properties of the real number line.

Sawyer, Walter W. 1961. *What is Calculus About?* New Mathematical Library no. 2. New York: L. W. Singer. Available through Mathematical Association of America.
> Captivating introduction to the subject. This book is best appreciated by students with no formal training in the subject, and supplies them with background not usually given them in the texts.

Zippin, Leo. 1962. *Uses of Infinity.* New Mathematical Library no. 7. Washington, D.C.: Mathematical Association of America.
Simple and readable introduction to the topic, with fascinating extensions and problems.

Recreational Mathematics

Although this area is not really suitable for formal development, many of its gems can be extracted and displayed in classroom settings. These books offer much material which is accessible to students with almost no mathematical background.

Berlekamp, Elwyn R., John H. Conway, and Richard K. Guy. 1982. *Winning Ways for Your Mathematical Plays.* New York: Academic.
Ostensibly a book on mathematical games. Some of them are not yet completely analyzed. Many of them will liven up the classroom. And all of them open exciting new areas of exploration.

Bunch, Bryan H. 1982. *Mathematical Fallacies and Paradoxes.* New York: Van Nostrand Reinhold.
A collection of clinkers. Sometimes it is as important in solving a problem to know what won't work as what will.

Frey, Alexander H., Jr., and David Singmaster. 1982. *Handbook of Cubik Math.* Hillside, N.J.: Enslow.
Not just a solution to Rubik's cube, but a solid introduction to the mathematics of groups and geometry that lies behind the object which has been called "the single most useful teaching tool for higher mathematics."

Gardner, Martin. 1977. *Mathematical Carnival.* New York: Vintage.
————. 1979. *Mathematical Circus.* New York: Knopf.
————. 1983. *Wheels, Life, and Other Mathematical Amusements.* New York: W. H. Freeman.
————. 1986. *Knotted Doughnuts and Other Mathematical Entertainments.* New York: W. H. Freeman.
————. 1987. *Time Travel and Other Mathematical Bewilderments.* New York: W. H. Freeman.
Collections of the author's columns from *Scientific American.* Gardner collects some of the most exciting ideas around and gives us lucid yet intriguing expositions. More of Gardner's books are listed under Resource Materials in Ch. 13, Recreational Mathematics.

Hofstadter, Douglas R. 1979. *Gödel, Escher, Bach: An Eternal Golden Braid*. New York: Basic Books.

Ostensibly an exposition of Gödel's famous theorem on undecidable propositions. Along the way, the author touches on topics in mathematics and computer science that are of paramount importance in their own right. Sometimes contrived, sometimes simple, but always intriguing.

————. 1985. *Metamagical Themas: Questing for the Essence of Mind and Pattern*. New York: Basic Books.

A fascinating look into a creative mind. This series of articles, originally from *Scientific American*, blends modern mathematics, computer science, and mathematical recreation. Many articles offer fascinating possibilities for enrichment topics and problem posing.

Klarner, David A., ed. 1981. *The Mathematical Gardner*. Boston: Prindle, Weber & Schmidt.

Essays and articles in honor of Martin Gardner, and very much in his style.

Morrison, Philip, and Phylis Morrison. 1982. *Powers of Ten*. Redding, Conn.: Scientific American Library. San Francisco, Calif.: distributed by W. H. Freeman.

A deep appreciation of an elementary topic. Accessible to young children. But even the most jaded scientist can get a fresh appreciation of the real numbers as a tool for describing the universe.

Schuh, Frederik. 1968. *The Master Book of Mathematical Recreations*. Translated by F. Göbel. Translation edited by T. H. O'Beirne. New York: Dover.

The closest thing we have to a complete reference. This book contains solutions to all the old chestnuts, as well as some twists that are not so well-known.

Singmaster, David. 1981. *Notes on Rubik's "Magic Cube."* Hillside, N.J.: Enslow.

Working notes of a master. Rather than working toward a solution of the cube (which can easily be found elsewhere), the author explores the intuitions and mathematics behind such solutions.

Computer Science

Although this area is considered a related but distinct field, it can yet serve as a source for problems and results requiring mathematical explanation.

Knuth, Donald E. 1968- . *The Art of Computer Programming*. 3 vols. Vol. 1: *Fundamental Algorithms*. 2nd ed. 1973. Vol. 2: *Semi Numerical Algorithms*. 2nd ed. 1981. Vol. 3: *Sorting and Searching*. 1973. Reading, Mass.: Addison-Wesley.

> Another encyclopedic work. Much material is suitable only for specialists; however, many problems and examples can be worked in a purely mathematical setting. This book fills a wide gap in the mathematical literature.

History

Many teachers have noticed that students struggling to comprehend a difficult topic make the same errors and follow the same paths as the mathematicians who first developed the topics. Of course, student progress is quicker, since the path has already been trod. But in guiding our students, we can learn a lot from a recollection of what the difficulties were. And in stretching their understanding, we can ask the same embarrassing questions that the original researchers encountered. We can profit from the mistakes of the past, as well as the successes.

Aaboe, Asger. 1964. *Episodes From the Early History of Mathematics*. New Mathematical Library no. 13. Washington, D.C.: Mathematical Association of America.

> From the Babylonians to late Greek times, the author selects samples of thought that will go well with modern students' experiences.

Bell, Eric Temple. 1937. *Men of Mathematics*. New York: Simon & Schuster.

> A major resource. This book gives us insight into the personalities and work of the great mathematicians. Some of the stories told are apocryphal, but even as canards they have become classic.

Dickson, Leonard E. 1975. *History of the Theory of Numbers*. New York: Chelsea.

> A comprehensive survey, combining exposition with history. Incidents from the history of number theory are often repeated in the classroom with gifted students.

Edwards, Harold M. 1978. Fermat's Last Theorem. *Scientific American* 239 (4) (October 1978): 104-122.

> A comprehensive history of the problem. Still unsolved, it has stimulated more mathematical thought than many questions that were grappled with more success. Aside from this important lesson, the reader will find many classroom ideas in this article.

Grinstein, Louise S., and Paul J. Campbell, eds. 1987. *Women of Mathematics: A Biobibliographic Sourcebook*. Westport, Conn.: Greenwood.

> Biographical essays of women mathematicians past and present. Essential for helping assure girls gifted and talented in mathematics that they *can* surmount whatever the obstacles and become mathematicians. (PJC & LSG)

Hallerberg, Arthur H., et al., eds. 1969. *NCTM Yearbook 31*.

> Teachers and other educators contribute ideas and experiences.

Kline, Morris. 1972. *Mathematical Thought from Ancient to Modern Times*. Oxford, England: Oxford University Press.

> Encyclopedic in scope. Almost every topic of current interest in mathematics is treated here. A good starting point for further investigation.

Pedagogy

Books by teachers and for teachers. Some emphasize classroom experience, while others stress research about the classroom.

Bartkovich, Kevin G., and William C. George. 1980. *Teaching the Gifted and Talented in the Mathematics Classroom*. Washington, D.C.: National Education Association.

> Some insights from research in the area.

Kennedy, Leonard M. 1970. *Guiding Children to Mathematical Discovery*. Belmont, Calif.: Wadsworth.

> Mostly for elementary education. A selection of activities and methods to open children to mathematical modes of inquiry.

Maletsky, Evan M., and Christian R. Hirsch, eds. 1981. *Activities from The Mathematics Teacher*. Reston, Va.: National Council of Teachers of Mathematics.

> A wealth of suggestions for hands-on activities, mostly for the elementary grades.

Ridge, H.L., and J.S. Renzulli. 1981. Teaching mathematics to the talented and gifted. In *The Mathematical Education of Exceptional Children and Youth: An Interdisciplinary Approach*, edited by Vincent J. Glennon. Reston, Va.: National Council of Teachers of Mathematics.

> Survey of literature and research, mostly involving methods and curricula already in use.

17. Sex-Related Differences and Mathematics

LINDSAY A. TARTRE
ELIZABETH FENNEMA
MARGARET R. MEYER

The Problem Identified

The roots of some of the research concerning sex-related differences can be found in economic reality—dollars and cents. Early in the recent feminist movement, studies showed that women as a group earned less than men. Many people wore buttons that displayed the statistic that women earned about 59¢ for every dollar that men earned. Social activists and others, such as Sheila Tobias (1976) and John Ernest (1976), were eager to understand why women earned less than men.

As a result of many studies researchers eventually focused on two explanations. Either individual employers were paying women less than men for the same jobs, or women were not in the high-paying occupations as much as men were. Both explanations appeared to be true. While legislation and social pressure could change the former, the latter problem was much more difficult to understand. Why would men, more than women, choose to enter high-paying careers? Which careers paid well? Which did not?

The pattern that began to emerge from research was that men, more than women, tended to enter the technical and scientific careers — engineering and computer science, for example — and the common denominator for those careers appeared to be mathematics preparation. Lucy Sells (1975) called mathematics "the critical filter" for preparation for many careers.

As the primary source for mathematics preparation, the schools have since become the focus of much of the research concerning the causes and possible interventions to eliminate inequities in mathematics. Two measures of the magnitude of the problem in schools which have been studied extensively are enrollment patterns and mathematics achievement.

Enrollment Patterns

Since one year each of algebra and geometry are often required for college entrance, enrollment patterns for those courses have tended to be similar for girls and boys, although fewer students take geometry than algebra I. The percentage of students enrolled, both boys and girls, drops substantially for the more advanced courses beyond geometry. However, differences between girls and boys have been observed in the number and level of mathematics courses taken during those critical high-school years. These differences in mathematics preparation could also be reflected in the possible options for college majors later.

Armstrong (1985), in a national survey of seventeen-year-olds conducted in 1978, found few sex-related differences in mathematics participation for the low-level high school mathematics courses. However, she found that "significantly more females took business or accounting mathematics while significantly more males took algebra II and probability/statistics" (p. 72). Although not statistically significant, Armstrong also found that "almost 4% more males took trigonometry; 5% more took computer programming and 3% more took calculus" (p. 72).

The pattern of more boys than girls continuing to take mathematics in the later years of high school has been observed in other studies. The National Assessment of Educational Progress (NAEP) report (1983) compared the third national assessment data from 1982 to the second national assessment data from 1978. Although the percent of boys enrolled continued to be higher than for girls for all mathematics courses beyond geometry, there was an indication that those differences were decreasing. For example, in 1978, 38% of the boys had taken at least one-half year of algebra II while only 36% of the girls had. By 1982 the percentage for boys was 39 and for girls, 38. In 1978, only 3.1% of the girls had taken precalculus or calculus; by 1982, the percentage was 3.6. The boys' enrollment remained unchanged during this time, with 4.7% of the boys taking precalculus or calculus.

Mathematics Achievement

In addition to focusing on which mathematics courses students are taking, research has also explored how students perform in mathematics. Fennema and Carpenter (1981) examining sex-related differences in mathematics achievement for the second NAEP, found that across mathematical topics "the averages for females on the knowledge and skills exercises tended to be slightly higher and the understanding and applications averages somewhat higher for males" (p. 555). This pattern, showing females performing better than males for low-level cognitive tasks and males performing better than females for high-level cognitive tasks, is consistent with other research and was reinforced when the researchers examined the critical topics of number and numeration. "Females scored higher on lower level number and numeration skills at ages 9 and 13. Males scored higher on multistep word problems in this content area at all ages" (p. 556).

Several years ago many people believed that if girls and boys enrolled in advanced mathematics courses in equal numbers, sex-related differences in mathematics would disappear. There have been indications recently, however, that the answer is not that simple. Fennema and Carpenter (1981) found achievement differences when students were grouped by course background.

> For each course background category, male achievement exceeded that of females. It should be noted that the magnitude of the difference increased consistently in relation to the amount of mathematics taken. In other words, the difference between 17-year-old females and males was smallest for students who had not taken algebra I; the size of the difference was greater for students who had taken algebra I; it was even greater for students who had taken geometry; and the trend continued through courses beyond second-year algebra. (p. 555)

Intervenable Factors

We have described sex-related differences which have been found in mathematics course enrollment and achievement. We now turn to the issue of why those differences exist. Is there, as some have suggested, an innate predisposition to mathematics that causes the resulting sex-related differences? Or, are there learnable skills and factors that influence the outcomes? This "nature versus nurture" argument has raged for a long time and is unlikely to be resolved in the foreseeable future, if at all. Both genetics and experience probably play roles in the development of each child. As teachers, we cannot change genetics. However, we should be concerned with factors that can be developed or changed to help students move toward their potentials.

These intervenable factors include cognitive skills and affective factors found to be associated with mathematics learning. Other factors have been identified through the dynamics of the classroom.

Cognitive Skills

The two types of cognitive skills that have shown high correlations with many mathematics tasks and have been studied extensively are verbal skills and spatial skills.

Verbal skills have been studied for many years in many forms, from vocabulary tests to tests of expository writing. Sometimes a test of verbal skill has been used as a type of IQ measure. The results have been mixed as well. Several studies concerning sex-related differences in verbal skills and mathematics have found no differences.

Many other studies have found a pattern of sex-related differences that points up a peculiar inconsistency. Several types of verbal skills have been found to correlate positively with a wide variety of mathematics tasks. As has been discussed, if sex-related differences are found for mathematics tasks, they tend to favor males. However, if sex-related differences have been found for verbal skills, they tend to favor females. One possible explanation for this inconsistency is that verbal skills may tend to be more "important" for girls' understanding of mathematics than for boys. Several research reports have cited higher correlations between verbal skills and mathematics for girls than for boys (Connor and Serbin (1985), for example).

The other type of cognitive skills whose relationship with mathematics has been studied extensively is spatial skill. Many different mental activities have been included under the term "spatial." Among those activities are such diverse skills as referring to a picture to solve a problem, mentally rotating a cube in space or being able to find your way out of a maze. Spatial skills

> include those mental skills concerned with understanding, manipulating, reorganizing or interpreting relationships in space and generally are classified into two types: spatial visualization, which requires that the subject mentally manipulate all or part of an object, and spatial orientation, which requires that the subject readjust her/his perspective to become consistent with a representation of an object presented visually. (Tartre 1984, xv)

Research has found sex-related differences favoring males for both spatial visualization and spatial orientation tasks, particularly after adolescence. In addition, many mathematics activities have been found to correlate positively with many different spatial tasks. Since sex-related differences in mathematics also tend to favor males, many people have speculated that the sex-related differences found in mathematics are due, at least in part, to differences in spatial skill. However, research has not yet established that link. In fact, two recent research studies have shown that males who scored low on a spatial test (low-spatial males) tended to perform as well, if not better, than high-spatial males on a variety of mathematics tasks (Fennema and Tartre 1985, Tartre 1984). In those studies, the high-spatial females tended to perform as well as the male groups. However, the low-spatial females did not perform as well as the other groups on several mathematics tasks. Much more research concerning both verbal and spatial skills needs to be done before the relationships among those cognitive skills, mathematics, and gender can be clearly understood.

Affective Factors

Affective factors are more difficult to measure and their influence more difficult to assess than cognitive skills. However, three factors that have been investigated and appear to be important to the learning of mathematics are: confidence, perceived usefulness, and how students attribute success and failure.

Confidence has been shown to be a good predictor of success in mathematics. In some studies, the correlation of mathematics achievement with confidence was almost as high as achievement's correlation with the verbal and spatial cognitive factors discussed earlier. How students feel about themselves and about their ability to do mathematics can ultimately influence how well they succeed or whether they even try. Several research studies have indicated that boys tend to be more confident in their ability to do mathematics than girls. Even when achievement means show no significant differences, several studies have reported significant sex-related differences in confidence favoring males.

Another factor that has been shown to relate to mathematics achievement is how useful to one's future life mathematics is perceived to be. Again, if sex-related differences have been found, boys tend to report more frequently than girls that mathematics will be useful to them. The future usefulness of mathematics is often reported by students as one of the major reasons they chose to continue to take mathematics courses.

How students attribute their successes and failures in mathematics has been explored by researchers also. Much of the research has been built from a framework with four categories developed by Weiner (1974).

Those categories are ability, effort, task difficulty, and luck. These categories were classified along two dimensions: locus of control and stability. For example, ability is considered to be stable and is internal to the student. However, luck is unstable and is external to the student.

A continuum from "learned-helpless" to "mastery-oriented" has been developed from observing attributional patterns. Learned-helpless indicates someone who tends to attribute success in mathematics to effort or to some external force and attributes failure to ability. Mastery-oriented indicates someone who tends to attribute success in mathematics to ability and attributes failure to effort. Sex-related differences have been found in attributional patterns with girls tending to be more learned-helpless and boys tending to be more mastery-oriented.

Attributional patterns of success and failure in mathematics have been linked to achievement and continued participation in mathematics.

> The importance of attributions is in the individual's expectation for success on similar tasks in the future. For example, if a student attributes failure to lack of ability then they have little reason to expect success in the future since ability is considered stable. On the other hand an attribution of failure to lack of effort does not preclude success in the future, since effort is within the control of the individual and can be adjusted to make success possible. (Meyer 1985, 5)

Classroom Interactions

In addition to looking at individuals and groups of students in terms of cognitive and affective factors to try to understand sex-related differences in mathematics, the dynamics of the classroom have been explored as well.

> Thus far, most of the research that has looked to the classroom as a possible source of ... [sex-related] differences, has focused on the differential treatment received by males and females in the classroom, primarily in terms of teacher-student interactions. Observational studies have been conducted in both elementary and secondary level mathematics classes and it has been consistently found that boys receive more favorable treatment than girls. (Koehler 1985)

Fennema and Reyes (1982) reporting on a three-year longitudinal study of sixth- through eighth-grade mathematics classes observed boys and girls who scored above the mean in mathematics achievement and who scored high or low on a scale that measured confidence toward doing mathematics. They found that for interactions in front of the entire class (public) between students and the teacher, the

> high confidence boys, more than any other group, initiated public interactions. At the same time, teachers initiated more public interactions with high confidence boys than any other group ... [In addition,] more so than the other groups, high confidence girls initiated few public interactions with their teachers. (p. 9)

Several possible explanations were given for the sex-related differences found in teacher-student interactions. Perhaps boys tend to be more salient in the classroom than girls. It is also possible that girls are less assertive or are less comfortable speaking in class than boys and therefore do not call out as much. This possibility was supported by the fact that "several statistically significant sex differences [were found] among the public categories but no statistically significant sex differences [were found] among the private [teacher with individual student] interaction categories" (p. 18).

Another explanation could be that girls know less about mathematics than boys do. However, no achievement difference was detected in this study by Fennema and Reyes (1982). The fact that no sex-related difference in achievement was found suggests that the relationship between teacher-student interactions and mathematics achievement is unclear. Koehler (1985) found that "indeed there was differential treatment occurring, and that most frequently this favored males, but that there was no apparent relationship between this differential treatment and male/female performance in algebra one" (p. 9). Perhaps differential treatment of students doesn't affect achievement; or perhaps researchers haven't yet tapped the source of that impact.

Our Part of the Solution

The discussion thus far has centered on the findings of the research concerning sex-related differences, which has helped identify problems and possible explanations of phenomena. The research has shown statistical mean differences or the trends of groups of students. But each of your students is not a group with means and standard deviations. Caring teachers with high expectations continue to approach each student according to her/his individual needs in an effort to help stretch that student to reach her/his potential. Some specific suggestions for teachers follow.

Self-Monitoring for Teachers

(a) Monitor your interactions with students. Are there girls or boys in your classes that you seldom interact with? Do you interact with students who don't have questions? What kinds of interactions do you engage in with students? What proportion of your interactions are praise? discipline? questions? or administrative activities, etc.?

(b) Monitor the involvement of your students in projects or other cooperative learning activities – as leaders, as doers, as followers. Monitor passive versus active participation.

(c) Evaluate your expectations of your students. What are your stereotypes? Try this activity – mentally picture a room full of each of the following groups: doctors, lawyers, engineers, veterinarians, dentists, secretaries, and sales clerks. Were the rooms balanced by sex? Which were? Which weren't?

People in Action

(a) Past: Mathematics is people. Continue to tell students about the people, both male and female, who have been involved in mathematics in the past.

(b) Present and Future: Show students women and men in many different careers to help students become aware of the options they have. We are not suggesting a one-shot "see the token-woman doctor," but rather a continuing program of observations of women and men in natural roles of career leadership in mathematics, business, engineering and other technical and scientific contexts.

REFERENCES

Armstrong, Jane M. 1985. A national assessment of participation and achievement of women in mathematics. In *Women and Mathematics: Balancing the Equation*, edited by Susan F. Chipman, Lorelei R. Brush, and Donna M. Wilson, 59-94. Hillsdale, N.J.: Erlbaum.

Connor, Jane M., and Lisa A. Serbin. 1985. Visual-spatial skill: Is it important for mathematics? Can it be taught? In *Women and Mathematics: Balancing* the Equation, edited by Susan F. Chipman, Lorelei R.

Brush, and Donna M. Wilson, 151-174. Hillsdale, N.J.: Erlbaum.

Ernest, John. 1976. _Mathematics and Sex._ Santa Barbara: University of California. Columbus, O.: ERIC/SMEAC. ERIC: ED 059 429.

Fennema, Elizabeth, and Thomas P. Carpenter. 1981. Sex-related differences in mathematics: Results from National Assessment. _Mathematics Teacher_ 74 (7) (October 1981): 554-559.

Fennema, Elizabeth, and Laurie H. Reyes. 1982. Sex and confidence level: Differences in participation in mathematics classroom processes. Paper presented at the annual meeting of the American Educational Research Association, New York, April 1982.

Fennema, Elizabeth, and Lindsay A. Tartre. 1985. The use of spatial visualization in mathematics by girls and boys. _Journal for Research in Mathematics Education_ 16 (3) (May 1985): 184-206.

Koehler, Mary Schatz. 1985. Sex-related differences in achievement and effective mathematics teaching in algebra one classes. Paper presented at the annual meeting of the American Educational Research Association, Chicago, April 1985.

Meyer, Margaret R. 1985. Predicting females' and males' achievement and participation in high school mathematics: A study of attitudes and attributions. Paper presented at the annual meeting of the American Educational Research Association, Chicago, April 1985.

National Assessment of Educational Progress. 1983. _The Third National Mathematics Assessment: Results, Trends, and Issues._ Report No. 13-MA-01. Denver, Col.: Education Commission of the States. Columbus, O.: ERIC/SMEAC. ERIC: ED 228049.

Sells, Lucy W. 1975. Sex, ethnic and field differences in doctoral outcomes. Ph.D. diss., University of California, Berkeley.

Tartre, Lindsay A. 1984. _The Role of Spatial Orientation Skill in the Solution of Mathematics Problems and Associated Sex-Related Differences._ Ph.D. diss. University of Wisconsin-Madison.

Tobias, Sheila. 1976. Math Anxiety. _Ms. Magazine_ (January 1976).

Columbus, O.: ERIC/SMEAC. ERIC: EJ 152 210.

Weiner, Bernard, comp. 1974. *Achievement Motivation and Attribution Theory*. Morristown, N.J.: General Learning.

BIBLIOGRAPHY

American Institute for Research. 1982. *Sourcebook of Measures of Women's Educational Equity*. Washington, D.C.: U.S. Department of Education, Women's Educational Equity Act.

> This sourcebook contains information about a large number of instruments that could be used to assess behaviors, attitudes, knowledge, etc., related to educational equity. It is in a format that is easy to use with numerous ways to find the reviewed instruments. While this resource does not contain the instruments, it does indicate how they can be obtained (pp. 17-45 present ten different measures of attitude toward mathematics).

Askew, Judy. 1982. *The Sky's the Limit in Math-Related Careers*. Washington, D.C.: U.S. Department of Education, Women's Educational Equity Act. Columbus, O.: ERIC/SMEAC. ERIC: ED 233899.

> This book is meant to be read by students to acquaint them with jobs that use mathematical training. It is based upon responses of women working in these jobs. The areas covered are computers, engineering, finance, mathematics education, research mathematics, and statistics. It gives names and addresses of women interviewed in the book to be used as a resource list.

Ball, Patricia G., Mary Ellen McLoughlin, and Nan E. Scott. 1981. *Exploring Educational Equity: Sex-Affirmative Guide for Counseling and Teaching*. Washington, D.C.: U.S. Department of Education, Women's Educational Equity Act. Columbus, O.: ERIC/SMEAC. ERIC: ED 215242.

> This resource consists of five curriculum units designed for use in either a college classroom or professional workshop setting:
> - New Techniques for Counseling Women: for graduate students in education, psychology, social work, nursing, or medicine. Purpose is to provide means by which students can become familiar with techniques for counseling women.
> - Sex Bias in Interest Measurement: upper level undergraduate or graduate; technical in nature, four lessons.
> - Women in Higher Education: purpose is to explore the position of women in higher education, graduate level.
> - Sex-Affirmative Action in Education: workshop guide for a day-long in-service session for public school teachers and counselors on issues of sex-role stereotyping and sex bias in the education setting.

- Assertiveness Training for Job-Seeking Skills: A workshop to teach others to handle workshops that teach assertive job-seeking skills.

Blum, Lenore. 1980. _Expanding your Horizons in Science and Mathematics_. Washington, D.C.: U.S. Department of Education, Women's Educational Equity Act.

This is a handbook that describes how to plan, conduct, and evaluate conferences for young women to encourage them to consider careers in science and technology. The emphasis is on exposure to role models and career information. The first half of the book considers the components of a day-long workshop and includes the conference brochures, etc. Startling statements, pp. 42-43 (though somewhat dated — 1978). Includes facilitator's guide.

Christensen, Twila. 1982. _The Whole Person Book (II): Guide to Preservice Training_. Washington, D.C.: U.S. Department of Education, Women's Educational Equity Act.

Materials and lessons to assist counseling or teacher education students in acquiring a basic understanding of sex-role stereotyping as it relates to career choice and development. There are six 3-hour modules each containing support materials, activities, and facilitator's notes. Includes a focus on male stereotypes as well as female. Module F is particularly good for "change agents" in school (see pp. 147-151, 131-146).

Cotera, Martha P. 1982. _Checklists for Counteracting Race and Sex Bias in Educational Materials_. Washington, D.C.: U.S. Department of Education, Women's Educational Equity Act. Columbus, O.: ERIC/SMEAC. ERIC: ED 221612.

This handbook contains guidelines for evaluating instructional materials for race and sex bias. Pp. 17-18 look specifically at stereotyping in mathematics and science texts and materials. In addition to the evaluation guidelines that are geared to more specific subject areas, there are also more general checklists aimed at evaluating instructional materials for bias regardless of subject area (pp. 25-30).

Downie, Diane, Twila Slesnick, and J. Stenmark. 1981. _Math for Girls and Other Problem Solvers_. Berkeley, Calif.: Equals Math/ Science Network, Lawrence Hall of Science.

This teacher's guide presents curriculum ideas for eight days' worth of classes. The material/activities are divided into five different strands focused on four problem-solving skills and a career component. It has two goals: to improve attitudes and to develop skills. Each day could serve as an independent ninety-minute or two-hour workshop or activities could be organized by strand. Designed for elementary and middle school level.

Fennema, Elizabeth. 1981. _Multiplying Options and Subtracting Bias_.

Reston, Va.: National Council of Teachers of Mathematics.

A videotape and workshop intervention program designed to eliminate sexism from mathematics education. Four 30-minute full-color videotapes narrated by Marlo Thomas. Each videotape is aimed at a specific junior/senior high school audience (students, teachers, parents, guidance counselors). A variety of formats are used — candid interviews, dramatic vignettes, and expert testimony — to address the problem of mathematics avoidance and suggest some possible solutions. A 192-page facilitator's guide provides an overview of the workshops. Has detailed instructions on how the facilitator can prepare for conducting the workshops, as well as four separate step-by-step sets of workshop instructions for each of the target audiences.

Fleming, Elyse S. 1979. *Project Choice*. Washington, D.C.: U.S. Department of Education, Women's Educational Equity Act.

This resource outlines a fourteen-week program to broaden the career options of talented adolescent (grade 11) women. Based on a diagnostic-prescriptive design, this program seeks to identify those personal and cultural barriers that may interfere with the realization of potential and then engage students in activities designed to overcome the particular impediments to fulfillment. It contains materials for assessing the effects of the 14-week program as well as full bibliography divided by topic.

Gilgert, Mary. 1982. *Choices and Changes*. Washington, D.C.: U.S. Department of Education, Women's Educational Equity Act.

Contains twenty-nine interviews with people in nontraditional careers. Pictures show the individuals in their jobs. Attention is given to showing minorities and handicapped persons, as well as women. Would be good to have in a classroom for students to read. For teachers, it could serve as an impetus for exploring alternative career options with their students.

Grinstein, Louise S., and Paul J. Campbell, eds. 1987. *Women of Mathematics: A Biobibliographic Sourcebook*. Westport, Conn.: Greenwood.

Biographies and scientific accomplishments of 43 women mathematicians, including a number now living. Includes bibliographies of works by and works about each biographical subject. (PJC & LSG)

Hansen, L. Sunny. 1980. *Born Free: Training Packet to Reduce Sex-role Stereotyping in Career Development*. Washington, D.C.: U.S. Department of Education, Women's Educational Equity Act. Columbus, O.: ERIC/SMEAC. ERIC: ED 204646, ED 204648.

The packet contains numerous independent strategies (activities) designed to increase the awareness of teachers, counselors, administrators, and parents of the ways in which they consciously and unconsciously inhibit or facilitate career options for children, youths, and adults. The strategies are divided into groups on the basis of the intended goal they address, and can be combined to fit the audience and the time available. Each strategy is rated on the basis of

parent/educator appropriateness, level of group trust required, level of awareness of career development, level of awareness of sex-role issues. Also included
is the amount of time required and a list of other materials required.

Hardeman, Carole H. 1982. *MATHCO*. Washington, D.C.: U.S. Department of Education, Women's Educational Equity Act. Columbus, O.:
ERIC/SMEAC. ERIC: ED 233900 – ED 233905.

This resource includes five teaching modules: Careers, Patterns, Mathematics in Your World, Everyday Mathematics, and Mathematics and Science. It
is designed to teach mathematics skills, demonstrate interrelationships between
mathematics and other subjects, and provided exposure to a wide variety of math-
ematics-related careers. Materials are appropriate not only for mathematics, but
also for language and fine arts, science, and social studies classes. Designed for
elementary and middle-school levels. Includes film or filmstrip, audiotape,
facilitator's guide, posters.

Hellsner, Esther. 1979. *ASPIRE: Awareness of Sexual Prejudice is the
Responsibility of Educators*. Washington, D.C.: U.S. Department of
Education, Women's Educational Equity Act.

Four modules: Sex-Role Socialization, Sexism in Education, Evaluating Instructional Materials, and Strategies for Change. Each module consists of a set
of activities for educators, and could stand alone or with others in a series. Also
included in each module is a set of readings based on the module topic and notes
to the facilitator.

Kaseberg, Alice, Nancy Kreinberg, and Diane Downie. 1980. *Equals*.
Berkeley, Calif.: Equals Math/Science Network, Lawrence Hall of Science.

This handbook is intended to assist educators in conducting in-service programs and to introduce Equals materials into the classroom. The workshop
model has three components: increasing awareness of sex differences in education and career choices, developing problem-solving skills in mathematics,
encouraging career aspirations. These three components and associated activities are covered in three separate chapters. Another chapter considers the
mechanics of an Equals workshop and another the implementing of Equals in
the classroom.

Klinman, Debra. 1979. *Teacher Skill Guide for Combating Sexism*.
Washington, D.C.: U.S. Department of Education, Women's Educational
Equity Act.

This program has been designed for use as either a sequential workshop
series or a college-level course. Consists of 13 training modules, each containing
a workshop design, handouts, background reading, and a classroom activities
booklet.

Kravitz, Ida. 1982. *Equity Lessons for Elementary School*. Washington,

D.C.: U.S. Department of Education, Women's Educational Equity Act.

This item contains ten lessons designed to develop in the elementary/middle school student an awareness of the many facets of sex-role stereotyping. The concept areas of the lessons correspond to the general areas of the basic elementary social studies curriculum. Each lesson includes: grade level, objectives, materials, procedures, and follow-up activities. Appendix contains guidelines for the selection of books and other instructional aids.

――――. 1982. *Equity Lessons for Secondary School*. Washington, D.C.: U.S. Department of Education, Women's Educational Equity Act.

Contains 11 lessons designed to develop in the secondary student an awareness of the many facets of sex-role stereotyping. The lessons are organized into three mini-units: recognizing and challenging stereotyping, a century of struggle: the women's rights movement in the U.S., and women who worked for justice in American society. Included in the appendix are guidelines for the selection of books and other instructional aids.

Nilsen, Alleen P. 1980. *Changing Words in a Changing World*. Washington, D.C.: U.S. Department of Education, Women's Educational Equity Act. Columbus, O.: ERIC/SMEAC. ERIC: ED 198556, ED 198557.

Activities and discussion topics (1-3 pages each) aimed at challenging students (teachers) to explore the basic elements and effects of communication. Gives practical guidelines on how to use non-exclusive language (pp. 23-25, 51-56). Good for raising consciousness on sexist language. Includes facilitator's guide. Contains curricular ideas and material for staff development.

Osen, Lynn M. 1974. *Women in Mathematics*. Cambridge, Mass.: MIT Press.

Contains the biographies of eight women mathematicians over the period 370 to 1935. The stated goals of the author were to "trace the impact women have had on the development of mathematical thought, to profile the lives of these women, and to explore the social context within which they worked."

Perl, Teri. 1978. *Math Equals: Biographies of Women Mathematicians Plus Related Activities*. Menlo Park, Calif.: Addison-Wesley.

This book contains nine biographies of women mathematicians. Following each biography is an introduction to the area of mathematics in which the woman worked. The activities are very intriguing and they provide an accessible entry into nontraditional mathematics, i.e., that usually not taught in secondary school.

Sadker, Myra P., and David M. Sadker. 1979. *Beyond Pictures and Pronouns: Sexism in Teacher Education Textbooks*. Washington, D.C.: U.S. Department of Education, Women's Educational Equity Act.

This is an analysis by subject of 24 teacher education texts published from 1973 to 1978. The authors note a pervasive and subtle sex bias (pp. 29-34 reviews three mathematics and three science methods books). Also included are sex equity guidelines for authors and editors to use in the revision and development of textbooks, and a selected annotated bibliography on sexism in education.

————. 1982. *Sex Equity Handbook for Schools: Guide for Sex Equity Trainers*. New York: Longman.

There are two items in this resource: a trainer's guide and a handbook. The trainer's guide provides the basics of training, plans for two sex equity workshops, and answers to some of the most commonly asked questions that arise in sex equity training. The handbook includes, among other things, discussion and guidelines regarding overcoming sex bias in classroom interaction and confronting sex bias in instructional materials, 22 lesson plans that deal with a variety of sex equity issues, and a resource directory.

Skolnick, Joan, Carol Langbort, and Lucille Day. 1982. *How to Encourage Girls in Math and Science: Strategies for Parents and Educators*. Englewood Cliffs, N.J.: Prentice-Hall.

The first four chapters are directed at parents and educators and are focused on the problem of girls avoiding mathematics and science. They are easily read and contain a good summary of relevant research. Contains references. Starting in Chapter 5 there is set of mathematics and science activities. Spatial visualization is given much attention. Some of the activities include interesting ways of integrating career information with mathematics.

Sprung, Barbara. 1980. *Maximizing Young Children's Potential*. Washington, D.C.: U.S. Department of Education, Women's Educational Equity Act.

Contains activities and resources to be used with preschool/early elementary teachers in a workshop format. Contains a checklist for evaluating sexism in children's books (p. 55) and a checklist for a nonsexist classroom (p. 39). Focus is on curriculum, literature, and language.

Stein, Dorothy. 1978. *Thinking and Doing: Overcoming Sex-Role Stereotyping in Education*. Washington, D.C.: U.S. Department of Education, Women's Educational Equity Act.

Contains four sections, each of which could stand alone as a workshop topic. The format is based upon the theory of Piaget. Contradictions and conflicts are presented via "problem situations" in group discussions. It is expected that by hearing differing opinions and responses, new, better ways of thinking will be recognized. The appendix contains a section for counselors. A section on workshop evaluation is included.

Weiss, Iris R. 1982. *Exploring Careers in Science and Engineering*. Research Triangle Park, N.C.: Research Triangle Institute.

There are four parts to this resource:
1)Class activities booklet, 12 activities, grades 4-9
2)Filmstrip with audiotape that highlights the diversity of scientific careers

and the appropriateness of them regardless of sex and race. Encourages the taking of mathematics to keep options open.

3)Booklet of resource materials for teachers. These resources are referred to in the classroom activities.

4)Poster set: 15 posters (15" x 20") that show real men and women of various races in science careers. Handicapped individuals are also shown.

Wisconsin Department of Public Instruction. 1977. *Freedom for Individual Development.* **Washington, D.C.: U.S. Department of Education, Women's Educational Equity Act.**

This in-service training program has as a primary goal that of sensitizing participants to the prevalence of sex-role stereotypes. The program consists of a trainer's guide and four in-service training modules: School/Community Relations, Vocational Education, Teaching Methods, and Counseling and Guidance. Each module contains instructions for a group trainer, activities for group work, background readings, evaluation tools, and a resource bibliography.

18. The Imperative of Teacher Education — Inservice After Preservice

CALVIN T. LONG

We intend to argue that if the educational enterprise is to be fully effective, it is imperative that teachers be involved in inservice activities on a regular and continuing basis. Contrapositively, if inservice activities are not a part of the regular ongoing activities of practicing teachers, then they are certain steadily to lose vitality and eventually to become sterile and largely ineffective.

What Is Inservice?

The commonly-held view is that inservice education for teachers consists of those collegiate or school based programs of professional study in which teachers are involved after they have been certified to teach and are actively employed by a school. These include workshops, seminars, formal courses, institutes, and after-school and summer activities. This definition is too narrow; we would include personal reading and self-study, as well as involvement in conferences and other job-related activities of local, regional, and national professional organizations.

Our nation is currently experiencing a serious shortage of qualified mathematics teachers, particularly in the secondary schools. The result is that many teachers certified to teach subjects other than mathematics are being pressed into service as teachers of mathematics. These teachers are unprepared for the task they are being asked to perform, and the results are entirely predictable. Thus the term *inservice education* must be further broadened to include appropriate efforts to provide opportunity for inadequately prepared teachers to be brought up to certification (or licensing) levels of competence and beyond.

In general, then, we will use the term inservice to refer to personal and institutional staff development activities applied to people already teaching mathematics in a school, whether they are certified to do so or not. Some of these activities can and should be sponsored by and carried out in the school systems where the teachers are employed. Some activities may be more appropriately carried out by colleges and universities—some at the expense of the teachers, and some at the expense of the school or state. Other activities are best carried out by appropriate professional organizations of mathematics teachers.

Finally, we attempt to distinguish between the terms *mathematics teacher* and *teacher of mathematics*. The choice of terms is arbitrary but the distinction is real and important, and we will be consistent in our usage throughout the remainder of the discussion. Briefly, we use *teacher of mathematics* to refer to a person who teaches mathematics, whether qualified or licensed to do so or not. The term *mathematics teacher* will refer to a person who teaches mathematics and is qualified to do so.

Preservice Expectations

To outline what ought to comprise the mathematics portion of the preservice training of teachers, i.e., the training persons would be expected to obtain in order to be certified or licensed to teach, we refer to two documents (National Council of Teachers of Mathematics (NCTM) 1981; Mathematical Association of America (MAA) 1983). These documents set a standard currently prevalent in the United States.

Recommendations cited for teachers of the junior-high-school grades (ages 12-14) are one course each in

- calculus, including both differentiation and integration;
- geometry, including informal approaches, axiomatics, and formal proof;
- computer science, using a high-level language;
- abstract algebra, including some number theory;
- applications and mathematical modeling, with topics from such fields as the natural sciences, the social sciences, business, and engineering;
- probability and statistics;
- methods of teaching junior-high-school mathematics, including methods of diagnosis and remediation.

For teachers of senior high school (ages 14-18), the following are recommended:

- three courses in calculus

and a course each in

- computer science, using a high-level language
- linear algebra
- abstract algebra
- geometry including Euclidean and other geometries
- probability and statistics
- applications and mathematical modeling, with topics from such fields as the natural sciences, the social sciences, business, and engineering
- the history of mathematics
- selected topics from the high-school curriculum, taught from an advanced standpoint and reflecting the mathematical concepts, generalizations, and applications as they relate to the school curriculum
- methods of teaching high-school mathematics, including methods of diagnosis and remediation;

and at least one course chosen from among

- differential equations
- number theory
- combinatorial analysis
- graph theory
- logic and foundations
- mathematical programming
- other applied mathematics.

Why Inservice?

The primary goal of any inservice program for teachers is the improvement of instruction. In the following discussion more specific objectives are dealt with.

To provide teachers with the time, means, and support for developing their professional competencies.

It is almost universally accepted in industry that a newly-hired engineer fresh from his or her university experience will be given on-the-job training for a period of at least a year and then subsequently as the need arises. Nor is this a denigration of the university experience. Rather it is recognition of the fact that formal and general university training cannot hope to substitute for hands-on experience, and that personnel must be constantly inserviced if they are to cope successfully with change. This is no less true for teachers than it is for engineers.

Unlike the situation of the engineer in industry, the burden for inservice education for teachers has been borne largely by teachers themselves, through enrollment in programs at colleges and universities. More recently, and appropriately, school districts are beginning to realize that it is important and often more effective to address local problems with locally-based inservice programs, complete with a variety of incentives to ensure acceptance and participation by teachers.

Inservice cannot be a one-way street. In order for improved goals to be achieved, there must be a balance of both responsibility and commitment on the part of teachers, school systems, and state and local governments.

To assist teachers to learn new pedagogical skills.

No single method of teaching a particular mathematical idea is best for all students and for all teachers. Teaching approaches are both student-dependent and teacher-dependent. It behooves every teacher to command a battery of different techniques for the teaching of each mathematical idea. The preservice experience does not allow time for the teacher to learn all possible strategies; and, of course, new strategies are constantly being developed. Continuing inservice experiences where new strategies can be learned may take a variety of forms ranging from seminars where local teachers discuss and share methods, to workshops arranged by the school system and perhaps featuring a visiting expert discussing new research.

To enhance teachers' perceptions of mathematics.

The attitude of many teachers of mathematics leaves a great deal to be desired. Some teachers see mathematics at best as a useful and necessary tool students will need for success in life. Other teachers frequently see mathematics at worst as mystifying, extraordinarily difficult and distasteful, and something to be avoided to the greatest possible extent. Many teachers of mathematics lack any appreciation of the cultural significance of mathematics, of its intellectual richness, of its inherent beauty, and of the remarkably subtle interconnections among its various parts. We maintain that this cannot be so of *successful* mathematics teachers. Such teachers must and do like mathematics to the point of enthusiasm and are therefore able to present the subject to students in an exciting and interesting way. It is perhaps an overstatement to assert that it is impossible to teach a student anything. But it is certainly true that it is far better to inspire students to *want* to learn. There *is* a beauty and a poetry in mathematics; and if teachers can catch this view, they will surely do a far better job of inspiring their students to want to learn.

To provide a means of quality control and improvement of the existing curriculum in a school system.

It would be a mistake for any school system to think that it had achieved the optimal mathematics curriculum. Similarly, it would be a mistake to presume that the quality of a good system, once in place, will remain high by inertia. If the same curriculum is taught in the same way year after year, teachers are almost sure to suffer from ennui; and the teaching will lose its vigor and vitality. The curriculum will only maintain its quality if it receives constant scrutiny from the teaching faculty with a view toward making adjustments in style and content, updating, and imaginatively adding "spice." Again, this calls for inservice education within the school system, probably in the form of study groups or task forces of teachers to review the teaching, content, and sequencing of the various courses. It also calls for experimentation on the part of individual teachers or groups of teachers, to see if new courses or new techniques might not be more effective than those in current use.

In particular, if major changes are to be made in the curriculum, it is imperative that inservice activities take place in order to prepare for the change (Berman and McLaughlin 1975; Rand Corporation n.d.; Taba 1965).

There are those who would claim that the so-called revolution in school mathematics in the late 1950s and 1960s in the United States never really took place, and to a considerable extent this is true. The "new math" curriculum was perceived to have been developed primarily by research-oriented university mathematicians and handed down from above. Though efforts were made to secure local input, these were largely cosmetic. In fact, there was little local input, there was considerable teacher fear and resistance, and the curriculum today is only marginally different from what it was twenty years ago. Significant and successful curricular change requires extensive inservice education, as well as serious local teacher input and on-site development of materials. Teachers thus involved in producing curricular change have a vested interest in seeing that change succeeds. Also, having had a hand in developing the new curriculum they are much more knowledgeable about the contents of the curriculum and how it might best be taught. Finally, the involvement in the new development is bound to produce as a by-product increased understanding of mathematics, improved pedagogical skill, and new zest for teaching – all highly desirable results.

To improve school resource utilization.

Inservice education is for teachers, but we have just seen how the involvement of teachers in the study of any program in which they are involved can positively effect the execution of that program. Thus, inservice education for teachers might well be directed at more efficient use of teacher time, at more efficient physical plant utilization or utilization of community resources. Without such inservice involvement of teachers, administrators may exhort and dictate; but little change will actually take place. With teacher input, it is quite likely that even better courses of action will be found and, as with curricular innovation, teachers will have a vested interest in seeing that the new plans are effectively implemented.

To enhance leadership development.

In the last twenty years, literally thousands of teachers have been involved in developing their talents in professional activities of all types, sponsored singly or jointly by school systems, governmental agencies, professional societies, and colleges and universities. Well-planned inservice programs on a local level might well tap this pool of talent to the distinct advantage of other local teachers. In the process, local schools might well discover and develop local educational leaders who could distinctly benefit their programs.

This notion squares well with two ideas currently receiving considerable attention – merit pay for teachers, and the creation of the formal rank of master teacher. At present the only opportunity for upward mobility for teachers is to move out of the classroom and into administration. The obvious effect of this situation is frequently to remove the best teachers from the classroom, to the detriment of the instructional program. A master-teacher program would allow talented teachers to seek career advancement by providing needed leadership in the improvement of both curriculum and instruction – areas consistent with their primary interest and professional expertise.

Inservice for the Underprepared

If minimal standards for training mathematics teachers are at all reasonable and if there are teachers of mathematics who do not meet these standards, then it follows that inservice education must be provided to allow these teachers to satisfy the desired criteria. Indeed, teachers of mathematics who do not meet such criteria should be *required* to do so by the cognizant school and government officials, since it is impossible to teach in a meaningful and effective way material you do not understand well yourself or that you do not understand how to teach.

Inservice education for such teachers should be college- or university-based and should be extensive and complete. There is no short cut to developing the necessary understandings and skills; those who believe otherwise are only deluding themselves.

Inservice for the "Prepared"

Those who meet some set of minimal standards like those referred to under "Preservice Expectations" above are presumably certified by an appropriate agency as qualified to teach. It might reasonably be asked why inservice education is necessary for them.

The teaching and learning of mathematics is so complex that no amount of preservice training can be expected to be sufficient for a lifetime of teaching. This is so even of those teachers who proceed beyond basic requirements to take the traditional master's degrees that provide for preferred status and increased salaries. Mathematics, as a body of material, grows. Uses of mathematics change. Changes in technology make old skills and content obsolete and make other skills and content increasingly important. Teachers who grew up with slide rules, log and trig tables, and mechanical calculators suddenly find themselves confronted by programmable calculators and sophisticated electronic computers that can even perform such feats as symbolic differentiation and integration in calculus.

Teaching technology is constantly changing; and teachers who used to rely almost solely on chalk and the blackboard must now cope with a bewildering array of manipulatives and audio-visual devices, as well as such still-developing techniques as computer-assisted instruction and computer-controlled laser disks. Also, educational and psychological research continues to provide new insights into the ways in which children learn mathematics and these new understandings need to be translated into classroom practice.

Teachers recognize the need for such programs. We have seen repeatedly the results of needs assessments in school districts in which teachers indicate feelings of inadequacy, particularly in such areas as problem solving, applications, and the use of calculators and computers in instruction. Of course, some teachers can and do return to colleges and universities in efforts to keep themselves up-to-date and to acquire new competencies. If, however, a school system desires to address its instructional problems comprehensively and uniformly, and if it desires to make inservice education attractive to and more available to its faculty, then it must institute and promote local inservice programs as well.

Because of the overriding importance of inservice education to the entire educational enterprise, it may be necessary for the federal government to mount continuing programs of inservice education, complete with stipends and other inducements, to attract and hold teachers in the profession, in the face of the severe competition for talent presented by industry and business.

BIBLIOGRAPHY

SALLY I. LIPSEY

AFT Task Force on the Future of Education. 1986. *The Revolution That Is Overdue: Looking Toward the Future of Teaching and Learning*. Washington, D.C.: American Federation of Teachers.

Recommendations for restructuring teacher education.

Austin, Joe Dan. 1978. Let's teach research evaluation. *School Science and Mathematics* 78 (5) (May-June 1978): 425-430.

Cites need for teachers to study research evaluation and how it might be done, and need for researchers to keep the classroom teacher in mind when selecting research problems and writing reports.

Balka, Don S. 1986. Characteristics of outstanding secondary school mathematics teachers. *School Science and Mathematics* 86 (4) (April 1986): 322-326.

Letters of support for nominees for Presidential Awards in Mathematics Teaching display a consensus about the teacher qualities that are most admired.

Bany, Bruce P., and W. Clifford Carbno. 1981. Preferred inservice activities among teachers of elementary school mathematics. *Alberta Journal of Educational Research* 27 (1) (March 1981): 57-73.

Results of a questionnaire that elicited teacher preferences among nine types of inservice activities. Traditional inservice training is often at variance with teacher preferences.

Battista, Michael T. 1986. The relationship of mathematics anxiety and mathematical knowledge to the learning of mathematical pedagogy by preservice elementary teachers. *School Science and Mathematics* 86 (1) (January 1986): 10-19.

A study involving 38 preservice teachers, relating their mathematical knowledge to results of methods course exams and teaching performance.

Bender, Louis W., and Maureen D. Lukenbill. 1984. Let's begin with ourselves. *Community and Junior College Journal* 55 (2) (October 1984): 16-18.

Notes policies developed by different states for inservice refreshment of junior college faculty, including networks with business and industry. Recommendations for the future.

Berman, Paul, and M.W. McLaughlin. 1975. The findings in review. In *Federal Programs Supporting Educational Change*, by Paul Berman et al., vol. 4. Santa Monica, Calif.: Rand Corporation.

Elaboration of the Rand Corporation study (n.d.). (CTL)

Bitter, Gary G. 1980. Calculator teacher attitudes improved through inservice education. *School Science and Mathematics* 80 (4) (April 1980): 323-326.

Finds "hands-on" calculator workshops effective in improving teachers' abilities with the calculator and their attitudes towards using them in the classroom.

———, and Jerald L. Mikesell. 1975. Materials, competence, and confidence: Products of a district mathematics laboratory. *Arithmetic Teacher* 22 (2) (February 1975): 114-116.

Describes a teacher-involvement program consisting of the establishment of a mathematics laboratory, inservice education, and development of curriculum and materials. Teachers were pleased with the opportunity to prepare materials for immediate use in their classrooms.

Burger, William F., Lee Jenkins, Margaret L. Moore, Gary L. Musser, and Karen Clark Smith. 1983. Teacher preparation – A coordinated approach. *Arithmetic Teacher* 30 (8) (April 1983): 21-22.
Describes a program at Oregon State U, based on recommendations by CUPM, NCTM, and others.

Bush, William S. 1986. Preservice teachers' sources of decisions in teaching secondary mathematics. *Journal for Research in Mathematics Education* 17 (1) (January 1986): 21-30.

Campbell, Patricia F., and Grayson H. Wheatley. 1983. A model for helping student teachers. *Mathematics Teacher* 76 (1) (January 1983): 60-63.
Cites need to recognize the phases through which student teachers go, in order to supervise them with greater effectiveness.

Carnegie Forum on Education and the Economy. Task Force on Teaching as a Profession. 1986. *A Nation Prepared: Teachers for the 21st Century.* Washington, D.C.: Carnegie Forum on Education and the Economy.
Recommends a national board of professional standards to certify teachers completing a rigorous assessment process.

Committee on the Mathematical Education of Teachers. 1984. Statement on retraining of elementary and high school teachers. Washington, D.C.: Mathematical Association of America.
Points out the importance of high standards for programs to prepare teachers from other disciplines to teach mathematics.

Committee on the Teaching of Undergraduate Mathematics. 1979. *College Mathematics: Suggestions on How to Teach It.* Washington, D.C.: Mathematical Association of America.
Booklet with tips for first-time college teachers. (PJC & LSG)

Corbitt, Mary Kay, ed. 1985. The impact of computing technology on school mathematics: Report of an NCTM conference. *Mathematics Teacher* 78 (4) (April 1985): 243-250.
Results of a 1984 conference representing government, commercial, and academic interests, including recommendations for changes in curriculum, instruction, and teacher education. Emphasizes the need for preservice and inservice programs to "model the desired changes."

Crouse, Richard J., and Clifford W. Sloyer, comps. 1987. *Mathemati-*

cal Questions from the Classroom. Providence, R.I.: Janson.
> Compilation of questions raised by students, with suggested replies, from junior-high mathematics through advanced topics in secondary mathematics. (PJC & LSG)

Davidson, Neil. 1977. A demonstration of terrible teaching techniques. *Mathematics Teacher* 70 (6) (September 1977): 545-546.
> Uses an "antimodel" instructor to stimulate discussion about teaching errors.

Davis, Edward J. 1983. Teacher education: Helping preservice teachers to teach mathematical concepts. *Arithmetic Teacher* 31 (1) (September 1983): 8-9.
> Peer teaching and micro-teaching techniques combined with a prescribed lesson format are recommended.

Davis, Ronald M. 1985. Relevancy and revitalization: Retaining quality and vitality in two-year college mathematics faculty. In *New Directions in Two-Year College Mathematics*, edited by Donald J. Albers, Stephen B. Rodi, and Ann E. Watkins, 381-392. New York: Springer-Verlag.
> Mainly on the importance of inservice training for two-year college teachers. Some hints about how to do so.

Dawson, A. J. 1978. Criteria for the creation of inservice education programs. *Canadian Journal of Education* 3 (1) (1978): 49-60.
> Describes a set of inservice activities in mathematics, reading, and foreign languages operating in the Vancouver region. Also propounds a philosophy on which teacher education should be based.

Dossey, John A. 1981. The current status of preservice elementary teacher-education programs. *Arithmetic Teacher* 29 (1) (September 1981): 24-26.
> Report of a national study, via questionnaire, of mathematics programs for preservice elementary teachers conducted in 1977 by the NCTM, involving mathematics content, methods, and practicum components. Recommended as baseline to measure changes in teacher education.

―――. 1984. Preservice elementary mathematics education: A complete program. *Arithmetic Teacher* 31 (7) (March 1984): 6-8.
> Three aspects (content, methods, and clinical experiences) are described. The author emphasizes the importance of integrating all these aspects but leaves it to the reader to carry this out.

Elliott, Peggy G. 1981. Begin reading inservice with math teachers.

Educational Leadership 38 (5) (February 1981): 412.

> Notes importance of reading techniques for math teachers, including needs of students in reading mathematics problems, and needs of teachers to understand how reading mathematics is different from reading other content areas.

Flener, Frederick. 1986. Teacher training and teacher inservice: The underpinnings of mathematics teaching in England. *School Science and Mathematics* 86 (1) (January 1986): 51-60.

> Major differences between professional education programs for primary school teachers and pure science programs for secondary school teachers at the preservice level. Importance of teacher centers for a wide variety of inservice activities.

Gibb, E. Glenadine, Huston T. Karnes, and F. Lynwood Wren. 1970. The education of teachers of mathematics. In *NCTM Yearbook 32*, 301-350.

> History of preservice and inservice education in the U.S. from 1823 to 1970, beginning with the first normal school and its program. Reports of committees and commissions, their surveys and recommendations.

Harty, Harold. 1978. A field-based professional development complex: One approach to future preservice-inservice teacher preparation. *Peabody Journal of Education* 55 (July 1978): 337-345.

> Notes limitations of traditional teacher preparation programs and offers prescriptions for change involving a professional development complex, designed and maintained by a wide variety of institutions.

————. 1980. Some collective thoughts on nontraditional inservice preparation of school-based professionals. *Contemporary Education* 51 (2) (Winter 1980): 74-78.

> Report of an informal meeting of teachers, administrators, and school of education faculty including suggestions for inservice programs other than traditional university offerings.

————, and Larry G. Enochs. 1985. Toward reshaping the inservice education of science teachers. *School Science and Mathematics* 85 (2) (February 1985): 125-135.

> Examines need for and problems with current inservice education. Suggests goals and research.

Hawk, Parmalee P., Charles R. Coble, and Melvin Swanson. 1985. Certification: It does matter. *Journal of Teacher Education* 36 (3) (May/June 1985): 13-15.

> A pilot study comparing teachers certified in mathematics with teachers who teach mathematics but are certified in other fields as to student achievement and

professional skills.

Hendrickson, Dean, and Milt Virant. 1978. A study of needs for further learning as seen by teachers of secondary school mathematics. *School Science and Mathematics* 78 (8) (December 1978): 655-664.
    Results of a survey (by questionnaire of 140 teachers), classified according to subject areas, experience levels, and training levels.

Hoffmann, Joseph R. 1984. Preservice education: New expectations for teachers of mathematics. *Teacher Education Quarterly* 11 (1) (Winter 1984): 31-36.
    Recommendations of the California Commission on Teacher Credentialing for the training of teachers.

Hollis, Loye Y. 1985. A summer professional growth experience. *Arithmetic Teacher* 32 (9) (May 1985): 16-17.
    Describes a summer inservice program combining theoretical discussions with practical approaches, involving unit planning, manipulative materials, and problem solving.

Holmes Group. 1986. *Tomorrow's Teachers*. East Lansing, Mich.: Holmes Group. Columbus, O.: ERIC/SMEAC. ERIC: ED 270454.
    Urges more substantive education for education candidates.

House, Peggy. 1975. Balancing the equation on CBTE. *Mathematics Teacher* 68 (6) (October 1975): 519-524.
    Characterizes competency-based teacher education (CBTE) programs and associated problems.

Hovey, Sheryl. 1986. Teachers at the center. *American Educator* 10 (3) (Fall 1986): 26-30.
    A new type of staff development program in Pittsburgh suitable for mathematics teachers.

Huffman, Harry, and Ingrid Dooms. 1976. Career education: A business and office career setting for mathematics teachers. *School Science and Mathematics* 76 (4) (April 1976): 338-346.
    Resource guides to help mathematics teachers provide career education while covering the standard curriculum.

Jamski, William D. 1977. A comparison of one aspect of the certification of secondary mathematics teachers from 1957 to 1974. *School Science and Mathematics* 77 (8) (December 1977): 681-682.
    Data showing that the certification requirement for mathematics courses in-

creased and became more uniform throughout the U.S.

Jones, Phillip S., and Arthur F. Coxford, Jr. 1970. Mathematics in the evolving schools. In *NCTM Yearbook 32*, 11-89.
> History of pedagogy; overview of teacher training from 1832 to 1970, including references to the first public normal school and the first methods book.

Kagan, Martin H., and Pinchas Tamir. 1977. Participation in and views concerning inservice training among high school science and mathematics teachers in Israel: A survey. *School Science and Mathematics* 77 (1) (January 1977): 31-46.
> Used a questionnaire to ascertain extent of inservice activity in Israel. Supports idea of teacher centers.

Kennedy, Joe. 1975. Operation two birds. *School Science and Mathematics* 75 (6) (October 1975): 541-542.
> Peer teaching by prospective secondary-school mathematics teachers has several beneficial effects.

Kerr, Donald R., Jr., and Frank K. Lester, Jr. 1982. A new look at the professional training of secondary school mathematics teachers. *Educational Studies in Mathematics* 13 (4) (November 1982): 431-441.
> How to combine in a teacher-education program solid mathematical content with discussions of related secondary school material, emphasizing major themes. Modernizing content and methods.

Korthagen, Fred A. J. 1985. Reflective teaching and preservice teacher education in the Netherlands. *Journal of Teacher Education* 36 (5) (September/October 1985): 11-15.
> Reflection on one's own experiences is a prescribed part of the teacher education program. Reflection is stimulated by logbooks, role playing, discussions, reports.

Krulik, Stephen, and Jesse A. Rudnick. 1982. Teaching problem solving to preservice teachers. *Arithmetic Teacher* 29 (6) (February 1982): 42-45.
> Techniques for problem solving and for teaching it to teachers and students.

Kullman, David E. 1978. A unit box for secondary school mathematics teachers. *School Science and Mathematics* 78 (5) (May-June 1978): 374-378.
> Describes involving prospective teachers in the varied activities associated with preparation of a curriculum unit, leading to a usable collection of materials.

————. 1981. Math is where you find it. _School Science and Mathematics_ 81 (1) (January 1981): 42-50.

 Report of an NSF Pre-College Teacher Development Project on applications of secondary school mathematics, including astronomy, optics, art, music, stamps, electronics, sports, travel, autos, bicycles, kites.

Larson, Carol N. 1983. Techniques for developing positive attitudes in preservice teachers. _Arithmetic Teacher_ 31 (2) (October 1983): 8-9.

 How to deal with feelings about mathematics in a methods course. Suggestions include open discussions, small group mathematics activities, and diversity of approaches for problem solving.

Leake, Lowell, Jr. 1976. A model for a methods course. _School Science and Mathematics_ 76 (3) (March 1976): 193-199.

 Use of the contract system.

Lipsey, Sally I. 1972. Student teachers ask for help. _Mathematics Teacher_ 65 (2) (February 1972): 137-138.

 A pool of questions submitted by student teachers provided data on what most concerned them and served as motivation for class discussions.

Long, Calvin T. 1985. The academic training of two-year college mathematics faculty. In _New Directions in Two-Year College Mathematics_, edited by Donald J. Albers, Stephen B. Rodi, and Ann E. Watkins, 394-403. New York: Springer-Verlag.

 Recommendations for the mathematical and pedagogical training of two-year college instructors on the preservice and inservice levels. Although the master's degree is considered sufficient, the doctor of arts degree is also discussed and illustrated.

Lukenbill, Jeffrey D. 1982. Faculty and program development go hand in hand. _Community and Junior College Journal_ 52 (6) (March 1982): 16-18.

 Science and other faculty working together on new courses; faculty development seminars.

Lukenbill, Maureen. 1982. Outlook: National Council for Staff, Program, and Organizational Development. _Community and Junior College Journal_ 52 (6) (March 1982): 10.

 Purposes of the Council.

Makurat, Phil. 1975. The development of a math teacher center. _Contemporary Education_ 47 (Fall 1975): 35-38.

 Goals and activities of a group of teachers involved in pursuit of improvement of instruction, in Milwaukee, Wisconsin.

Mathematical Association of America. 1983. *Recommendations on the Mathematical Preparation of Teachers.* Washington, D.C.: Mathematical Association of Association.

> This document is essentially parallel and complementary to the entry for the National Council of Teachers of Mathematics (1981). Together they set the standard in the process of being adopted in the U.S. today. (CTL)

————. 1987. Statement on the Holmes and Carnegie reports on teacher preparation. Washington, D.C.: Mathematical Association of America.

> Endorsement of some recommendations of national reports on teacher training, including establishment of a national standards and certification board, plus additional recommendations that "prospective teachers of mathematics in grades 9-12 should major in a mathematical science with a program of study that follows [(Mathematical Association of America 1983)]." (PJC & LSG)

McQualter, J. W. 1986. Becoming a mathematics teacher: The use of personal construct theory. *Educational Studies in Mathematics* 17 (1) (February 1986): 1-14.

> Describes "personal construct theory" and its use in teacher self-evaluation and in studying how teachers think and what they know, their decision-making procedures. Reports on studies done in 1981-1983 with general discussion of results but no specifics as to who was involved.

Merseth, Katherine K. 1985. Harvard Graduate School midcareer mathematics and science program. *Journal of College Science Teaching* 14 (4) (February 1985): 239-241.

> Description of a relatively new program enabling midcareer professionals to become certified as mathematics or science secondary school teachers and in-service teachers to upgrade their skills.

Michigan Council of Teachers of Mathematics. 1976. Program for training mathematics teachers. *Mathematics Teacher* 69 (1) (January 1976): 74-78.

> Report of MCTM committee to develop specifications for the training of a teacher of secondary mathematics.

Mitzel, Harold E., ed. 1982. Faculty development. In *Encyclopedia of Educational Research*, 5th ed., vol. 2, 646-655. New York: Macmillan.

> Factors affecting the emergence of faculty development programs, models and strategies for such programs, reports of results.

————. 1982. Inservice teacher education. In *Encyclopedia of Educational Research*, 5th ed., vol. 2, 883-890. New York: Macmillan.

History, importance, and content of inservice programs, research and evaluation and their limitations.

Mitzman, B. 1976. Seeking a cure for "mathephobia." *American Education* 12 (2) (March 1976): 10-14.

How the Oregon System in Mathematics Education used workshops, resource centers, mathematics consultants, and laboratory demonstrations for preservice and inservice training of teachers.

National Council of Teachers of Mathematics. 1981. *Guidelines for the Preparation of Teachers of Mathematics*. Reston, Va.: National Council of Teachers of Mathematics.

This document has been adopted by the National Council for the Accreditation of Teacher Education (NCATE) as the official standard for colleges and universities that train teachers. Contains recommendations for all levels of mathematics teachers through senior high school as well as suggested course outlines and suggested requirements outside of mathematics. (CTL)

Nelson, Barbara Scott. 1986. Collaboration for colleagueship: A program in support of teachers. *Educational Leadership* 43 (5) (February 1986): 50-52.

Report of a Ford Foundation Project to develop "mathematics collaboratives" — groups of professionals from schools, industry, universities, museums, joining together in each of nine cities on a variety of projects in mathematics education.

O'Daffer, Phares G. 1981. How teacher educators can use the *Arithmetic Teacher*. *Arithmetic Teacher* 29 (2) (October 1981): 6-57.

Suggestions include handouts, assignments, reports, and ratings.

Olson, Melfried. 1982. Through the portal: Inservice mathematics teacher education at the University of Wyoming. *Journal of Research and Development in Education* 15 (4) (Summer 1982): 81-83.

Relates ten years of experience with a successful statewide teacher--education collaborative, which has continued to function and expand beyond the period of federal funding and is being emulated elsewhere.

Perlez, Jane. 1986. New rules drawing a different breed of teacher. *New York Times* (August 4, 1986): B1.

Worthwhile effects of ending requirements for education courses as prerequisites for teaching.

Professional Development and Status Advisory Committee. 1985. *Professional Development Programs for Teachers of Mathematics.* Washington, D.C.: National Council of Teachers of Mathematics.

Guidelines for inservice "professional development programs that enhance" teaching skills and knowledge.

Rand Corporation. *Evaluation of Federal Programs Supporting Educational Change.* Unpublished executive summary. Washington, D.C.: U.S. Office of Education.

A report on an investigation into strategies to promote innovations in the schools, which was conducted by the Rand Corporation. The study found that the implementation strategies selected to carry out a project vitally influence project outcomes. In particular, the strategies that significantly promoted teacher change included staff training, frequent regular meetings, and local materials development. If any one of these elements was not present in a project's implementation approach the project's perceived success and the amount of teacher change was reduced. (CTL)

Reynolds, R. F. 1986. Take the NEWMAST cure (NASA Educational Workshops for Mathematics and Science Teachers). *Science Teacher* 53 (3) (March 1986): 32-33.

Science and mathematics teachers of grades 7-12 work with NASA scientists and engineers on projects of their own choosing.

Rodriguez, Roy C., and Irene V. Rodriguez. 1986. Attracting and retraining Hispanics in math and science teacher education. *Teacher Educator* 21 (4) (Spring 1986): 9-15.

Rubba, Peter A., and Jerry P. Becker. 1985. Qualities secondary school principals examine when hiring mathematics and science teachers. *School Science and Mathematics* 85 (4) (April 1985): 271-278.

Results of a questionnaire that may be of interest to teacher trainers who wish to know which qualities are most highly prized by principals.

Sachdev, Sohindar. 1977. Mathematics foundations and philosophy of mathematics in teacher education. *Improving College and University Teaching* 25 (4) (Autumn 1977): 205-206.

Report of a study of 82 teacher education programs to ascertain the role of courses in foundations and philosophy.

Sadowski, Barbara R. 1983. A model for preparing teachers to teach with the microcomputer. *Arithmetic Teacher* 30 (6) (February 1983): 24-25, 62-63.

Suggestions, based on fifty workshops conducted with teachers at every grade level, for inservice and preservice training.

Sharp, Karen Tobey. 1985. Current continuing education needs of two-year college mathematics faculty must be met! In *New Directions in Two-Year College Mathematics*, edited by Donald J. Albers, Stephen B. Rodi, and Ann E. Watkins, 406-421. New York: Springer-Verlag.
> Cites need for inservice training of two-year college mathematics instructors. Offers many suggestions for providing this training, utilizing academic, business and government support and activities.

Smith, Lyle R., and Mary L. Cotten. 1980. Effect of lesson vagueness and discontinuity on student achievement and attitudes. *Journal of Educational Psychology* 72 (5) (October 1980): 670-675.
> Report of an experiment with 100 seventh-graders studying plane geometry. Results suggest procedures for teacher training and evaluation.

Stannard, William. 1982. A statewide model: Inservice mathematics teacher education by the Montana Council of Teachers of Mathematics. *Journal of Research and Development in Education* 15 (4) (Summer 1982): 84-86.
> Based on Wyoming model (see Olson 1982), this inservice program is run by the MCTM rather than a university, with certain beneficial administrative results.

Taba, Hilda. 1965. Techniques of inservice training. *Social Education* 29 (7) (November 1965): 464-476.
> Indicates that the more radical the changes that are expected in teaching strategies, the greater the necessity that inservice training consider the sequential steps involved in producing such changes and provide both the time and the help in producing them. Points out that much of teacher resistance comes from the fact that exhortations to make changes are not always accompanied with the help to acquire the skills needed to make these changes with psychological comfort and without the threat and risk of making errors. Reshaping curriculum and instruction is not a matter that can be accomplished in a 6-week summer workshop or a series of monthly meetings during the year. A more methodical way is required, plus time to change old habits and to develop new ideas and put them into practice. (CTL)

Trafton, Paul R. 1984. Mathematics educators: Establishing working relationships with schools. *Arithmetic Teacher* 31 (8) (April 1984): 6-7.
> How and why mathematics educators should be involved in school activities.

Willoughby, Stephen S. 1986. Master teacher certification. *Mathematics Teacher* 79 (3) (March 1986): 160-161.
> Choice and responsibilities of master teachers.

Willson, Victor L., and Antoine M. Garibaldi. 1976. The association between teacher participation in NSF institutes and student achievement. *Journal of Research in Science Teaching* 13 (5) (September 1976): 431-439.

> Claims impossibility of conducting a well-controlled experiment; offers consistent results from the best data available.

Willson, Victor L., and Frances Lawrenz. 1980. Relationship between teacher participation in NSF institutes and student attitudes and perception of the classroom learning environment. *Journal of Research in Science Teaching* 17 (4) (July 1980): 289-294.

> Results indicate a small effect of NSF institutes on student attitudes, providing support for inservice activity by secondary, mathematics and science teachers.

19. Trends in Secondary and Two-year College Education

WADE ELLIS, JR.

Introduction

Women and men trained and skilled in the use of mathematics in science, technology, and industry are in great demand in our society. As we increasingly use science and technology to invent, develop and produce new products and improve the performance and reduce the production costs of existing products, this demand will continue to increase. The use of computers to store and manage large amounts of data has increased the need for individuals with the mathematical tools and skills to analyze this data. Moreover, computer technology itself seems to have an unending appetite for mathematically-trained men and women. Even as we use old mathematical ideas and techniques more successfully in every aspect of our society, our need to search for, find, and disseminate new mathematical ideas and techniques increases.

Despite many difficult problems, mathematics education must respond to this demand for more mathematically-trained individuals.

Teachers

First, the size of the reservoir of mathematically trained high school and community college teachers is decreasing. This is caused both by the low prestige of the teaching profession in our society and the low salaries that teachers are paid. Though the low prestige of teachers is well documented, its principal cause is not. The supervision and training of mathematics teachers has been left to specialists in teaching who are not specialists in mathematics. Mathematics, of course, is not the only discipline in which this has occurred. The idea that a mastery of teaching techniques will allow the good teacher to teach anything (regardless of content area education) is as bankrupt as the idea, once prevalent in industry, that anyone can manage anything as long as the management techniques are mastered.

Many teachers are well-trained in mathematics and are doing an excellent job in the classroom. Many more, however, have not been properly trained in mathematics and must teach in rigid ways to avoid exposing their ignorance. No amount of additional training in the form of courses that focus on presentation methods or psychological and sociological aspects of teaching can compensate for a lack of mathematical maturity and understanding. Rigidity and ignorance breed contempt. Contempt for teachers leads to a loss of prestige. A clear, long-term remedy for this problem is to increase our expectation of teacher trainees to include higher initial-quality standards and to include more mathematics in their training supervised and given by mathematicians.

We need to pay our teachers more. Teachers do not make as much money as they did in the early 1970s. At that time, however, they were making much more than they were making as a group in the 1950s. In the past teachers were expected to give to the community, and they did. Now teachers expect (as they should) the same financial rewards that lawyers, doctors, engineers, real estate agents, and other similarly trained and dedicated professionals receive. This is especially true in mathematics, where the lure of great wealth and prestige has begun to tempt seasoned teachers away from the classroom and into the computer industry. Their pay must reflect the salary scales of other professionals. In return, teachers must expect to be more professional: they must know more, they must do more, and they must expect more from themselves and their students. This cannot occur, of course, unless more and better training and retraining can be provided to new teachers entering the profession and to our current stock of teachers.

The litany of environmental and psychological burdens that teachers in many of our schools must endure need not be repeated here. We do not pay lawyers and doctors handsomely and then require them to work in less than an excellent environment. A recognition that teaching our young is an important activity that should be done in an enjoyable environment will eliminate the need to repeat this litany in the coming years.

Financial and environmental factors are magnified when we begin to talk about teacher recruitment and training. Those with the mathematical talent and experience to become teachers are not encouraged by the working environment and financial prospects that teaching currently offers. For prospective community college teachers completing a bachelor's degree, the choice is easy: either take an immediate job in the defense industry at $30,000 with salary reviews every six months, or continue in school two more years for a master's degree and hope for a starting salary of $20,000 and a fixed year-by-year salary scale. Moreover, some of the available industrial jobs offer fun and excitement on the cutting edge of technology, where teaching offers adolescent students and the same "dry," 200-year-old mathematical formulas and theorems. What would you choose? Of course, this is not to say that there are not enormous internal rewards in teaching that we should exploit in recruiting teachers from the best students in our mathematics classes. Given the current social setting, however, how many young and energetic teachers can we expect to attract?

In the short term, we have to depend upon the often overworked, tired, and financially harried teacher for the new thrust in mathematics education. We must concern ourselves with motivating, retraining, updating, and rewarding our current teachers, since they are really all we have for the next five to ten years. For the future, there must be a trend toward higher salaries, better working conditions, and more prestige for school teachers in general and mathematics teachers in particular.

The decreasing size of the teacher reservoir in mathematics is masked by schemes developed by educational managers (from the state education offices to the school boards, principals, and teacher organizations) to show that teachers are certified rather than qualified. Two such techniques are (1) to make the middle schools include the ninth grade, where algebra is taught, and then teach the algebra classes with K-8 certified teachers who are not content area specialists; (2) to use either teachers with lifetime teach-everything K-14 certificates or the provisions of state law that allow teachers to teach 40% to 60% of their load outside their content-area specialty. In such situations the education establishment, including teacher organizations, can point with pride to the fact that there are no uncertified teachers in the district, county, or state. That it is difficult to determine qualification is not denied; nevertheless, it is wrong to use phony systems of certification as a substitute.

Students

With the increasing complexity of our society, the individual citizen will need to be more flexible; and education assists individuals in being flexible. Individuals will hold different jobs in their lifetimes. Many of these jobs will require skills based on a knowledge of mathematics; and, as the need for retraining increases, the need for intermittent use of mathematics in retraining periods will increase as well. Even if one spends an entire career in the same industry, some additional training will often be required. The new training may require a need for quantitative analysis of problems. Of course, some of the mathematics that will be encountered in a working lifetime has not yet been discovered. Hence, when retraining occurs, the student must be able to learn new ideas and skills as well as recall old ones.

As we recreate our educational system to reflect the new needs of lifelong learning, we must of course restructure what and how we teach in the secondary schools — the initial education for further training later in life. First, we must recognize that high-school (and college) students have changed. Many more students begin their work lives earlier and work longer hours while attending school than in the past. This might be referred to as "lifelong work," as a counterpart to "lifelong learning." As students work more, they will, in general, have less time to devote to their studies. Homework at home may be a thing of the past.

Since we must aspire to teach students to learn on their own and to solve problems on their own, we probably should turn away from the time-honored tradition of lecturing our students and become more oriented toward guided learning environment and worktext approaches to the learning of mathematics. Our students seem to be more interested in immediate returns on investments of time and energy (much as our society is). We should perhaps cater to this desire.

Teaching Techniques

The need for problem solving approaches to the teaching of mathematics is frequently heard at mathematics meetings and read in education journals. Unfortunately, this approach can be perverted into a list of steps for solving a particular set of problems (coin problems, for example). Such lists of steps are only useful as a problem solving technique if the students themselves have recognized that there is a class of problems that can be solved using the same basic algorithm — an algorithm or set of steps that they themselves have created. The textbooks that carefully spell out how to work a certain kind of problem rob students of the opportunity to exercise and develop their own problem-solving techniques and abilities.

The guided learning environments in many worktexts are indeed a step toward helping students learn to deal with new material on their own, working and reading alone or in groups. These guided learning environments must, however, turn away from the prescribed lists of steps and turn toward helping the students to develop their own set of steps. The new teaching and learning environment in the secondary schools may not cover as much material or content, but it will leave the students with the intellectual tools for learning new material in later years when retraining in new mathematical content is required.

In this learning environment, there will be a strong bias toward mastery learning in the sense that only ideas and concepts central to learning mathematics must be presented and learned. A partial understanding of these essential ideas and analytic tools will not be nearly enough.

The computer will be of substantial assistance in presenting new ideas. It is one of the analytic tools a student should understand in working with mathematically oriented problems. The computer can provide enormous numbers of examples for students as they investigate mathematical ideas, and it can serve as a problem solving tool by allowing students to model real life situations easily and accurately. In addition, the computer can be used to deliver remedial drill and practice exercises based on the new learning theory that is emerging from empirical studies of how and what people learn in studying mathematics.

Changing Content

The mathematical ideas and skills that are important are changing. Until quite recently, the mathematics that was thought necessary to teach in high school and the first two years of college was the mathematics needed in a physics or engineering setting. With the coming of computers, with the ability to store, keep track of, and manage large masses of data, other mathematical methods of analyzing quantitative data have become important. Though the traditional topics are still useful and important, not all students should learn mathematics that is intended for the physicist or engineer. Statistical concepts that were all but unknown in high-school mathematics courses twenty years ago should become more prevalent in the curriculum. Aspects of algebra that are important to computer science should become more important and more readily available to high-school and college students. Finally, mathematical modeling with a computer will become a standard topic in high school and the first two years of college.

As mathematical topics that are accessible to high school students and students with an intermediate algebra background jostle for a place in the curriculum, computer symbolic algebra (the calculation with symbols rather than just numbers) will begin to become an important method of dealing with complex symbolic manipulations in algebra, calculus, differential equations, and linear algebra. It will be exciting to watch the evolution of the standard calculus courses once the algebraic manipulations become routine machine activities. We should see a much greater emphasis on understanding and problem solving as the manipulative skills needed to perform complex operations correctly are handed over to machines.

Teacher Training

Teacher training must change dramatically in the coming years. More mathematics must be included in undergraduate training. Each student must have exposure to methods of using computers to teach mathematics. Mathematical modeling courses with a strong computer component must be a required part of teacher training. New courses in learning theory must be developed and taught. Small-group dynamics must become a part of the curriculum, perhaps through courses where small-group cooperative effort is required in a mathematics course. Each student must have a firm grasp of how to use a computer to assist in solving mathematics and other types of real-world problems.

But these items speak to the future. What are we going to do now to improve the quality and content of instruction in the high schools and community colleges? Here the answer is easy but its implementation hard. The teachers that are in place now must have access to the items mentioned above in a way that does not abuse, threaten, or insult them. If the curriculum is to change, then the instructors must change. We cannot wait for the current teachers to retire. We must begin a strong (and expensive) effort to retrain and update those troupers that are in the field now. A most attractive method for doing this is to encourage teachers, through release time from their jobs during the school year and in the summer, to work on new curricula in study groups at their own high schools and colleges. The National Science Foundation is not afraid to pay college professors to do research in the summer on their own. We should not be afraid to pay high-school and community-college teachers to perform research on how to better teach our children, especially if we demand that they be accountable for our children's performance in mathematics.

Summary

We are confronted with a great challenge in mathematics education. Let us hope we have the courage, stamina, and intelligence to meet the challenge to provide quality education and instruction for our citizens in the face of changes in mathematics and society.

BIBLIOGRAPHY

Bibliographic entries are subdivided into

- Books
- Articles.

Books

Albers, Donald J., Stephen B. Rodi, and Ann E. Watkins, eds. 1985. *New Directions in Two-Year College Mathematics.* New York: Springer-Verlag.

    A collection of papers presented at a conference of this name. Contains a series of recommendations which strongly supports the need to combat teacher burnout and to incorporate more statistical and applied mathematics into the two-year-college curriculum.

Begle, Edward G. 1979. *Critical Variables in Mathematics Education: Findings from a Survey of the Empirical Literature.* Edited by James W. Wilson and Jeremy Kilpatrick. Washington, D.C.: Mathematical Association of America and the National Council of Teachers of Mathematics.

Dorling, Alison R., ed. 1977. *Use of Mathematical Literature.* London: Butterworths.

    Contains a description of the ways in which the mathematical literature can be used. Important in that there is so much literature now, with so many uses, that we must begin to teach our students (as well as teachers and fellow workers) how to use mathematical resources.

Fey, James T., ed. 1984. *Computing & Mathematics: The Impact on Secondary School Curricula.* Reston, Va.: National Council of Teachers of Mathematics.

    An excellent collection of articles cataloging the need for the use of computers in every branch of secondary and community college mathematics instruction. Includes a bibliography.

Griffiths, Hubert B., and Albert G. Howson. 1974. *Mathematics: Society and Curricula.* London: Cambridge University Press.
A British view of the state of mathematics and mathematics education.

Hamming, Richard W. 1985. *Methods of Mathematics Applied to Calculus, Probability, and Statistics.* Englewood Cliffs, N.J.: Prentice-Hall.
A nontraditional first-year college mathematics textbook for science and engineering majors. An important and interesting effort by a prominent mathematician to change the content and direction of mathematics as taught in the first two years of college. Essential reading, especially the prologue.

Hansen, Viggo P., and Marilyn J. Zweng, eds. 1984. *NCTM 1984 Yearbook.*
An excellent series of articles on the computer and its possible uses and impact on mathematics education. Contains an extensive annotated bibliography.

Hilton, Peter J., and Gail S. Young, eds. 1982. *New Directions in Applied Mathematics.* New York: Springer-Verlag.
Important for the preface, which gives a cogent argument for the importance of computer driven applied mathematics with the historical framework of mathematics as handmaiden to the sciences.

Howard, Homer. 1941. *Mathematics Teachers' Views on Certain Issues in the Teaching of Mathematics.* New York: Teachers College, Columbia University.
A snapshot of what issues in mathematics education have captured center stage in the past.

Howson, Albert G., and J.-P. Kahane. 1986. *The Influence of Computers and Informatics on Mathematics and Its Teaching.* ICMI Study Series: Strasbourg 1985. London: Cambridge University Press.
A summary of the Strasbourg symposium on using computers in the teaching of mathematics, especially computer symbolic algebra systems.

Kline, Morris. 1977. *Why the Professor Can't Teach: Mathematics and the Dilemma of University Education.* New York: St. Martin's.
A spirited criticism of the standard curriculum and methods of teaching it.

Lindquist, Mary Montgomery, ed. 1980. *Selected Issues in Mathematics Education.* Berkeley, Calif.: McCutchan.
A teacher's perspective on mathematics education. Valuable for giving the

day to day, lesson by lesson, problems faced by elementary and high-school teachers today.

Morris, Robert, ed. 1980, 1981. *Studies in Mathematics Education.* Vol. 1, 1980. Vol 2, 1981. Paris: United Nations Educational, Scientific and Cultural Organization (UNESCO).

    Gives a more global view of the problems facing mathematics education. Clearly sets forth the applied side of mathematics in the applied vs. pure mathematics controversy.

Panel on Undergraduate Education in Mathematics of the Committee on Support of Research in the Mathematical Sciences (COSRIMS) of the National Research Council. 1968. *The Mathematical Sciences: Undergraduate Education: A Report.* Washington, D.C.: National Academy of Sciences.

    An excellent casebook of problems that face mathematics education. Though the book is not recent, some of the panel members are still major players in mathematics education, especially John Kemeny, Henry Pollak, and Robert Wisner.

Papert, Seymour. 1980. *Mindstorms: Children, Computers, and Powerful Ideas.* New York: Basic Books.

    A spirited attack on the way we teach mathematics to children and other students.

Post, Dudley L. 1970. *The Use of Computers in Secondary School Mathematics.* Newburyport, Mass.: Entelek.

    Describes and discusses the issues in using computers in secondary school in 1970. The discussion of equipment is a bit dated as one might expect. It does, however, give a good summary of the teaching issues that still exist in trying to use computers in education.

Ralston, Anthony, and Gail S. Young, eds. 1983. *The Future of College Mathematics.* New York: Springer-Verlag.

    An outgrowth of the Williamstown Conference sponsored by the Sloan Foundation. Contains the seminal papers that launched the concerted effort by the Sloan Foundation to change the first two years of college mathematics to reflect the needs of computer science (algebra, logic, and combinatorics) over the traditional needs of physics and engineering (the limit process).

Seyfert, Warren C., ed. 1968. *The Continuing Revolution in Mathematics.* Washington, D.C.: National Council of Teachers of Mathematics. Reprinted from the *Bulletin of the National Association of Secondary-School Principals* no. 327 (April 1968).

    An important view of the problems facing mathematics education, from the perspective of school administrators.

Taylor, John L., ed. 1984. *Teacher Shortage in Science and Mathematics: Myths, Realities and Research.* Washington, D.C.: National Institute of Education.

Proceedings of a conference sponsored by the National Institute of Education. Gives all the details of the teacher shortage in mathematics and discusses some of the possible remedies. Important as a document blessed by the federal government.

Wain, G.T. 1978. *Mathematical Education.* New York: Van Nostrand Reinhold Company.

A British view of the structure of the mathematics and what effect it should have on the curriculum in mathematics at the primary and secondary levels.

Articles

Akst, Geoffrey R. 1985. Reflections on basic mathematics programs in the two-year college. In Albers et al. (1985), pp. 141-158.

Proposes guidelines for increasing the effectiveness of the mathematics curriculum at two-year colleges. Focuses on protecting the integrity of the college degree while providing appropriate skills and student assistance in the curriculum.

Capps, Joan P. 1984. Mathematics laboratory and personalized system of instruction: A workshop presentation. Columbus, O.: ERIC/ SMEAC. ERIC: ED 246969.

Describes Personalized System of Instruction (PSI) used at Somerset County (N.J.) College Mathematics Laboratory. Critical to the program are peer tutors and proctors who immediately evaluate student work and then tutor, counsel, and encourage the students.

————. 1984. Mathematics laboratory report: Activities during academic year 1983-1984 and plans for academic year 1984-1985. Columbus, O.: ERIC/ SMEAC. ERIC: ED 246968.

Sets forth the successful elements and problems encountered in the initial year of the Mathematics Laboratory at Somerset County (N.J.) College. Indicates solutions to be instituted in the second year which include holding workshops for teachers and students, providing videotaped instructional materials and supplementary course materials, and a research design for evaluating the laboratory.

————. 1984. Individualized instruction programs and learning centers. Columbus, O.: ERIC/SMEAC. ERIC: ED 246967.

Proposes future development of the Mathematics Laboratory at Somerset County (N.J.) College and developmental mathematics courses.

Carl, Iris M. 1984. Finding--and keeping--good math and science teachers. Columbus, O.: ERIC/SMEAC. ERIC: ED 251329.

Houston Independent School District's attempt to alleviate the shortage of good mathematics and science teachers. The program involves recruitment from inside the district as well as throughout the country and includes a differential salary structure and incentive pay for various categories of professional growth and educational progress.

Carnevale, Thomas A. 1978. Qualifications of the two-year college mathematics teacher: What are they, what should they be? Paper presented at the Annual Meeting of the National Council of Teachers of Mathematics, San Diego, Calif., April 1978. Columbus, O.: ERIC/SMEAC. ERIC: ED 176817.

In order to teach the diverse community college mathematics student body, a master's degree must be the minimum qualification. However, it is suggested that a broader understanding of mathematics and its role in society is also requisite. In addition, instructors should have an understanding of the issues in two-year mathematics instruction, theories of learning as related to mathematics instruction, and the use of mathematics in other disciplines. Instructors need formal and informal opportunities for professional development such as short courses, summer programs, regional and local seminars, and departmental seminars to renew instructor enthusiasm and to provide the opportunity for discussion of current issues and problems.

Case, Bettye Anne, and Jerome A. Goldstein. 1985. Coordinating curriculum in two-year colleges with baccalaureate institutions. In Albers et al. (1985), 439-454.

Coordination between two-year and four-year institutions is essential to successful student transfer. This includes formal and informal communication between the institutions with support from professional mathematics societies.

Cohen, Arthur M. 1985. Mathematics in today's community college. In Albers et al. (1985), 1-20.

Addresses the changes in the community college over the last 20 years, especially in the types of students and their needs, and how these changes affect course offerings, curriculum deficiencies, and testing/placement programs. Reports on individual college attempts to handle high attrition, mathematics anxiety, and mathematics laboratories. Reviews the professional characteristics of two-year-college mathematics instructors. Discusses the future of mathematics with respect to faculty, curriculum, and students' skills.

Coole, Walter A. 1975. Oleanna math program materials. Columbus,

O.: ERIC/SMEAC. ERIC: ED 103088.

A collection of course outlines, syllabi, and test materials for auto-tutorial courses from pre-algebra through differential and integral calculus. Students determine levels of entry into the program coursework by performance on the Student Decision Placement Test, which is included.

Covington, Helen C., and Terry Tiballi. 1982. Using Bloom's taxonomy for precision planning and creative teaching in the developmental math classroom. Paper presented at the Western College Reading Association Convention, San Diego, Calif.: April 3, 1982. Columbus, O.: ERIC/SMEAC. ERIC: ED 221253.

Describes the process of applying Bloom's Taxonomy of Educational Objectives to developmental mathematics classes. Provides a framework to help students overcome mathematics anxiety and help the instructor in planning lessons and teaching creatively. A detailed lesson example involving teaching quadratic equations is presented. The appendices provide additional lesson plans for study of set notation, solving right triangles, and sketching curves.

Crepin, Dorothy M. 1981. A developmental mathematics program for community college students. Columbus, O.: ERIC/SMEAC. ERIC: ED 210076.

Lower Columbia College found high attrition in its Review Mathematics course and so instituted extensive curriculum changes. Extensive placement testing was instituted. In an effort to guide students through a comfortable non-threatening path to regular classroom mathematics, a course was developed at the arithmetic level for students with limited mathematics concepts. The Review course was designed to include self-paced, competency-based, variable credit instruction. A one-credit Mathematics Anxiety course was instituted, as was an Introduction to Algebraic Concepts. The new Elementary Algebra course was extended over two quarters.

Curnutt, Larry. 1985. Let's keep the "college" in our community colleges: Mathematics for college transfer. In Albers et al. (1985), pp. 21-29.

Discusses the need for continued education of an informed faculty as the most important part of revising the mathematics curriculum in the community college where preparing students for transfer is a significant portion of the faculty task.

Davis, Ronald M. 1985. Relevancy and revitalization: Retaining quality and vitality in two-year college mathematics faculty. In Albers et al. (1985), pp. 381-392.

In addition to retraining faculty to meet the challenges of the 1980s and 1990s, the new knowledge must be incorporated as new approaches and methods into existing courses. Faculty vitality will be necessary to cope with the changing student body which will require non-traditional environments and instruction. Faculty will need the support of society (i.e., industry, government, foundations) as well as redefinition by the colleges themselves in terms of faculty workload, remuneration, and the role of the faculty at the college.

Dolan, Lawrence. 1983. Affective characteristics of the adult learner: A study of mastery based instruction. *Community/Junior College Quarterly of Research and Practice* 7 (4) (July-September 1983): 367-378.

Reports on the use of mastery learning techniques for the adult learner.

Doversberger, Betty. 1970. An analysis of the practices in the teaching of technical mathematics and technical physics in Illinois junior colleges, Phase I. Columbus, O.: ERIC/ SMEAC. ERIC: ED 061933.

The results of this study indicate that courses should be applications-oriented rather than theoretical; instructors should have industrial experience; and the mathematics and physics courses should be offered in the technology department. Students who have deficiencies when they enter should receive more psychological support.

Drum, Randell L., and Tim J. Wells. 1984. A survey of teachers' opinions and practices regarding the teaching of problem solving skills. Columbus, O.: ERIC/ SMEAC. ERIC: ED 240075.

A survey of Texas teachers that indicates that most believed they were good problem solvers though it had not been encouraged in their college training or subsequent inservice. While most did not stress problem solving in their own classrooms, those who did were older, with more years of experience, and belonged to professional subject area associations.

Dyer, Patricia A., ed. 1981. American Mathematical Association of Two-Year Colleges Developmental Mathematics Curriculum Committee: Annual Report. Santa Rosa, Calif.: American Mathematical Association of Two-Year Colleges. Columbus, O.: ERIC/SMEAC. ERIC: ED 208924.

This annual report of the Developmental Mathematics Curriculum Committee (DMCC) of the American Mathematical Association of Two-Year Colleges (AMATYC) includes seven subcommittee reports that follow DMCC's goals and objectives for 1981 through 1986. Subcommittee reports include findings on the impact of calculator usage in the two-year colleges; establish minimum level of mathematics literacy for all college-level students; outline methods to encourage information exchange between DMCC and AMATYC; provide recommendations on two-year college instructor qualifications; and list standards to identify suitable tests.

Eldersveld, Paul J. 1983. Factors related to success and failure in developmental mathematics in the community college. *Community/ Junior College Quarterly of Research and Practice* 7 (2) (January-March 1983): 161-174.

Reports on the determinants for success/failure of developmental mathematics students in eight Illinois Community Colleges.

An evaluative study of the student completion rate for mathematics 1403 (A, B, C). 1984. Columbus, O.: ERIC/SMEAC. ERIC: ED 248911.

Analyzes factors affecting student completion rates in the remedial mathematics program which includes arithmetic, beginning algebra, and intermediate algebra. The report indicates possible improvements to the program and includes detailed findings of the study.

Freshman mathematics course descriptions, Texas colleges and universities. 1966. Bulletin 662. Austin, Tex.: Texas Education Agency. Columbus, O.: ERIC/SMEAC. ERIC: ED 015723.

A comprehensive handbook for students and faculty outlining entrance requirements including mathematics courses, graduation requirements in mathematics for general and specialized majors, short descriptions of mathematics courses, and information on examination procedures, provisions for repeating coursework, and methods used in determining course grades.

Friedlander, Jack. 1979. Developmental mathematics. Junior College Resource Review. ERIC Clearinghouse for Junior College Information, August 1979. Columbus, O.: ERIC/SMEAC. ERIC: ED 172894.

A review of studies of developmental mathematics programs in two-year colleges. Points out inconsistencies in policies regarding credit and problems of avoidance of basic mathematics by students, as well as inadequate levels of achievement and high attrition rates. Indicates the need for recruiting and training motivated and interested instructors and then providing support to develop instructional methods and materials and evaluation programs.

Friesen, Chuck. 1974. An analysis of general education mathematics programs in two-year colleges. A research report. Columbus, O.: ERIC/SMEAC. ERIC: ED 094841.

An attempt to determine common requirements and differences in the two-year colleges mathematics general education requirements in the North Central Accrediting area.

Gash, Philip. 1983. Remedial math and language arts study: Effectiveness of remedial classes in a rural Northern California community college district. Columbus, O.: ERIC/ SMEAC. ERIC: ED 241091.

Correlates class completion, return rates, units completed, and GPA for remedial students enrolled in mathematics and language arts. Correlations are given for Fall 1981, Spring 1982, and Fall 1982.

Goldston, Ruth. 1983. Math 100 survey, Fall 1982. Columbus, O.: ERIC/ SMEAC. ERIC: ED 237146.

Based on responses of students in the basic mathematics course. Includes demographic data and weighted information on students' attitudes toward mathematics. Reveals the pass rate for women was 55%, for men, 41%; a strong positive attitude toward mathematics correlated strongly with success in the course, but a negative attitude did not correlate strongly with failure; the number of units carried combined with work load did not correlate significantly with success in the course.

Gordon, Sheldon P. 1985. Discrete topics in the undergraduate curriculum: How big a step should we take? In Albers, et al. (1985), pp. 225-242.

Discusses the reasons for teaching discrete mathematics topics; analyzes advantages and disadvantages of introducing discrete topics in particular courses; reviews trends in teaching mathematics, specifically, the calculus sequence, applied calculus, differential equations and linear algebra, finite mathematics, statistics, mathematics for liberal arts students, remedial mathematics, and geometry.

Gormley, Tyrone D. 1978. Some considerations in combining traditional and non-traditional methods of instruction in a mathematics program. Paper presented at the Annual Meeting of the American Mathematical Association of Two-Year Colleges, Houston, Tex., October 10-14, 1978. Columbus, O.: ERIC/SMEAC. ERIC: ED 162679.

Outlines the characteristics of students and courses relative to teaching methods and specific elements of the mathematics curriculum. Includes a list of textbooks and a bibliography.

Guthrie, James W., and Ami Zusman. 1982. Teacher supply and demand in mathematics and science. *Phi Delta Kappan* 64 (1) (September 1982): 28-33.

Suggests that differential pay, inservice staff development, school-industry cooperation, improved work environments and CAI (computer-assisted instruction) may be partial solutions to the current shortage of mathematics and science teachers.

Hansen, Viggo P. 1983. Using media to teach math. *Instructional Innovator* 28 (6) (September 1983): 25-26.

Addresses the need to develop strong mathematics curriculum while making effective use of computers.

Hector, Judith H. 1983. A base rate approach to evaluating developmental mathematics and English courses at a community college. Columbus, O.: ERIC/ SMEAC. ERIC: ED 229087.

The evaluation of Walters State Community College's developmental mathematics and English courses. Data were collected and compared on students' success rate with later college-level courses; success rates of developmental students compared with non-developmental students; and relationship of developmental and college-level course grades.

Heller, Barbara R., and Stanley Kogelman. 1982. Project MART (Mathematics Anxiety Reduction Training) III: Encouraging the dissemination and use of instructional materials to counteract student math avoidance. New York: Institute for Research and Development in Occupational Education, City University of New York, November 1982. Columbus, O.: ERIC/SMEAC. ERIC: ED 223430.

Project MART has attempted to help faculty understand student mathematics anxiety and avoidance and to provide solutions for them to handle this anxiety in their own classroom interactions. The report includes a complete guide for mathematics instructors wishing to provide a workshop dealing with mathematics anxiety/avoidance.

Hering, William M., and Elsie W. Gee. 1984. Collaboration in applying research to teacher education. San Francisco, Calif.: Far West Lab for Educational Research and Development, April 1984. Columbus, O.: ERIC/ SMEAC. ERIC: ED 244934.

Describes two teacher-education projects: one for elementary-school teacher education and one for secondary-school mathematics teacher education. Both included implementation plans to improve teacher education.

Houston, Charles A., and Robert W. Hoyer. 1976. Virginia Community College mathematics curriculum study (1975-1976). Columbus, O.: ERIC/ SMEAC. ERIC: ED 116767.

A survey of Virginia four-year college and university mathematics offerings correlated with the course descriptions in the Virginia Community College Curriculum Guidelines (VCCCG); validation of the correlation was supplied by chairpersons of mathematics departments. Lists of textbooks used at the community and four-year colleges are included.

Howard, Bessie C. 1982. Mathematics in content areas. MICA. A teacher training approach. Columbus, O.: ERIC/SMEAC. ERIC: ED 213694.

Presents inservice mathematics programs for elementary teachers and secondary teachers to help them implement mathematical concepts in content areas. The secondary program culminates in a team-teaching approach to mathematics applications.

————. 1983. Mathematics Teacher Resource Development. Final Report 1982-1983. E.C.I.A. Chapter 2. Columbus, O.: ERIC/SMEAC. ERIC: ED 239866.

The final report on the District of Columbia's attempt to recruit and develop mathematics teachers. Programs involved potential district mathematics teachers, teachers who needed additional credits for certification, and those who needed skills upgrading. The program was offered through the District Mathematics Department and local universities.

Jacobs, Judith E. 1983. Equity through mathematics: Everyone's responsibility. *Mathematics Teacher* 76 (7) (October 1983): 463-464.

Points out that mathematics will be the "critical filter" in deciding who gets the higher paying jobs. Without motivation to get into mathematics, women and minorities will suffer.

Johnson, Marvin L. 1984. Computer literacy at the community college — way to start. *Mathematics and Computer Education* 18 (2) (Spring 1984): 89-92.

Computer literacy should be broken into three levels: knowing something; being able to do something with software; and writing one's own programs. If students are to become computer literate, the faculty must also be computer literate. Suggestions are included to develop faculty computer literacy.

Kane, Michael, and Cheryl Chase. 1983. Staff development. Background papers for the Task Force on Education for Economic Growth. Working Paper No. TF-83-4. Denver, Colo.: Education Commission of the States, Task Force on Education for Economic Growth, July 1983. Columbus, O.: ERIC/SMEAC. ERIC: ED 243873.

Outlines some successful staff development programs carried out in various parts of the United States — New York, Texas, Maryland, Colorado, Nebraska, North Carolina, and Vermont.

Lawrisuk, Paul. 1971. Committing curricular heresy. *Two-Year College Mathematics Journal* 2 (1) (Spring 1971): 58-64.

Presents a two-year college mathematics curriculum in which students can avail themselves of short courses of six and 12 weeks in length.

Leake, Lowell. 1983. What every secondary school mathematics teacher should read — twenty-four opinions. *Mathematics Teacher* 76 (2) (February 1983): 128-133.

A compilation of the items that 24 male mathematicians believe should be read by every secondary mathematics teacher. George Pólya wins the most-popular-author spot.

Leitzel, Joan R. 1983. Improving school-university articulation in Ohio. *Mathematics Teacher* 76 (8) (November 1983): 610-616.

A discussion of the low mathematics placement scores (1965-1975) and how Ohio State University has begun to make high school students aware of their skill levels *before they go to college.*

Maier, Gene. 1983. We have a choice. *Mathematics Teacher* 76 (6) (September 1983): 386-387.

> The revolution from paper and pencil mathematics to electronics mathematics brings new directions, dilemmas, freedom, and excitement to the classroom.

Maurer, Stephen B. 1985. The algorithmic way of life is best. *College Mathematics Journal* 16 (1) (January 1985): 2-18.

> A strong argument for the presentation of mathematics from an algorithmic point of view. Comments from other mathematicians are included.

―――. 1985. The lessons of Williamstown. In Albers et al. (1985), 255-270.

> Reviews areas of agreement and disagreement during July 1982 conference at Williams College. Points out the increased interest in discrete mathematics; the reasons for resistance to change in the curriculum; the author's observations about what first-year and second-year students should know; and options available in developing courses for non-transfer students.

Melton, Roger H. 1976. Algebraic and trigonometric equations with applications. A study guide of the science and engineering technician curriculum. Columbus, O.: ERIC/SMEAC. ERIC: ED 207787.

> Interdisciplinary curriculum study guide entitled Science and Engineering Technician (SET) for use in training technicians in the applications of electronic instruments. Includes elements from chemistry, physics, mathematics, mechanical technology, and electronic technology.

Newman, Anne. 1984. Computer training helps Appalachians compete. *Appalachia 17* (3) (January-April 1984): 20-26.

> Describes two programs funded by the Appalachian Regional Commission to foster computer literacy. In Mississippi, microcomputers were used to provide training for mathematics, science, and vocational education teachers. In West Virginia, vocational education students were trained in word processing, spreadsheet usage and database management.

Ohlemeier, Bill J. 1972. Mini-math courses at Barton County. *Junior College Journal* 42 (5) (February 1972): 36-37.

> Students at Barton County Community College (Kansas) are able to zero-in on their specific needs in the mathematics curriculum using 15 mini-courses.

Orr, Eleanor Wilson. 1987. *Twice as Less: Black English and the Performance of Black Students in Mathematics and Science.* New York: Norton. Review: *New York Times Book Review* (1 November 1987): 12-13.

> Emphasizes the linguistic aspect of learning mathematics. (PJC & LSG)

Queensborough Community College. 1976. Training program for teachers of technical mathematics in two-year curricula. Columbus, O.: ERIC/SMEAC. ERIC: ED 131869.

A handbook for developing curricula oriented to the concrete rather than abstract needs of students in electrical, mechanical, design drafting technology, and technical physics. Includes sections on reading and study skills development as well as general management of the classroom.

Ralston, Anthony. 1984, 1985. Will discrete mathematics surpass calculus in importance? *College Mathematics Journal* 15 (5) (November 1984): 371-382; 16 (1) (January 1985): 19-21.

An argument for the place of discrete mathematics in the first two years of college mathematics. Comments by other mathematicians are included.

Rendon, Laura. 1981. Basic skills: Responding to the task with effective innovative programs. Columbus, O.: ERIC/ SMEAC. ERIC: ED 213460.

Reviews issues in community college basic skills instruction. Two model programs are outlined: the interdisciplinary Coordinated Bilingual Bicultural Studies Program at Laredo (Tex.) Junior College, and the Ford Foundation sponsored Mathematics Intervention Project for Hispanic Students conducted by the Border College Consortium. The Mathematics Intervention Program uses faculty, counselors, peers, and parents in an attempt to introduce Hispanics to mathematics and science.

Rising, Gerald R. 1983. Separate computer science from mathematics. *Mathematics Teacher* 76 (8) (November 1983): 554-555.

An argument that establishing separate entity computer science departments would better serve both science and humanities.

Roberts, Fred. 1984. The introductory mathematics curriculum: Misleading, outdated, and unfair. *College Mathematics Journal* 15 (5) (November 1984): 383-399.

An attack on the standard curriculum and teaching methods found in the first two years of college mathematics. Comments by other mathematicians are included.

Rotman, Jack W. 1984. Developmental mathematics and the Lansing Community College Math Lab. Lansing, Mich.: Lansing Community College, September 1984.

A review of recent research and applicability to Lansing Community College's self-paced mastery learning mathematics laboratory. The literature review covers areas of developmental mathematics and mastery learning ranging over such topics as program objectives, cultural bias, achievement and sex, modular/variable credit programs, instructional methods, personalized instruction, mathematics anxiety, and differentiated staffing. Includes an annotated bibliography.

Say, Elaine. 1983. A shortage of mathematics teachers in Houston. *Mathematics Teacher* 76 (9) (December 1983): 644-645.

> One high school district's approach to the mathematics teacher shortage — extra pay incentives and district-paid teacher retraining — to provide quality staffing both in basic skills and mathematics skills.

Schonberger, Ann K. 1981. Gender differences in solving mathematics problems among two-year college students in a developmental algebra class and related factors. Columbus, O.: ERIC/SMEAC. ERIC: ED 214602.

> A study at the University of Maine at Orono involving students who had completed two-year programs or tested out of a developmental algebra course. The study examined gender differences in ability areas such as mathematical problem-solving, visual/spatial, and abstract reasoning. The report details methodology, limitations and findings, provides suggestions for further research, and suggests the implications for instruction.

Schwanke, Dean. 1982. Educating secondary school teachers. *Journal of Teacher Education* 33 (1) (January-February 1982): 59-62.

> The selected annotated bibliography is divided into five categories dealing with secondary teacher preparation and the students who enter the secondary-teaching education programs. One category deals specifically with mathematics and science teacher preparation.

Self, Samuel L. 1975. Community College Technical Mathematics Project. Final Report. College of Education, Texas A and M University, College Station, Tex., December 1975. Columbus, O.: ERIC/SMEAC. ERIC: ED 137511.

> Mathematical concepts required for vocational/technical training were identified and arranged into sequential units and curriculum materials were developed for each unit. Extensive appendices include the taxonomy of competencies and examples of mini-modules.

Sharp, Karen Tobey. 1984. Meeting the challenge: Implications for *Educating Americans for the 21st Century* for two-year colleges. Columbus, O.: ERIC/ SMEAC. ERIC: ED 248935.

> Reviews the plan of action recommended by the National Science Board Commission on Pre-College Education in Mathematics, Science, and Technology. Discusses the special implications for the two-year college.

―――. 1985. Current continuing education needs of two-year college mathematics faculty must be met. In Albers et al. (1985), 405-422.

Discusses ways faculty continuing education can be done in the face of rapidly-changing technology and enrollment patterns. Argues that retraining must be complemented with such things as released time, sabbatical leaves, and tuition reimbursement. Faculty continuing education proposals include expanded government-funded teacher training programs; faculty training through professional societies; funding by business and industry in training programs and vacation employment; and increased efforts by colleges and faculty themselves.

Sobel, Max A. 1983. The crisis in mathematics education. *Educational Horizons* 61 (2) (Winter 1983): 52, 55-56.

Includes recommendations of the NCTM in this discussion of the shortage of qualified mathematics teachers and the decline in student achievement.

Steen, Lynn Arthur. 1987. Mathematics education: A predictor of scientific competitiveness. *Science* 237 (17 July 1987): 251-252, 302.

"Evidence suggests that our mathematics classrooms, like our smokestack industries, no longer provide adequate support for modern society." This provocative essay by the former president of the Mathematical Association of America cites comparisons with other countries, notes the impact computers have yet to have, and concludes with a manifesto including the principles:

- Only teachers who like mathematics should teach mathematics
- Only tests that measure higher order thinking skills should be used to assess mathematics
- The chief objective of school mathematics should be to build student confidence
- Mathematics in the schools should be linked to science in the schools.

(PJC & LSG)

Suydam, Marilyn N. 1984. What research says: Microcomputers and mathematics instruction. *School Science and Mathematics* 84 (4) (April 1984): 337-343.

Includes comments on selecting a microcomputer and software as well as using computers in research. Suggests ways to use computers in mathematics classrooms.

Taylor, B. Ross. 1983. Equity in mathematics: A case study. *Mathematics Teacher* 76 (1) (January 1983): 12-17.

An account of the Minneapolis Public Schools' program for recruiting and encouraging minorities (Native Americans and blacks) in mathematics.

Thompson, Carla J., and Joyce E. Friske. 1984. CLIMB: A two-year approach to technology in mathematics. *Journal of Computers in Mathematics and Science Teaching* 3 (2) (Winter 1984): 13-15.

The Center for Learning and Instruction in Mathematics-concept Building is discussed as a practical approach to meeting the needs of the adult learner.

U.S. General Accounting Office. 1984. New Directions for Federal Programs to Aid Mathematics and Science Teaching. Columbus, O.: ERIC/SMEAC. ERIC: ED 241300.

The GAO sees retraining teachers in other fields a better alternative in the face of the teacher shortage than inservice training for mathematics and science teachers because, it says, inservice training doesn't seem to improve student performance.

Usiskin, Zalman. 1984. Mathematics is getting easier. *Mathematics Teacher* 77 (2) (February 1984): 82-83. Reaction by George R. Vick. 77 (6) (September 1984): 406.

Mathematics teachers are implored to give up paper-and-pencil activities in favor of using the wonderful aids that exist--calculators, computers and canned programs, and value tables. Usiskin says there is much more to be learned in mathematics and it's getting easier. Instructors will not be able to keep this a secret from the students forever.

Wagner, Laura. 1984. Implementation of teacher education and computer centers in California: Results of first year descriptive study. California State Department of Education, Sacramento, Calif.: Office of Staff Development, April 1984. Columbus, O.: ERIC/SMEAC. ERIC: ED 243831.

A four-section summary of the first year of implementation of 15 California regional centers for teacher training. Section I discusses study methodology; Section II is a summary of services; Section III is three case studies; and Section IV is the analysis and discussion.

Warren, William C., and James R. Mahoney. 1985. Occupational education and mathematics: Ownership makes the difference. In Albers et al. (1985), 101-118.

Identifies and discusses areas of interaction between mathematics departments and vocational-technical education departments. Addresses the problems and issues in these areas with suggested solutions focusing on "ownership," defined as the responsibility of the instructor, department, and/or college for the success or deficiencies of the students.

Washington, Allyn J. 1985. Technical mathematics in two-year college programs. In Albers et al. (1985), 119-130.

Provides an overview of the current status of technical and vocational mathematics in two-year colleges. Suggests basic topics to be included in a good mathematics background in conjunction with other components of vocational and technical programs. Discusses the place of calculators and computers in these courses. Suggests ways to interest faculty in teaching these classes as well as updating and upgrading technical mathematics instructors.

Wiebe, James H. 1983. Needed: Good mathematics tutorial software for microcomputers. *School Science and Mathematics* 83 (4) (April 1983): 281-292.

> Discusses in detail both learning and curriculum considerations for developing tutorial software to be used in mathematics instruction.

Willoughby, Stephen S. 1984. President's report: Mathematics education 1984: Orwell or well? *Mathematics Teacher* 77 (7) (October 1984): 575-582.

> Willoughby, then President of the NCTM, cites the lack of support from society as well as the government and school administrators for current problems in education. He comments on proposals to increase the number of mathematics teachers, to upgrade the quality of teacher education and the quality of textbooks.

20. Resources

PAMELA TRIM

After reading the essays on the important topics in the preceding chapters, some readers may desire additional sources for information on these, as well as other topics related to mathematics education. In an effort to provide them, this chapter lists

- Organizations
- Newsletters
- Periodicals
- NCTM Yearbooks
- Films/Videotapes
- General References
- Selected Distributors and Publishers

which may assist in the search for pertinent resources.

Readers are reminded that listings of this nature can never be comprehensive, and many valuable resources for information may be found outside these listings. For example, although for the most part the organizations listed are national organizations, there are many regional and local organizations with inestimable resources. In addition, there are numerous international organizations and publications that should not be overlooked in the search for current information. Many large corporations also supply information on such topics as mathematical applications, mathematics-oriented careers, as well as others. Furthermore, some nonprofit foundations furnish resources for the mathematically gifted.

Another important resource for information that should not be overlooked is a local college or university. Departments of mathematics, computer science, and mathematics education may assist with specialized libraries and/or resource personnel. Technical institutes can also be of great assistance, particularly in the area of mathematical applications. There is no question that there is an abundance of resources available to mathematics educators today. We hope the listings that follow will encourage their utilization to the fullest advantage.

ORGANIZATIONS

Aerospace Education Foundation
1750 Pennsylvania Avenue N.W.
Washington, DC 20006

Provides curriculum materials on vocational/technical courses developed by the military. Affiliated with the Air Force Association.

American Association for the Advancement of Science (AAAS)
1333 H Street, N.W.
Washington, DC 20005

A comprehensive scientific organization that includes a section on computing and mathematics. Sponsors mathematics education projects such as free film series.

American Library Association
50 East Huron Street
Chicago, IL 60611

Includes Young Adult Services division that can provide information on book and non-book materials for teenagers and young adults.

American Mathematical Association of Two-Year Colleges
    (AMATYC)
Austin Community College
Box 2285
Austin, TX 78768

A national organization for two-year-college mathematics educators. Publishes a newsletter and *AMATYC Review*, which provide for the exchange of mathematical ideas and programs. Sponsors the Two-Year College Mathematics League Competition. Affiliated with numerous state organizations.

American Mathematical Society (AMS)
P.O. Box 6248
Providence, RI 02940

Professional society of mathematicians and educators. Emphasizes mathematical scholarship and research. Provides career information.

American Newspaper Publishers Association Foundation
The Newspaper Center
Box 17407
Dulles International Airport
Washington, DC 20041

Publishes and distributes "Using the newspaper in secondary mathematics" to secondary mathematics teachers. This 13-page paper illustrates the use of the newspaper as a learning resource, through a series of meaningful activities.

American Society for Engineering Education
11 Dupont Circle, Suite 200
Washington, DC 20036

Professional society for engineering educators, including those at junior colleges and technical institutes. Emphasizes education and research in engineering and related fields, such as science and mathematics.

American Statistical Association (ASA)
806 15th Street, N.W., Suite 640
Washington, DC 20005

Professional society for individuals interested in all areas of statistics. Includes a section on education. Provides career information. Publications include a newsletter and *American Statistician*.

Association for Computing Machinery (ACM)
11 West 42nd Street
New York, NY 10036

Promotes the advancement of information processing. Includes a committee on education, which publishes curriculum recommendations. Numerous publications.

Association for Educational Communications and Technology
 (AECT)
1126 16th Street, N.W.
Washington, DC 20036

Dedicated to the improvement of education through the use of communication media in instruction. Maintains archives of materials and equipment.

Association for Symbolic Logic
Department of Mathematics
1409 West Green Street
University of Illinois
Urbana, IL 61801

Professional society for individuals interested in formal or mathematical logic. Publishes *Journal of Symbolic Logic*.

Association for Women in Mathematics
P.O. Box 78
Wellesley College
Wellesley, MA 02181

Dedicated to making women aware of opportunities in the field of mathematics. Sponsors a speakers bureau. Publishes booklets on the speakers bureau and on career opportunities, and a newsletter.

Association of Teachers of Mathematics
King's Chambers
Queens Street
Derby DE1 3DA
England

Publications include the journal *Mathematics Teaching*.

Canadian Mathematical Society
577 King Edward, Suite 109
Ottawa, Ontario
Canada K1N 6N5

Consortium for Mathematics and Its Applications (COMAP Inc.)
60 Lowell Street
Arlington, MA 02174

A non-profit membership corporation dedicated to the improvement of mathematics education. Emphasizes mathematical applications. Develops and disseminates instructional materials for undergraduate and secondary mathematics. Publications include the newsletter *Consortium* as well as the *UMAP Journal*.

Council for Exceptional Children
1920 Association Drive
Reston, VA 22091

Provides various types of print and non-print material on the education of exceptional children and youths. Publications include the journal *Teaching Exceptional Children*.

Educational Film Library Association (EFLA)
45 John Street, Suite 301
New York, NY 10038

Publishes information and evaluations of educational films and videotapes.

EPIE Institute
P.O. Box 839
Water Mill, NY 11976

Provides user data on instructional materials including microcomputer hardware and courseware. Publishes the *Educational Software Selector* as well as *EPIEgram: Equipment* and *EPIEgram: Materials*.

ERIC Clearinghouse on Science, Mathematics, and
   Environmental Education
Ohio State University
1200 Chamber Road, 3rd Floor
Columbus, OH 43212

National clearinghouse for information on science and mathematics.

Foundation for Exceptional Children
1920 Association Drive
Reston, VA 22091

Deals with education of gifted and handicapped children. Publishes *Focus* as well as other educational materials.

Foundation for Gifted and Creative Children
395 Diamond Hill Road
Warwick, RI 02886

Concerned with the education of gifted and creative children. Services include workshops, specialized library, and newsletter.

Institute of Electrical and Electronics Engineers (IEEE)
345 East 47th Street
New York, NY 10017

Educational activities include aid to student organizations, promotion of scholarship through awards and career information. Publications include *IEEE Computer Society Education Newsletter*.

Institute of Mathematical Statistics
3401 Investment Boulevard, Suite 6
Hayward, CA 94545

Professional organization for individuals interested in mathematical statistics and probability theory. Publishes lecture notes and monograph series.

Jets, Inc.
c/o United Engineering Center
345 East 47th Street
New York, NY 10017

A national high-school organization for students interested in engineering and applied science. Provides career guidance and sponsors numerous student activities.

The Madison Project
Curriculum Laboratory
1212 West Springfield
University of Illinois-Urbana
Urbana, IL 61801

Develops and implements curricula for mathematics education from preschool through high school. Prepares print and non-print course materials. Publishes the *Journal of Mathematical Behavior*.

Mathematical Association of America (MAA)
1529 18th Street, N.W.
Washington, DC 20036

A national organization for college mathematics educators and professionals who use mathematics. Concerned with the teaching of undergraduate mathematics. Sponsors annual high-school mathematics contests. Publications include *American Mathematical Monthly*, *College Mathematics Journal*, *Mathematics Magazine*, and the newsletter *Focus*. Provides career information.

Math Science Network
c/o Mills College
Oakland, CA 94613

Especially interested in promoting women in mathematics. Sponsors "Expanding Your Horizons in Science and Mathematics," a career conference for young women in high school. Provides programs and printed materials on mathematical careers. Sponsors EQUALS, a teacher education program.

Mu Alpha Theta
601 Elm Avenue
Room 423
Norman, OK 73019

An honorary high-school and two-year-college mathematics society. Publishes the *Mathematical Log* and numerous inexpensive recreational materials.

National Aeronautics and Space Administration (NASA)
400 Maryland Avenue, S.W.
Washington, DC 20546

Provides speakers, films, publications and exhibit services through individual NASA installations. Publications list and career information available.

National Council of Teachers of Mathematics (NCTM)
1906 Association Drive
Reston, VA 22091

Organization for K-12, two-year-college and teacher-education college personnel. Publications include *Arithmetic Teacher, Journal for Research in Mathematics Education, Mathematics Teacher*, a newsletter, and yearbooks. Provides career information. Publication list is available free.

National Information Center for Educational Media
P.O. Box 40130
Albuquerque, NM 87196

Provides a computerized catalogue of audio-visual educational materials.

National Institute of Education
1200 19th Street, N.W.
Washington, DC 20208

Provides information and resources in education. Especially interested in research for upgrading basic skills in reading and mathematics.

National Oceanic and Atmospheric Administration
Assessment Information Services Center
Library and Information Services
Federal Building 4
Suitland, MD 20233

Maintains collection of printed materials and a computer information service on mathematics, computer science, satellite technology, and atmospheric physics. Makes interlibrary loans.

National Science Foundation (NSF)
1800 G Street, N.W.
Washington, DC 20550

Promotes science by funding research and educational programs. Sponsors conferences and workshops. Specifically encourages proposals aimed at strengthening mathematics instruction. Detailed brochures available from Division of Teacher Enhancement and Informal Science Education.

New Zealand Statistical Association
P.O. Box 1731
Wellington, New Zealand

Publishes *New Zealand Mathematics Magazine.*

School Science and Mathematics Association
126 Life Science Building
Bowling Green State University
Bowling Green, OH 43403

Organization for elementary through college science and mathematics teachers. Provides information on instructional materials and methods. Publications include *School Science and Mathematics*.

Society for Industrial and Applied Mathematics (SIAM)
1405 Architects Building
117 South 17th Street
Philadelphia, PA 19103

Emphasizes applications of mathematics. Sponsors visiting lecturer program. Provides career information. Publishes periodicals and the newsletter *SIAM News*.

Society of Actuaries
500 Park Boulevard
Itasca, IL 60143

Professional organization for actuaries. Provides career information.

Women and Mathematics Education
c/o Judith Jacobs
Education Department
George Mason University
Fairfax, VA 22030

Interested in the mathematical education of girls and women. Provides clearinghouse for resources and a speakers bureau. Publishes a newsletter.

Woodrow Wilson National Fellowship Foundation
Box 642
Princeton, NJ 08542

Administers faculty development programs for teachers of high-school mathematics.

NEWSLETTERS

CONSORTIUM
Consortium for Mathematics and Its Applications (COMAP, Inc.)
60 Lowell Street
Arlington, MA 02174

Available free of charge to any secondary school teacher. Includes pull-out lessons, mathematical news, articles, teaching hints, puzzles and games and a section on computers.

EPIEgram: EQUIPMENT
EPIEgram: MATERIALS
EPIE Institute
P.O. Box 620
Stony Brook, NY 11790

ETC TARGETS
CN 6745
Princeton, NJ 08541-6745

Newsletter of the Educational Technology Center, a consortium of organizations which focus on technology in education. Subscriptions are free on request.

FOCUS
Mathematical Association of America
1529 18th Street, N.W.
Washington, DC 20036

Newsletter of The Mathematical Association of America.

GIFTED CHILDREN'S NEWSLETTER
P.O. Box 115
Sewell, NJ 08080

IEEE COMPUTER SOCIETY EDUCATION NEWSLETTER
Institute of Electrical and Electronics Engineers
345 East 47th Street
New York, NY 10017

INTERNATIONAL STATISTICAL EDUCATION NEWSLETTER
International Statistical Institute
428 Prinses Beatrixlaan
P.O. Box 950
2270 AZ Voorburg
Netherlands

A free newsletter containing information about committees, programs, and projects in teaching statistics at both precollege and college levels from around the world. (AEW)

NEWS BULLETIN
National Council of Teachers of Mathematics
1906 Association Drive
Reston, VA 22091

Contains news briefs, announcements and "Students Math Notes," an instructive recreational section for students.

NEWSLETTER
Association for Women in Mathematics
828 Washington Street
Wellesley College
Wellesley, MA 02181

NEWSLETTER
Women and Mathematics Education
c/o Judith Jacobs
Education Department
George Mason University
Fairfax, VA 22030

PLACEMENT TEST NEWSLETTER
Placement Test Program (PTP)
Mathematical Association of America
1529 18th Street, NW
Washington, DC 20036

Facilitates the exchange of information testing among PTP users. The PTP program provides placement tests in mathematics for entering college students and for high-school juniors wishing a prognosis of their mathematics placement in college. (More information about PTP can be found in the "User's Guide: The Placement Test Program of the Mathematical Association of America.") The newsletter include articles reporting experiences and statistics obtained in the placement testing program on specific campuses. The newsletter is also used to keep PTP users informed of program developments. (AOG & JWK)

RANDOM NEWS
Centre for Statistical Education
25 Broomgrove Road
Sheffield S1O 2NA
England

A free newsletter containing information about workshops for secondary teachers and publications of the Centre. (AEW)

SIAM NEWS
Society for Industrial and Applied Mathematics
1405 Architects Building
117 South 17th Street
Philadelphia, PA 19103

STATISTICS TEACHER NETWORK NEWSLETTER
American Statistical Association —
  National Council of Teachers of Mathematics
Joint Committee on Curriculum in Statistics and Probability
806 15th Street N.W., Suite 640
Washington, DC 20005

  A free newsletter containing contributions from secondary teachers across the U.S. and Canada on projects they have begun, state curriculum guidelines, conferences on teaching statistics and probability, new products and publications, and other information valuable to secondary teachers of statistics. (AEW)

PERIODICALS

ABACUS
Springer-Verlag New York, Inc.
P.O. Box 2485
Secaucus, NJ 07094

  A popular journal about computing, computer science, and computer technology, intended not only for professionals in those fields but also for knowledgeable and interested amateurs.

AMATYC REVIEW
State Technical Institute at Memphis
5983 Macon Cove
Memphis, TN 38134

  Published by the American Mathematical Association of Two-Year Colleges. Devoted to two-year college mathematics education. Contains sections on problem solving, book reviews, and computer software.

AMERICAN MATHEMATICAL MONTHLY
Mathematical Association of America
1529 18th Street NW
Washington, DC 20036

  There is a cumulative index for volumes 1-80 (1894-1973).

AMERICAN STATISTICIAN
American Statistical Association
806 15th Street, N.W., Suite 640
Washington, DC 20005

> Most of the articles are at too high a level for the typical teacher of elementary statistics and probability. However, there is a "Teacher's Corner" and valuable sections on new teaching materials and on statistical computing. (AEW)

ARITHMETIC TEACHER
National Council of Teachers of Mathematics
1906 Association Drive
Reston, VA 22091

> Designed to aid mathematics instruction in grades K-8. Cumulative author, title, and subject indices exist for 1954-1973 and 1974-1983.

BYTE
BYTE Publications
70 Main Street
Peterborough, NH 03458

CALCULATOR/COMPUTER MAGAZINE
Dymax
P.O. Box 310
Department 27
Menlo Park, CA 94025

CLASSROOM COMPUTER LEARNING
Peter, Li, Inc.
2451 East River Road
Dayton, OH, 45439

CLASSROOM COMPUTER NEWS
P.O. Box 266
Cambridge, MA 02138

COLLEGE MATHEMATICS JOURNAL
(formerly TWO-YEAR COLLEGE MATHEMATICS JOURNAL)
Mathematical Association of America
1529 18th Street, N.W.
Washington, DC 20036

> Devoted to all aspects of mathematics instruction in the first two years of college.

COMPUTE!
P.O. Box 10955
Des Moines, IA 50950
Contains articles for home, educational, and recreational computing, book reviews and program listings.

COMPUTING TEACHER (formerly OREGON COMPUTING TEACHER)
International Council for Computers in Education (ICCE)
University of Oregon
1787 Agate Street
Eugene, OR 97403
Concerned with computers in instruction.

CREATIVE CHILD AND ADULT QUARTERLY
National Association for Creative Children and Adults
8080 Springvalley Drive
Cincinnati, OH 45236

CRUX MATHEMATICORUM
Canadian Mathematical Society
577 King Edward Avenue, Suite 109
Ottawa, Ontario K1N 6N5
Canada
Problem-solving journal "at the senior secondary and university under-graduate levels for those who practise or teach mathematics."

CURRICULUM REVIEW
Curriculum Advisory Service
517 S. Jefferson
Chicago, IL 60607
Contains articles on trends in curriculum development. Evaluates textbooks and supplementary material in all areas K-12.

DISCOVER
P.O. Box 359105
Palm Coast, FL 32035-9105
A source for miscellaneous problems and puzzles (see "Mind Benders" and "Brain Bogglers" columns by M. Steuben) (BA & OC)

EDUCATIONAL HORIZONS
4101 East Third Street
Bloomington, IN 47401

Published by Pi Lambda Theta, a national honor and professional society in education. Contains articles of interest in all areas of education.

EDUCATIONAL LEADERSHIP
Association for Supervision and Curriculum Development (ASCD)
225 North Washington Street
Alexandria, VA 22314

Concerned with curriculum, instruction, and supervision in grades K-12. Contains sections on textbook selection, book reviews, and resources.

THE EDUCATIONAL SOFTWARE SELECTOR (TESS)
EPIE Institute
P.O. Box 839
Water Mill, NY 11976

Contains information (as well as some ratings) on educational software products for microcomputers.

EDUCATIONAL STUDIES IN MATHEMATICS
D. Reidel Publishing Company
Box 17
3300 AA Dordrecht
Netherlands

GAMES MAGAZINE
1350 Avenue of Americas
New York, NY

Devoted to puzzles and games, most of a nonmathematical nature. Usually includes a page of logic problems as well as number of other features of mathematical interest. (BA & OC)

GIFTED CHILD QUARTERLY
National Association for Gifted Children
5100 North Edgewood Drive
St. Paul, MN 55112

Contains articles on curriculum research and evaluation, counseling, and programs for the gifted.

HANDS ON!
Technical Education Research Centers (TERC)
1696 Massachusetts Ave.
Cambridge, MA 02138

INSTRUCTOR AND TEACHER
(formerly two separate journals: INSTRUCTOR and TEACHER)
Instructor Publications
545 Fifth Avenue
New York, NY 10017

Most appropriate for kindergarten through junior high school, contains sections on "take out and use" materials, computers and software, freebies, and book reviews.

JOURNAL FOR RESEARCH IN MATHEMATICS EDUCATION
National Council of Teachers of Mathematics
1906 Association Drive
Reston, VA 22091

Contains research reports and articles. Critiques articles and books concerned with mathematics education at all levels.

JOURNAL OF COMPUTERS IN MATHEMATICS AND
  SCIENCE TEACHING
Association for Computers in Mathematics and Science Teaching
P.O. Box 4455
Austin, TX 78765

JOURNAL OF DEVELOPMENTAL EDUCATION
Center of Developmental Education
Appalachian State University
Boone, NC 28608

Contains some articles on developmental mathematics programs in post-secondary education.

JOURNAL OF EDUCATIONAL PSYCHOLOGY
American Psychological Association
1400 North Uhle Street
Arlington, VA 22201

Contains some articles on mathematical learning and cognition in an educational setting.

JOURNAL OF EDUCATIONAL RESEARCH
Heldref Publications
Suite 504
4000 Albemarle Street, N.W.
Washington, DC 20016

Some issues contain articles on research in mathematics education.

JOURNAL OF MATHEMATICAL BEHAVIOR
P.O. Box 2095, Station A
Champaign, IL 61820
Published by the Madison Project (See ORGANIZATIONS).

JOURNAL OF RECREATIONAL MATHEMATICS
Baywood
Farmingdale, NY
Contains articles about mathematical games and other recreational problems and puzzles. Much of the material included is intended for an audience with some mathematical maturity. There is a cumulative index for vols. 1-10 (1968-1978). (BA & OC)

JOURNAL OF UNDERGRADUATE MATHEMATICS
Guilford College
Department of Mathematics
Greensboro, NC 27410

LEARNING
P.O. Box 2580
Boulder, CO 80322
Most appropriate for kindergarten through junior high school, emphasizes creative teaching. Contains reviews, resources and reader exchanges.

MATHEMATICAL GAZETTE
The Mathematical Association
Leicester
England
Contains some articles of recreational interest as well as a regular problems column. (BA & OC)

MATHEMATICAL INTELLIGENCER
Springer-Verlag New York Inc.
P.O. Box 2485
Secaucus, NJ 07094

MATHEMATICS AND COMPUTER EDUCATION
(formerly MATYC JOURNAL)
P.O. Box 158
Old Bethpage, Long Island
New York, NY 11804

Concerned with mathematics and computer education in senior high school and the first two years of college. Contains a problem department and book and software reviews.

MATHEMATICS MAGAZINE
Mathematical Association of America
1529 18th Street, N.W.
Washington, DC 20006

There is a cumulative index for volumes 1-50 (1926-1977).

MATHEMATICS TEACHER
National Council of Teachers of Mathematics
1906 Association Drive
Reston, VA 22091

Designed to aid mathematics instruction in junior-high schools, senior high schools, two-year colleges, and teacher-education colleges. Contains activities, and sections on "sharing teaching ideas," courseware reviews, new products, publications and new projects. There are cumulative author, title, and subject indexes for 1908-1965 and 1966-1975.

MATHEMATICS TEACHING
Association of Teachers of Mathematics
King's Chambers
Queens Street
Derby DE1 3DA
England

MICROQUESTS
Martin-Bearden
P.O. Box 337
Grapevine, TX 76051

Published for upper-elementary and junior-high-school students who use Logo.

PERSONAL COMPUTING
1050 Commonwealth Avenue
Boston, MA 02215

PHI DELTA KAPPAN
8th and Union
P.O. Box 789
Bloomington, IN 47402

Some issues contain articles on research and trends in mathematics education.

PI MU EPSILON JOURNAL
Pi Mu Epsilon Fraternity
South Dakota School of Mines & Technology
Rapid City, SD 57701

RESOURCES IN EDUCATION
Superintendent of Documents
United States Government Printing Office
Washington, DC 20402

SCHOOL SCIENCE AND MATHEMATICS
School Science and Mathematics Association
126 Life Science Building
Bowling Green State University
Bowling Green, OH 43403

Contains a problem section as well as book and software reviews. There is a cumulative subject index for 1901-1960 (vol. 61 no. 9, pt. II of II).

SCIENTIFIC AMERICAN
415 Madison Avenue
New York, NY 10017

Contains articles about mathematical games and other recreational problems and puzzles. The "Mathematical Games" column by M. Gardner appeared 1957-1981. (BA & OC)

TEACHING EXCEPTIONAL CHILDREN
The Council for Exceptional Children
1920 Association Drive
Reston, VA 22091

Contains practical information for teachers working with exceptional children. Includes instructional methods and materials.

TEACHING STATISTICS
Department of Probability and Statistics
University of Sheffield
Sheffield, S1O 2TN
England

Similar in level, style, and readability to *Mathematics Teacher*. Many articles translate directly into classroom lessons. A collection, *The Best of Teaching Statistics* (1986), is available from the same address. (AEW)

TECHNOLOGY REVIEW
Massachusetts Institute of Technology
Alumni Association
Cambridge, MA 02139
  A source for miscellaneous problems and puzzles (see "Puzzle Corner"
column by A. Gottlieb). (BA & OC)

T.H.E. JOURNAL
Information Synergy
P.O. Box 15126
Santa Ana, CA 92705-0126

UMAP JOURNAL
Consortium for Mathematics and Its Applications (COMAP, Inc.)
60 Lowell Street
Arlington, MA 02174
  Contains selected UMAP Modules, articles on applications of mathematics,
reviews, explanations of current mathematical jargon, as well as articles on the
history of mathematics and its applications. (JRC)

YEARBOOKS PUBLISHED BY THE
NATIONAL COUNCIL OF TEACHERS OF MATHEMATICS

A General Survey of Progress in the Last Twenty-five Years. Yearbook
1 (1926). Edited by Charles M. Austin, et al. New York: Bureau of
Publications, Teachers College, Columbia University.

Curriculum Problems in Teaching Mathematics. Yearbook 2 (1927).
Edited by William D. Reeve, et al. New York: Bureau of Publications,
Teachers College, Columbia University.

Selected Topics in the Teaching of Mathematics. Yearbook 3 (1928).
Edited by John R. Clark and William D. Reeve. New York: Bureau of
Publications, Teachers College, Columbia University.

*Significant Changes and Trends in the Teaching of Mathematics
throughout the World since 1910.* Yearbook 4 (1929). Edited by William
D. Reeve. New York: Bureau of Publications, Teachers College, Columbia University.

The Teaching of Geometry. Yearbook 5 (1930). Edited by William D. Reeve. New York: Bureau of Publications, Teachers College, Columbia University.

Mathematics in Modern Life. Yearbook 6 (1931). Edited by William D. Reeve. New York: Bureau of Publications, Teachers College, Columbia University.

The Teaching of Algebra. Yearbook 7 (1932). Edited by William D. Reeve. New York: Bureau of Publications, Teachers College, Columbia University.

The Teaching of Mathematics in the Secondary School. Yearbook 8 (1933). Edited by William D. Reeve. New York: Bureau of Publications, Teachers College, Columbia University.

Relational and Functional Thinking in Mathematics. Yearbook 9 (1934). Herbert Russell Hamley. New York: Bureau of Publications, Teachers College, Columbia University.

The Teaching of Arithmetic. Yearbook 10 (1935). Edited by William D. Reeve. New York: Bureau of Publications, Teachers College, Columbia University.

The Place of Mathematics in Modern Education. Yearbook 11 (1936). Edited by William D. Reeve. New York: Bureau of Publications, Teachers College, Columbia University. Reprint 1966. Washington, D.C.: NCTM.

Approximate Computation. Yearbook 12 (1937). Aaron Bakst. New York: Bureau of Publications, Teachers College, Columbia University. Reprint. 1966. Washington, D.C.: NCTM.

The Nature of Proof. Yearbook 13 (1938). Harold P. Fawcett. New York: Bureau of Publications, Teachers College, Columbia University. Reprint. 1966. Washington, D.C.: NCTM.

The Training of Mathematics Teachers for Secondary Schools in England and Wales and in the United States. Yearbook 14 (1939). Edited by Ivan Stewart Turner. New York: Bureau of Publications, Teachers College, Columbia University.

The Place of Mathematics in Secondary Education: The Final Report of the Joint Commission of the MAA and the NCTM. Yearbook 15 (1940). Edited by William D. Reeve. New York: Bureau of Publications, Teachers College, Columbia University.

Arithmetic in General Education. Yearbook 16 (1941). Edited by William D. Reeve. New York: Bureau of Publications, Teachers College, Columbia University.

A Source Book of Mathematical Applications. Yearbook 17 (1942). Compiled by Edwin G. Olds, et al. New York: Bureau of Publications, Teachers College, Columbia University.

Multi-Sensory Aids in the Teaching of Mathematics. Yearbook 18 (1945). Edited by William D. Reeve. New York: Bureau of Publications, Teachers College, Columbia University.

Surveying Instruments: Their History and Classroom Use. Yearbook 19 (1947). Edmond R. Kiely. New York: Bureau of Publications, Teachers College, Columbia University.

The Metric System of Weights and Measures. Yearbook 20 (1948) Compiled by J.T. Johnson, et al., New York: Bureau of Publications, Teachers College, Columbia University.

The Learning of Mathematics: Its Theory and Practice. Yearbook 21 (1953). Edited by Howard F. Fehr. Washington, D.C.: NCTM.

Emerging Practices in Mathematics Education. Yearbook 22 (1954). Edited by John R. Clark. Washington, D.C.: NCTM.

Insights into Modern Mathematics. Yearbook 23 (1957). Edited by F. Lynwood Wren, et al. Washington, D.C.: NCTM.

The Growth of Mathematical Ideas Grades K-12. Yearbook 24 (1959). Edited by Phillip S. Jones, et al. Washington, D.C.: NCTM.

Instruction in Arithmetic. Yearbook 25 (1960). Edited by Foster E. Grossnickle, et al. Washington, D.C.: NCTM.

Evaluation in Mathematics. Yearbook 26 (1961). Edited by Donavan A. Johnson, et al. Washington, D.C.: NCTM.

Enrichment Mathematics for the Grades. Yearbook 27 (1963). Edited by Julius H. Hlavaty. Washington, D.C.: NCTM.

Enrichment Mathematics for High School. Yearbook 28 (1963). Edited by Julius H. Hlavaty, et al. Washington, D.C.: NCTM.

Topics in Mathematics for Elementary School Teachers. Yearbook 29 (1964). Edited by Lenore John, et al. Washington, D.C.: NCTM.

More Topics in Mathematics for Elementary School Teachers. Yearbook 30 (1969). Edited by Edwin F. Beckenbach, et al. Washington, D.C.: NCTM.

Historical Topics for the Mathematics Classroom. Yearbook 31 (1969). Edited by Arthur H. Hallerberg, et al. Washington, D.C.: NCTM.

A History of Mathematics Education in the United States and Canada. Yearbook 32 (1970). Edited by Phillip S. Jones. Washington, D.C.: NCTM.

The Teaching of Secondary School Mathematics. Yearbook 33 (1970). Edited by Myron F. Rosskopf. Washington, D.C.: NCTM.

Instructional Aids in Mathematics. Yearbook 34 (1973) Edited by Emil J. Berger. Washington, D.C.: NCTM.

The Slow Learner in Mathematics. Yearbook 35 (1972). Edited by William C. Lowry. Washington, D.C.: NCTM.

Geometry in the Mathematics Curriculum. Yearbook 36 (1973). Edited by Kenneth B. Henderson. Reston, Va.: NCTM.

Mathematics Learning in Early Childhood. Yearbook 37 (1975). Edited by Joseph N. Payne. Reston, Va.: NCTM.

Measurement in School Mathematics. Yearbook 38 (1976). Edited by Doyal Nelson and Robert E. Reys. Reston, Va.: NCTM.

Organizing for Mathematics Instruction. Yearbook 39 (1977). Edited by F. Joe Crosswhite and Robert E. Reys. Reston, Va.: NCTM.

Developing Computational Skills. 1978 Yearbook. Edited by Marilyn N. Suydam and Robert E. Reys. Reston, Va.: NCTM.

Applications in School Mathematics. 1979 Yearbook. Edited by Sidney Sharron and Robert E. Reys. Reston, Va.: NCTM.

Problem Solving in School Mathematics. 1980 Yearbook. Edited by Stephen Krulik and Robert E. Reys. Reston, Va.: NCTM.

Teaching Statistics and Probability. 1981 Yearbook. Edited by Albert P. Shulte and James R. Smart. Reston, Va.: NCTM.

Mathematics for the Middle Grades (5-9). 1982 Yearbook. Edited by Linda Silvey and James R. Smart. Reston, Va.: NCTM.

The Agenda in Action. 1983 Yearbook. Edited by Gwen Shufelt and James R. Smart. Reston, Va.: NCTM.

Computers in Mathematics Education. 1984 Yearbook. Edited by Viggo P. Hansen and Marilyn Zweng. Reston, Va.: NCTM.

The Secondary School Mathematics Curriculum. 1985 Yearbook. Edited by Christian R. Hirsch and Marilyn J. Zweng. Reston, Va.: NCTM.

Estimation and Mental Computation 1986 Yearbook. Edited by Harold L. Schoen and Marilyn J. Zweng. Reston, Va.: NCTM.

Learning and Teaching Geometry. 1987 Yearbook. Edited by Mary Lindquist. Reston, Va.: NCTM.

FILMS/VIDEOTAPES

Bestgen, Barbara J., and Robert E. Reys. 1982. *Films in the Mathematics Classroom.* Reston, Va.: National Council of Teachers of Mathematics.

Lists appropriate films. Reviews and rates each.

Schneider, David I. 1980. *An Annotated Bibliography of Films and Videotapes for College Mathematics.* Washington, D.C.: Mathematical Association of America.

> Provides description of mathematics films and videotapes. Listed by distributor but also indexed by subject as well as title.

GENERAL REFERENCES

Gaffney, Matthew P., and Lynn Arthur Steen, with Paul J. Campbell. 1976. *Annotated Bibliography of Expository Writing in the Mathematical Sciences.* Washington, D.C.: Mathematical Association of America.

> Organized by topic, this book gives references to some of the most successful expositions of individual topics in mathematics. Many entries discuss very advanced material, but there is a lot here on any level higher than elementary algebra. (MES)

Posamentier, Alfred S., and Jay Stepelman. 1986. *Teaching Secondary School Mathematics, Techniques and Enrichment Units.* 2nd ed. Columbus, Ohio: Charles E. Merrill. (DWS)

Schaaf, William L. 1970-1978. *A Bibliography of Recreational Mathematics.* 4 vols. Reston, Va.: National Council of Teachers of Mathematics.

> Many articles and notes, gleaned from all areas of mathematics. Emphasis is on material not directly related to classroom or textbook exposition. (MES)

Sobel, Max A., and Evan M. Maletsky. 1975. *Teaching Mathematics: A Sourcebook of Aids, Activities and Strategies.* Englewood Cliffs, N.J.: Prentice-Hall. (DWS)

SELECTED DISTRIBUTORS/PUBLISHERS
(Compiled by DWS and RSC)

For distributors and publishers not listed, please see *Books in Print.*

A.R. Davis & Co.
P.O. Box 24424
San Jose, CA 95154-4424
> Supplemental books.

Activity Resources Company, Inc.
P.O. Box 4875
Hayward, CA 94540
415-782-1300
Books, activities, models, puzzles (mostly elementary).

Addison-Wesley
Reading, MA 01867
617-944-3700

Allyn & Bacon
Rockleigh, NJ 07647
800-526-4799, 201-768-7200

Annenberg/CPB Collection
1213 Wilmette Avenue
Wilmette, IL 60091

Avant-Garde
37B Commercial Blvd.
Novato, CA 94947

BMDP Statistical Software
1964 Westwood Blvd., Suite 202
Los Angeles, CA 90025
213-475-5700

Broderbund Software
17 Paul Drive
San Rafael, CA 94903-2101
415-479-1700
Computer software.

Brooks/Cole Publishing Co.
Monterey, CA 93940
800-354-9706

Carolina Biological Supply Company (CABISCO)
2700 York Road
Burlington, NC 27215
800-334-5551

Books, blackboard aids, drawing tools, posters, filmstrips.

The Center for Humanities, Inc.
Communications Park, Box 1000
Mount Kisco, NY 10549-0010
800-431-1242
Slide/filmstrip/cassette series.

COMPress
P.O. Box 102
Wentworth, NH 03282
603-764-5831

CONDUIT
The University of Iowa
Oakdale Campus
Iowa City, IA 52242
319-353-5789

Steven R. Conrad
Box 1090
Manhasset, NY 11030

Control Data Publishing Co., Inc.
Higher Education Marketing MNB04A
3601 West 77th St.
Bloomington, MN 55435
800-328-1109, ext. 1446
Computer software.

Cosine
P.O. Box 2017
West Lafayette, IN 47906

Creative Publications
5005 West 110th Street
Oak Lawn, IL 60453
800-624-0822
Books, blocks, posters, drawing aids, models, computer software, puzzles, Miras, geoboards, measuring devices.

Cuisenaire Co. of America, Inc.
12 Church St., Box D
New Rochelle, NY 10805
914-235-0900
> Books, blocks, tiles, geoboards, measuring and drawing aids, models, Miras.

Dale Seymour Publications
P.O. Box 10888
Palo Alto, CA 94303
800-USA-1100
> Books, activities, posters, drawing aids, computer software.

Dayott Associates
12508 Over Ridge Road
Potomac, MD 20854

Delta Education
Box M, Mathematics Department
Nashua, NY 03061-6102
800-258-1302
> Books, blocks, geoboards, drawing aids, polyhedra, activities.

Dick Blick
Box 1267
Galesburg, IL 61401
800-447-8192
> Construction and drawing aids (full line of art supplies).

Educational Audio Visual Inc.
Pleasantville, NY 10570
800-431-2196
> Overhead projector transparencies, filmstrip/cassette series, computer software.

Educulture, Inc.
1 Dubuque Plaza
Dubuque, IA 52001-9990
800-553-4858
> Microcomputer software, instructional cassette/study guides.

Eye Gate Media
3333 Elston Avenue
Chicago, IL 60618
800-621-8086
   Filmstrip/cassette series.

Gamco Industries, Inc. (Mathmaster)
P.O. Box 310X5
Big Spring, TX 79721
800-351-1404
   Filmstrip/cassette series; overhead transparencies, demonstration models,
microcomputer software, construction/ graphing aids.

Geodestix
P.O. Box 5179
Spokane, WA 99205
   D-Stix rods and connectors for building frame models.

Geyer Instructional Aids Co., Inc.
P.O. Box 10060
Fort Wayne, IN 46850
219-745-5408
   Mathematical chalkboards, posters, books, construction aids, demonstration models, theorem demonstrators; largest and most varied selection of
geometry aids.

Imported Publications
320 W. Ohio St.
Chicago, IL 60610-4175
800-345-2665
   Books, primarily English translations of publications from Eastern Europe
and the USSR.

Intellectual Software
562 Boston Avenue
Bridgeport, CT 06610

J. Weston Walch, Publisher
P.O. Box 658
Portland, ME 04104-0658
800-341-6094
   Activity worksheets, microcomputer software, posters.

Kadon Enterprises, Inc.
1227 Lorene Dr., Suite 16
Pasadena, MD 21122
301-437-2163
Various wooden and plastic puzzles and games (including pentaminoes and pentacubes.)

Kern International, Inc.
433 Washington St.
P.O. Box 1029
Duxbury, MA 02331
617-934-0445

Key Curriculum Project
P.O. Box 2304
Berkeley, CA 94702

Krell Software Corporation
1320 Stony Brook Road
Stony Brook, NY 11790
516-751-5139

Lano Company
9001 Gross Road
Dexter, MI 48130
313-426-4860
Blackboard and overhead projector aids—grids, theorem demonstrators, construction aids, polyhedra, plastic demonstrator models, filmstrips.

Learning Arts
P.O. Box 179
Wichita, KS 67201
316-682-6594
Educational computer software, filmstrip/cassette series

MCE, Inc.
157 S. Kalamazoo Mall, Suite 250
Kalamazoo, MI 49007
800-421-4157, 616-345-8681

MECC
3490 Lexington Ave. N.
St. Paul, MN 55112
612-481-3500

Metier
P.O. Box 51204
San Jose, CA 95151
415-270-3011

Microcomputer Workshops
225 Westchester Ave.
Port Chester, NY 10573

Microsoft, Inc.
10700 Northrup Way
Box 97200
Bellevue, WA 98009
206-828-8080

Microteach Corp.
P.O. Box 2946
South Bend, IN 46680-2946
219-234-3224
   Computer software.

Minimath Projects
Box 2505
2626 Lakeview
Chicago, IL 60614
312-348-0514
   String design and polyhedra kits.

Modulo Éditeur
233 Avenue Dunbar
Ville Mont-Royal
Québec H3P 2H4
Canada

Northwest Analytical, Inc.
520 NW Davis
Portland, OR 97209
503-224-7727

Opportunities for Learning, Inc.
20417 Nordhoff St.
Dept. Y85P
Chatsworth, CA 91311
818-341-2535
Microcomputer software, activity books, posters.

Polydron USA
700 Fee Fee Road
St. Louis, MO 63043

Prentice-Hall
Englewood Cliffs, NJ 07632
201-592-2000

Pythagorean Press
P.O. Box 162
Bradford, MA 01830

Queue, Inc.
562 Boston Avenue
Bridgeport, CT 06610
800-232-2224
Microcomputer software.

Rhombics
36 Pleasant Street
Watertown, MA 02172

Software Arts
27 Mica Lane
Wellesley, MA 02181

Spectrum Educational Supplies Limited
8 Denison Street
Markham, Ontario L3R 2P2
Canada
416-475-6250
    Books, models, puzzles, tiles, geoboards, Miras, drawing aids.

SPSS, Inc.
444 N. Michigan Ave.
Chicago, IL 60611
312-329-2400

B.M. Stewart
4494 Wausau Road
Okemos, MI

Sunburst Communications
Room D D75
39 Washington Ave.
Pleasantville, NY 10570-9971
800-431-1934
    Educational computer courseware.

Symmetrics, Inc.
P.O. Box 401
Atkinson, NH 03811

Tarquin Publications
Stradbroke, Diss
Norfolk IP21 5JP
England
037 984 218
    Books, models, puzzles, posters, drawing aids, S.M.P., and Leapfrog materials.

Time-Life Video
Distribution Center
100 Eisenhower Drive
P.O. Box 644
Paramus, NJ 07653
800-526-4663
    Videotapes.

TV Ontario
Suite 163
4825 LBJ Freeway
Dallas, TX 75234

Abbreviations

AAAS	American Association for the Advancement of Science
ACM	Association for Computing Machinery
ADCIS	Association for Development of Computer-Based Instructional Systems
AECT	Association for Education Communications and Technology
AEDS	Association for Educational Data Systems
AI	Artificial Intelligence
AIM	Applications in Mathematics
AM	Automated Mathematician
AMATYC	American Mathematical Association of Two-Year Colleges
AMS	American Mathematical Society
AP	Advanced Placement
ASA	American Statistical Association
ASCD	Association for Supervision and Curriculum Development
ASPIRE	Awareness of Sexual Prejudice Is the Responsibility of Educators
CAI	Computer Assisted Instruction
CBMS	Conference Board of the Mathematical Sciences
CBTE	Competency Based Teacher Education
CCSP	College Curriculum Support Project
CEEB	College Entrance Examination Board
CIMSE	Computers in Mathematics and Science Education
CLIMB	Center for Learning and Instruction in Mathematics-Concept Building
COMAP	Consortium for Mathematics and Its Applications
COSRIMS	Committee on Support of Research in the Mathematical Sciences
CPB	Corporation for Public Broadcasting
CSMP	Comprehensive School Mathematics Program
CTUM	Committee on Teaching Undergraduate Mathematics
CUPM	Committee on the Undergraduate Program in Mathematics
DMCC	Developmental Mathematics Curriculum Committee
DSM	Diagnostic and Statistical Manual

ECIA	Education Consolidation Improvement Act (1981)
EFLA	Educational Film Library Association
EH	Emotionally Handicapped
EMR	Educable Mentally Retarded
EPIC	Exploration Programs in Calculus
EPIE	Educational Products Information Exchange
ESN	Educationally Subnormal
ETC	Educational Technology Center
ETS	Educational Testing Service
FRG	Federal Republic of Germany
GAO	General Accounting Office
GPA	Grade Point Average
GPO	Government Printing Office
HiMAP	High School Mathematics Applications Project
ICCE	International Council for Computers in Education
ICD	International Classification of Diseases
ICME	International Congress on Mathematical Education
ICMI	International Commission on Mathematical Instruction
IEEE	Institute of Electrical and Electronics Engineers
IPI	Individually Prescribed Instruction
ISBN	International Standard Book Number
LD	Learning Disabled
MAA	Mathematical Association of America
MART	Mathematics Anxiety Reduction Training
MAWIS	Mathematics At Work In Society
MCTM	Michigan Council of Teachers of Mathematics, Montana Council of Teachers of Mathematics
MECC	Minnesota Educational Computing Consortium
MICA	Mathematics in Content Areas
MMA	Metropolitan Museum of Art
MSCA	McCarthy Scales of Children's Abilities
NACOME	National Advisory Committee on Mathematical Education
NAEP	National Assessment of Educational Progress
NASA	National Aeronautics and Space Administration
NASSP	National Association of Secondary-School Principals
NCATE	National Council for the Accreditation of Teacher Education
NCSM	National Council of Supervisors of Mathematics
NCTM	National Council of Teachers of Mathematics
NEA	National Education Association
NECC	National Educational Computer Conference

NFER	National Foundation for Educational Research
NSB	National Science Board
NSF	National Science Foundation
OEEC	Organisation for European Economic Cooperation
PL	Public Law
PRISM	Priorities in School Mathematics
PSI	Personalized System of Instruction
PTP	Placement Test Program
SAT	Scholastic Aptitude Tests
SET	Science and Engineering Technician
SIAM	Society for Industrial and Applied Mathematics
SMP	School Mathematics Project
SMSG	School Mathematics Study Group
SOLO	Structure of the Observed Learning Outcomes
TEAM	Teaching Experiential Applied Mathematics
TESS	The Educational Software Selector
UICSM	University of Illinois Committee on School Mathematics
UMAP	Undergraduate Mathematics and Its Applications Project
UMMap	University of Maryland Mathematics Project
UNESCO	United Nations Educational, Scientific and Cultural Organization
USBE	United States Bureau of Education

Author Index

Subject Index

How This Book Was Produced

The chapters of this book were either sent to the editors in magnetic form or optically scanned into the computer. The manuscript was edited on IBM-PC-compatible computers, design and layout were accomplished with Xerox Ventura™ desktop publishing software, and the camera-ready page originals were printed on a Hewlett-Packard LaserJet +. The typefaces are Dutch and Swiss. The designer and typographer was David R. Heesen, Head of Secretarial Services at Beloit College.